The American Prose Poem

The American
Prose Poem

Poetic Form and the Boundaries of Genre

Michel Delville

University Press of Florida

Gainesville · Tallahassee · Tampa · Boca Raton

Pensacola · Orlando · Miami · Jacksonville

Copyright 1998 by the Board of Regents of the State of Florida
Printed in the United States of America on acid-free paper
All rights reserved

03 02 01 00 99 98 6 5 4 3 2 1

Library of Congress Cataloging-in-Publication Data
Delville, Michel, 1969–
The American prose poem: poetic form and the boundaries of genre / Michel Delville
p. cm.
Includes bibliographical references and index.
ISBN 0-8130-1591-X (alk. paper)
1. Prose poems, American—History and criticism. 2. Literary form.
3. Poetics. I. Title.
PS309.P67D45 1998 97-43641
811—dc 21

The University Press of Florida is the scholarly publishing agency for the State
University System of Florida, comprised of Florida A&M University, Florida Atlantic
University, Florida International University, Florida State University, University of
Central Florida, University of Florida, University of North Florida, University of
South Florida, and University of West Florida.

University Press of Florida
15 Northwest 15th Street
Gainesville, FL 32611
http://nersp.nerdc.ufl.edu/~upf

To my father,
Gilbert Delville

Contents

Preface

In this book I offer a critical analysis of the emergence and evolution of a genre that has not yet received the attention it deserves, despite the growing interest it has generated among poets and critics in the last twenty or thirty years. It will be apparent to all who read on that the purpose of this study is not to provide an exhaustive account of the history of the American prose poem. Nor have I even attempted to cover in detail all the poets I consider to be important representatives of a consciously cultivated tradition of poetry written in prose. Given the myriad possible candidates, I have chosen to deal with a limited number of works, each of which epitomizes a crucial pattern of development in the history of the genre.

There are a number of risks involved in this project. One is that one can only deal with poets judged either representative of a certain "trend" or too idiosyncratic to be ignored. Another is that the critic's interest in a particular genre may cause the uniqueness and complexity of individual works to be lost. I have tried to guard against these dangers by grounding my analysis in a series of close readings of individual poems, on the one hand, and in a theoretical discussion of the very notion of genre on the other.

To many readers and critics, the prose poem is a piece of prose that wants to be a poem and derives at least part of its meaning from its ability to defeat our generic expectations. Seen from that angle, its subversive potential—as well as its propensity to transcend traditional distinctions between the lyric, the narrative, the critical essay, and a variety of other genres and subgenres—appears as only one example of what postmodern aesthetics diagnoses as the arbitrariness and instability of generic boundaries. The current popularity of the genre can thus be seen as resulting, at least in part, from its self-proclaimed hybridity and the ensuing sense of freedom afforded to prose poets—a feature the prose poem shares with a number of other centaurial neologisms, such as the "poetic novel," the "lyric short story," or, more recently, the paraliterary works of Barthes, Baudrillard, and Derrida. Needless to add that one of the chief merits of such early representatives of the genre as Gertrude Stein, Sherwood Anderson, or Kenneth Patchen is that they prefigured the current fashion for hybrid forms long before it became an integral part of the academic agenda.

It seems to me that one of the most challenging features of the prose poem is its potential for reclaiming a number of functions and modes usually considered to be the privilege of prose literature. Starting from the assumption that poetry can gain from such a renewed interaction with other literary genres—and as no reading of the prose poem would be complete without a sense of the various norms and traditions prose poets are writing within or against—I have tried to account for the prose poem's strategic position in the history of contemporary literature as well as its efforts to engage with a number of essential concerns that have occupied writers and critics throughout the twentieth century. As I seek to demonstrate in this book, it is precisely at a time when writers and critics have come to subvert or disregard traditional generic taxonomies that the need for critical and theoretical works dealing with the specific implications of such transgressions establishes itself with a vengeance. This field of study creates an interface between the aesthetic and the nonaesthetic (linguistic, social, ideological, material, philosophical) foundations of all literary texts, and that is the one I attempt to explore here.

As to the prose poem's discursive and formal hybridity, I read it as a clear indication of poetry's capacity to challenge the power of genre as a gesture of authority and to transgress accepted rules and boundaries for the purpose of forcing us to contemplate those rules and boundaries. Perhaps more important, many writers have turned to the prose poem because of its ability to reflect upon the methods, aspirations, and internal contradictions of poetry and thereby invite us to ask questions that address the problems of dominance and subversion, tradition and innovation. These related concerns are most apparent in the work of many prose poets who take an interest in the problematics of genre and gender, ideology, politics, sociolinguistics, and in the theory of discourse. Clearly, in the works of these writers, the prose poem is motivated not just by a desire to expand the formal, structural, and thematic range of poetic language, but also by a need to generate terms that emphasize the historical nature of dominant notions of genre and form. What is at stake here is the extent to which poetry, like any other discourse or cultural practice, can have claims to larger concerns in the world outside the text.

This book is addressed to those who care about such matters. For the general reader or student of American poetry, I hope it also has the merit of providing an in-depth critical survey of the contemporary prose poem and introducing readings of writers whose works deserve to be examined and appreciated in their own right, quite independently from whatever generic labels are attached to them.

During the writing of this book, many people have been supportive of my efforts. I wish to express my gratitude to Professor Pierre Michel of the University of Liège for his discerning reading of the entire book, especially for suggestions on how to organize some cumbersome material. Among my Liège colleagues of the last six years, I also wish to thank Andrew Norris and Christine Pagnoulle, who carefully read and proofread a considerable part of the manuscript, for their early and generous interest in this project. Specific thanks are due to Peter Johnson, whose unflinching enthusiasm, encouragement, and support helped to make the whole enterprise possible; to Bruce Michelson, who gave this study a long and searching critique for which I am very grateful; to Charles Bernstein, who brought his expertise to bear on the closing part of this book; to an anonymous reader for the University Press of Florida, whose insights helped inform the final revision; and to Sally Antrobus, who helped to ready the final manuscript for the press. I would also like to thank the following people who read my dissertation or discussed its issues with me, providing both advice and encouragement: Maxine Chernoff, Russell Edson, Hena Maes-Jelinek, Paule Mertens-Fonck, Danielle Bajomée, Elisabeth Waltregny, Stephen Adams, Joe Amato, Solvej Balle, Michael Benedikt, the late Bernard Benstock, Clark Coolidge, John Frayne, Madeline Gins, Philip Graham, Luc Herman, William Kulik, Robert Leroy, Paulette Michel-Michot, Bob Perelman, Charles Simic, Fiona Templeton, and Rosmarie Waldrop. Many thanks also to Carine Melkom-Mardorossian and Valérie Bada for various forms of assistance during the last stages of the study.

Portions of this work in earlier forms have been tested on colleagues and audiences at several institutions in the United States, Great Britain, and Belgium. Without the help and interest of these individuals and institutions, the present book would not have met the challenge of open debate. Short portions of the text have appeared in earlier, somewhat different incarnations. Sections of chapter 2 were first published in *The Prose Poem: An International Journal* 7 (1998). Some of the material in chapter 3 originally appeared in *The Contact and the Culmination*, edited by Marc Delrez and Bénédicte Ledent (Liège: L3, 1997), and in *Writing (on) Short Stories*, edited by Christine Pagnoulle (Liège: L3, 1997). The section on *Giacomo Joyce* is forthcoming in the *James Joyce Quarterly*. I am grateful to the editors of these books and journals for their encouragement and advice.

Special thanks are also due to the Fonds National de la Recherche Scientifique for granting me two terms of study leave in which to conduct research on the prose poem at the University of Illinois and for funding a final period of research at Brown University.

And finally, I am greatly indebted to my mother, Lucia Delville-Furlanetto; to my father, Gilbert Delville, to whom this book is dedicated; to my brother, Gilbert Delville, Jr., for instilling into me a passion for art in all its diverse forms; and to Elisabeth, who assisted this project with continuing love and patience.

Acknowledgments

Excerpts from *Giacomo Joyce* and *Epiphanies* by James Joyce. Quoted with the permission of the Estate of James Joyce, © The Estate of James Joyce: *Epiphanies* 1956—*Giacomo Joyce* 1959 and 1967/68.

"Hysteria" from *Collected Poems 1909–1962* by T. S. Eliot, © 1963, 1964 by T. S. Eliot. Reprinted by permission of Faber and Faber Ltd and Harcourt Brace & Company.

"Illustrations of Madness" and "Pharmacie du Soleil" by Harry Crosby. Excerpt from "Entity" by Paul Bowles. Quoted with permission of Black Sparrow Press.

Excerpt from "Monologue" by Eugene Jolas. Excerpt from "Faula and Flauna" by Theo Rutra. Reprinted by permission of Tina and Betsy Jolas.

"Mademoiselle Comet" from *Progress of Stories* by Laura (Riding) Jackson. Reprinted by permission of the Board of Literary Management of the late Laura (Riding) Jackson.

Excerpts from *Tender Buttons* and other works by Gertrude Stein. Reprinted by permission of the Estate of Gertrude Stein.

"Family Portrait" from *The Collected Poems of Kenneth Patchen*, © 1949, 1957 by New Directions Publishing Corp. Reprinted by permission of New Directions Publishing Corp.

"Personality" from *Chicago Poems* by Carl Sandburg, © 1916 by Holt, Rinehart and Winston Inc. and renewed 1944 by Carl Sandburg. Reprinted by permission of Harcourt Brace & Company.

Excerpts from *Mid-American Chants* and *A New Testament* by Sherwood Anderson. Reprinted by permission of the trustees of the Sherwood Anderson Literary Estate.

Excerpts from *The Collected Poems of Arturo Giovannitti* by Arturo Giovannitti. Reprinted by courtesy of E. Clemente & Sons, Publishers.

Excerpts from *The Famous Boating Party* and *Poemscapes* by Kenneth Patchen. Reprinted by permission of Miriam Patchen.

"Burning" by Michael Delp, from the anthology, *Epiphanies: The Prose Poem Now* (George Myers, ed.). Reprinted by permission of the author.

"Through the Streets of My Own Labyrinth" from *Under a Glass Bell* by Anaïs Nin, © 1948 by Anaïs Nin. Reprinted by permission of Peter Owen Ltd, London.

"The Reaper" from *Houses and Travellers* by W. S. Merwin, © 1977 by W. S. Merwin. Reprinted by permission of Georges Borchardt, Inc.

Excerpts from *The Wounded Breakfast* and *The Intuitive Journey* by Russell Edson. Reprinted by permission of the author.

"The Driver" by David Ignatow, from *The Prose Poem: An International Anthology* (Michael Benedikt, ed.). Reprinted by permission of the author.

Excerpts from *Ballade* and *Visions infernales* by Max Jacob, © 1970 Éditions Gallimard, Paris. Reprinted by permission of Éditions Gallimard.

"The Departure" from *Franz Kafka: The Complete Stories* (Nahum N. Glatzer, ed.) by Franz Kafka, © 1946, 1947, 1948, 1954, 1958, 1971 by Schocken Books, Inc. Reprinted by permission of Schocken Books, distributed by Pantheon Books, a division of Random House, Inc.

"Portable Thoughts" and "Invitation to Previously Uninvited Guests" by Michael Benedikt, first published in *Mole Notes* (Wesleyan University Press, 1971), © 1971 by Michael Benedikt. Revisions printed by permission of the author who retains copyright. "The Politics of Metaphor and "Travel Notes" by Michael Benedikt, first published in *Mole Notes* (Wesleyan University press, 1971), © 1971 by Michael Benedikt. "The Melancholy Moralist" by Michael Benedikt, first published in Night Cries (Wesleyan University Press, 1976), © 1976 by Michael Benedikt. Reprinted by permission of the author who retains copyright.

"A Stone Taking Notes" from *Truth, War, and the Dream-Game* by Lawrence Fixel, © 1991 by Lawrence Fixel. Reprinted by permission of Coffee House Press.

Excerpts from *Utopia TV Store* and *Leap Year Day* by Maxine Chernoff. Reprinted by permission of the author.

"Women's Novels," "An Affair with Raymond Chandler" and "Bad News" are part of the collection *Good Bones and Simple Murders* by Margaret Atwood, © 1994 O.W. Toad Ltd., published in the U.S. by Bantam, Doubleday, Dell. Reprinted by permission of the author.

Excerpts from *The Morning Glory* and *This Body Is Made of Camphor and Gopherwood* by Robert Bly. Reprinted by permission of the author.

Excerpts from "Le Ministre" from *Le Grand recueil* by Francis Ponge, ©

1961 Éditions Gallimard, Paris. Excerpts from "L'Objet, c'est la poétique" from *Nouveau recueil* by Francis Ponge, © 1967 Éditions Gallimard, Paris. Reprinted by permission of Éditions Gallimard.

"Talking to Myself," "My own House" and "I'm a Depressed Poem" from *New and Collected Poems: 1970–1985* by David Ignatow. Reprinted by permission of Wesleyan University Press.

Excerpts from *The World Doesn't End* by Charles Simic, © 1989, 1988, 1987, 1986, 1985 by Charles Simic. Reprinted by permission of Harcourt Brace & Company.

Excerpts from "Naked in Arcadia," "Medici Slot Machine," "Untitled (Bébé Marie), early 1940s" and "Totemism" from *Dime-Store Alchemy* by Charles Simic, © 1992 by Charles Simic. First published by The Ecco Press in 1992. Reprinted by permission of the publisher.

Excerpt from "Fork" from *Dismantling the Silence* by Charles Simic, © 1971 by Charles Simic. Reprinted by permission of George Braziller, Inc.

Excerpt from *PCOET* by David Melnick, © 1975 by David Melnick. Reprinted by permission of the author.

Excerpt from *Sentences* by Robert Grenier, © 1978 by Robert Grenier. Reprinted by permission of the author.

Excerpt from *Paradise* by Ron Silliman, © 1985 by Ron Silliman.

Excerpt from *Discipline* by Craig Watson, © 1986 by Craig Watson. Reprinted by permission of Burning Deck Press.

Excerpts from *My Life* (Los Angeles: Sun & Moon Press, 1987) by Lyn Hejinian, pp. 53, 54–55, © 1980, 1987 by Lyn Hejinian. Reprinted by permission of the publisher. Excerpt from *Writing Is an Aid to Memory* (Los Angeles: Sun & Moon Press, 1996), © 1996, 1978 by Lyn Hejinian. Reprinted by permission of the publisher and the author.

Excerpts from *Lawn of Excluded Middle* by Rosmarie Waldrop, © 1993 by Rosmarie Waldrop. Reprinted by permission of the author.

Excerpt from *Never Without One* by Diane Ward, © 1984 by Diane Ward. Reprinted by permission of Segue Foundation and the author.

Excerpt from *Our Nuclear Heritage* by James Sherry (Los Angeles: Sun & Moon Press, 1991), pp. 50–51, © 1991 by James Sherry. Reprinted by permission of the publisher.

Excerpts from *1–10* by Barrett Watten, © 1980 by Barrett Watten. Reprinted by permission of the author.

Excerpts from *Windows* by Kit Robinson, © 1985 by Kit Robinson. Reprinted by permission of the author.

Excerpt from *gIFTS: The Martyrology Book(s) 7 &* by bp Nichol, © 1990

The Estate of bp Nichol. Reprinted by permission of Eleanor Nichol for the Estate of bp Nichol.

"The Dog Man" by Lydia Davis, first published in *boundary 2* 14.1/2 (1984), © 1984 by Lydia Davis. Reprinted by permission of the author.

Selections from "Spring Drawing" taken from *Human Wishes* by Robert Hass, © 1989 by Robert Hass. First published by The Ecco Press in 1989. Reprinted by permission of the publisher.

Introduction
The Prose Poem and the Ideology of Genre

Verse is everywhere in language where there is rhythm, everywhere,
except on posters and page four of the newspapers. In the genre which we
call prose there is verse of every conceivable rhythm, some of it admirable.
But in reality there is no prose: there is the alphabet, and then there are
verse forms, more or less rigid, more or less diffuse. In every attempt at
style there is versification.

Stéphane Mallarmé, "Réponses à des enquêtes"

All that is not prose is verse,
and all that is not verse is prose.

Molière, *Le Bourgeois gentilhomme*

Since its first official appearance in nineteenth-century France with Charles
Baudelaire's celebrated *Paris Spleen* (begun in 1855 and first published in
full in 1869), the prose poem, "the literary genre with an oxymoron for a
name" (M. Riffaterre 117), has not ceased to puzzle readers and critics
alike. In his famous preface to the collection, Baudelaire himself nevertheless sought to put forward a first definition of the genre as "the miracle of
a poetic prose, musical though rhythmless and rhymeless, flexible yet rugged enough to identify with the lyrical impulses of the soul, the ebbs and
flows of reverie, the pangs of conscience" (*Poems* 25). Baudelaire's *Paris
Spleen* was one of the first significant attempts by a major representative of
the Western canon to question the then widely accepted formal and phonic
premises of poetry, namely the presence of rhyme and meter. In the English-
speaking world, the prose poem and other forms of "poetic prose" were
later cherished by the British Decadents as an ideal form in which to fulfill
their craving for syntactic intricacies and stylistic mannerisms. Since then,
the prose poem in English has veered off in various directions as antipodal
as Gertrude Stein's Cubist vignettes in *Tender Buttons*, Sherwood Anderson's Whitmanesque hymns in *Mid-American Chants*, and more recently
Robert Bly's "Deep Image" poems or the postgeneric experiments of the
new American avant-garde known as the "Language poetry" group. Baudelaire's generic *enfant terrible* now seems to have developed almost as
many trends as there are poets practicing it, so that any attempt at a single,
monolithic definition of the genre would be doomed to failure.[1]

As suggested by the diversity of stylistic, modal, and methodological approaches to the genre represented in this study, the history of the contemporary prose poem in English is, to a large extent, the history of the successive attempts by poets to redefine the parameters governing our expectations of what a poem (or a prose poem) should look or sound like. If we turn to specialized reference works, such as the *Princeton Encyclopedia of Poetry and Poetics,* we find the following detailed description of what a prose poem should and should not be:

> PROSE POEM (poem in prose). A composition able to have any or all the features of the lyric, except that it is put on the page—though not conceived of—as prose. It differs from poetic prose in that it is short and compact, from free verse in that it has no line breaks, from a short prose passage in that it has, usually, more pronounced rhythms, sonorous effects, imagery, and density of expression. It may contain even inner rhyme and metrical runs. Its length, generally, is from half a page (one or two paragraphs) to three or four pages, i.e., that of the average lyrical poem. If it is any longer, the tensions and impact are forfeited, and it becomes—more or less poetic—prose. The term "prose poem" has been applied irresponsibly to anything from the Bible to a novel by Faulkner, but should be used only to designate a highly conscious (sometimes even self-conscious) art form.

Other definitions in the same vein include Martin Gray's description of the genre as a "short work of poetic prose, resembling a poem because of its ornate language and imagery, and because it stands on its own, and lacks narrative: like a lyric poem but not subjected to the patterning of metre." For M. H. Abrams, Baudelaire's *Paris Spleen,* Rimbaud's *Illuminations,* and a number of "excerptible passages" from Pater's prose essays "approximate the form that in the nineteenth century was called the prose poem: densely compact, pronouncedly rhythmic, and highly sonorous compositions which are written as a continuous sequence of sentences without line breaks."

The common denominator of these various definitions is a conception of the prose poem defined from the perspective of poetry, one which brings forward two distinct but interrelated assumptions concerning the nature of "the poetic." The first of these assumptions, to which we will turn later, relies on an all-too-common equation of poetic language with the lyric; it postulates that a poem should be a relatively short piece of writing concerned primarily with the expression of feelings. The second hypothesis posits that the degree of stylistic and imagistic "density" of poetry allegedly distinguishes it from the dull, commonplace, matter-of-fact language of prose. Since poetry, as Ursula K. Le Guin memorably put it, is "the beautiful dumb blonde, all words," and prose the "smart brunette with glasses, all ideas" (109), the first task of a prose poet should be to reproduce the rhythmic, sonorous, and stylistic richness commonly associated with poetic language through the medium of prose.

According to such a view, poetic language is primarily characterized by a more "vehement" usage of the same stylistic devices present in literary prose. As Roland Barthes argues in *Writing Degree Zero,* these strictly stylistic considerations still rely on the classical conception of poetry as "merely an ornamental variation of prose," a mode which is felt to be "a minimal form of speech, the most economical vehicle for thought." In the following double equation, Barthes uses the letters *a, b,* and *c* for "certain attributes of language, which are useless but decorative, such as meter, rhyme or the ritual of images":

Poetry = Prose + a + b + c
Prose = Poetry - a - b - c

In the classical period, Barthes comments, the difference is clearly not one of essence but one of quantity, as poetry and prose are "neither more nor less separated than two different numbers, contiguous like them, but dissimilar because of the very difference in their magnitudes" (*Reader* 53). This conception of poetry as a measurable degree of stylistic and imagistic "decorativeness" always already present in any literary work—whether written in prose or in verse—has remained, until recently, a basic tenet in contemporary literary criticism. As Jean Cohen claims in *Structure du langage poétique,* "prose is only a moderate kind of poetry." Poetry, by contrast, is seen as "the most passionate form of literature, the paroxysmic degree of style. Style is one. It comprises a finite number of figures, always the same. From prose to poetry and from one state of poetry to another, the difference is only in the audacity with which language employs the processes virtually inscribed within its structure" (149).

As we will see, Cohen's notion of poetic language, a relativistic variant of Coleridge's "homely definitions of prose and poetry" ("prose = words in their best order; poetry = the best words in their best order"), cannot do justice to the history of the contemporary prose poem, the subversive potential of which is certainly not based exclusively on an attempt to emulate the stylistic fertility of traditional "poetic" language. However, the most problematic aspect shared by Cohen's theory and the aforegoing definitions of the prose poem as a piece of "poeticized" prose is that traditional categories associated with the "poetic"—including metaphorical density, stylistic sophistication, and lyric intimacy—have long ceased to be the convenient hallmarks that, at the time of Oscar Wilde and Walter Pater, enabled one to separate the wheat from the chaff by making the difference between "poetic prose" and the undecorative, utilitarian matter-of-factness of "prosaic" prose. Now that ordinary language and diction have gained acceptance into the canon of American poetry, one is entitled to wonder about the possible survival of formal, phonic, or thematic standards of poeticity in view of the progressive narrowing of the contemporary poetry reader's "horizon of expectations," to use Hans Robert Jauss' famous expression.

How are we to approach a prose text labeled as poetry at a time when traditional notions of poetic language have become so problematic? Despite the advent of free verse and the subsequent obsolescence of metric and stylistic criteria for distinguishing poetry from prose, the prose poem has paradoxically continued to be regarded by many as a rather disturbing, if not downright illegitimate mode of literary expression. Though it would no longer seem necessary to refute essentialist notions of genre, the relatively unexpected commotion caused in the poetic and critical establishment by Charles Simic's 1990 Pulitzer Prize–winning collection of prose poems, *The World Doesn't End*,[2] suggests that a number of prescriptive norms about the formal premises of poetry continue to prevail, even in a country which was among the first to free poetic expression from both stylistic sophistication and prosodic convention. At a time when verse and poetry are no longer necessarily synonymous, the survival of a certain number of formal expectations and prescriptive boundaries between literary genres nonetheless remains the uncertain ground from which the prose poem still manages to draw a significant part of its subversive and, some would argue, political potential. What is more, the recent renewal of interest by both writers and critics in the prose poem, a "formless" genre par excellence, has greatly contributed to relegitimizing debates concerning the specific attributes of poeticity resisted or transgressed by prose poets. As the following chapters show, the allegedly "genreless" or "postgeneric" space of the prose poem has given a new significance and a new relevance to the notion of genre itself.

*   *   *

The prose poem was first introduced to the English-speaking public by Stuart Merrill's *Pastels in Prose,* a collection of French prose poems in English translation published in New York in 1890. In the years that followed the appearance of Merrill's anthology, the prose poem began to arouse the interest of a whole generation of British Decadent writers. The main representatives of the British prose poem in the final years of the nineteenth century included Ernest Dowson, the Scottish author William Sharp (a.k.a. Fiona Macleod), and Oscar Wilde, whose parable-like *Poems in Prose* (1894) are the first instance of a consciously cultivated tradition of the prose poem in English. In the general climate of self-conscious Aestheticism that characterized the work of these writers in the 1880s and 1890s, the prose poem—which was then viewed as barely distinguishable from other experiments with "poetic prose," such as the "artistic" prose of Walter Pater's essays on Renaissance art—almost naturally became a preferred form for the kind of painstaking artifice and stylistic sophistication favored by the fin-de-siècle generation. The typical Decadent prose poem combines a colorful, heavily stylized vocabulary with a deceptively simple, self-consciously archaic diction often inspired by the King James Bible. Like many prose poems written at the heyday of British Aestheticism, William Sharp's "Orchil" also makes use of a number of formal features, such as the use of repetitions and alliterations, which were meant to approximate the musical quality of traditional verse:[3]

> I dreamed of Orchil, the dim goddess who is under the brown earth, in a vast cavern, where she weaves at two looms. With one hand she weaves life upward through the grass; with the other she weaves death downward through the mould; and the sound of the weaving is Eternity, and the name of it in the green world is Time. And, through all, Orchil weaves the weft of Eternal Beauty, that passeth not, though her soul is Change.
>
> This is my comfort, O Beauty that art of Time, who am faint and hopeless in the strong sound of that other Weaving, where Orchil, the dim goddess, sits dreaming at her loom under the brown earth. (Füger 60)

One of the first critical responses to such a conception of the prose poem as a piece of stylized and "poeticized" prose (Ernest Dowson's 1899 collection of prose poems was quite appropriately named *Decorations in Prose*) was voiced by T. S. Eliot in 1917. In an essay entitled "The Borderline of Prose," Eliot reacted against the prose poems of Richard Aldington, which he saw as a disguised attempt to revive the stylistic preciousness and technical "charlatanism" ("Borderline" 158) of the Decadents. In contrast with the prose poems of Baudelaire's *Paris Spleen* and the "pure prose" of

Rimbaud's *Illuminations,* which he admired, Eliot condemned Aldington's hybrid prose poems on the ground that they "seem[ed] to hesitate between two media" (159). As became clear in a second essay on the subject, published in 1921, Eliot objected less to the prose poets' endeavors to create a hybrid genre than to the terms *prose poem* and *prose poetry* themselves, to which he preferred the more neutral expression *short prose* ("Prose and Verse" 6). That Eliot's fierce condemnation of the formal hybridity of the prose poem did much to discourage other early modernist poets from even trying their hand at the genre is beyond any doubt—if Eliot had been the lesser poet, and Aldington one of the most respected and influential men of letters of his time, the history of the contemporary prose poem in English might have taken a totally different turn. Be that as it may, Eliot cannot be blamed for dismissing a tradition that, besides Aldington's rather undistinguished "impressionistic" sketches, had so far produced little more than a handful of neo-Ossianic hymns and Wildean "poetic parables." Indeed, one of the more positive implications of Eliot's rejection of Aldington's prose poems was that the modern prose poem needed to rid itself of the stigmata of the Decadent school and its reliance on "outward" attributes of poeticity.

As we will see, an alternative to the stylistic "charlatanism" of the Decadents can already be detected in Eliot's one published prose poem, "Hysteria" (1915), the matter-of-fact tone and unlyrical content of which distinguish it from any previous tradition of the prose poem in English and make it an interesting precursor of the so-called fabulist trend examined in chapter 3. However, the process of emancipation of the contemporary prose poem from its fin-de-siècle heritage was a slow and difficult one. A typical example of the ambivalent relationship of early modernist writers with the prose lyric was Amy Lowell's "polyphonic prose," which was based on "the long, flowing cadence of oratorical prose" (xii) and the poetic quality of which relied on "the recurrence of a dominant thought or image, coming in irregularly and in varying words, but still giving the spherical effect . . . imperative in all poetry" (xv). The circular, contrapuntal patterns of Lowell's polyphonic prose (which first appeared in the volume *Can Grande's Castle* in 1918 and was originally inspired by Paul Fort's experiments with "rhythmic prose") made it to a large extent a continuation of, rather than a departure from, the Decadent tradition of the prose poem, which amounted to a transposition of metrical and phonic constraints of verse onto the medium of prose—like its fin-de-siècle counterparts, Lowell's polyphonic prose still aspired to the "musical" condition of the verse lyric.

Lowell's insistence on "the absolute adequacy of the manner of a passage [of polyphonic prose] to the thought it embodies" (xi), however, also makes *Can Grande's Castle* an early example of an American variation on the Baudelairian project to create a prose supple enough to be able to reproduce "the lyrical impulses of the soul, the ebbs and flows of reverie, the pangs of conscience" (*Spleen* 24). At a time when British and American novelists were becoming increasingly interested in registering the full spectrum of mental life (what William James had described in his *Principles of Psychology* [1890] as "the stream of thought, of consciousness, or of subjective life" [Bradbury 197]), it is hardly surprising that the first genuinely modern experiments with the short prose lyric were carried out by two major representatives of the stream-of-consciousness novel: James Joyce and Gertrude Stein. As is shown in the prologue to this study, Joyce's early "dream epiphanies" (1900–1904) constitute the first modern attempt to use the prose poem as a vehicle for approaching the capricious "flow" of consciousness and the process of subjective experience from the side of the lyric.

*   *   *

"What is?" laments the disappearance of the poem—another catastrophe.
By announcing that which is just as it is, a question salutes the birth of prose.
Jacques Derrida, "Che cos'è la poesia"

If most modernist writers still regarded the prose poem as a rather marginal phenomenon and a mere curiosity for Francophiles, a recent "revival" of the genre in the United States is attested to by the publication, over the past twenty-five years, of numerous volumes of prose poems, notably by some of America's most distinguished poets, such as Robert Bly, Rosmarie Waldrop, or Charles Simic. Still, only recently have American critics started to show an interest in the prose poem as a genre. Unfortunately, the two studies published so far on the prose poem in English, Stephen Fredman's *Poet's Prose* and Margueritte Murphy's *A Tradition of Subversion,* focus on a limited number of contemporary writers whose works are by no means representative of the wide variety of items currently published and received as prose poems in countless collections and poetry magazines.[4] With the exception of Gertrude Stein's *Tender Buttons,* William Carlos Williams' *Improvisations,* and Robert Bly's *The Morning Glory,* the great majority of the works dealt with in the present study—and which are nevertheless generally credited with having given the prose poem in English its *lettres de noblesse*—have been consistently neglected by literary criticism, both in Europe and in the United States, even by the few critics who have so far written on the genre.

In addition to providing an analysis of several canonical or noncanonical collections all too often ignored by critics, I offer a general survey of the contemporary prose poem in English, in the course of which the work of numerous "minor" or occasional contemporary writers of prose poems—including such established writers as Sherwood Anderson, Kenneth Patchen, and W. S. Merwin—are dealt with more briefly. My intention, however, is not to produce an exhaustive chronological account of the development of the modern prose poem in English but, rather, to describe a number of important directions taken by the genre as it has been defined and redefined by its practitioners throughout the twentieth century.[5] In this respect, I approach the notion of genre itself as a historical rather than a theoretical category—that is, by drawing inductively on an existing body of contemporary works labeled, marketed, or simply received as prose poems, rather than by establishing a prescriptive construct that would precondition my attempts to come to terms with the texts themselves.[6] Whenever possible, the following chapters privilege the issue of "generic intentionality" through an investigation of the various creative and theoretical approaches the prose poets themselves apply to their own work and the work of others.

With the exception of Stephen Fredman in his groundbreaking *Poet's Prose: The Crisis in American Verse,* the critics who have so far attempted to account for the potential for innovation of the prose poem as a genre have done so by referring to a single, synthetic system of interpretation. Michael Riffaterre, for instance, defines the text's relation to a selected "intertext" as the single, invariant constitutive feature of the genre; Jonathan Monroe in *A Poverty of Objects* and Margueritte Murphy in *A Tradition of Subversion* rely on Mikhail Bakhtin's theories on the novel in emphasizing the prose poem's inherently "dialogical" and "heteroglot" nature. Both studies describe the genre as the locus of convergence or conflict of various discourses, which in turn reflect a variety of extradiscursive realities, including a number of specific social, political, and ideological agendas. Ultimately, they suggest that the prose poem exists mainly by reference to other genres, which it tends to include or exclude, subscribe to or subvert.

To some extent, this emphasis on the inherently intertextual and heteroglot dynamics of the prose poem is indispensable in the context of a form whose very name suggests its ambivalent status as a genre writing across other genres—a self-consciously deviant form, the aesthetic orientation and subversive potential of which are necessarily founded on a number of discursive and typographical violations. One way of coming to terms with the inherent duality of the prose poem therefore consists in attending to the specific generic conventions alternately introduced and negated by the genre. Instead of resorting to a single interpretive strategy, however, in the present study I consider the contemporary prose poem—approached in the light of its multiple love-hate relationships with dominant aesthetic and extra-aesthetic discourses—as representative of how individual works can subvert the very codes and narratives by which they exist and can expose them as the product of specific historical moments. Consequently, the prose poem is also addressed as emblematic of how literary genres conceal traces of their own underlying aesthetic contradictions, including the fact that such metagenres as "poetry," "narrative," and the "lyric" are always already contaminated by the traces of other generic categories they tend to subscribe to or exclude. Special attention is given to the various transgeneric experiments carried out by contemporary prose poets in the context of a simultaneous move in twentieth-century literature toward a hypothetical *degree zero* of genre. In this respect, also, traditional generic categories and labels pertaining to "prosaic" as opposed to "poetic" works (including the elusive distinction between newcomers like the "short short story" or "sudden fiction" and a certain kind of prose poem with a strong narrative line) appear as just another familiar narrative the prose poem tends to subvert and deconstruct by virtue of its own shamelessly hybrid modalities.

* * *

In a recent study entitled *The Power of Genre*, the critic Adena Rosmarin claims that "a genre is chosen or defined to fit neither a historical nor a theoretical reality but to serve a pragmatic end" (49–50). Rosmarin's subsequent call for a revised theory of genre as a critical instrument and a tool for the interpretation of individual texts is symptomatic of the current crisis of legitimization undergone by genre theory and criticism. At a time when the notion of "generic instability" has become an accomplished fact in both postmodern aesthetics and poststructuralist theory, the taxonomic logic often associated with genre studies indeed appears still to be caught in the throes of its former existence as a prescriptive discourse. The retrieval and revaluation of forgotten, minor and marginal genres, the preoccupation with intertextuality and pastiche, and the desire for cross-cultural and cross-discursive forms all testify to a new network of complications, contradictions, and paradoxes not easily containable within the symmetrical hierarchies and paradigms of traditional genre theories.

In the midst of this postgeneric chaos, the prose poem remains a relatively young genre still in the process of self-definition, a formal abstraction whose changing methods and ambitions are exceptionally difficult to define and formulate. By testing the validity of our assumptions concerning the nature and function of both poetic and prosaic language, the prose poem inevitably leads us to investigate a number of specific postulates underlying the act of defining genres and, above all, of tracing boundaries between them. In the absence of any transhistorical definition of the prose poem, descriptive—and essentially modal—orientations will be preferred to the prescriptive generic taxonomies of mainstream genre theory, which, more often than not, still stubbornly perpetuates the sacrosanct poetry/ verse/lyric triad. More generally, I here consider the notion of genre itself as necessarily founded on a semi-arbitrary link between a label and its "content." As Tzvetan Todorov reminds us, there is no "pure" (or even purely "lyric," "epic," or "dramatic") genre, and even a "new" genre automatically exists by reference to one or several previously existing ones (*Genres* 15). Since a particular genre does not exist exclusively by virtue of its own constitutive features but also—and above all—in terms of its relationship with other norms, labels, or discursive conventions, a literary work always possesses a given generic value both within and without each of the genres, subgenres, and modes of representation it belongs to, "straddles," or subverts.

Whoever acknowledges the necessity to recognize the specific norms transgressed or eluded by the prose poem will easily identify the underlying contradiction of a number of recent theories proclaiming the alleged "post-" or "nongeneric" nature of the genre. In this respect, neither Michael Davidson's "nongeneric" prose ("After Sentence" 3) nor Stephen Fredman's description of the prose poem as "a kind of 'last genre'," purporting to effect what Octavio Paz calls "the mixture and ultimate abolition of genres" in Western literature (Fredman 5), can adequately account for the subversive potential of the works discussed here, which can be regarded as so many creative transactions at work both within and against a specific set of generic and discursive conventions.

As suggested, an alternative to both traditional generic systems and Fredman's theory concerning the postgeneric status of the prose poem consists in seeing beyond the existence of generic boundaries as such in order to look for similarities and differences between individual works. As Paul Hernadi writes, arguing for a radical reconsideration of the basic axioms of genre theory, "things may be similar in *different respects*" (4). This relativistic concept of similarity, which Hernadi himself inherited from Karl R. Popper's *Logic of Scientific Discovery,* provides a useful methodological starting point for a descriptive study of generic *features* present, to a certain extent, in any literary work. Heeding Popper's advice, critics confronted with such an elusive genre as the prose poem will cease to rely on the claims to universal validity of traditional generic distinctions. Instead, they will seek to account for the rhetorical gesture(s) involved in the act of composing and labeling a piece of prose as a prose poem, as well as for the complex interplay between its synchronic and diachronic positions in the history of modern literature.

*   *   *

Jonathan Monroe defines the literary and historical significance of the prose poem as "above all that of a critical, self-critical, utopian genre, a genre that tests the limits of genre" (16). The prose poem, he adds, "aspires to be poetic/literary language's own coming to self-consciousness, the place where poet and reader alike become critically aware of the writer's language" (35–36). By putting the accent on the genre's status as a self-consciously deviant form, Monroe raises the issue of the possibility of a *mise en abyme* of genericness by an individual literary work. The question, according to Jacques Derrida, becomes whether a writer is actually practicing a genre, so to speak, "from within" or "from without":

> What are we doing when, to practice a "genre," we quote a genre, represent it, stage it, expose its generic law, analyze it practically? Are we still practicing the genre? Does the work still belong to the genre it re-cites? But inversely, how could we make a genre work without referring to it [quasi-]quotationally, indicating at some point, "See, this is a work of such-and-such a genre"? Such an indication does not belong to the genre and makes the statement of belonging an ironical exercise. It interrupts the belonging of which it is a necessary condition. (*Reader* 259)

Seen from that angle, the act of writing and labeling a literary work is necessarily inscribed in a network of differential relationships between signifiers that are constantly quoting and requoting themselves and each other, sometimes—but not always—in a subversive or parodic fashion. Since a particular genre always exceeds the very formal, thematic, and presentational restrictions that generate it, the supplemental quality of generic labels themselves necessarily makes them subject to an ironical treatment within the individual work. With the interplay of such ironical citations as its object, genre theory, once it has been redefined into a differential practice, can derive new heuristic strategies from the ashes of its now obsoleted prescriptive foundations. In the context of the present work, what Derrida calls the "law of genre"—a "principle of contamination, a law of impurity, a parasitical economy" (*Acts* 227) denying the self-contained integrity of any discourse—seems an adequate model for a descriptive approach to the prose poem, a genre which, more than any other genre, constantly gestures to its own constructedness and, more broadly, to what poststructuralism generally diagnoses as the arbitrariness and undecidability of boundaries.

As we will see, however, a full investigation of the genre-testing potential of the prose poem cannot be limited to describing its intertextual and interdiscursive strategies without accounting for the exact circumstances of its composition and reception. Among my major aims here indeed is to demonstrate that one method of coming to terms with such hybrid "boundary works" (Morson 48) as the prose poem consists in speaking of genre not as a given "thing" but as the expression of a relationship between a reader and a text. Only in such a way can one hope to redefine the taxonomic categories of traditional genre theory into a genuine instrument of exegesis, one which remains justified and valuable if it facilitates continuing insight into the art itself.

*　　*　　*

As the following chapters make clear, the various intergeneric transactions at work in the contemporary prose poem in English often involve the reclamation of a number of nonlyric and nonliterary modes and discourses. Jonathan Holden has provided a convincing analysis of the possibility of reclaiming for poetry the right to explore the syntactic and semantic possibilities of public, utilitarian prose from the point of view of verse. His thought-provoking *The Fate of American Poetry* examines the different ways in which verse forms can or cannot investigate a number of functions, modes, and subject matters that seem to be monopolized by prose genres. After exploring the didactic and storytelling orientations of American poetry, as well as how these specific orientations distinguish themselves from their equivalents in didactic prose and prose narratives, Holden proceeds to discuss the potential for discursiveness of verse poetry as opposed to that of "nonfiction prose." Comparing a passage of expository prose with a verse adaptation of it, Holden contrasts the self-contained isolatedness of the lineated version with the contextual discursiveness of the prose original. "The rhetorical markers and the diction of prose," he concludes, "have the effect of subtly qualifying each proposition by placing it in a larger context than would be implied by the verse version":

The urbanity and sense of wisdom that the best prose affords derives, in large part, from its unhurried and generous admission into discourse of other possible contexts. That is the opposite of lyric poetry. When Coleridge, in his *Biographia Literaria,* argues that in poetry "every passion has its proper pulse," he is assuming that the subject matter of poetry deals, in large part, with "passion." But "passion," it would seem self-evident, is a state of mind in which the subject rules out all possible actions except one, in which mental activity proceeds in a drastically limited context. It becomes obsessive. The speaker of an impassioned lyric does not pause to put things into perspective. In fact, a condition for the success of lyric, and of song, is that it convince the audience, during the interval of the song's duration, to forget any other perspectives. As Barbara Herrnstein Smith put it memorably, in *Poetic Closure:* "A poem must carry its own context on its back." (117)

Holden's approach—which is strictly limited to verse and does not acknowledge the existence of generic hybrids as such—is based on a formal and comparative analysis of the structural and rhetorical potential of lineated poetry as opposed to that of prose. His examination of functional negotiations between verse and prose forms, however, can profitably be extended to the question of whether generic, functional or modal (as opposed to merely structural) categories like "poetry" or the "lyric" can reterritorialize other genres, functions and modes which have come to be associated more or less exclusively with prose literature. As the works of Russell Edson, Michael Benedikt, and other neo-Surrealist prose poets demonstrate, the admission of narrative development or abstract discursiveness into a lyric format is still typical of many prose poems written in the United States today. These prose poems, which question a number of basic assumptions concerning the self-contained "presence" of the lyric mode, also tend to develop affinities with short discursive or narrative forms, whether literary or nonliterary, such as the fable, the parable, the dream narrative, the aphorism, the journal entry, the *pensée,* the dictionary definition, or even the stand-up comedy joke—at the end of these various intergeneric negotiations, what may have resulted in a sort of "anti-genre," or a shapeless polymodal jumble, generally emerges as a self-conscious and creative compromise between two or among several conflicting sets of linguistic codes and conventions.

The notion of a unified and self-present lyric discourse—impervious to its social, political, psychological context or simply to its very textual or linguistic premises—is also challenged, in various ways, by most of the prose poets discussed in the present study. As Jonathan Monroe has argued, referring to the potential of the genre for dialogizing what Bakhtin called the "monological" tendency of the lyric, the prose poem "stands in direct opposition to the notion of a pure, self-contained 'poetic' speech that would betray no sense of historicity or of the social determinations of its own language" (Monroe 35). The range of methods used by prose poets in order to achieve this reintegration of the lyric into a larger constellation of literary and extraliterary contexts is as diverse as that of the various skills and ambitions displayed by the literary periods, movements, writers, and individual prose poems discussed here. Despite an enormous diversity of styles and approaches to the genre, a number of major methodological trajectories nevertheless emerge from the polymorphous and often rather sporadic history of the contemporary prose poem in English. Besides a general tendency to destabilize traditional generic boundaries, these recurrent features include a taste for (self-)parody, an awareness of the necessity to reinscribe the lyric self into a network of personal or public narratives, and a desire to turn the act of writing and the workings of consciousness itself into objects of investigation.

*　　*　　*

Even though they were published posthumously and therefore cannot be granted a historically central or founding place within the genre, James Joyce's "lyrical" epiphanies (1900–1904)—examined in the prologue—emerge as an early attempt to move the prose lyric away from the stylistic intricacies of the British Decadents and to carry out Baudelaire's project to reproduce the complex and discontinuous rhythms of consciousness. Considered in the light of Stephen Daedalus' theory of genres in *A Portrait* and of Barthes' notion of the *romanesque,* Joyce's posthumous *Giacomo Joyce* also enacts the formal struggle between lyric (self-)presence and narrative continuity that was to characterize the genre throughout the twentieth century. By withholding the pressures of both narrative linearity and poetic closure, Joyce's prose fragments eventually result in a "writerly" variant of the traditional lyric, one which attends to nothing less than the movement of desire itself.

Early representatives of a modern, post-Decadent tradition of the American prose lyric are examined in part I. In this respect, also, Joyce's interest in the dialectics of the conscious and unconscious mind makes his "dream epiphanies" an interesting forerunner of the Surrealist "dreamscapes" favored by the *transition* poets discussed in chapter 1. In the absence of a powerful alternative to the epigonic *exercices de style* of the neo-Decadents, the only hope of revitalizing the prose poem had to come from outside the English-speaking world. Indeed, it was not until the advent of a real international avant-garde, influenced by the aesthetics of French Surrealism, that the prose poem in English started to win its credentials. In particular, the birth of the Paris-based English-language magazine *transition* (1927–38), which published all of the major French Surrealists in translation, coincided with a renewal of interest by American writers in the prose poem. Since the Surrealist movement attracted little attention in Anglo-Saxon literary circles before the late 1930s, *transition* also became a unique interface between the French Surrealist movement and a number of expatriate writers then part of literary Paris.[7] At a time when the individual consciousness itself began to be perceived as increasingly fragmented and self-divided, Eugene Jolas' "Proclamation" of the "Revolution of the Word" (1929) favored an approach to the lyric characterized by discontinuity and associational transitions such as were used, in the realm of fiction, in the so-called stream-of-consciousness novel. Long after *écriture automatique* had become somewhat old-fashioned even within the circles of French Surrealist pioneers, the work of a number of writers published in *transition* continued to retain some of the original impulses of *Les Champs magnétiques* (1920), which included, besides a renewed attention to the workings of the subconscious mind, a sense of "writing as process" insisting not so much on the content or subject matter of the poem as on what André Breton called "the actual functioning of thought" (*Manifestos* 26).

More than fifteen years before Jolas' manifesto of the Revolution of the Word, Gertrude Stein, another member of the American community in Paris, had already perceived that another, perhaps even more radical way of renewing the strength of poetry lay in a discovery of the "poetic" potential of descriptive and argumentative syntax. Her early portraits and still lifes laid the foundations of a self-conscious critique of the claims to transparency of mimetic and utilitarian prose, which paved the way for the postlyric mode recently developed by the so-called Language poets. A precursor of a certain form of postmodern poetry rather than a typical representative of the modernist avant-garde, Stein's *Tender Buttons* (1914) argues both for a total reexamination of the use-value of prose and a radical questioning of the aspirations to figurativeness of poetic language.

My discussion of Sherwood Anderson's *Mid-American Chants* (1918) in chapter 2 provides the terms for an analysis of the development of a popular (or "low modernist") tradition of the prose poem represented by a number of texts largely written out of the canon of American literature. Whereas Anderson's prose "chants" seek to accommodate a vision of the collective self and the expression of subjective feelings, Kenneth Patchen's dissonant stylistic medleys in *The Famous Boating Party* (1954) prefigure the playful intergeneric fantasies that were to become the hallmarks of the absurdist "narratives of consciousness" of Russell Edson and Michael Benedikt. Patchen's first experiments with the prose poem in the late 1940s can also be seen as a kind of "missing link" in the history of the contemporary prose poem, which vanishes almost completely from the Anglo-American literary scene after the heyday of Jolas' *transition,* only to reappear in the United States in the 1960s.

Part II is devoted to some of the best-known representatives of this so-called "American prose poem revival," including pioneers such as Russell Edson, Robert Bly, and Michael Benedikt, as well as a number of newcomers such as Charles Simic and Canadian writer Margaret Atwood. Chapter 3, which centers on the fabulist (or Jacobean) trend of the prose poem made famous by Russell Edson, begins with a theoretical examination of the relationship between the narrative prose poem and recent generic neologisms such as sudden fiction and the short short story. I then proceed to consider to what extent the metapoetic foregrounding of discourse and writing-as-process that characterizes the fabulist prose poem is linked with an understanding of poetic language as a deviant use of the language of rational logic and a number of specific conventions underlying discursive or narrative genres. In this perspective, special attention will be given to how the didactic aims and moral certainties traditionally attached to the fable and the parable become engulfed in the turmoil of Edson's poetics of metafictional fabulation and "paradox." Margaret Atwood's prose poems and "short shorts" use a number of other parodic and metapoetic strategies in order to debunk the various sociolinguistic assumptions underlying diverse literary and nonliterary narratives. Her more specifically feminist concern with the textual and existential constraints imposed upon the feminine self argues for an approach to both genre and gender as cultural formulae lodged at the intersection of literary and ideological discourses.

Bly's "thing poems," discussed in chapter 4, are emblematic of the preoccupation with objects that characterizes the work of a number of major representatives of the contemporary prose poem, such as Gertrude Stein and Francis Ponge. Unlike the majority of the works discussed in this study, however, the work of Robert Bly displays a strong distrust of abstraction and discursiveness. The assumptions of artlessness and immediacy that constitute the premises of Bly's poetics of the "Deep Image" also distinguish his work from the fabulist trend of the American prose poem, which on the whole tends toward the foregrounding of artifice and of the text's self-consciousness.

Charles Simic's 1990 Pulitzer Prize–winning *The World Doesn't End*, examined in chapter 5, is one of the most recent, and also one of the most accomplished, avatars of the American neo-Surrealist prose poem. Even though Simic's prose poems share some of the defining features of the fabulist prose poem (including a taste for black humor and tragicomical absurdities), their most important feature is an ability to create a successful blending of lyric, philosophical, and critical material. In *Dime-Store Alchemy*, a double homage to the art of Joseph Cornell and to the city of New York, Simic regards the modern city as a new spatial model for a redefinition of the poetic, which becomes a means of "making strange" objects or events we tend to perceive as trivial or prosaic.

Throughout the twentieth century, the prose poem has often been used as a means of questioning and redefining the methods, aims, and ideological significance habitually attributed to both poetry and prose. Nowhere in recent years has this tendency been more apparent than in the experiments of the so-called Language poetry movement. The language-centered dynamics of Ron Silliman's "New Prose Poem," examined in part III, are directly inspired by the work of Gertrude Stein. Like many other Language poets, Silliman indeed shares Stein's skepticism about the implicit relationship of language to reference and the transparent "naturalness" of descriptive and argumentative syntax. In the larger context of the development of postwar American poetry, Silliman's "New Prose Poem" also seeks to deconstruct Charles Olson's speech-based "open field" and to redefine it into a primarily scriptural medium. More generally, the Language poets' creative and theoretical project as a whole—which echoes Derrida's critique of Western logocentrism and the poststructuralist deconstruction of literary subjectivity—rejects any conception of poetry as a spontaneous, "natural" utterance and provides the terms for a lyric mode "with a difference," one which puts the accent on the inherent textuality of the lyric self. In the course of my analysis of the rejection of mimesis and referentiality advocated by the Language poets, I also look upon their deconstructive practices as an ambitious (if not altogether successful) reorientation of poetic practice toward social and political analysis. Finally, I consider the emphasis the Language movement lays on theoretical discussion and how it eventually leads to the erasure of traditional divisions between creative and utilitarian forms of writing. By deconstructing the very notion of genre as just another dominant "narrative" and by calling into question the naturalness of accepted boundaries between prose and poetry, the lyric and the narrative, or the literal and the figurative, the New Prose Poem emerges as the methodological culmination of the transgeneric experiments dealt with in the preceding chapters.

Prologue
James Joyce and the Novelistic Fragment

James Joyce's first meeting with William Butler Yeats took place in early October 1902 in the smoking room of a Dublin restaurant. According to Yeats' own account of the interview, Joyce, then a twenty-year-old undergraduate, claimed to have "thrown over metrical form" and succeeded in creating "a form so fluent that it would respond to the motions of the spirit" (Ellmann 102). That Joyce declined to call his prose sketches prose poems is hardly surprising, considering his well-known reluctance to be assimilated into any specific literary tradition. The term *prose poem* (which, in English literature, had so far been applied, somewhat loosely, to a variety of neo-Ossianic eclogues and Wildean *contes-poèmes*) probably appeared far too restrictive to the young man whom Richard Ellmann describes as already confident enough in his talents as a prose writer "to feel he might outdo George Moore, Hardy, and Turgenev, if not Tolstoy" (83). Be that as it may, Joyce's description of the "epiphany," despite its claims to novelty, reads like a quasi-verbatim rerun of Charles Baudelaire's famous definition of the genre as "the miracle of a poetic prose . . . flexible yet rugged enough to identify with the lyrical impulses of the soul" (*Poems* 25). A second, even more striking similarity between the Baudelairian prose poem and the Joycean epiphany lies in the capacity of both genres not only to render the fluidity of mental states but also to give shape to an essentially modern and urban reality. In *Stephen Hero* (the earlier version of *A Portrait of the Artist as a Young Man*), Stephen Daedalus, like Baudelaire's *flâneur*, likes to wander through the streets of his native city, gleaning moments of poetic inspiration from seemingly unimpressive and random events:

> He was passing through Eccles' St one evening, one misty evening . . . when a trivial incident set him composing some ardent verses which he entitled a "Vilanelle of the Temptress." A young lady was standing on the steps of one of those brown brick houses which seem

the very incarnation of Irish paralysis. A young gentleman was lean-
ing on the rusty railings of the area. Stephen as he passed on his quest
heard the following fragment of colloquy out of which he received an
impression keen enough to afflict his sensitiveness very severely.

The Young Lady—(drawling discreetly) . . . O, yes . . . I
    was . . . at the . . . cha . . . pel . . .
The Young Gentleman—(inaudibly) . . . I . . . (again
    inaudibly) . . . I . . .
The Young Lady—(softly) . . . O . . . but you're . . . ve
    . . . ry . . . wick . . . ed . . .

This triviality made him think of collecting many such moments
together in a book of epiphanies. By an epiphany he meant a sudden
spiritual manifestation, whether in the vulgarity of speech or of gesture or in a memorable phase of the mind itself. He believed that it
was for the man of letters to record these epiphanies with extreme
care, seeing that they themselves are the most delicate and evanescent
of moments. (*Stephen* 188)

Most of the forty surviving epiphanies were later adapted and used in
Joyce's more extended works of fiction.[1] Many critics have therefore
tended to consider them as merely preparatory material for Joyce's "ambitious" works. However, the neatly and carefully written manuscripts Joyce
left behind him—all of which seem to date from between 1902 and 1904—
leave no reason to believe that he did not originally consider them as literary achievements in their own right.[2] Joyce even played for a time with
the idea of gathering them in a volume and, in a letter sent to his brother
Stanislaus in 1903, referred to them as a single work simply entitled
"Epiphany" (*Letters* 2:28). In a brief, self-mocking remembrance, Stephen's reincarnation in *Ulysses* later dismissed the project as the product of
an arrogant and immature mind: "Remember your epiphanies on green
oval leaves, deeply deep, copies to be sent if you died to all the great librar-
ies of the world, including Alexandria? Someone was to read them there
after a few thousand years, a mahamanvantara. Pico della Mirandola like"
(*Ulysses* 41).

Stephen Daedalus' definition of the epiphany as "a sudden spiritual
manifestation, whether in the vulgarity of speech or of gesture or in a
memorable phase of the mind itself" points to the existence of two distinct

epiphanic modes reflected in the extant manuscripts themselves: the one consists in a brief dramatic dialogue, the other in a short descriptive or narrative sketch. While the "dramatic" epiphanies (which include Stephen's description of an overheard conversation in the passage quoted) arising from "the vulgarity of speech or gesture" are evidently preparatory, the "lyric" epiphanies (Scholes and Kain 3–4) are in the form of short but relatively self-contained vignettes, often inspired by a dream.

Joyce's early fascination with dreams, which he shared with a number of other Dublin poets such as George Russell and Yeats, suggests that at least one of the original impulses behind his short prose sketches was quite independent from his project to incorporate them into a larger narrative. Richard Ellmann is undoubtedly right in suggesting that, although Freud's *Traumdeutung* appeared in late 1899 (that is, shortly before Joyce wrote his first dream epiphanies), Joyce's interest in dreams was pre-Freudian "in that it look[ed] for revelation, not scientific explanation" (85).[3] This is not to say, however, that Joyce was not interested in the secret or latent meaning of the oneiric mind.[4] As his brother Stanislaus wrote, retrospectively, in *My Brother's Keeper,* "there is no hint . . . that [Joyce] considered dreams anything but an uncontrolled rehash of our waking thoughts, though he may have hoped they would reveal things our controlled thoughts unconsciously conceal" (S. Joyce 127). Considering the revelatory quality Stephen consistently ascribes to the epiphany, it seems very unlikely indeed that Joyce should have been interested solely in its potential for reproducing the basic rhythms of the unconscious. Just like the dramatic epiphanies, the dream narratives were supposed to deliver one or several "evanescent" moments of insight—the writer's task was to perceive and disclose their symbolic relevance in the outside world.

Epiphany #30 demonstrates clearly this dialogical process between the waking and the unconscious mind. Joyce's dream vision illustrates his conflicting feelings toward his mother country as well as his fear of spiritual imprisonment. More generally, it outlines the theme of the relationship of the artist to his family, culture, and race that was to preoccupy Joyce throughout the composition of *Stephen Hero* and *A Portrait of the Artist as a Young Man:*[5]

The spell of arms and voices—the white arms of roads, their promise of close embraces and the black arms of tall ships that stand against the moon, their tales of distant nations. They are held out to say: We are alone,—come. And the voices say with them, We are your

people. And the air is thick with their company as they call to me their
kinsman, making ready to go, shaking the wings of their exultant and
terrible youth. (*Poems* 190)

If one refers to Yeats' description of the epiphanies as "a beautiful
though immature and eccentric harmony of little prose descriptions and
meditations" (Ellmann 102), there is good reason to believe that all or most
of the pieces Joyce submitted to him belonged to the so-called "narrative"
or "lyric" species. Considering Joyce's own emphasis on the malleable flu-
ency of prose, the dream narrative evidently corresponds to the Baudelairian ideal of a form freed from the constraints of metrical verse, one
which is capable of reproducing the "actual" movement of consciousness
and accommodating the capricious narrative logic of the dream mind.

While some dream epiphanies, like "[The Spell of Arms of Voices]," are
certainly imagined and visionary, others seem rooted in the observation of
an everyday incident:

Dull clouds have covered the sky. Where three roads meet before a
swampy beach a big dog is recumbent. From time to time he lifts his
muzzle in the air and utters a prolonged sorrowful howl. People stop
to look at him and pass on; some remain, arrested, it may be, by that
lamentation in which they seem to hear the utterance of their own
sorrow that had once its voice but is now voiceless, a servant of labo-
rious days. Rain begins to fall. (Epiphany #8 [*Poems* 168])

Virtually nothing distinguishes this piece from even a fairly "realist"
passage excerpted from one of Joyce's works of fiction. In "[The Big
Dog]"—which Joyce himself interpreted to be about his brother Stanislaus
(*My Brother's Keeper* 136)—the dreamlike quality of the vignette arises
mainly from the absence of contextual elements. Since Joyce's "dreamscape" appears isolated and independent from a larger narrative or dramatic whole, the type of reading it imposes on its audience is one that
encourages what Jonathan Culler has called "the expectation of totality or
coherence" (170). In the same way as William Carlos Williams' famous
lyric "This Is Just to Say" turns from a note left on a kitchen table into a
self-contained poem as soon as it is set down on the page *as* a poem, the
intimidating margins of silence framing Joyce's epiphanies (which were
neatly and carefully calligraphed on separate sheets) invite a reading that
urges us to assume their inherent totality at the same time as it insists on
their incomplete and fragmentary nature.[6]

"Poems which succeed as fragments or as instances of incomplete totality," Culler writes, "depend for their success on the fact that our drive
towards totality enables us to recognize their gaps and discontinuities and
to give them a thematic value" (171). As a result of Joyce's emphasis on the
lyric quality of the piece, to the detriment of its narrative progress, the
reader has to rely almost exclusively on the (potentially) revelatory nature
of the epiphany in order to construe it into a self-contained whole. In "[The
Big Dog]," this particular interpretive strategy is consolidated by the inter-
vention of an authorial voice, commenting, albeit tentatively, on the reaction of the passers-by, and endowing the dreamscape with symbolic value.
More generally, the semi-allegorical significance of the dream scene is best
understood in the context of Stephen's project to transmute both the content of the subconscious mind and the raw material of "trivial" everyday
experience (here reunited in a single dreamt "incident") into a spiritual
"manifestation"; a moment of revelation or "inscape" at which the commonplace object delivers a sense of "sudden radiance," which here occurs
when the passers-by begin to see in the howling dog an emblem of their
own sorrowful lives.[7]

Giacomo Joyce: Fragments of a Lover's Discourse

> I have the illusion to suppose that by breaking up my discourse I cease to
> discourse in terms of the imaginary about myself, attenuating the risk of
> transcendence; but since the fragment (haiku, maxim, *pensée*, journal
> entry) is *finally* a rhetorical genre and since rhetoric is that layer of
> language which best presents itself to interpretation, by supposing I
> disperse myself I merely return, quite docilely, to the bed of the imaginary.
> Roland Barthes, *Roland Barthes by Roland Barthes*

By translating the liturgical meaning of the term *epiphany* into secular
(though still Platonic and essentialist) terms, the young Joyce purported to
redefine nothing less than the role of the modern artist, who would hence-
forth seek to grasp, record, and transcend the trivial, prosaic incidents and
realities of everyday life into moments of extraordinary aesthetic and spiritual significance. In Joyce's writings, however, the stress is often not so
much on the moment of insight as such as on the process of apprehension
of the object by the individual consciousness. The "apprehensive faculty"
of the artist is described by Stephen as "the gropings of a spiritual eye
which seeks to adjust its vision to an exact focus" (*Stephen* 189). "The
moment the focus is reached," Stephen adds, "the object is epiphanised"—
only then can the aesthete hope to recognize the thing in itself, "its soul, its
whatness" (190).

This double process of aestheticization and interpretation of the real also lies at the heart of *Giacomo Joyce,* a series of prose sketches Joyce wrote in Trieste between late 1911 and 1914, shortly before the publication of *A Portrait of the Artist as a Young Man* and at a time when he had already started to work on *Ulysses.* The manuscript comprises fifty fragments of variable length—ranging from a single line to a little more than one page—painstakingly transcribed onto eight oversized sheets of heavy sketching paper enclosed between the blue paper covers of a school notebook. When Joyce moved to Zurich in 1915, the sketchbook, which bore the name "Giacomo Joyce" on the front cover in an unidentified handwriting, was left behind in the care of Joyce's brother Stanislaus.[8] The small book remained unknown until 1956, when Richard Ellmann discovered it among Stanislaus' possessions. Although Ellmann's biography, published in 1959, featured a discussion of *Giacomo Joyce* (including a significant portion of it), the book first appeared in its entirety in an annotated edition issued by Viking Press in 1968.

Joyce never attempted to have his manuscript published, and the fragments were ultimately recycled to form pages of his longer works of fiction: both *A Portrait* and *Ulysses* contain direct or paraphrased borrowings from *Giacomo Joyce.* The amount of painstaking care that went into the calligraphy of the manuscript, however, leaves no room for doubt concerning its original status as an independent work. Furthermore, *Giacomo Joyce,* unlike Stephen's project of a "book of epiphanies" (*Stephen* 211), is not merely a florilegium of precious but disparate moments of revelation. It is a collection of lyric and narrative fragments all related to a single subject: Joyce's infatuation with one of his students in Trieste, whom Ellmann identifies as Amalia Popper, the daughter of a Triestine Jewish businessman.[9] The explicitly autobiographical character of the poem and the scabrousness of the subject eventually prevented Joyce from publishing the work in its original form. Nevertheless, other considerations of an aesthetic nature may have led Joyce to disown a work whose inherent poetics were irreconcilable with his current aesthetic development as a novelist. In other words, as I argue, Joyce's prose lyrics may have been aesthetically embarrassing as well as biographically compromising. My second purpose is to reexamine the position of *Giacomo Joyce,* within or outside the Joyce canon, in the context of Joyce's ongoing experimentations with both lyric and narrative form. In order to do so, I propose to look first at a number of rhetorical and phenomenological strategies as they operate in Joyce's use of the fragment as well as in his changing conception of the lyric self. The generic negotiations at work in *Giacomo Joyce* are also given special attention as they account for the text's ambivalent status as what Henriette Lazaridis Power calls a "maggot" (623), a formally and thematically unstable quirk whose hybrid poetics test the validity of our assumptions concerning Joyce's chief preoccupations as a poet and a novelist.

> Who? A pale face surrounded by heavy odorous furs. Her movements are shy and nervous. She uses quizzing-glasses.
> *Yes:* a brief syllable. A brief laugh. A brief beat of the eyelids. (*Giacomo* 1)

The opening lines of *Giacomo* are representative of the phenomenological premises of Joyce's fragments, which often originate in the brief but scrupulous observation of a specific part of the student's body. This particular aspect of Joyce's prose lyrics makes them akin to the epiphanies, the heuristic potential of which also results from the artist's apprehension of a given object or incident in its irreducible spatial and temporal particularity. According to Stephen, the first stage of the epiphanization of the real indeed consists in "divid[ing] the entire universe into two parts, the object, and the void which is not the object." The general presentation of the fragments—a series of short blocks of prose surrounded by white space—is particularly well suited to Stephen's desire to grasp the radical "integrity" of things for the sake of aesthetic illumination or Thomist *claritas* (*Stephen* 212).[10]

There is no dearth of books and articles on the literary and philosophical origins of the Joycean epiphany. As Ashton Nichols and other critics have shown, its revelatory value originates in the nineteenth century, notably in Wordsworth's "spots of time," Coleridge's "flashes," Shelley's "best and happiest moments," and Keats' "fine isolated verisimilitude," all of which similarly revealed the mind's ability to perceive the hidden meaning of ordinary events and situations. Another possible influence, that of Ignatius of Loyola, has, to my knowledge, escaped the attention of critics. Saint Ignatius of Loyola, to whom Giacomo appeals for help at the end of the thirteenth fragment (5), occupied a privileged position in Joyce's Jesuit education. One of his *Spiritual Exercises,* the "composition of place," which is mentioned in the third chapter of *A Portrait* (137), recommends meditating upon a physical object as a prelude to the contemplation of a spiritual truth. More than anything else, Loyola's insistence on the essential role played by the imagination in the self's attempts to recognize the heuristic potential of the physical world probably appealed to the young Joyce.

However that may be, Joyce's concern with the self-contained wholeness of the beheld object is as much characteristic of *Giacomo* as it is an essential element of Imagist poetry, a movement in which Joyce was briefly involved and the heyday of which roughly coincides with the composition of the *Giacomo* manuscript.[11] The Imagists' belief in economy of language and brevity of treatment, as well as their penchant for short, single images or objects presented for "direct apprehension," may indeed have inspired some of Joyce's shorter fragments, which—had they been presented in a versified form—would have fitted perfectly in an Imagist anthology:

A flower given by her to my daughter. Frail gift, frail giver, frail blue-veined child. (*Giacomo* 3)

Great bows on her slim bronze shoes: spurs of a pampered fowl. (8)

My words in her mind: cold polished stones sinking through a quagmire. (13)

The last two, haiku-like fragments bear a striking resemblance to Ezra Pound's "In a Station of the Metro" ("The apparition of these faces in the crowd; / Petals on a wet, black bough" [1913]), which also results from the juxtaposition of two images unconnected by any kind of comment or explanation. The unmediated apprehension, "hard and clear, never blurred or indefinite" (Jones 135) of images or objects, which *Giacomo* shares with Imagist poetry, is made possible by the asyndetic dynamics of the collection through which each single "image" acquires irreducible autonomy and is framed in a particular lyric moment.

The fragments quoted above clearly indicate that the very brevity of Joyce's prose lyrics functions as a constitutive part of Giacomo's discourse, which seeks to disclose the essential significance of a series of ephemeral impressions. The elusive, fragmented nature of Giacomo's observations illustrates a principle Roland Barthes was later to describe as one of the major manifestations of the pleasure of the text. Discussing his own taste for discontinuous writing, a tendency apparent in such works as *A Lover's Discourse* and *Roland Barthes*, Barthes explains that his mode of writing was "never lengthy, always proceeding by fragments, miniatures, paragraphs with titles, or articles." One implication of this, he continues, is that the fragment breaks up with what he calls "the smooth finish, the composition, discourse constructed to give a final meaning to what one says" (*Grain* 209). In the preface to *A Lover's Discourse* (revealingly entitled, in French, *Fragments d'un discours amoureux*), Barthes adds that "no logic links the figures (i.e., the incidents or schema in the book), determines their contiguity: the figures are nonsyntagmatic, nonnarrative, they are Erinyes; they stir, collide, subside, return, vanish with no more order than the flight of mosquitoes" (*Fragments* 7).

The resistance of Barthes' writings to narrative and logical linearity is symptomatic of his longing for a mode of discourse he calls the "novelistic" ("le romanesque"). The novelistic, Barthes insists, is a form distinct from the novel, in that it is no longer structured by coherent psychological characters and plot structures. "A mode of notation, investment, interest in daily reality, in people, in everything that happens in life" (*Grain* 222), the novelistic—which Barthes defines elsewhere as "simply that space where subtle, mobile desires can circulate" (*Bruissement* 394)—is concerned with the raw material of common, everyday experience uncontaminated by the pressure of narrative. For Barthes, the *actual* transformation of this novelistic material into a novel—a form of writing he sees as dominated by the "superego of continuity" (*Grain* 132)—is bound to lead to an impoverishment of the text's semantic and psychological open-endedness. In *Roland Barthes par Roland Barthes,* Barthes applies the principle of the novelistic fragment to the art of autobiography and comments that this process of disordering and discontinuing ("that science of apportionment, division, discontinuity, what I referred to somewhat ironically as 'arthrology'" [*Grain* 132]) inevitably entails a dispersal of the speaking or writing subject into a "circle of fragments." The possibility of finding psychological coherence in Barthes' fragments is precluded by the lack of narrative continuity in the discourse itself:

> To write by fragments: the fragments are then so many stones on the perimeter of a circle: I spread myself around: my whole little universe in crumbs; at the center, what? (*Roland Barthes* 92–93)

Barthes' conception of the fragment as disjunctive and anticlosural device—one that resists any extended narrative or syntagmatic development and ultimately results in the decentering of the writing self—proves particularly useful in the context of an analysis of the basic dynamics of Giacomo's discourse. The opening question ("Who?") already indicates the real subject matter of Joyce's fragments, for *Giacomo Joyce* is almost entirely dedicated to the narrator's ever-changing perceptions of his pupil, whom he perceives now as a charming specimen of fragile adolescent beauty ("Frail gift. Frail giver, frail blue-veined child" [*Giacomo* 3], "A cold frail hand: shyness, silence" [13]); now as a source of deadly threat

("She answers my sudden greeting by turning and averting her black basil-isk eyes." / "A starry snake has kissed me: a cold nightsnake. I am lost!" [15]). Giacomo's responses to the young woman follow contradictory patterns of admiration and contempt, submission and domination, desire and disgust. More often than not, they gravitate around a double diptych in which the student is alternately represented as (1) a virgin and a whore; (2) a woman and a child. In this respect, the constant juxtapositions of images of pallor and vividness, candor and sensuousness are facilitated by the inherently paratactic relationships between and within the fragments. Sometimes the juxtaposition occurs within a single sentence, as in "a pale face surrounded by heavy odorous furs" (1). Typically, Giacomo's doubly obsessive attraction to his pupil's virginity and the carnal act are channeled into a vision of endangered virginity and potential prostitution, as in the following juxtaposition of the pupil's assiduousness and the corrupted exuberance of the city's demimonde:

She listens: virgin most prudent.
. . . .
Here are wines all ambered, dying fallings of sweet airs, the proud pavan, kind gentlewomen wooing from their balconies with sucking mouths, the pox-fouled wenches and young wives that, gaily yielding to their ravishers, clip and clip again. (9)

The image of the "sucking mouths," which represents the menace of unbound sexuality, echoes another fragment in which the student's "long lewdly leering lips" are compared with "dark-blooded molluscs" (5). Giacomo's imaginary projections reach a masochistic climax when he envisions the possibility of his committing adultery with his pupil now married and turned into a "cold nightsnake" (15). At the very last moment, the dream vision is short-circuited by a desperate cry to Nora Barnacle:

Soft sucking lips kiss my left armpit: a coiling kiss on myriad veins. I burn! I crumple like a burning leaf! From my right armpit a fang of flame leaps out. A starry snake has kissed me: a cold nightsnake. I am lost!
—Nora!—(15)

The shifting nature of Giacomo's desire, which, simultaneously or alternately directed toward two different objects, oscillates between attraction and repulsion, is also apparent in his variations on the woman-child diptych. In the following fragment, for instance, the pale, frail child's aseptic innocence ("Her body has no smell: an odourless flower" [13]) is threatened, not only by marriage—and the loss of virginity followed by the possibility of adultery—but also by mortality itself:

> She walks before me along the corridor and as she walks a dark coil of her hair slowly uncoils and falls. Slowly uncoiling, falling hair. She does not know and walks before me, simple and proud. So did she walk by Dante in simple pride and so, stainless of blood and violation, the daughter of Cenci, Beatrice, to her death:

> ... *Tie*
> *My girdle for me and bind up this hair*
> *In any simple knot.*
> (11)

The image of Beatrice proudly passing Dante and the reference to another Beatrice, that of Shelley's *The Cenci* (the final quotation is from her death speech), introduce the themes, respectively, of love for a young girl and of incest. They reflect Giacomo's incapacity to express his feelings otherwise than by means of the related strategies of projection, juxtaposition, and narrative. Giacomo's comparison of the student with a series of famous female figures in literary history (he also casts her as Shakespeare's Ophelia, Ibsen's Hedda Gabler, and even Hawthorne's Hester Prynne) is also symptomatic of his repeated attempts to turn the desired object into an unattainable icon of secret worship.[12] By linking the young woman with these tragic literary figures, Giacomo implicitly casts himself as the male characters who worshipped them and were forced to conceal or disguise their love: Dante, Orsino, Hamlet, Ejlert Lövborg, and Arthur Dimmesdale. More generally, these literary allusions blur the borderlines of the student's bodily and textual identity while asserting it in a new paradoxical shape that mirrors Giacomo's own anxieties. As Vicki Mahaffey has pointed out, however, Giacomo's projections can also be seen as a reflection of Joyce's own aesthetic ambitions at the time of writing the *Giacomo* manuscript. "As the author of his own love story," she argues, "Joyce is able to compare himself, not only to five characters, both great and mean, but also to the artists who created them." Joyce is therefore able to "transform a 'failed' imaginary love affair into an important stage in his own artistic development" ("Giacomo" 407). In the same way as the young Stephen's "trivial incident" will wait to be transmuted into some "ardent verses," the young woman only exists in the world of Giacomo's imagination, where she stands as a "writerly" text opening itself up to all kinds of metamorphoses and interpretations. Like Stephen's epiphanies, the novelistic fragments of *Giacomo* show that the young Joyce consistently sought to translate his own experience into art by allowing his imaginative powers to interfere with his vision of the external world. The result of this method is a succession of heavily aestheticized sexual fantasies, increasingly divorced from the "real," observed reality that nourishes Giacomo's insatiable voyeurism.

On a formal and stylistic level, the conflicting nature of Giacomo's textual constructions is often mirrored in the juxtaposition of antipodal tones and modes of representation. Surreal visions or dreamscapes, impressionistic sketches (Giacomo's lady often appears shrouded in faint or shadowy light) coexist alongside more realistic passages, sometimes verging on the unsavory and the morbid. In the context of Joyce's career as a poet and a novelist, the stylistic and modal ambivalence of the prose lyrics of *Giacomo Joyce* appears to constitute a transitional stage between the restrained sophistication of his early verse lyrics in *Chamber Music* and the epico-burlesque prosaism of *Ulysses:*

A ricefield near Vercelli under creamy summer haze. The wings of her drooping hat shadow her false smile. Shadows streak her falsely smiling face, smitten by the hot creamy light, grey wheyhued shadows under the jawbones, streaks of eggyolk yellow on the moistened brow, rancid yellow humour lurking within the softened pulp of the eyes. (2)

Loggione. The sodden walls ooze a steamy damp. A symphony of smells fuses the mass of huddled human forms: sour reeks of armpits, nozzled oranges, melting breast ointments, mastick water, the breath of suppers of sulphurous garlic, foul phosphorescent farts, opoponax, the frank sweat of marriageable and married womankind, the soapy stink of men. . . . All night I have watched her, all night I shall see her: braided and pinnacled hair and olive face and calm soft eyes. A green fillet upon her hair and about her body a green-broidered gown: the hue of the illusion of the vegetable glass of nature and lush grass, the hair of graves. (12)

The first fragment is typical of Giacomo's ambivalent responses to the student's mysterious beauty, in that the description of the girl's serene pallor, emphasized by a subdued but pervasive light, irresistibly slips into a recognition of the potential for treason and corruption hidden beneath the varnish of virginal innocence. Typically, also, the young aesthete associates his distasteful vision of the *loggione* (gallery) in the second fragment with the threat of marriage, which appears to him as a condition of sordid, domestic vulgarity. Giacomo's admiration for the girl's meticulous submissiveness (her "meek supple tendonous neck" [3], "braided and pinnacled hair and calm soft eyes" [2]) alternates with a tone of mockery and contemptuous disdain for her carefree immaturity and her cold indifference to his attempts at seducing her:

> Once more in a chair by the window, happy words on her tongue, happy laughter. A bird twittering after storm, happy that its little foolish life has fluttered out of reach of the clutching fingers of an epileptic lord and giver of life, twittering happily, twittering and chirping happily. (11)

> My words in her mind: cold polished stones sinking through a quagmire. (13)

Here, Giacomo's infatuation (which constantly alternates between patterns of admiration and contempt, domination and submission) turns into a significantly embittered version of the neo-Elizabethan celebration of courtly love of *Chamber Music*. Yet, if Joyce's fragments take place primarily in Giacomo's imagination, the pupil's cold remoteness (she greets him "wintrily . . . darting at [him] for an instant out of her sluggish sidelong eyes a jet of liquorish venom," 15) can usefully be related to the real circumstances of Joyce's life in Trieste. Giacomo's sense of social inferiority climaxes in the "Loggione" scene quoted, in which the English teacher— sitting amid the smelly "mass of huddled human forms" of the gallery— contemplates his pupil's fragile beauty, inaccessibly nestled in the velvet luxury of the stalls. In order to compensate for his position of inferiority, Giacomo rewrites some of his unproductive encounters into scenarios of imaginary possession:

> She raises her arms in an effort to hook at the nape of her neck a gown of black veiling. She cannot: no, she cannot. She moves backwards towards me mutely. I raise my arms to help her: her arms fall. I hold the websoft edges of her gown and drawing them out to hook them I see through the opening of the black veil her lithe little body sheathed in an orange shift. It slips its ribbons of moorings at her shoulders and falls slowly: a lithe smooth naked body shimmering with silvery scales. It slips slowly over the slender buttocks of smooth polished silver and over their furrow, a tarnished silver shadow. . . . Fingers, cold and calm and moving. . . . A touch, a touch. (7)

As the fragments quoted above have shown, Giacomo's love story remains an affair of the eye that can only lead to various forms of imaginary—and primarily aesthetic—forms of gratification. Giacomo's attempts to transform the pupil into a textual construction lacking wholeness and identity go hand in hand with his incapacity to acknowledge and describe her otherwise than in terms of the clothes she is wearing or the parts of her body on which his attention momentarily focuses. The object of his desire appears successively not as a person but as "a pale face," "a brief beat of the eyelids" (1), "a skirt caught back by her sudden moving knee; a white lace edging of an underskirt lifted unduly; a leg-stretched web of stocking" (9), "slowly uncoiling falling hair" (11), "quiet and cold and pure fingers," or "a cold frail hand" and "dark langour-flooded eyes" (13). The frequent use of the indefinite pronoun further impersonalizes the young woman and confirms her status as a mere source of inspiration for Giacomo's visual fantasies.

Through the paratactic and synecdochial strategies at work in the fragments, the narrative of Giacomo's unacceptable desires ("the pages, foul and fair, on which my shame shall glow for ever" [13]) is shattered into pieces and the poem itself is converted into a puzzle, which can only be metonymically reconstructed. Typographically speaking, the synecdochial dismemberment and the subsequent objectification of the student is emphasized by the already reified *en bloc* composition of the prose fragments. In the same way that each block of prose is perceived by the reader as a frozen vision of restrained beauty, the young woman herself is ultimately ascribed the static, disembodied grace of a work of art.[13] Ironically enough, the poem ends with a heraldic transcription of the pupil's hat and umbrella and a final, disenchanted comment on the further reification of the desired object:

Unreadiness. A bare apartment. Torbid daylight. A long black piano: coffin of music. Poised on its edge a woman's hat, red-flowered, and umbrella, furled. Her arms: a casque, gules, and blunt spear on a field, sable.

Envoy: Love me, love my umbrella. (16)[14]

Genres and Modes: Joyce's Conflicting Poetics

In the light of Giacomo's ever-changing perceptions, *Giacomo Joyce*, which Ellmann describes as "Joyce's attempts at the education of a dark lady" (*Giacomo* xi), would, instead, be more aptly characterized as a fragmented and tortured hymn to the meanders of a narcissistic self racked by the all-powerful strategies of its imagination.[15] However, the synecdochial strategies at work in Joyce's vicarious celebration of the student's remote sensuousness do not serve merely to reflect the complexity of Giacomo's emotional turmoil. By placing the emphasis on the perceiving conscious-ness and its attempts to fictionalize the real, the fragmented form of Joyce's prose lyrics also entails a mise en abyme of the fragmentariness and decenteredness of the lyric self, whose conflicting feelings—just like the student's body—are scattered among a number of discrete, metonymically linked "lyric units." As a result of these multiple (self-)manipulations, Giacomo's discourse disintegrates into a succession of euphemized mo-ments and temporary resolutions, so that what begins as a fairly coherent and credible first-person lyric narrative (the "I-persona," after all, is named Jim and has a wife named Nora) becomes just another exercise in the trans-formation or epiphanization of the raw material of personal experience into art. The issue of the fictionalization of autobiographical material is raised several times in *Giacomo Joyce,* notably by the student herself (or is she merely being cast as a mouthpiece for Giacomo's lack of self-confidence as a writer?), who, after having "touched the pages, foul and fair, on which [his] shame shall glow for ever" (13), expresses her misgivings about the moral and intellectual integrity of Giacomo-Joyce's writings. Typically, the student's voice is interrupted by Giacomo's attempts to regain ironic con-trol over his material:

> She says that, had *The Portrait of the Artist* been frank only for frankness' sake, she would have asked why I had given it to her to read. O you would, would you? A lady of letters. (12)

In the context of his own development as an artist, Joyce's ambivalent relationship with the lyric mode in *Giacomo Joyce* raises the issue of the relationship between the fragments and the longer narrative productions into which they were later incorporated. In this respect, the fragmentary and paratactic dynamics of *Giacomo Joyce* can be linked with Joyce's in-creasingly radical critique of the unified wholeness and linear dynamics of the traditional nineteenth-century novel. As Vicki Mahaffey has remarked, the structural premises of Joyce's shorter works—his poems and epipha-nies, *Giacomo Joyce,* and *Exiles*—give us an outline of the basic design of all of their longer and better known counterparts. What Joyce's prose and verse lyrics share with his more extended works of fiction, she writes, is "the strategy of producing a longer and more complicated text by stringing together a series of formally self-contained units." Therefore, she contin-ues, "the minor works make it much more apparent that Joyce's technique—even in the longer texts—is in large part an imagist one, adapted from poetry to narrative and massively elaborated in the process" ("Joyce" 186). In this respect, an interesting parallel can be drawn between Joyce's novelistic prose lyrics and the definition of the prose poem put forward by Des Esseintes, the protagonist of Huysmans' *A Rebours* (1884). Des Esseintes, who sees the prose poem as "the concrete pith, the osmazome of literature, the essential oil of art," defines the genre as a concentrated and supremely writerly avatar of the novel: "Then the words chosen would be so unpermutable as to substitute for all the others; the adjective, placed in such an ingenious and so definitive a way that it could not be legally divested of its position, would open such perspectives that the reader could dream for weeks on end about its meaning, at the same time fixed and multiple, could take note of the present, reconstruct the past; could guess the future of the characters' souls, revealed by the light of that unique epithet" (320).

Despite its strong Decadent overtones (the emphasis on stylistic refinement and semantic ingeniousness, in particular), Des Esseintes' definition suggests that Huysmans, like Joyce, saw in the prose poem the possibility of turning the concentrated brevity and semantic ambiguity of poetic language into a means of expanding and complexifying the creation of plot and character. In this perspective, also, the prose lyrics of *Giacomo Joyce* enact the principle of contamination between narrative linearity and poetic closure, poetic ambiguity and novelistic verisimilitude that characterizes Joyce's work and, as we will see, the development of a modern tradition of the prose poem. The specific nature of the "elaboration" of the isolated lyric moments of *Giacomo Joyce* and the epiphanies into larger narrative units lies outside the scope of the present chapter. Suffice it to say, at this stage, that what in *Giacomo* remains primarily a means of articulating (albeit in a self-consciously manipulative fashion) the sudden bursts of the lyric self subsists in Joyce's fiction within a larger referential system obeying its own internal logic and in which the self tends to be engulfed in the more impersonal arts of irony, satire, allusion, parody, and pastiche. When Joyce left Trieste in 1915, leaving behind him the *Giacomo* manuscript, the fragment and the aesthetics of the first-person prose lyric had already been put aside to give way to the luxuriant anonymity of the third-person encyclopedic parody of *Ulysses*.[16]

In order to situate further Giacomo's prose fragments in the development of Joyce's poetics, we must turn to Stephen, who, toward the end of *A Portrait of the Artist as a Young Man*, develops his own theory of literary genres. According to Stephen, "art necessarily divides itself into three forms progressing from one to the next": the lyric form, in which the artist presents an image "in immediate relation to himself"; the epical form, in which the image is "in mediate relation to himself and others"; and the dramatic form, in which the image is "in immediate relation to others" (*A Portrait* 231–32):

> The lyric form is in fact the simplest verbal gesture of an instant of emotion, a rhythmical cry such as ages ago cheered on the man who pulled at the oar or dragged stones up a slope. He who utters it is more conscious of the instant of emotion than of he himself as feeling emotion. The simplest epical form is seen emerging out of lyric literature when the artist prolongs and broods upon himself as the centre of an epical event and this form progresses till the centre of emotional gravity is equidistant from the artist himself and from others. The narrative is no longer personal. The personality of the artist passes into the narration itself, flowing round and round the persons and the action like a vital sea. This progress you will see easily in that old English ballad Turpin Hero which begins in the first person and ends in the third person. The dramatic form is reached when the vitality which has flowed and eddied round each person fills every person with such vital force that he or she assumes a proper and intangible esthetic life. The personality of the artist, at first a cry or a cadence or a mood and then a fluid and lambent narrative, finally refines itself out of existence, impersonalises itself, so to speak. The esthetic image in the dramatic form is life purified in and reprojected from the human imagination. The mystery of esthetic like that of material creation is accomplished. The artist, like the God of the creation, remains within or behind or beyond or above his handiwork, invisible, refined out of existence, indifferent, paring his fingernails. (*A Portrait* 232–33)

As Gérard Genette has remarked, Stephen's theory is, in fact, a somewhat simplified version of August Wilhelm Schlegel's dialectical trinity (1801), according to which the "pure objectivity" of the epic and the "pure subjectivity" of the lyric should be interwoven into a single "dramatic" sequence. A few years later, Schelling reworked Schlegel's triad into a diachronic sequence much like Stephen's "progression" from the lyric to the dramatic. According to Schelling, art begins as a subjective utterance and has to raise itself to epic objectivity before it reaches the state of dramatic "identification," which he defines as "the synthesis of the universal and the particular" ("Introduction" 124). Clearly, Stephen subscribes to Schelling's notion of the dramatic mode as the supreme form of art. For

Stephen, however, the dramatic mode is not so much a synthesis of its lyric and epic counterparts as the ultimate stage of a process of emancipation of the work of art from its subjective premises. The superiority of the dramatic form therefore lies in its capacity to "refine" the raw material of personal experience and turn it into a work of impersonal, "intangible" finesse. In this sense, Stephen's theory reflects his commitment to a form of art that reveals the world in all its meaning, as well as his conception of the artist as a semi-angelic figure standing apart from the multitude (or what Joyce himself called the "rabblement"). Finally, Stephen's ideal of the dramatic mode is one in which the artist appears as a highly self-conscious craftsman—a condition antipodal to that of the lyric self described earlier as "more conscious of the instant of emotion" than of feeling emotion himself.[17]

Significantly enough, the word *epiphany,* which occurs at the most crucial point of the discourse on aesthetics in *Stephen Hero,* has disappeared altogether from Stephen's theories in the *Portrait.* This is hardly surprising since Stephen's "lyric" metaphor of the epiphany—which still laid the emphasis on the artist's personal apprehension, unmediated by irony and dramatic distance, of the "whatness" of a given object or incident—would have been inconsistent with Stephen's own "impersonal" theory (in the *Portrait*) of the progressive separation of the artist from the lyric impulse. In view of the development of Joyce's oeuvre as a whole, one may reasonably argue that Stephen is, at least to some extent, a fictional mouthpiece of the author's younger self and of his aesthetic convictions at the time. As suggested above, Joyce gradually abandoned the lyric mode in the years that followed the publication of Stephen's three-form theory of genres. In the context of Stephen's "three forms progressing from one to the next," it seems probable that Joyce's decision not to publish *Giacomo* was prompted by aesthetic as well as personal reasons. In the same way as Stephen's theory of the epiphany was replaced, in *A Portrait,* by another theory concerning the development of the poet away from the raw lyric impulse toward dramatic objectivity, Giacomo's lyric effusions—for all their paradoxical attempts to enact the *failure* of the constitution of the lyric self—were soon discarded in favor of the more controlled and detached mode of *Ulysses,* in which the parodic and ironic tenor indeed seems to correspond to Stephen's ideal of the artist-as-god, "refined out of existence, indifferent, paring his fingernails."

Thus, one way of approaching *Giacomo Joyce* is as an example of the type of lyric epiphanies the Stephen of *Stephen Hero* and, indeed, the young Joyce would have written and, by the time of *Ulysses,* abandoned. In this respect, also, *Giacomo Joyce* and the prose lyric, which stand at the junction of a lyric discourse already on the wane and the genesis of the "dramatic" novel, mark a turning point in Joyce's career. The very title of the manuscript, itself a dichotomy, carries the implications of a struggle between the lyrico-poetic writing of Joyce's early work—with its focus on the expression of transitory moods or momentary illuminations—and the ambitions of the mature novelist. Yet, if Joyce progressively moved away from lyric brevity toward the impersonality of the monumental dramatic novel, the fragments of *Giacomo* nevertheless testify to the existence of an alternative undercurrent in Joyce's poetics, one in which the lyric epiphany no longer seems to mediate between the mind and its object but is displaced onto the split consciousness of the speaker. Joyce's later return to poetry with *Pomes Penyeach,* a collection of thirteen formally conventional and overtly sentimental poems in verse published in 1927 (despite Ezra Pound's claim that the poems were not worth printing and belonged "in the Bible or in the family album with the portraits" [Ellmann 591]), confirms that his oeuvre was never really immune to a return of the lyric repressed. Similarly, the rather unexpected appearance of a poem from *Pomes Penyeach,* "Nightpiece," in an early draft of the parody romance of "Tristan and Isolde" in *Finnegans Wake* points to the ambivalent nature of Joyce's relationship with his own "poetic" works (*A First Draft* 210–11). Joyce, whose interest in poetry was always inseparable from his enthusiasm for music, never completely forsook the pre-ironic musicality of his early lyrics. Toward the end of the *Giacomo* manuscript, Joyce—who, a few months before his departure for Italy, had failed to raise enough money to tour England as a singer and a lute player (Ellmann 154–55)—writes what seems to be a rather bitter and disillusioned adieu to the frustrated ambitions of his youth, as well as a comment on the superiority of musical lyric over its literary counterpart:

Jan Pieters Sweelink. The quaint name of the old Dutch musician makes all beauty seem quaint and far. I hear his variations for the clavichord on an old air: *Youth has an end.* In the vague mist of old sounds a faint point of light appears: the speech of the soul is about to be heard. Youth has an end: the end is here. It will never be. You know that well. What then? Write it, damn you, write it! What else are you good for? (*Giacomo* 16)

In the course of his career as a novelist, Joyce tried to satisfy his penchant for the musical aspects of the lyric through the medium of prose. This tendency reaches a climax in *Finnegans Wake,* which Joyce—countering accusations of unnecessary obscurity—kept defending on the grounds that it was "pure music" and that the fact that it was "pleasing to the ear" was one of the book's justifications (Ellmann 702–3). In this perspective, the simple and nostalgic songs of *Chamber Music* and the sophisticated multilingual experiments of *Finnegans Wake* are not as diametrically opposed to each other as they may seem.

If Stephen's theory of genres provisionally sounds the knell of Giacomo's lyric impulses, it nonetheless offers a number of insights into the inherently heterogeneric quality of any literary work. Stephen's translation of the traditional triad into modal rather than strictly generic features, in particular, presents the lyric, the epic, and the dramatic not as mutually exclusive categories, but as different degrees of "genericness" coexisting within the same work, as exemplified in the absorption and the subsequent dissolution of the personal mode into its narrative extension in *Turpin Hero*. It would therefore be tempting to see the novelistic prose lyrics of *Giacomo Joyce*, as most critics have done, as so many lyric "snatches" destined to be recycled in the increasingly complex narrative structures of Joyce's later works of fiction. As the preceding discussion has shown, however, *Giacomo Joyce* should not be considered solely as a missing link in the development of Joyce's career as a novelist. By resisting the pressures of narrative linearity and poetic closure, Joyce's fragments also emerge as a new, hybrid form of lyric discourse, which seeks to embrace the complex and discontinuous nature of experience and memory and, eventually, offers itself up to the ludic authority of the reader's desire. In this respect, the essentially paratactic relationships between and within the prose blocks of *Giacomo* are once again reminiscent of Baudelaire's project of a "writerly" text *avant la lettre*—a literary work which, like the prose poems of *Paris Spleen*, is "both head and tail, alternately and reciprocally" (*Spleen* 23) and in which both the writer and the reader are free to participate in the construction and the dispersal of subjectivity, longing for no other form of narrative coherence than that of the movements of the mind itself. As the following chapters show, Joyce's desire to reproduce the actual movement of the perceiving consciousness, as well as his careful balancing and counterpointing of subjective and objective experience, prefigure a number of creative and phenomenological strategies that were to dominate the entire history of the contemporary prose poem.

PART I

The Birth of the Modern Prose Poem

1 · Gertrude Stein and the Expatriate Avant-Garde

The Prose Poem in Transition

In the years that followed World War I, Paris became synonymous with freedom of expression and behavior, at a time when many American artists were trying to escape from the atmosphere of intellectual inertia, private and public censorship, as well as the general lack of interest in and support of modern art prevailing in the United States. The new Parisian community of American writers included literary personalities as diverse as Ernest Hemingway, Hilda Doolittle (H.D.), Ezra Pound, Djuna Barnes, Eugene Jolas, and Gertrude Stein, who had left the United States as early as 1903 to settle with her brother Leo at 27 rue de Fleurus, leaving behind her a country she was later to describe as "early Victorian . . . a rich and well nourished home but not a place to work" (Fitch 218). These expatriate writers and some of their wealthier supporters soon created a number of small publishing houses and so-called little magazines in which they published their own and one another's work. Many of these small publications were short-lived, printed in limited editions, or even published at the author's expense.

Among the small journals, Eugene Jolas' *transition* (1927–38) was probably the one that best exemplified the international position of the new avant-garde. Born in New Jersey in 1894 of a French father and a German mother, Jolas was the perfect person to be in charge of a magazine purporting to become a forum for the cosmopolitan avant-garde and to present "the quintessence of the modern spirit in evolution" (Fitch 23). Jolas' magazine is now primarily remembered for serializing and defending the cause of James Joyce's *Finnegans Wake* (called at the time *Work in Progress*), after Marianne Moore's *The Dial,* Ford Madox Ford's *transatlantic review,* Ezra Pound's *The Exile,* and Wyndham Lewis' *The Enemy* had rejected it as either too obscure or downright obscene. During its eleven years of existence, however, *transition* published many other leading writers in the English language, such as Gertrude Stein, William Carlos Williams, Djuna Barnes, Hart Crane, H. D., Samuel Beckett, Paul Bowles,

Anaïs Nin, and Dylan Thomas. The great majority of the journal's contributors were American, and Jolas' most lasting achievement lies in his success at bringing American writing into contact with various European literary movements and currents of thought. While Jolas' editorials and manifestos reflected the influence of various European intellectual movements (including the theories of Freud, Nietzsche, Bergson, and Jung, whose essay "Psychology and Poetry" appeared in the June 1930 issue), the magazine also published many literary works in translation, mainly by French and German writers. These included Rainer Maria Rilke, Franz Kafka (then relatively unknown to the Anglo-Saxon public), André Gide, and, prominently, Paul Eluard, André Breton, Robert Desnos, and other French Surrealists who shared Jolas' fascination with dreams and the realm of the unconscious.

The master-word of the new international avant-garde was *new*. As the editor's notes to the June 1927 issue make clear, the *transition* poets, according to Jolas, were in search of "new words, new abstractions, new hieroglyphics, new symbols, new myths" that could assist them in their quest for "new outlets and new regions of probability." Following Jolas' conviction that "there [was] no hope for poetry unless there be disintegration first," originality and experimentation were soon raised to the status of supreme values. Like so many other modernist artists before him, Jolas felt the need to legitimize his work as both an editor and a writer by means of several manifestos, in which he proclaimed his break with all tradition and sought to channel the efforts of his various contributors into a cohesive force. His famous "Revolution of the Word Proclamation," which appeared in the June 1929 issue of *transition,* proclaimed the right of the "literary creator" to "disintegrate the primal matter of words imposed upon him by text-books and dictionaries" and rebel against "the hegemony of the banal word, monotonous syntax, static psychology [and] descriptive naturalism" (Fitch 19); with the disappearance of the very notion of consensual style, the modern writer was now free to develop his or her own particular technique, regardless of any predecessor.

Eugene Jolas' *transition* and the Revolution of the Word

The particular kind of "wild" modernism cultivated by Jolas and the other signatories to the "Revolution of the Word"[1]—with its commitment to an expressionistic, incantatory verbalism and various forms of stylistic and formal excessiveness—was diametrically opposed to the poetics of dispassionate irony and precise scrutiny advocated by Pound, Eliot, and other representatives of what is now commonly referred to as the "High Modernist" tradition. As Dougald McMillan has explained, Jolas' manifesto was also part of a reaction against the Imagists' tendency to consider words as an auxiliary mode of perception, often seen as deficient because it lacked the "objective directness" of Pound's visual aesthetics (123). Having freed themselves from the domination of Imagist precepts concerning art's representational vocation, Jolas' Revolutionaries of the Word were in a position to embark on an exploration of language for its own sake ("the 'litany of words' is admitted as an independent unit"), quite independently from any outside "referent." Lastly, Jolas' iconoclastic editorial policies also denied the necessity to write poetry with reference to a specific cultural "tradition," a stance most poets belonging to Eliot's generation considered as the only means by which the modern writer could combat what they saw as the stifling provincialism and intellectual sterility of Anglo-Saxon letters.

Jolas' project was strongly influenced by the aesthetics of French Surrealism, which were also informed by various forms of anxiety and skepticism concerning the validity of traditional strategies of expression and representation. His desire to "emancipate the creative elements from the present ideology" reminds us that the general disillusionment concerning the validity of both conventional notions of language and realist modes of representation was itself the result of a profound loss of faith in dominant social and cultural structures. As Shari Benstock points out, contrasting Jolas' liberalism with Pound's increasingly overt adherence to Fascism, "the Revolution of the Word was political as well as linguistic, challenging the more conservative principles on which early Modernism based itself and opening the way to a critique of the language of power" (372). As point number nine of Jolas' manifesto makes clear, however, this process of emancipation from the dominant ideology was also a necessary step toward a redefinition of the very notion of consciousness and its relationship to poetic language. At a time when the human mind had become an unstable notion (its wholeness had been definitively invalidated by Freud's discoveries on the unconscious or subliminal self), Jolas' Revolution of the Word clearly considered poetry the supreme medium through which truly "modern" writers were to give full expression to a consciousness they perceived as increasingly fragmented, discontinuous, and noncausal, sometimes to the point of obscurity and unintelligibility. Considering the repudiation of the language of conventional reference and causality advocated by the new avant-garde, the dream-narrative (of which Joyce's dream-epiphanies were an early, protomodernist instance) almost naturally became a favorite form among poets claiming to go back to the spirit of Rimbaud's "hallucination of the word." Jolas' "Monologue" was written at a time when the dream-narrative (or its nonnarrative avatar: the "dreamscape") had already become one of the preferred poetic subgenres of the French Surrealist group. It displays most of the hallmarks of the French Surrealist tradition of the prose poem initiated, in 1919, by the discovery of "automatic writing" and continued by Reverdy, Eluard, and Breton himself in the early 1920s. These included attention to the associative logic of the unconscious, and a conception of poetic language as a means of counteracting the hegemony of what Jolas called the "banal word," "static psychology," and "descriptive naturalism" (Fitch 19):

> I sleepwalk through the city and plunge into a golden smoke. What is my love for you, magical space and sinister time, when the dusk settles into marble and the owl is a categorical imperative? I left dream-staring puppets in a room, where the Ethiopian trembles at a blasphemy, and the sketch-book holds the contours of an atlas. The mother had a child in the dust and the lonely woman cried in a cafe. Then came a girl from out the autumnal solitude of her rooms, where she had stared at mirrors, and her silence was the dream of a midnight. Cool waters flowed under bridges and electric wires brought decay of flowers, tempests, portraits of nightmares, broken violins. Comrades walked tired into hurricanes. When the philosophies panted, and the symphonies ended in a shriek, stallions ground fire, and the bandits swilled brandy in an hallucinated den. The organ at the fair whimpered love-songs, but the funeral of the poor went past us with memories of loam. The trees became brass shining in sun. My waiting gulped bussed, tears, dust, drinks and sparrows. (133)[2]

Through the syntactic flow of the prose poem, unimpeded by the interruptive effect of line breaks, Jolas sought to render the capricious fluidity of subliminal states of consciousness while preserving the stylistic and metaphorical density usually associated with poetic language. Furthermore, "Monologue" suggests that Jolas' rejection of rationality and linear logic went hand in hand with a critique of the principles of order and causality underlying realist narrative. What is most remarkable about this particular kind of prose poem is its syntactic regularity, which encourages the reader's expectation of a straightforward narrative line. Yet, despite the persistence of grammatical orthodoxy, Jolas' prose poem introduces a series of characters and events but refuses to provide them with any definite context. Its uncanny, surreal quality derives precisely from the *tension* created between a conventional form and an irrational content. The ensuing friction between the unconscious and the conscious, the oneiric and the rational mind ("the owl is a categorical imperative") favors an aesthetic of irresolution and open-endedness. It also denies the determinist, utilitarian logic of narrative and descriptive realism. Following Jolas' Rimbaldian belief that "narrative [was] not a mere anecdote, but the projection of a metamorphosis of reality" (Fitch 19), the dream-narrative eventually tends to become its own universe, a form complete and integral unto itself, encouraging a response to the connotative (as opposed to denotative) function of language, a search for internal relationships rather than external referents. This autotelic quality of Jolas' prose is even more apparent in the following "sound poem" (entitled "Faula and Flona" and published under the pseudonym Theo Rutra), in which the emphasis is almost exclusively on the transformative powers of language:

> The lilygushes ring and ting the bilbels in the ivilley. Lilools sart slingslongdang into the clish of sun. The pool dries must. The morrowlei loors in the meaves. The sardinewungs flir flar and meere. A flishflashfling hoohoos and haas. Long shill the mellohoolooloos. The rangomane clanks jungling flight. The elegoat mickmecks and crools. A rabotick ringrangs the stam. A plutocrass with throat of steel. Then woor of meadowcalif's rout. The hedgeking gloos. And matemaids click fer dartalays. (34)

The sound poems reflect Jolas' faith in his "autonomous and unconfined" imagination, as well as his belief in an "a priori reality" located within poetic language itself ("the litany of words is admitted as an independent unit" [Fitch 19]). They also testify to his desire to emulate the instinctive, prelogical *Ursprache* he saw at work in Joyce's "Work in Progress." In Joyce's search for a multilingual language, along with his use of puns and portmanteau words, Jolas saw the key to an examination of the verbal alchemy of the "night mind" ("The Dream" 47). Jolas himself wrote a number of polylingual poems, in which he embarked on his own quest for a universal idiom through which he could record the interior reality of the unconscious mind.

As suggested by Jolas' "Monologue," many dreamscapes published in *transition* display a strong oratorical strain as well as a tendency to dwell on apocalyptic visions and various psychopathological states. Other representatives of this flamboyant, "hallucinated" trend of the prose poem–dreamscape include Edouard Roditi, Charles Henri Ford, Marius Lyle, and "Sun-poet" Harry Crosby, whose convulsive hymns to poetic madness constantly assert the primacy of the inner forces of the subconscious in the act of writing. By comparison with Jolas' associative dreamscapes, in which the self often appears as a mere observer whose gaze is carried about by myriads of incomprehensible circumstances, Crosby's prose poems often amount to a highly controlled and self-reflexive exercise. The following excerpt from "Illustrations of Madness" is a representative example of Crosby's hybrid poetics. The term *illustration,* which bears discursive as well as imagistic connotations, once again confirms that the dreamscape was not conceived of as a celebration of the irrational but rather as an attempt to create dialectical relationships between the waking and the unconscious mind:

> I can cause good sense to appear as insanity distort the wisest institutions of civilized society into the practices of barbarians and strain Christianity into a jest book.

> *   *   *

> My heart is a madhouse for the twin lunatics of her eyes.

> *   *   *

> I rejoice in that dangerous automatic liberty which deprives man of the volition which constitutes him a being responsible for his actions.

> *   *   *

> I have heard for days and nights on end the reverberation crashing in my head of all the skyscrapers and buildings of the world, the reverberation of the crashing of ships in the fog at sea, the reverberation of the crashing of iron thoughts on the cold floor of the brain.

> *   *   *

> There is in me the infernal fury of the Sun by means of which I practice atrocities on the philistines. The operation of my fury is instantaneous and I abandon them to the malignity of my scorn and ridicule. (102–3)

The obsessional, infuriated, and iconoclastic overtones of Crosby's "Illustrations of Madness" make it one of the most representative examples of the cult of uncompromising excessiveness promulgated by Jolas' Revolution of the Word via William Blake's precept that "the tigers of wrath are wiser than the horses of instruction." At their worst, both Crosby and Jolas tend to rely on apocalyptic clichés and a vacuous, standardized eroticism, which led them to publish work that today seems of little value, even within the boundaries of the magazine's manifestos. The stylized, over-wrought gothicism pervading many of their prose poems—which often results in a mechanized expression of *mal du siècle* and revolt—can be seen as symptomatic of the failure of the "wild modernist" avant-garde truly to go beyond their repudiation of the power of traditional forms and consensual languages to represent the inner world of feeling and consciousness. As suggested above, the Revolution of the Word was an attempt to escape from what Jolas perceived as the stifling causal and discursive logic of dominant ideological narratives. The formal ambiguity of the prose poem—which parallels the dualism of conscious and unconscious, reason and intuition, manifest and latent meaning of the dreamscape—was hailed by the *transition* poets as an ideal medium for a "liberation" of the language of prose from the fetters of reason. However, the exalted, convulsive expression of individual experience characterizing many poems and prose poems published in Jolas' magazine, far from bridging the gap between the self's waking and dreaming life, is often obscured by a bitter, gloomy outlook resulting from various forms of alienation and internal self-division. In a manner reminiscent of the "panting philosophies" of Jolas' "Monologue," Paul Bowles' "Entity," for example, puts the accent on the uncertainty and elusiveness of expression. The result is a form of writing in which the Blakean self praised by Jolas' manifesto appears in a neurotic, self-consciously debased form, irremediably overwhelmed by the anarchic powers of the liberated Word:[3]

> Eradicate, if you can, the adaptability of my nature to joy. It is our heritage, this abandoned cerise;—perhaps the only one we have left. The steel of now cannot be rounded like letters of the system into laughing hordes of misunderstanding. We cannot permit these unflinching bones to perform such elegies. There may be falsehoods about ponds. Last week occurred a strange step. Paradise stalked, and seizing a trombone from the wall, stumbled. In this way all such margins weaken. ("Entity" 219)

The Narrative of Consciousness

Hostile to both the bourgeois logic of everyday reality and the humanist conception of a self-present unified self, the dreamscape inaugurated a form of "narrative of consciousness" that is still one of the major submodes of the contemporary prose poem. The infinitely extensible paragraph—with its capacity to drag the reader along the syncopated stream of the poet's rambling thoughts—proved ideal for the kind of oneiric and hallucinated contents favored by many *transition* poets, who shared a preoccupation with the subterranean, inner rhythms of mental life. The prevailing influence on this specific subgenre of the prose poem is that of Henri Bergson. As Christopher Butler reminds us, Bergson's theories on the dynamics of subjective experience had a tremendous impact on the notion of time in modernist art, "particularly by sustaining the idea . . . that subjective experience has a peculiar rhythmic character" (142). According to Bergson, intuition—unlike intelligence, the purpose of which can only be materialistic and utilitarian—enables us to comprehend the life of the spirit itself and to experience what he calls "pure duration." Bergson's definition of intuition insists on the primacy of creative experience and, above all, on the existence of a "pure" memory retaining the totality of our conscious states and fusing the past and the present into an organic whole.

This particular aspect of Bergson's theory illuminates similar attempts in literature to recreate the multiple intersections and superimpositions of images, memories, and emotions that make up the processes of consciousness and dream. The Bergsonian treatment of time as pure duration (that is, as a datum of consciousness immediately and intuitively perceived), which also underlies Jolas' provocative motto that "time is a tyranny to be abolished," led to the kaleidoscopic, mosaiclike word sequences occurring in William Carlos Williams' "improvisations," inaugurated with *Kora in Hell* in 1920. Even though the term *improvisation* was originally meant to accommodate a variety of modes and subject matters, Williams' prose poems usually consist of a nonlogically constructed concatenation of thoughts and images, a succession of fragmentary moments following an aesthetic of ellipsis and fracture, which Williams himself defined as "the disjointing process" (*Imaginations* 285). The two major literary influences behind Williams' art of improvisation are the Dadaists' early experiments with automatic writing and the *Illuminations* of Arthur Rimbaud, who, more than thirty years before, had found in the prose poem a means to celebrate the "sacred disorder" of the spirit (Rimbaud 141). As Williams made clear in his prologue to *Kora in Hell,* however, the improvisations were not meant as an American remake of any previous tradition of the prose poem. On the contrary, they were part of Williams' project to develop a form of modernism with specifically American objectives.[4] At a time when Williams felt profoundly dissatisfied with the lack of a flourishing avant-garde tradition in the United States, the improvisations were indeed primarily a pretext for an exploration of the poetic possibilities of the American idiom. The apparent lack of firm artistic control of Williams' verbal collages, as well as the frequent intrusion of direct quotation into the "narrator's" thoughts, make him a precursor of the popular, speech-based poetics characterizing Kenneth Patchen's jazzy fantasies, examined in chapter 3. More than anything, the urgent and intimate tone of the Improvisations did much to liberate the prose poem from the "aestheticist" tradition condemned by T. S. Eliot and to turn prose poems into a means of verbalizing specific modern concerns and realities.

Williams' speech-based form of "simultaneist" prose was developed by a number of other writers in the 1920s, notably by Djuna Barnes and e.e. cummings, whose rhapsodic city vignettes in & (1925) read like a radical rewriting of Williams' disjointing process. Formally speaking, of course, Williams' prose poems resemble a number of late modernist avatars of the stream-of-consciousness technique (some of Williams' early *Improvisations* were serialized in *The Little Review* at the same time as Joyce's *Ulysses*), which also challenge the linear, syllogistic movement of traditional narrative and descriptive prose. Yet, while most modernist novelists sought to describe the process of thought and memory for the purpose of narration and characterization, Williams and other prose poets attempted to adapt experimentalist modes of expression to the tracking of "actual" mental processes per se. In this sense, their rejection of "bourgeois" realist accounts of the external world ironically paves the way for a new mimetic art, one reflecting their desire to capture and represent the contingent and fluctuating rhythms of consciousness through a form itself protean and freed from the restrictions of traditional metric patterns.

The Prose Poem and the Reclamation of Public Language

For all his critique of the referential power of language and his commitment to a poetry divorced from both linguistic and social conventions, Jolas believed in an intrinsic, "a priori" reality present in any verbal utterance. His conception of poetic language as an act of pure expression and, ultimately, a form of life in itself still subscribes to the Mallarmean notion of the autonomy of the work of art. The poem becomes a private universe in which meaning is seen as residing in the words themselves rather than in their relationship to an external reality. This tendency toward the separation of art and life, which certainly calls into question the *transition* poets' assertion of art's relevance in social and political contexts, is even more apparent in Jolas' proclamation of the "Vertigral Age," published in 1933, in which he definitively turns his back on modernity and sees once more in the transfigurative power of dreams the only means by which to restore a lost unity with the primeval strata of life. In reaction against what he calls "the collapse of mechanistic utopia" (in which "[man's] senses moved in the dull rotation of blind forces"), Jolas exhorts his followers to engage in a quest for "a primitive grammar, the stammering that approaches the language of God" (128).

W. C. Williams' *Improvisations* suggest that one alternative to Jolas' "pure poetry" lay in a poetic investigation of the effects of modernity upon the individual consciousness. In the 1920s and 1930s, the writings of other experimental prose poets displayed a renewed interest not only in the experience of the mechanical age but also in the poetic potential of the language of modern science and technology. Harry Crosby's semiconcrete "Pharmacie du Soleil," for example, consists exclusively of an uninterrupted series of metalloid elements:

> calcium   iron   hydrogen   sodium   nickel
> magnesium   cobalt   silicon   aluminium
> titanium   chromium   strontium   manganese
> vanadium   barium   carbon   scandium   ytrium
> zirconium   molybdenum   lanthanum   niobium
> palladium   neodymium   copper   zinc   cadmium
> cerium   glucinum   germanium   rhodium   silver
> tin   lead   erbium   potassium   iridium
> tantalum   osmium   thorium   platinum   tungsten
> ruthenium   uranium
>
> (*Chariot* 27)

Crosby's "Pharmacie du Soleil" does not confine itself to undermining the metaphorical and subjectivist premises of the lyric mode—it also sets out to challenge accepted boundaries between public and private, utilitarian and poetic language. As Clive Scott has remarked, this process works both ways. Commenting on two lines from Jules Laforgue's "L'Hiver qui vient" ("Le sobre et le vespéral mystère hebdomadaire / Des statistiques sanitaires"), he writes that Laforgue's poem "demonstrate[s] what much Modernist poetry demonstrates, that any scientific or technical term is poetically viable as long as it is thought of not in connection with a discipline but as a 'rare' combination of vowels and consonants with an exotic etymology, and that poetic diction is as much a technical jargon as any other" (359). If Crosby's poem illustrates that a new kind of poetic decorum can be invented within the new "exotic" terminology of modern technologies, the long prose sequences of Abraham Lincoln Gillespie suggest that the polysemantic potential of poetry can be recreated on the basis of such borrowings from the language of discursive prose:

> What's been dough-clogging the sieve-process of the Speak-Mind, what's been shunting off part WORDprecip of the *original* flashsear-Consciousness *QUANTITY* of Images, that polygonating Impact-series of the was-aspected Ideation? Surely the psyche apprehends other than the 2'd sorts of these clashMeets, (5) other than Ap-plauseSeek-Impactage sirop'd in grammar-seequenced fledgeling-Pla-cates!

> There, possibly, we have it: The aforementioned asyet bleedplead-Need, Grammar'd communication. GRAYMAR. Academic Buga-boo, stuffshirt-PaunchPace-Idealiser, Nujol-Insidiate pettisogging us in GET-drippy Complace-brewing HigherConschPretense—lard-rousing our slobAdmire of a Mind's jello-sieving us neat preciperies of 2-imaged [(]2i.e. dingle series of but ONCE-impacting) line jam-clashtwangs. This maybe locates the Americo-perennial Bodeheims. (3)

> (5) Rather apprehends contrajostles of PhotoMinim-IMPORT particles. (9)

In this passage from "Textighter Eye-Ploy or Hothouse Bromidik" (first published in the March 1928 issue of *transition*), Gillespie clearly goes beyond the rejection of rationality advocated by Jolas and his followers in the name of the "pure" poetic flow of the unconscious mind. Rather, he proceeds to question nothing less than the capacity of language to make sense. Gillespie's pun-laden parody of interpretive rhetoric challenges our expectations of argumentative coherence in order to draw our attention to the artificiality and constructedness of analytical discourses. By reproducing the polysemic ambiguity of poetic language within the realm of utilitarian prose, Gillespie's theoretico-poetic project prefigures the Language poets' dissolution of boundaries between the literal and the figurative discussed in part III of the present study. In order to comprehend fully the prose poem's subversion of the use-value of culturally inherited discourses, as well as its self-conscious misappropriation of utilitarian languages for the purpose of poetic creativity, we must now turn to the work of Gertrude Stein.

Redefining the Poetic: Gertrude Stein's Portraits and Still Lifes

What is poetry and if you know
what poetry is what is prose.

Gertrude Stein, "Poetry and Grammar"

A regular contributor to Jolas' *transition,* Gertrude Stein is now generally remembered as one of the most uncompromisingly experimental writers of the modernist era. The beginnings of her career as a prose writer, however, were still very much inscribed in the tradition of nineteenth-century novel writing. *Q.E.D.* (composed in 1903; published in 1950), her first significant piece of creative writing, is a relatively conventional work of fiction centered on the consciousness of a central character named Adele and following a linear narrative line.[5] Stein's explorations of the individual consciousness, which were strongly influenced by the novels of Henry James, are continued in *Three Lives* (c. 1905–6; 1909), her first published work, which details the intellectual and emotional life of three servant girls. In *Three Lives,* however, Stein departs from the conventions of realistic fiction—including the use of traditionally structured plots and settings—in order to focus almost exclusively on the mental processes of her protagonists. But *Three Lives* is also characterized by a tendency toward a certain form of abstraction. Unlike the protagonists of Victorian and Edwardian novels, Stein's characters are indeed described not with reference to a specific social background or context but in terms of personality types. The main influence on Stein's use of "flat" types was that of William James, under whose directorship Stein studied at the Harvard psychology laboratory and whose theories imparted to her an interest in psychological universals that was to dominate her entire creative life.

The next milestone in Stein's career as a prose writer is *The Making of Americans* (1902–11; 1925), which was written at a time when she became concerned not so much with characterological types themselves as with the way in which these "universals" could be used in order to listen to the "rhythm of each human being" (*Look* 89). Stein's main center of attention therefore became the very nature of human personality. The finished product was a thousand-page-long book focusing on an immigrant family, the Herslands, and attempting to define the "bottom nature" of the American people. Stein's concern with the essence of "Americanness," however, was only one aspect of a much more ambitious task, for her real intention was to describe nothing less than "every kind of human being that ever was or is or would be living" (88). To this end, she progressively abandoned all the basic elements of the conventional nineteenth-century novel, including plot, character, and sociohistorical background. At the same time, she began to give herself increasingly to abstract considerations and eventually had her own narrative consciousness take over not just the story but also the very subject of the narrative. *The Making of Americans* was followed by the unfinished *A Long Gay Book* (c. 1910–12; 1932), a second experiment in absolute comprehensiveness, in which Stein's interest shifted from "every possible kind of human being" to "every possible kind of pairs of human beings" (*Look* 91). Yet soon after completing *The Making of Americans,* Stein had already discovered that, after all, "it was not an enormously long thing to do to describe every one" (94), and consequently she turned her attention to shorter narrative or descriptive forms. In the portraits and "still lifes"—which constitute Stein's contribution to the genesis of the modern prose poem—the endless, all-inclusive flow of her earlier prose was definitively abandoned and was supplanted by a new compositional unit: the paragraph.

Despite their more limited length and scope, the portraits are still in concordance with Stein's earlier attempt to render in words "the rhythm of anybody's personality" (105). "Picasso" (1909; 1912) is an early example of what one might call Stein's art of "impersonal" portraiture:

> One whom some were certainly following was one who was completely charming. One whom some were certainly following was one who was charming. One whom some were following was one who was completely charming. One whom some were following was one who was certainly completely charming.
>
> Some were certainly following and were certain that the one they were then following was one working and was one bringing out of himself then something. Some were certainly following and were certain that the one they were then following was one bringing out of himself then something that was coming to be a heavy thing, a solid thing and a complete thing.
>
> One whom some were certainly following was one working and certainly was one bringing something out of himself then and was one who had been all his living had been one having something coming out of him.
>
> Something had been coming out of him, certainly it had been coming out of him, certainly it was something, certainly it had been coming out of him and it had meaning, a charming meaning, a solid meaning, a struggling meaning, a clear meaning.
>
> One whom some were certainly following and some were certainly following him, one whom some were certainly following was one certainly working. (213)

As is the case in most of her portraits, Stein does not seek to depict her "subject" in a conventional or realistic way and, instead, attempts to diagram certain actions or qualities of the person described that seem to point to a number of ill-defined personality "essentials." The anonymous pronouns "one," "some," and "something"—which abound in many of the early portraits—further emphasize the semi-abstract quality of the piece, which, on the whole, tends to concentrate on a series of discrete ideas or situations, rather than on a specific "character." In a manner reminiscent of *The Making of Americans,* Stein attempts to understand human beings not through the observation of meaningful, "realist" details but in terms of general characterological types present in *any* individual. This feature confirms Stein's desire to depersonalize her subject or, rather, to systematize personality with reference to collective and universal categories.

"Picasso" is typical of Stein's early portraits in that it contains a limited number of semantic units, each paragraph being centered on a particular concept, which is itself subjected to a number of structural and syntactic variations. Many of Stein's portraits indeed "function" on the basis of a series of incremental variations on a particular detail or feature. This specificity of focus can be accounted for by Stein's interest in Cubist painting, which also tends to select a particular detail of a whole and describe it from a variety of perspectives. The redundant character of Stein's syntax can also partly be ascribed to her interest in the rhythms of everyday conversation, on which she claimed many of her portraits were based and which are largely responsible for what has been called Stein's stylistic "primitivism." However, Stein herself described this "repetition with variation" technique as a literary equivalent of the cinema, in which "[she] was making a continuous succession of the statement of what the person was until I had not many things but one thing" (106). This "cinematic" effect is achieved through a process of semantic accretion in which the succession of similar enunciations with slight but pertinent additions, subtractions, variations, and permutations create the peculiarly insistent, litany-like rhythm characterizing many of Stein's early portraits. Just as in a film, she reminds us, "no two pictures are exactly alike each one is just that much different from the one before" (106). Each paragraph thus introduces a particular theme, idea, or key word alternately posited, negated, and made more complex. The result is not meant to appear as a succession of discrete utterances but as a single entity that the reader should perceive as the "continuously moving picture of any one" (105)—this "flowing" quality of Stein's prose is further enhanced by her penchant for the continuous present. Her comparison of her prose with the cinema clearly indicates that her portraits, even though they display a certain degree of "abstractness," are far from being strictly a-referential or a-descriptive: such apparent "nonsense" is still being written with a view to expressing a specific succession of actions or psychological states. While the opening passage, for instance, seeks to render Picasso's aura of prestige and his success with his admirers or "followers," the rest of the excerpt seems to imply, among other things, that his whole life is devoted to his art.

In the remaining paragraphs of her three-page-long portrait of Picasso, Stein continues to describe the painter on the basis of a number of obsessively recurrent motifs, while adding new information concerning her ambivalent response to his work (which she successively characterizes as solid, charming, lovely, perplexing, disconcerting, simple, clear, complicated, interesting, disturbing, repellent, and a "very pretty thing" [214]). The portrait ends with what has long been interpreted as Stein's assessment of a character weakness in Picasso ("He was not ever completely working"; 215), which somehow casts doubt on the followers' confidence in the painter's total commitment to his work.[6] Generally speaking, Stein's piece, despite its many departures from any previous tradition of the portrait, still manages to render some general sense of Picasso's personality and his relationship with his followers.

Many of Stein's portraits attempt not so much to convey specific psychological states of the portrayed person as to explore the metonymic relationships existing between him/her and diverse elements of a specific physical and psychological context. "Ada" (1910; 1922 in *Geography and Plays*), Stein's famous portrait of Alice Toklas, starts with a description of the Toklas family as a whole and does not mention Alice herself until the end of the fourth paragraph; even then, Stein goes on describing her almost exclusively in terms of her connections with the other members of the family, thus giving expression to the "many relations who lived in them" (*Reader* 102). Around 1912, Stein even began a series of "group portraits" (some of which were later to be included in *A Long Gay Book*), in the course of which various personal or contextual relationships between persons and things started to prevail even further over the psychological types themselves. "Two Women" (1911?; 1925) is a typical example of Stein's interest in pairs of men and women, an interest coexisting with her more habitual cinematic technique of repetition with incrementation:

There are often two of them, both women. There were two of them, two women. There were two of them, both women. There were two of them. They were both women. There were two women and they were sisters. They both went on living. They were often together then when they were living. They were very often not together when they were living. One was the elder and one was the younger. They always knew this thing, they always knew that one was the elder and one was the younger. They were both living and they both went on living. They were together and they were then both living. They were then both going on living. They were not together and they were both living and they both went on living then. They sometimes were together, they sometimes were not together. One was older and one was younger. (*Reader* 105)

A quick comparison between "Two Women" and any sample of poetry discussed in the first part of this chapter would reveal the extent to which Stein's own particular kind of experimentalism went against what can be referred to as the "mainstream" of the modernist avant-garde represented by Jolas' Revolution of the Word. While her abstract and relational poetics were clearly incompatible with Jolas' belief in a reality intrinsically contained in the word, Stein's poetic project was also antipodal to Joyce's cult of popular and literary allusion. As Shari Benstock observes, Stein remained unimpressed by *Finnegans Wake,* "feeling that the very bankruptcy of linguistic meaning was evidenced in Joyce's need to shore up meaning through multilingual puns" (375). By contrast with Joyce's interest in culturally and historically inherited semantic traces, Stein's own "revolution" was based on an exploration of the grammatical and syntactic principles regulating everyday language. For her, meaning was, above all, the product of relations of words to each other and to a particular context. The only possibility for creative agency within a reified language therefore lay in a subversion of the syllogistic movement of prose at the level of the sentence, the paragraph, and the work as a whole. Stein's use of her famous repetition-with-variation technique in "Picasso" and "Two Women," for instance, questions the taken-for-granted transparency of the referential chain by constantly challenging our expectations of semantic closure.

As we will see, other key aspects of Stein's poetic project—which include a conception of writing as process, a commitment to "literalness" as opposed to metaphorical depth, and an emphasis on the medium rather than on the subject of a literary work—make her a precursor of a certain form of postmodern poetry rather than a typical representative of "far-out" modernism. Still, the influence of her experimental techniques on a number of contemporary writers must not be underestimated. Whereas the much-discussed "metonymic narratives" of Sherwood Anderson and Ernest Hemingway were largely derived from Stein's use of repetition, Laura Riding's "Mademoiselle Comet" (published in 1928 in *transition*) recalls the semi-abstract quality of Stein's portraits:

We, then, having complete power, removed all the amusements that did not amuse us. We were then at least not hopelessly not amused. We inculcated in ourselves an amusability not qualified by standards developed from amusements that failed to amuse. Our standards, that is, were impossibly high.

And yet we were not hopeless. We were ascetically humorous, in fact. And so when Mademoiselle Comet came among us we were somewhat at a loss. For Mademoiselle Comet was a really professional entertainer. She came from where she came to make us look.

But Mademoiselle Comet was different. We could not help looking. But she more than amused. She was a perfect oddity. The fact that she was entertaining had no psychological connection with the fact that we were watching her. She was a creature of pure pleasure. She was a phenomenon; whose humorous slant did not sympathetically attack us; being a slant of independence not comedy. Her long bright hair was dead. She could not be loved.

Therefore Mademoiselle Comet became our entertainment. And she more than amused; we loved her. Having complete power, we placed her in a leading position, where we could observe her better. We were not amused. We were ascetically humorous. Thus we aged properly. We did not, like mirth-stricken children, die. Rather, we could not remember that we had ever been alive. We too had long bright dead hair. Mademoiselle Comet performed, we looked always a last time. We too performed, became really professional entertainers. Our ascetically humorous slant became more and more a slant of independence, less and less a slant of rejected comedy. With Mademoiselle Comet we became a troupe, creatures of pure pleasure, more than amused, more than amusing, looker-entertainers, Mademoiselle Comet's train of cold light. We were the phenomenal word *fun*, Mademoiselle Comet leading. Fun was our visible property. We appeared, a comet and its tail, with deadly powerfulness to ourselves. We collided. We swallowed and were swallowed, more than amused. Mademoiselle, because of the position we had put her in with our complete power, alone survived. Her long bright dead hair covered her. Our long bright dead hair covered us. Her long bright dead hair alone survived; universe of pure pleasure, never tangled, never combed. She could not be loved. We loved her. Our long bright dead hair alone survived. We alone survived, having complete power. Our standards, that is, were impossibly high; and brilliant Mademoiselle Comet, a professional entertainer, satisfied them. Our standards alone survived, being impossibly high. (207–8)

On a superficial level, "Mademoiselle Comet" displays the most essential features of a "typical" Steinian portrait, including the technique of repetition with incrementation leading to structural variations upon a single theme or motif; here, that of "entertainment," "amusability," or "impossibly high standards." As in the Stein pieces discussed, we are not presented with a fully fledged individual but, rather, with a number of psychological states—this same concern with characterological abstraction led another *transition* poet, Herman Spector, to describe one of his characters as "ordinarily clean and nice and fat and eyes" (177). We do not really know in what way "Mademoiselle Comet" is "entertaining," nor are we told, for example, about her physical appearance, her motives, or the precise circumstances of her arrival ("She came from where she came to make us look").

Even though her use of repetition may seem indebted to Stein, Riding's treatment of character remains very much her own. Her most essential contribution to the history of the "abstract" narrative indeed lies in a redistribution of subjective and predicative structures that leads to several alternative (ir-)resolutions at the same time as its seeks to redefine the self-pursuing logic of its own discourse. The point here is not to describe specific personality types or to define the "bottom nature" of a particular character. Instead, Riding's own particular brand of "primitivism" relishes the contrast between an extreme clarity and simplicity of diction and an increased indeterminacy of content. This Riding achieves through a series of disconcertingly direct and factual statements, alternately confirmed and negated, leading to further complexities and ambiguities. The somewhat puzzling premises of Riding's "portrait"—anonymous "ascetically humorous" we-personae (or should the "we" be understood as a singular royal "we"?) introducing themselves and describing their standards for being entertained as "impossibly high"—are further complicated by a number of unexpected juxtapositions and rhetorical oddities ("a phenomenon; whose humorous slant did not sympathetically attack us") interfering with the apparent orthodoxy of Riding's straightforward, argumentative tone. On the whole, "Mademoiselle Comet" resists the conventions underlying both "illusionistic" description and conventional narrative, apparently subscribing to them in order to subvert them "from within." Eventually, it is the fusion and transformation of identities that becomes the subject of Riding's narrative as the "entertained" we-speakers are turned into "looker-entertainers," only to become part of the "long bright dead hair" of the (literalized) comet's tail.

Tender Buttons and Stein's Redefinition of Poetic Language

In "Picasso," "Two Women," and a number of other pieces written in the same period, Stein's concern with relationships is turned into a mode of representation in itself.[7] In her portrait of Carl Van Vechten, written two years after "Picasso," Stein's subject appears in an even more depersonalized form, this time depicted exclusively in relation to the clothes he is wearing and various objects and pieces of furniture surrounding him:

One.
In the ample checked fur in the back and in the house, in the by next cloth and inner, in the chest, in mean wind.
One.
In the best might last and wind that. In the best might last and wind in the best might last.
Ages, ages, all what sat.
One.
In the gold presently, in the gold presently unsuddenly and decapsized and dewalking.
In the gold coming in.
     ONE.
One.
None in stable, none at ghosts, none in the latter spot.
     ONE.
One.
An oil in a can, an oil and a vial with a thousand stems. An oil in a cup and a steel sofa.
One.
An oil in a cup and a woolen coin, a woolen card and a best satin.
A water house and a hut to speak, a water house and entirely water, water and water. (*Reader* 274)

"One: Carl Van Vechten" (1913; 1922) is emblematic of Stein's shift of interest from personality to context, which is a major impulse behind *Tender Buttons* (1913; 1914), a collection of "still lifes" written at a time when

Stein had become increasingly engrossed in the observation of objects rather than human beings. This gradual change is largely to be put down to her intention to "express what something was, a little by talking and listening to that thing, but a great deal by looking at that thing" (*Look* 114). *Tender Buttons* is divided into three sections. The first two, "Objects" and "Food," contain 108 short prose entries, their length ranging from a single line to a little more than a page.[8] "Rooms," the third part of the collection, is a long, uninterrupted prose sequence consisting of relatively autonomous paragraphs. Even though the exact subject matter of the whole collection is hard, if not impossible, to ascertain, the titles of Stein's entries prepare the reader for a description of Victorian domestic interiors. The still lifes of the first section, for instance, include "descriptions" of a carafe, a cushion, a box, a piece of coffee, a red stamp, a cloak, a red dress, and an umbrella. In *Tender Buttons*, however, Stein's style moves away from the initial, cinematic technique of repetition-with-variation toward a more absolute form of abstractionism. While the portraits still delivered a fairly precise description of specific characterological types, it is generally impossible to relate the contents of Stein's still lifes to the objects mentioned in their titles. The following description of "Glazed Glitter" signals her radical departure from any mimetic—or even strictly descriptive—tradition of the still life:

GLAZED GLITTER

Nickel, what is nickel, it is originally rid of a cover.

The change in that is that red weakens an hour. The change has come. There is no search. But there is, there is that hope and that interpretation and sometime, surely any is unwelcome, sometime there is breath and there will be a sinecure and charming very charming is that clean and cleansing. Certainly glittering is handsome and convincing.

There is no gratitude in mercy and in medicine. There can be breakages in Japanese. That is no programme. That is no color chosen. It was chosen yesterday, that showed spitting and perhaps washing and polishing. It certainly showed no obligation and perhaps if borrowing is not natural there is some use in giving. (*Look* 161)

Stein's still lifes (this one is excerpted from the "Objects" section) emerge as the ultimate—and arguably the last—development of the tradition of the object-poem, which Stein attempts to release from the very assumptions of transitiveness and referentiality that supported its existence perhaps more than that of any other poetic genre. Even though the titles of the entries still make it clear that Stein's poetics of "looking" are rooted in the observation of mostly trivial objects and everyday matters, the objects themselves often seem to exist mainly as a springboard for the observer's abstract reflections. In a similar way, the descriptive or definitional impulse announced in the poem's heading is subsequently undermined by the semantic vagueness of the entry itself. Stein's poem, however, maintains an illusion of referentiality through a syntax whose apparent orthodoxy ironically foregrounds its actual indeterminacy. Even though Stein's description is not exactly what one could expect from a definition of a "glazed glitter" or a "nickel," it still occasionally *seems* to refer to a stable, constitutive, contextualizable referent (involving, for instance, the polishing of a tarnished silver coin). Similarly, if the twelve sentences that compose Stein's still life do not seem to follow a clear logical sequence, the syntax used throughout is, most of the time, grammatically correct and appears to have retained—at least superficially—all the attributes of a quite straightforward piece of argumentative prose. In an extract such as this one, the a-semantic or a-referential quality of Stein's prose is attributable not so much to syntactic or lexical difficulties as to the absence of contextual hints that might enable the reader to construe the entry into a "meaningful" whole.

Still, what directly concerns us here is that the vignettes of *Tender Buttons* were, as Stein herself repeatedly insisted, the result of her investigation not of prose but of *poetic* language and what she perceived as poetry's reliance on "nouns." In a lecture entitled "Poetry and Grammar" given in the United States during her 1934 lecture tour, Stein commented that

> in coming to avoid nouns a great deal happens and has happened. It was one of the things that happened in a book I called *Tender Buttons*.
>
> In *The Making of Americans* a long very long prose book made up of sentences and paragraphs . . . I said I had gotten rid of nouns and adjectives as much as possible by the method of living in adverbs in verbs in pronouns, in adverbial clauses written or implied and in conjunctions.
>
> But after I had gone as far as I could in these long sentences and paragraphs that had come to do something else I then began very short things and in doing very short things I resolutely realized nouns and decided not to get around them but to meet them, to handle in short to refuse them by using them and in that way my real acquaintance with poetry was begun. (*Look* 136–37)

Stein's refusal of "nouns" must not be taken at face value, for it extends well beyond strictly grammatical considerations. For Stein, nouns are the means by which we ascribe meaning to reality and thereby establish fixed relationships between signifier and signified. Stein's distrust of the referential power of words ("the sign that means that really means a necessary betrayal" [168]) parallels her pessimistic view of the evolution of poetic language, which she sees as a gradual process of erosion of its capacity to represent reality adequately. "When the language was new," she argues, "as it was with Chaucer and Homer, the poet could use the name of a thing and the thing was really there" (7); "the completeness was in the use" (41). "After hundreds of years had gone by and thousands of poems had been written," she goes on, "he could call on those words and find that they were just wornout literary words." The ensuing "long period" in which "confusion" arises and writers start to "confuse what they are saying with the words they are choosing" (44) signaled the progressive separation of poetic language from the reality to which it is striving to refer. To the modern poet, this utilitarian, quasi-performative power of words to summon reality into being that Stein calls "the excitedness of pure being" is irremediably lost.

As a result of the failure of language to create one-to-one relationships between signifier and signified, the name-giving, reality-defining function of words is precisely what the contemporary poet should strive to question and subvert ("poetry is doing nothing but using losing refusing and pleasing and betraying and caressing nouns" [138]). As poetry, however, is "entirely based on the noun," this can only occur if one decides to "refuse nouns by using them" in order to meet them on their own ground and question their use-value. The best example of this is Stein's famous line "A rose is a rose is a rose is a rose," its main purpose being to avoid losing "the enjoyment of naming" (139), which disappears as soon as you know a thing by its name.[9] Poetic language therefore becomes a means of disrupting reified relationships within so-called referential or utilitarian language in order to revitalize it and "make it new": Stein's ambition, so she claimed, was to make the rose appear "red for the first time in English poetry for a hundred years" (7).

The "abstract" still lifes of *Tender Buttons* suggest that a possible alternative to both the separation of signifier and signified and the reification of poetic language is to break the chains linking words to specific signified realities in conventional, "utilitarian" language (the realm of prose, not of poetry). Only in such a way can the contemporary poet hope to "bring back vitality to the noun" (7). It should be noted, however, that Stein's "refusing by using" differs from other avant-gardist attempts to "defamiliarize" language or celebrate the acoustic charms of the "word as such." In many ways, *Tender Buttons* can indeed be seen as part of the general disillusion concerning language as a referential, meaning-producing tool, which was an important impulse behind, for example, Velimir Khlebnikov's *zaum* and especially behind the Dada movement. Stein, however, definitely veers away from a number of major premises of Dada, including its uncompromising confidence in the value of "spontaneous" utterances, chance operations, and absolute formal indeterminacy. (The question of whether Dada writing does or does not stand up to its own claims to absolute indeterminacy is, needless to say, equally open to argument.) Her lack of interest in the workings of the unconscious mind, in particular, is well attested. Even in her early years as an undergraduate student at the Harvard psychology laboratory where she worked under Hugo Münsterberg and, more importantly, William James, she was more interested in the latter's research on the relationship between specific states of mind and parts of speech than in his early experiments with automatic writing. As Elizabeth Sprigg has pointed out, "the conscious, just before it was superseded, through the influence of Freud, by the unconscious—although never for Gertrude Stein" was her main preoccupation (*Look* 14). As suggested above, Stein may have been one of the most experimental writers of the modernist era, but she also remained in many ways a child of the nineteenth century, as is clear, for instance, from her empiricist and positivist faith in the power of literature (and her own talent) to write "a history of everyone" and attend to "the daily life the complete daily life and the things shut in with that complete daily life" (35). Such claims to absolute comprehensiveness are indeed diametrically opposed to the postwar pessimism that was to pervade the whole history of modernist aesthetics, including Dada's nihilist stance, which extends, beyond language, to all moral and epistemological certainties: "I destroy the drawers of the brain, and those of the social fabric" (Tzara 2).

To the Dadaists' cult of absolute freedom of expression and, later, the Surrealists' associative "free flow," Stein opposes her own peculiar but unmistakable litany-like "rhythm," a form of "poetic" prose which still functions with reference to a tradition of conventionally descriptive and argumentative prose syntax. The "voice" of Stein's prose, as it appears in *Tender Buttons* and in the portraits discussed here, does not seek to give free rein to the poet's free-wheeling associations. Rather, it appears to be constantly listening to itself and its own strategies of (self-)expression—according to Stein herself, "being one who is at the same time talking and listening" was precisely what "[made] one a genius" (*Look* 102).

The Prose Poem and Nonillusionistic Writing

The subject. A lemon beside an orange is no longer a lemon, the orange is no longer an orange; they have become fruit.

Georges Braque

At the end of her essay "Poetry and Grammar," Stein advances her own tentative conclusion on this process of defamiliarization of the poetic medium. "Here was the question," she writes, "if in poetry one could lose the noun as I had really truly lost it in prose would there be any difference between poetry and prose" (145–46). I want to argue that Stein's hybrid vignettes testify to an important *functional* difference between poetic and prosaic language, one that extends well beyond the stylistic or modal premises of what is commonly understood as "prose" or "poetry." In this context, Roman Jakobson's research on the nature of poetic language provides a useful model for examining not only the dynamics of Stein's *Tender Buttons* but also the whole development of the contemporary prose poem in English from the formal mannerisms of the Decadents to the language-oriented experiments of the Language poets. In his seminal essay "Two Aspects of Language and Two Types of Aphasic Disturbances" (1956), Jakobson describes language as oscillating between the two antipodal processes of selection and combination—the former is described as metaphoric, the latter as metonymic. Jakobson clearly considers metaphor and metonymy as two complementary aspects of *any* discourse, as speech implies "a selection of certain linguistic entities and their combination into linguistic units of a higher degree of complexity" (97). Any linguistic utterance thus develops along both the axis of similarity (the substitution of one word or idea for another) and that of contiguity (the sequential arrangement of the signifying chain). "Under the influence of a cultural pattern, personality, and verbal style," however, "preference is given to one of the two processes over the other" (110). Jakobson later proceeds to apply his theory to specific trends or movements in Western art. The metaphoric conception underlying Surrealism, for example, is to be distinguished from the metonymic orientation of Cubism, "where the object is transformed into a set of synecdoches." Cinema, unlike drama, is basically metonymic but some filmmakers nevertheless make use of metaphoric techniques, such as Charlie Chaplin's "lap dissolves," which Jakobson describes as "filmic similes." In the sphere of literature, Jakobson opposes Romanticism and Symbolism to the tradition of realist writing: "The primacy of the metaphoric process in the literary schools of Romanticism and Symbolism has been repeatedly acknowledged, but it is still insufficiently realized that it is the predominance of metonymy which underlies and actually predetermines the so-called Realist trend, which belongs to an intermediary stage between the decline of Romanticism and the rise of Symbolism and is opposed to both" (111).

Jakobson concludes his essay by extending his argument to the difference between poetry and prose per se and proposes that poetic language, regardless of any specific school or period, tends toward the metaphoric pole. While prose is essentially forwarded by contiguity, "the principle of similarity underlies poetry; the metrical parallelism of lines or the phonic equivalence of rhyming words prompts the question of semantic similarity and contrast." This metrical and phonological patterning, Jakobson concludes, makes metaphor "the line of least resistance" for poetry (114). In another essay entitled "Linguistics and Poetics" (1958), Jakobson defines the poetic or "aesthetic" function of language more specifically as the superimposition of similarity upon contiguity: "*The poetic function projects the principle of equivalence from the axis of selection into the axis of combination*" (71). Poetic language is therefore neither antimetonymic nor exclusively metaphoric. Instead, it seeks to transpose the substitutional dynamics of metaphoric language onto the metonymic speech act.

Two important consequences of the superimposition of similarity upon contiguity are directly relevant to Stein's *Tender Buttons*. The first is that it imparts to poetry "its thoroughly symbolic, multiplex, polysemantic essence" (85). The poetic function of language thus introduces ambiguity into the referential chain and, thereby, problematizes the very creation of meaning. As a result, it undermines not only accepted connections between signifier and signified but also the "naturalness" of realist prose, which relies on metonymic (or "contextual") relationships between signifiers in order to create meaning. The second essential quality Jakobson associates with the poetic function is its nonreferential and essentially self-conscious (and self-questioning) nature. Poetry—or, rather, Jakobson insists, the poetic or "aesthetic" function of language which is present, to some extent, in any verbal utterance—draws attention to the material and phonetic properties of the words themselves. As is the case in Stein's prose, this is done at the expense of their capacity to depict or refer to a particular reality, for poetry, by promoting "the palpability of signs, deepens the fundamental dichotomy of signs and objects" (70). Here, too, Jakobson's characteriza-

tion of poetic language as medium-oriented strongly resembles Stein's definition of contemporary poetry as characterized by its self-reflexive and
subversive use of "nouns"—in both cases, poetic language is therefore a
means of "bringing back vitality to the noun" by privileging the formal
quality of words over their denotative power.

Seen in the light of Jakobson's theory, the "poeticity" of Stein's *Tender
Buttons* can thus be seen as residing in its attempts to subvert the premises
of realist, descriptive (and, as we will see, argumentative) prose from
within. The only imperfection in Jakobson's bipolar model—at least from
the point of view of the present study—is that it still takes for granted that
poetry is necessarily written in verse. His favorite subjects of analysis are
not Gertrude Stein or Stéphane Mallarmé but G. M. Hopkins, Edgar Allan
Poe, and Charles Baudelaire (as the author, of course, of *Les Fleurs du mal*,
not of *Le Spleen de Paris*). More generally, "Linguistics and Poetics" does
not refer to a single example of *vers libre*. As a result, the only means of
projecting equivalence onto the combinatory axis remains, for Jakobson,
the "*mounting* of the metrical form upon the usual speech form," which
"necessarily gives the experience of a double, ambiguous shape to anyone
who is familiar with the given language and with verse" (80). The principle
of equivalence therefore relies exclusively on the phonic and structural parallelism created by rhyme and/or meter: "In poetry one syllable is equalized
with another syllable of the same sequence; word stress is assumed to equal
word stress, as unstress equals unstress" (71). Referring to Hopkins' definition of verse as "speech wholly or partially repeating the same figure of
sound" (72), Jakobson also argues that ambiguity essentially arises from
the contrapuntal tension created between two different "rhythms," that of
metric accentuality and that of the language of everyday life. For instance,
rhyme, by drawing together words similar in sound but different in meaning, defamiliarizes their habitual referential and contextual value. Jakobson is thus interested not so much in the decorative value of rhyme and
meter as in their capacity to question the use-value of language: "poeticalness is not a supplementation of discourse with rhetorical adornment
but a total reevaluation of the discourse and of all its components whatsoever" (93). Since it is carried out exclusively within the realm of prose,
Stein's use of the poetic or "complexifying" function of language cannot
rely on a similar discrepancy between two distinct phonetic patterns and,
therefore, has to be based on significantly different premises.[10]

In view of Jakobson's insistence on complexity and polysemy, however,
one could argue that the poetic character of Stein's prose pieces lies in their
rejection of the basic assumptions underlying traditional mimetic writing

and in their endless redistributions of competitive relationships at both the metaphorical (or substitutive) and the metonymic (or combinative) level. Stein's prose defies interpretation precisely because it subverts the very metalinguistic code and, more generally, the social consensus according to which most people call a spade a spade (or a poem a poem) and use language to mean "what it says." By resisting the power of prose syntax to "name" its object and undermining the reader's attempts to naturalize the text into a conventional piece of descriptive prose, Stein also uses the opportunity to ask what a poem (or a prose poem) really is:

A CARAFE, THAT IS A BLIND GLASS

A kind in glass and a cousin, a spectacle and nothing strange a single hurt color and an arrangement in a system to pointing. All this and not ordinary, not unordered in not resembling. The difference is spreading. (161)

Another direct equivalent of Jakobson's "rhythmic" tension lies in Stein's subversive use of discursive rhetoric and the language of logic. As we have seen and will see, Stein's still lifes are often called abstract precisely because their various parts refuse to form the contextual or "meaningful" metonymic whole we are likely to expect from a sample of descriptive or argumentative prose. The somewhat "teasing" quality of Stein's prose arises from the fact that it still pretends to create conventionally descriptive metonymic chains even as it forcefully resists description in the strict sense. This Stein often achieves through her consistent use of outward attributes of logical thought. The semblance of argumentative orthodoxy maintained throughout the whole collection proves quite clearly that Stein's intention is not to deny the metonymic chain itself but, rather, the various ways in which we seek to "put it to good use" for the purpose of description or logical argumentation.

In this sense, the prose of *Tender Buttons* radically differs from aphasic language, to which it has often been compared. David Lodge (who was the first to perceive the relevance of Jakobson's bipolar model in the context of the work of Gertrude Stein) has commented that to "neglect [the contiguous] side of language completely removes the writer from the realm of prose fiction—and in Stein's case from the realm of meaningful communication, to an extent rare in Modernism" (489). "Even Joyce in *Finnegans Wake*," Lodge continues, "or, later, Samuel Beckett in 'Ping' (1967), though they exemplify many of the features pushed far towards the metaphorical pole (e.g. the disappearance of grammatically functional words, conjunctions, prepositions, pronouns, articles), still preserve through word-order a tenuous narrative and logical continuity" (489). Stein's prose in *Tender Buttons,* by contrast, results in a kind of discourse that resembles the speech of aphasics suffering from what Jakobson terms "Contiguity disorder or Contextual deficiency, where 'syntactic rules organizing words into a higher unit are lost' and sentences degenerate into a 'a mere word-heap'" (488). Lodge quotes Stein's vignette "Apple" as an example of such deficiencies at the combinatory level:

> Apple plum, carpet streak, seed calm, coloured wine, calm seen, cold cream, best shake, potato, potato and no gold work with pet, a green seen is called bake and change sweet is bready, a little piece a little piece please.
> A little piece please. Cane again to the presupposed and ready eu-calyptus tree, count out sherry and ripe plates and little corners of a kind of ham. This is use. (187)

What is problematic about Lodge's argument is that "Apple" is in no way representative of Stein's collection as a whole. A quick look at the other entries considered so far indicates that *Tender Buttons* is by no means devoid of articles, prepositions, conjunctions, and pronouns; in fact, even Lodge's example contains several such linking words. Not only do Stein's sentences abound in hypotactic (or "grammatically functional") words, they also generally follow a fairly orthodox syntactic order. In this, they still succeed in maintaining a semblance of syntagmatic continuity and logical consistency. To interpret *Tender Buttons* as an equivalent of Jakobson's Contiguity disorder is to miss the point of a kind of writing that seeks precisely to work at the level of both metaphor *and* metonymy and to subvert the very mechanisms ruling the creation of meaning.[11]

In "Poetry and Grammar," Stein accounts for her preference for certain grammatical units and her rejection of others. After dismissing question marks as "uninteresting" (128) and commas as "servile" and "having no life of their own" (131), Stein proceeds to acount for her "passion" for active present verbs, adverbs, articles, conjunctions, and above all preposi-tions, which can "live a long life being really being nothing" and which you can "be continuously using and everlastingly enjoying" (127). Prepositions are not aimed at defining or naming things. They create meaning through the discovery of relationships between signifiers, rather than by bridging the gap between signifier and signified. Once again, Stein does not refer so much to syntactic elements as such as to a specific use of language, which results in what she suggestively described in "A Carafe, That Is a Blind Glass" as "a system to pointing." In a similar way, the closing sentence of "A Carafe"—an interesting precursor of deconstructive thought—argues for a definition of meaning as the result of *differences* "spreading" between different objects or signs. While the repetition-with-variation technique of the early portraits emphasized this aspect mainly at the level of the syntax, the differential poetics underlying *Tender Buttons* extends to the way in which the human mind perceives and construes its immediate surroundings:

> Why is the name changed. The name is changed because in the little space there is a tree, in some space there are no trees, in every space there is a hint of more, all this causes the decision. ("Rooms" [202])

Stein's attempts to undermine the taken-for-granted syllogistic transparency of descriptive or "realist" discourse (in which, according to Jakobson, a thing is described with reference to a credible context created by a network of metonymically related units) eventually leads her to ascribe a new functional vocation to the signifying chain, in which the act of naming itself becomes an elusive category essentially based on connotation rather than denotation. Ultimately, the mimetic impulses of prose ("An imitation, more imitation, imitation succeed imitations" [182]) are replaced by an interrogation not only of the poetic but of art itself and the conditions in which it is produced and received, as evoked by Stein's Duchampian ready-made in "Asparagus" ("Asparagus in a lean in a lean to hot. This makes it art and it is wet wet weather wet weather wet" [190]). Language, in *Tender Buttons,* thus ceases to be a representational or definitional tool as the word sequence, to quote Marjorie Perloff, tends to express "a way of happening rather than an account of what has happened, a way of looking rather than a description of how things look" (*Poetics* 85). Stein's translation of the very process of description into an essentially phenomenological activity recalls the techniques used by the Cubist painters she admired and to which her work has often been compared. On a superficial level, Stein's still lifes share with Cubist painting a propensity to reduce their subjects to simplified or stylized geometrical patterns ("A single climb to a line, a straight exchange to a cane" ["A Method of a Cloak" 164]), sometimes to the point of dissolving them into a space of one-dimensional elusiveness:

A BLUE COAT

A blue coat is guided guided away, guided and guided away, that is
the particular color that is used for that length and not with any
width not even more than a shadow. (167)

Another "Cubist" strain identified in Stein's prose in *Tender buttons* is
the absence of firm distinctions between different physical realms and semantic fields, including persons and objects ("a kind in glass and a cousin"
[161]), fluid and solid bodies (Stein's "tender buttons" have been described
by some critics as literary equivalents of Dali's *montres molles*), figure and
ground ("a whole is inside a part" [195]) or the abstract and the concrete
("the one way to use custom is to use soap and silk for cleaning" [163]).
Sometimes, language itself is mixed with the physical world in a manner
reminiscent of the early *papiers collés* of Georges Braque and Pablo Picasso
("suppose the rest of the message is mixed with a very long slender needle"
[166]). As a result of this radical blurring of boundaries between language
and the outside world, and in the absence of a fixed, prescriptive center of
referentiality ("act so there is no use in a centre" [196]), the focus of Stein's
prose pieces is displaced further away from a description of the objects
themselves onto an examination of the very process of "change" and mutability that constantly interferes with the act of naming:

A SUBSTANCE IN A CUSHION

The change of color is likely and a difference a very little difference is
prepared. Sugar is not a vegetable. (162)

Depthlessness and Literalness

The many parallels that can be drawn between the prose of *Tender Buttons*
and the techniques of Cubist painting led David Lodge to argue that Stein's
vignettes, though "sometimes described as 'Cubist' in technique . . . are in
fact closer to Surrealist art, Surrealism being metaphoric and Cubism metonymic in Jakobson's scheme" (496).[12] Lodge's objection to Cubist interpretations of *Tender Buttons* is largely based on his own perception of
Stein's "Symbolist" pursuit of "the thing in itself" and of her method of
composition ("looking at anything until something that was not the name
of that thing but was in a way that actual thing would come to be written")
as "one of selection and substitution in Jakobson's sense." Lodge's remark

certainly has the merit of indirectly bringing out a much overlooked contradiction between the essentialist premises and the uncompromising experimentalism that characterize Stein's *oeuvre* as a whole. In this perspective, one has to acknowledge that Stein's current reputation as a precursor of the postmodern avant-garde and a "deconstructive" writer *avant la lettre* has largely overshadowed her significantly more old-fashioned belief in the possibility of the human mind capturing the *essence* of a particular reality. As we will see, this contradiction can be put down to her uncomfortable position in the history of contemporary literature as both a child of nineteenth-century positivism and one of modernism's most dedicated representatives. However, I find it difficult to agree—even by strictly Jakobsonian standards and despite Lodge's concession that Stein's metaphoric poetics are "entirely private, and the result therefore inscrutable"—that pieces such as "A Carafe" and "Glazed Glitter" genuinely function at the metaphorical level and are therefore chiefly concerned with "the perception of similarities" (488). If one goes beyond Jakobson's Surrealism vs. Cubism dichotomy and bears in mind Stein's desire to defamiliarize the word, one could argue that her prose poems seek not so much to reject the metonymic chain as such as to question the validity of any kind of taken-for-granted, reified relationship between a thing and its environment. Such are indeed the hallmarks of "realist" and, more generally, illusionistic art that the still lifes of *Tender Buttons* and Stein's work as a whole constantly attempt to undermine. In this respect, they do not necessarily function at a metaphoric level but, on the contrary, still focus on the metonymic (or combinative) axis of language, albeit in a subversive fashion. In the same way, it can be argued that the prose vignettes of *Tender Buttons,* even though they have often been hailed as a precursor of Barthes' "writerly" text, nevertheless adhere to orthodox syntax and modes of representation (the definition and the still life), which implies that Stein does not seek so much to achieve "writerliness" as such as to upset the "readerliness" of conventional prose. The semic diagram I propose in part III suggests that Stein's prose vignettes are still very much concerned with questioning the nature of fixed reference and normative syntax. This subversive quality of *Tender Buttons* is conspicuously absent from Lodge's discussion of Stein's prose, mainly because he tends to mistake what he perceives as the absence of metonymic links for the presence of metaphorical relationships.

Another aspect of Stein's work that invalidates Lodge's characterization of her poetics as post-Symbolist and proto-Surrealist is its concern with surfaces, and its consequent resistance to the various forms of allegorical depth or spiritual transcendence that are still central to both Baudelaire's

theory of correspondences and Breton's *écriture automatique.* In a remarkable essay published as early as 1927 in *transition,* Laura Riding was the
first (and, regrettably, one of the last) to emphasize this essential aspect of
Stein's poetics. According to Riding, Stein's unique contribution to the
early modernist period (or, more precisely, that peculiar "wild" modernist
trend discussed earlier and then often labeled as the "new barbarism") was
not really her doing away with any and all poetic conventions, from the
primacy of "sentiment" to the use of heightened imagery, or even the "ob-
solete" rules of grammar. The most innovative aspect of Stein's poetics,
Riding's essay suggests, was her capacity to take "everything around her
very literally and many things for granted which others have not been naive
enough to take so" ("The New Barbarism" 158).

A PURSE

A purse was not green, it was not straw color, it was hardly seen and
it had a use a long use and the chain, the chain was never missing, it
was not misplaced, it showed that it was open, that is all that it
showed. (169)

"A Purse" is characteristic of Stein's rejection of the metaphorically
laden foundations of conventionally poetic language and of her relish in
the literal ordinariness of everyday life. Stein's objects do not refer to anything but themselves and are completely devoid of such transcendental
depth as was condemned by Riding as a form of disguised Romanticism.
This feature was, at the time, radically opposed to "the devotion of the
modern barbarian to originality," which Riding saw as "the most serious
flaw in his metaphysical technique," whether in the form of the disguised
Romanticism lurking in the poetry of Ezra Pound or in T. E. Hulme's "dei-
fication of pessimism, a sentimental abstraction of despair" (157). Similarly, the sober, strangely level-headed tone of Stein's prose does not leave
any room for the kind of self-celebrating despair and alienation we find in
the work of most of the poets published in the same avant-garde forums in
the 1920s and 1930s. Instead, what we have in *Tender Buttons* is a kind of
writing in which the self, far from expressing its sense of alienation from
the things around it, casts a cold eye on its environment, which it perceives
in strictly spatial and, ultimately, analytical terms.

The disappearance of the lyric self, however, indirectly announces the
supremacy of the author's voice openly displaying its strategies of self-ver-
balization and insisting on its constant struggle with the concrete material-

ity of language. A direct result of Stein's method of "composition as explanation" in *Tender Buttons* is indeed that the *writing* I is more present than ever, only in a form completely different from what one would expect from a poetic sketch or even from the then burgeoning form of the *Dinggedicht*. Unlike, for instance, Rainer Maria Rilke's *Neue Gedichte* (1907)—the first modern and fully developed occurrence of the so-called "object poem"— Stein's still lifes do not seek to represent the object as self-sufficient and impervious to change and time (in Rilke's own words: in a pure state of being "separated from chance and time" [Preminger 194]). Far from denying or downplaying the presence of the observer, they underline his/her role in defining the various terms and parameters of the description, which, in Stein's poetics of "looking," is founded on a recognition of the inevitable mutability of the thing observed. Stein therefore does not seek to impose a particular view of reality onto the reader but insists, instead, on the necessity of letting the phenomenal world open itself up to an infinite number of alternatives:

NOTHING ELEGANT

A charm a single charm is doubtful. If the red is rose and there is a gate surrounding it, if inside is let in and there places change then certainly something is upright. It is earnest.(164)

Indeed, what remains most "doubtful" throughout *Tender Buttons* and Stein's work as a whole is the possibility of attending to a single representation of the same phenomenon. "A rose is a rose is a rose is a rose," and no given thing can be known or used in the same way ("the use of this is manifold" [166]) according to when and how it is looked at and verbalized. The image of the gate surrounding the rose in the ironically named "Nothing Elegant" may suggest that conventional "referential" language attempts to deny what Stein perceives as the irreducible proteanism of the outside world. Once again, Stein's emphasis on change and mutability distinguishes her still lifes from other contemporary attempts to write poems based on the observation of a particular object. While the Imagists, for example, sought to capture the essence of a static, petrified epiphanic moment (what Pound called "an intellectual and emotional complex in an instant of time"), the vignettes of *Tender Buttons* represent reality in a state of flux and tend to make the act of perception their very subject matter. Things therefore cease to hold their identity in themselves (Stein's essentialist pursuit of "the thing in itself" notwithstanding) and are subordinated to an analysis of medium and perspective.[13] As we will see, Stein's poetics of mutability, as well as her "naive" interest in surfaces, also make her a precursor of the specific kind of postmodern "depthlessness" that characterizes the new American avant-garde known as the Language poets.

The Mutability of Meaning and the Need of Clamor

Despite the overall resistance of Stein's still lifes to both description and narrative in the conventional sense, a certain "internal" logic is safeguarded through a consistent development of specific "motifs" running through the whole collection. As the passages discussed so far suggest, these constants include a number of physical or geometrical elements (such as lines, curves, blank spaces, and color) or recurrent concepts (including the idea of change or the process of spreading), all of which are in some way linked with her interest in painting and what was defined earlier as Stein's Cubist poetics. More generally, Stein's interest in physical and semantic mutability undermines the general atmosphere of Victorian cleanliness and propriety that pervades the whole collection and constitutes its one and only unquestionable subject matter:

BREAKFAST

A change, a final change includes potatoes. This is no authority for the abuse of cheese. What language can instruct any fellow.

A shining breakfast, a breakfast shining, no dispute, no practice, nothing, nothing at all.

A sudden slice changes the whole plate, it does so suddenly.

An imitation, more imitation, imitation succeeds imitations.

Anything that is decent, anything that is present, a calm and a cook and more singularly still a shelter, all these show the need of clamor. What is the custom, the custom is in the centre. (182–83)

Stein's assertion of "the need of clamor," her subversive treatment of the formal, aseptic decency (and "custom") of Victorian interiors goes hand in hand with her refusal to write the kind of prose poems that would meet the usual criteria of stylistic and imagistic decorativeness then widely accepted as one of the hallmarks of the genre—at least as it was practiced by its turn-of-the century representatives, such as Oscar Wilde or Ernest Dowson. One should also keep in mind that Stein spent her whole lifetime as a writer trying to react against any kind of "poetic decorum" and the premodern conception according to which "a thing irritating annoying stimulating" is denied "all quality of beauty" (23).

The question now arises, once again, of what Stein's vignettes actually may seek to represent or simply convey, albeit in an obscure or oblique fashion. Some critics have ventured a number of interpretations concerning various buried or coded subtexts allegedly hidden behind the abstract varnish of Stein's areferential prose. While Allegra Stewart, for instance, sees *Tender Buttons* as an expression of Stein's deep religious feelings, others, like Neil Schmitz, argue for an interpretation of the work based on various "private" narratives, including her lesbianism. In such interpretations *à clef* of the biographical foundations of Stein's prose, the abstractness of Stein's so-called Cubist pieces is more often than not regarded as a euphemistic device, if not a disguised form of self-censorship. However, considering the specific aesthetic concerns Stein was obsessed with throughout her whole life, as well as her hubris concerning the essential role she felt she had to play in the evolution of modern literature, it is hard to imagine that her *main* intention in writing experimental prose was to give, say, a euphemized expression to her relationship with Alice B. Toklas. By this, I do not mean to dismiss all interpretations of the buried narratives present in some or all of Stein's works; my feeling is that some of the most successful pieces collected in *Tender Buttons,* such as, for example, "This Is This Dress, Aider" or "Single Fish" have strong homoerotic overtones:

SINGLE FISH

Single fish single fish single fish egg-plant single fish sight.
A sweet win and not less noisy than saddle and more ploughing and nearly well painted by little things so.
Please shade it a play. It is necessary and beside the large sort is puff.
Every way oakly, please prune it near. It is so found.
It is not the same. (188)

In addition—and even though certain interpretations of Stein's subtextual politics may seem more far-fetched than others—numerous examples show that her aesthetic concerns and her general, Cubist-inspired defense of the "internal" autonomy of art was not necessarily incompatible with the expression of specific political concerns. While a later work such as *Brewsie and Willie* (1945; 1946) deals (perhaps too explicitly) with the author's partisanship for the American GIs who came to France with the army of liberation, even so-called abstract prose sequences such as "Lifting Belly" (1915; 1953) and "Patriarchal Poetry" (1927; 1953) are clearly informed by various social and political issues. The same could be argued about a number of recurrent motifs of *Tender Buttons,* some of which, as I have suggested, subvert a number of basic icons of Victorian domesticity. Such examples remind us that Stein, although she is still better known for her experiments with nonillusionistic writing, was probably one of the few public figures capable, as early as 1934, of describing the insular and colonialist prejudices of nineteenth-century English literature in the following terms: "If you live a daily island life and live it everyday and own everything or enough to call it everything outside the island you are naturally not interested in completion, but you are naturally interested in telling about how you own everything" (45).

Far from denying the potential presence of a number of hidden codes and narratives in a text such as *Tender Buttons,* I have tried to show that Stein was, among other things, trying to concentrate on the different ways in which she could redefine the parameters according to which the then fine arts Establishment decreed what was "poetic" and what was not. This, we have seen, Stein achieved precisely by putting the emphasis on medium over subject, material over content, as well as through her groundbreaking explorations of the *process* of composition of a literary work. In this perspective, the very syntactic and semantic elusiveness of Stein's vignettes suggests that the politics of desire which inform them (and which, again, are not incompatible with the more specifically lesbian narrative they are often associated with) are based on a never-to-be-fulfilled—and therefore eternally pleasurable—language-oriented craving:

A BOX

> Out of kindness comes redness and out of rudeness comes rapid same question, out of an eye comes research, out of selection comes painful cattle. So then the order is that a white way of being round is something suggesting a pin and it is disappointing, it is not, it is so rudimentary to be analysed and see a fine substance strangely, it is so earnest to have a green point not to red but to point again. (163)

The nonmimetic playfulness of Stein's poetic language bears striking resemblances to Jacques Lacan's definition of desire as an infinite extension of the metonymic chain, one which does not seek to bridge the gap between signifier and signified (the domain of knowledge, as opposed to desire, according to Lacan) but favors, instead, an endless paratactic displacement from signifier to signifier. Like the dynamics of Lacanian desire, Stein's "system to pointing" (161) favors a rhetoric of free play that maintains the gap between language and being and thus rejects the reifying strategies of reference and description. It urges words to "point again" and again at a being that always lies outside (or beyond) the act of "naming," which for both Stein and Lacan stands for the satisfaction and the subsequent reification of desire.[14] Ultimately, Stein's writing seeks to represent nothing less than the process of representation itself ("Celery tastes tastes" [190]) and to discover "a way of naming things that would not invent names, but mean names without naming them" (141).

2 · Popular Modernism and the American Prose Poem
From Sherwood Anderson to Kenneth Patchen

PERSONALITY
Musings of a Police Reporter in the Identification Bureau

You have loved forty women, but you have only one thumb.
You have led a hundred secret lives, but you mark only one thumb.
You go round the world and fight in a thousand wars and win all
    the world's honors, but when you come back home the print of
    the one thumb your mother gave you is the same print of thumb
    you had in the old home when your mother kissed you and said
    good-by.
Out of the whirling womb of time come millions of men and their
    feet crowd the earth and they cut one another's throats for room
    to stand and among them all are not two thumbs alike.
Somewhere is a Great God of Thumbs who can tell the inside story
    of this.

On a strictly formal level, "Personality," one of Carl Sandburg's famous *Chicago Poems* (1916), signals an interesting move away from the Whitmanesque long line resulting in a mixed form halfway between free verse and the prose poem. By forsaking Whitman's endlessly paratactic flow (including the usual comma at the end of each line) and choosing the full-length sentence as his basic rhythmic and compositional unit, Sandburg reworked the traditional indented line into a more extended whole that comes as close as anything to a syntactically self-contained prose paragraph.[1]

Sandburg's transformation of the Whitmanian line into a hybrid sentence-paragraph (a form which remained a major formal premise of Sandburg's work from the early years of *Chicago Poems* to the later experiments of *The People, Yes* [1936]) was not an altogether unprecedented phenomenon.[2] Two years before the appearance of *Chicago Poems*, Italian-American poet and social activist Arturo Giovannitti (1884–1959) had already used the sentence-paragraph to convert a similar mixture of lyric fervor and prosaic sobriety into a poetic expression of his socialist convictions.[3] "The Walker," one of the most powerful poems of Giovannitti's *Arrows in the Gale* (1914), is a remarkable example of such a synthesis of personal feeling and political commitment. The poem was inspired by Giovannitti's own time in prison awaiting trial for leading the famous Lawrence, Massachusetts, strike of textile workers in 1912. Typically, "The Walker" displays an acute sense of individual experience endowed with a collective significance by the author's penchant for consciousness-raising discursiveness:

> Wonderful is the supreme wisdom of the jail that makes all think the same thought. Marvelous is the providence of the law that equalizes all, even in mind and sentiment. Fallen is the last barrier of privilege, the aristocracy of the intellect. The democracy of reason has leveled all the two hundred minds to the common surface of the same thought.
> I, who have never killed, think like the murderer;
> I, who have never stolen, reason like the thief;
> I think, reason, wish, hope, doubt, wait like the hired assassin, the embezzler, the forger, the counterfeiter, the incestuous, the raper, the drunkard, the prostitute, the pimp, I, I who used to think of love and life and flowers and song and beauty and the ideal. (151)

Giovannitti's predilection for the prose poem form can also be put down to his tendency to secularize the rhetoric energy and the didactic potential of popular religious genres, like the parable or the sermon, and put them at the service of his socialist convictions. Similar strategies of poetic *détournement* are also apparent in "The Sermon of the Common," in which Giovannitti parodies the Sermon on the Mount in order to turn the conservative rhetoric of the Beatitudes into an exhortation to social revolt ("Blessed are the strong in freedom's spirit: for theirs is the kingdom of the earth. Blessed are they that mourn their martyred dead: for they shall avenge them upon their murderers and be comforted. Blessed are the rebels: for they shall reconquer the earth. Blessed are they which do hunger and thirst after equality: for they shall eat the fruit of their labor" [193]).

More generally, the issue at stake in Giovannitti's "The Walker" is that of poetry's cultural and political role and its critical engagement with society itself, for the main subject matter of "The Walker" is a principle of social exclusion and confinement of the individual, which is an integral part of the workings of modern democracy. The poem's mode, however, remains consistently lyrical, in that it is concerned, above all, with the individual consciousness and its attempts to deal with the social and intellectual equalizing brought about by the "wisdom of the jail" and its "democracy of reason." In the context of poetic practice, the aesthetic and ideological values grudgingly dismissed by the prisoner ("love and life and flowers and song and beauty and the ideal") are precisely those which were promulgated by the cultural Establishment as being the privileged subject of poetry—a genre then understood not as a place to comment on the subject's position in social life but, rather, as an idealized and self-contained domain in which the lyric I could break away from the contingencies of society by surrendering to the gentle, decorative, and sentimental power of song.

By reading the political consciousness of the lyric self through the lens of its social and historical environment, Giovannitti had already anticipated the major methodological determinants of Sherwood Anderson's early experiments with the prose poem form.[4] Of the forty-nine pieces included in Anderson's *Mid-American Chants* (1918), eighteen are written in prose. Like Sandburg's *Chicago Poems* and Giovannitti's *Arrows in the Gale,* Anderson's prose poems, a stylistic alternative to Whitman's long, unrhymed, declamatory line, owe as much to the declamatory conversationalism of the latter as to the prosodic techniques of the King James Bible. The biblical rhythms and turns of style in the opening poem of the collection, "The Cornfields," include a limited lexicon, a stark but repetitious diction, a fondness for syntactic and thematic parallelisms, and an austere explicitness, which often has the effect of moderating the author's occasionally over-sententious postures:

> I am pregnant with song. My body aches but does not betray me. I will sing songs and hide them away. I will tear them into bits and throw them in the street. The streets of my city are full of dark holes. I will hide my songs in the holes of the streets.

> In the darkness of the night I awoke and the bands that bind me were broken. I was determined to bring old things into the land of the new. A sacred vessel I found and ran with it into the fields, into the long fields where the corn rustles.

> All the people of my time were bound with chains. They had forgotten the long fields and the standing corn. They had forgotten the west winds.

Into the cities my people had gathered. They had become dizzy with words. Words had choked them. They could not breathe. (*Mid-American* 11)

For all their stilted exaltation and dignified didacticism, Anderson's prose poems—published at a time when the reputation of the Chicago "Renaissance" (and of "populist" poets Carl Sandburg, Vachel Lindsay, and Edgar Lee Masters, in particular) was at its peak—also exhibit a concern with the rhythms of midwestern everyday life and idiomatic speech that makes them the first (and, arguably, the last) significant example of a populist tradition of the prose lyric. As a whole, the collection displays a heroic, hymnal (and, as we will see, ultimately unsuccessful) effort to sing both the poetic and the working-class self into contemporary history and myth:[5]

On the bridges, on the bridges, swooping and rising, whirling and circling. Back to the bridges, always the bridges.

I'll talk forever. I'm damned if I'll sing. Don't you see that mine is not a singing people. We're just a lot of muddy things caught up by the stream. You can't fool us. Don't we know ourselves?

Here we are, out here in Chicago. You think we're not humble? You're a liar. We are like the sewage of our tow, swept up stream by a kind of mechanical triumph—that's what we are.

On the bridges. On the bridges. Wagons and motors, horses and men—not flying—just tearing along and swearing.

By God we'll love each other or die trying. We'll get to understanding, too. In some grim way our own song shall work through.
("Song of the Soul of Chicago" [62])

The mixture of biblical solemnity and raw colloquialism characterizing the *Mid-American Chants* records Anderson's duplicitous desire to sing both the poet's bardic self and his midwestern roots. Again, in this respect, the influence of Carl Sandburg cannot be overemphasized. Still, despite the obvious formal and thematic similarities between Sandburg's *Chicago Poems* and Anderson's *Mid-American Chants,* the latter distinctly lacks the former's triumphant assertiveness. Sandburg could still capture and exalt both the ugliness and the unlimited vitality of urban life and celebrate his vision of Chicago as a "city with lifted head singing so proud to be alive and coarse and strong and cunning" (35). In contrast, Anderson's chants—despite occasional notes of joyful affirmation in which he calls attention to the health and vitality once possessed by a mythic, preindustrial America—are torn between a socialist faith in the future of the American people and a pessimistic response to the depopulation of the rural Midwest. In addition, they are more often than not colored by a tragic awareness of the poet's inability to redeem the squalid reality of the overcrowded modern city. Characteristically, the singer's endeavors to celebrate himself and his people in "Song of the Soul of Chicago" succumb to the anonymous forces of modern, industrialized society. Eventually, the lyric expression of the individual "I," irremediably replaced by a collective "we," is absorbed into a grim vision of social and individual dismay in industrialized America:

> We'll stay down in the muddy depths of our stream. We will. There can't any poet come out here and sit on the shaky rail of our ugly bridges and sing us into paradise.

> We're finding out. That's what I want to say. We'll get at our own thing out here or die for it. We're going down, numberless thousands of us, into ugly oblivion. We know that.

> But say, bards, you keep off our bridges. Keep out of our dreams, dreamers. We want to give this democracy thing they talk so big about a whirl. We want to see if we are any good out here—we Americans from all over hell. That's what we want. (62–63)

Neither the self nor the community can be adequately sung by the "bards" and the "dreamers," the official representatives of a predominantly genteel, idealistic, and aristocratic tradition completely severed from the squalid reality of the industrialized working city. More specifically, the speaker's determination not to "sing" anymore but to "talk forever" is at once an implicit warning against the potential for idealization and aestheticization of mainstream poetry—as well as the inflated optimism distilled by the rhetoric of the political Establishment ("this democracy thing they talk so big about")—and an appeal for a new literary medium, more adapted to the proletarian cause. Although the precise nature of this new medium is left unclear, one of the answers to Anderson's dilemma clearly lies in an adaptation of lyric poetry to a social content that, until the efforts of Anderson, Sandburg, and other popular modernists associated or not with the Chicago Renaissance, had been almost systematically foreign to it.

In the passage quoted from "The Cornfields," Anderson makes it clear that his own songs are meant to liberate the heart and mind of the city dweller, who—severed from the sacred fertility of "the long fields and the standing corn"—has become "dizzy with words" and behaves like "a confused child in a confused world" (13). In his foreword to the collection, however, Anderson comments on the inherent inadequacy of his chants and, more largely, on the failure of poetry to verbalize the multiple private and public alienations brought about by the industrial age:

> I do not believe that we people of mid-western America, immersed as we are in affairs, hurried and harried through life by the terrible engine—industrialism—have come to the time of song. To me it seems that song belongs with and has its birth in the memory of older things than we know. In the beaten paths of life, when many generations of men have walked the streets of a city or wandered at night in the hills of an old land, the singer arises. . . . In Middle America men are awakening. Like awkward and untrained boys we begin to turn toward maturity and with our awakening we hunger for song. But in our towns and fields there are few memories of haunted places. Here we stand in roaring city streets, on steaming coal heaps, in the shadow of factories from which comes only the grinding roar of machines. We do not sing but mutter in the darkness. Our lips are cracked with dust and with the heat of furnaces. We but mutter and feel our way toward the promise of a song. (7–8)

Anderson's vision of the modern industrialized self is one of sordid estrangement from the basic sources of midwestern life and traditions. His nostalgia for preindustrial lore and the unmediated experience of rural life is contrasted with the self-alienating dynamics of urban working conditions, in which poetry and language itself seem to have lost their power as a prophetic, or even simply communicative, tool. In "Song of Industrial America," for instance, the voice of the bard, along with that of the factory workers, is drowned out into sordid inarticulateness by the all-engulfing roar of the Machine Age:[6]

> First there are the broken things—myself and the others. I don't mind that—I'm gone—shot to pieces. I'm part of the scheme—I'm the broken end of a song myself. We are all that, here in the West, here in

Chicago. Tongues clatter against teeth. There's nothing but shrill screams and a rattle. That had to be—it's part of the scheme. (15)

Like the bard-prophet in "Song of Theodore," who, invoking "the spirit of the old priests," briefly appears as a charismatic leader aspiring to re-deem mankind in a Dionysism embrace but inevitably fails ("I am a priest and my head is not shaven. I sit in my room and my doors are bolted. I tremble and am afraid" [25]), Anderson's poetic persona is systematically reduced to silence by his environment and the historical imperatives of modernity. Anderson's project to give public expression to the collective consciousness of the common people was eventually undermined by the general lack of critical and commercial success of the *Mid-American Chants*. His prose poems never reached more than a limited number of sophisticated readers quite untouched by the working conditions described in "Song of the Soul of Chicago."

If the epistemological pessimism that pervades Anderson's hymnal self-portraits is best understood in its social and historical context (which in-cludes, besides the growth of industrialism, the involvement of the United States in World War I, as suggested by the presence of several war poems in the collection), Anderson's distrust of the power of poetry to sing the indus-trialized world and the alienated modern self into redemption also under-lines his attempt to distance himself from a tradition that, since Whitman's *Leaves of Grass*, had been torn between a personal and a social vocation: the creation of a hymn to the triumph of individualism, on the one hand, and a democratic, national, and epic rewriting of America and the Ameri-can people into new potentialities, on the other. In the political and eco-nomic desolation of the Depression years, Whitman's project to sing the self through the community, and the community through the self, became all the more problematic. The conflicting impulses of Whitman's poetic utopia, however, are still to be found not only in its contemporary avatars (such as Hart Crane's industrial revision of Whitman's epic in *The Bridge*) but also in the most radically proletarian poetry of the period, rooted as it was in a conception of art as a collective enterprise subjected to an imper-sonal notion of historical evolution. Cary Nelson has commented on the "special status granted poetry even among some of the most relentless ad-vocates of a proletarian literature," which accounts for the compatibility of Anderson's relentless self-celebration—as well as his stylistic and formal experiments—with the social and political aims of the *Mid-American Chants*. "Unlike proletarian fiction," Nelson writes, "poetry was rarely pressed to abandon all marks of stylistic and political idiosyncracy," so that "even writers who generally had little patience with what they considered the bourgeois cult of individualism left considerable space for poetry to register individual experience, conflicts about political commitment, and linguistic effects that suggest the peculiarity of an individual language" (150). Such a compromise between the private and the public value of poetic language is detectable in the work of many prominent writers devoted to the proletarian cause. Mike Gold, for instance, whose impatience with the bourgeois cult of individualism is apparent in his criticism of many modernist poets (including Gertrude Stein, whose work he described as "an example of the most extreme subjectivism of the contemporary bourgeois artist" and of "the same kind of orgy and spiritual abandon that marks the life of the whole leisure class"), nevertheless saw in a synthesis of lyric mysticism and political commitment "the contradiction . . . and the secret of communism" (quoted in C. Nelson 150–51).

In this respect, the formal and thematic premises of Anderson's *Mid-American Chants* argue for an approach to poetic language (this time not equated with versified form) as a cultural formula lodged at the intersection of aesthetic and social institutions, one which establishes relationships between the subjective self and the specifics of a cultural community. Anderson's strategic retreat into the prose lyric indirectly illustrates the complex dialectics underlying the political and aesthetic orientation of contemporary works of poetry trying to accommodate a socially conscious vision of modern society and the expression of subjective anxieties. As I have suggested, the *Mid-American Chants* appear as the site of a conflict between the idealized and stylized position of the Poet-as-Prophet and the pragmatic cultural uses to which poetic discourse may be put. The conflicting impulses at work in Anderson's prose-poetic project are, to some extent, observable in the history of poetry itself, which, despite its historical links with social and political resistance or conservatism, is still generally thought of as an autonomous textual domain impervious to the contingencies of "real," everyday life. In the context of this study, Anderson's chants, oscillating between the circularity of song and the continuity of prose, emerge as the structural enactment of the struggle between lyric self-containedness and epic contingence that has dominated the prose poem throughout the twentieth century. In the early history of the contemporary prose poem, this struggle over the private and public functions of poetry is best reflected in the paradoxical copresence in the same decade of two essentially opposite tendencies—one primarily aesthetic and reclusive, the other antagonistic and socially committed—embodied by Stein and Anderson. Where Stein's prose poems attempt to subvert the use-value of prose and dissolve it into the polysemic undecidability of poetic language, Anderson seeks to endow poetry with a new use-value, that of bridging the gap between personal and social comment.

The kind of "revolutionary feeling" characterizing the *Mid-American Chants,* a formal synthesis of prosaic discursiveness and lyric mysticism, can also be seen as a logical (if only provisional) resolution of Anderson's aspirations as a prose writer. Despite the fairly uneven quality of the collection—and, more generally, of Anderson's poetic work as a whole—the *Chants* constitute an interesting episode in his career, in that they stand as an early example of his sustained interest in experiments with short prose pieces. Anderson's short prose lyrics, which were published shortly after his first two "populist" novels (*Windy McPherson's Son* [1916] and *Marching Men* [1917]) were indeed soon to be followed by the more picturesque idiosyncracies of *Winesburg, Ohio* (1919), in which he was to find his true poetic voice. Moving away from the universal considerations and the anti-Whitmanesque self-deprecating poses of the *Chants* to a deeper, self-forgetful investigation of individual lives, Anderson's miniature grotesques are his real lasting achievement in experimental writing. In *Winesburg, Ohio,* he was to create a unique, unclassifiable genre of his own, in which he would successfully reconcile his original talents as a fiction writer with his aspirations to lyric conciseness.[7]

Anderson's experiments with the prose poem, however, continued to coexist with his ambitions as a novelist and short story writer, as demonstrated by his later return to the form with *A New Testament* (1927), a second collection of short, dramatic prose "songs" inspired by an even more scrupulous study of biblical prosody. In these later chants, the Whitmanesque exaltation of the *Mid-American Chants* is tempered by the presence of a number of quieter and more meditative parabolist riddles and descriptive vignettes. The sobriety of style, sometimes bordering on the archetypal, and the restrained lyricism distinguishing the best among Anderson's prose poems make them akin to two earlier works with which he was more than probably familiar when he started to work on *A New Testament:* Oscar Wilde's *Poems in Prose* (1894)—another deliberate attempt at emulating the prose style of the King James Bible—and Khalil Gibran's prose parables collected in *The Prophet* (1923), which instantly met with tremendous enthusiasm in American literary circles.

Proletarian Realism and Americanness

Kenneth Patchen's first book of poetry, *Before the Brave* (1936), established him as the paragon of the "proletarian" poet. A disciple of Lindsay and Sandburg (whose long folk epic *The People, Yes* appeared that same year), Patchen embodies the renewal of populist values and political radicalism that followed the Wall Street Crash of 1929. His early poetry is typical of the kind of uncompromising political commitment and awareness of the social responsibilities of the artist that was to characterize the work of several other poets of the Depression years—notably Kenneth Fearing and Archibald MacLeish—and, to a certain extent, the rest of Patchen's own career.

Patchen's first experiments with the prose poem—notably in *Panels for the Walls of Heaven* (1946) and *Red Wine and Yellow Hair* (1949)—coincide with an increased interest in formal experiments, which were to include various kinds of concrete and semiconcrete poetry as well as several attempts at blending poetry with nonliterary mediums like painting or music. All these aspects of Patchen's oeuvre are typical of a work-in-progress aspiring to a conception of art as emancipated from such notions as "high" and "low" culture, as well as from a number of accepted boundaries between various poetic and nonliterary genres. A number of prose poems written in the late 1940s, however, are clearly still in keeping with the tradition of "proletarian realism" governing his early free verse. Among them, "Family Portrait," a prose poem contained in the collection *Red Wine and Yellow Hair,* stands out:

Great tarry wings splatter softly up out of the rotting yolk of sun. In the millyard the statue of an old bastard with a craggy grin is turning shit-colored above the bowed heads of the new shift crunching in between the piles of slag. . . . That's my father washing at the kitchen sink. The grimy water runs into the matted hair of his belly. The smell of Lava soap and sweat adds its seasoning to the ham and cabbage. On the other side of town a train whistles. Tearing shadows fill the steaming room. Wind rushes out of my old man with the sound of a thunderclap, and my sister vigorously rattles the lid of a pot. In the parlor my grandfather lies, two days dead. "Aye, and the only statue for him's a spade in 'is stumpy teeth now."—"A lapful of withered nuts to make the muckin grasses grow . . ."

—"Hush you are, for here be the priest with his collar so tidy and so straight."—"Liked his bit of drink, he did, God take the long thirst out of his soul and all." I remember once after a brush with Mrs Hannan, who happened to be passing hard under his window one morning, he told me, "Ah, there's only one thing worse than the rich, my lad . . . and that's the poor, and that's the ruckin, lyin, unmannerin, snivelin poor, my lad!" and a great whip of tobacco juice lashed out into the dust of the road. On, on into the small hours

went the singing and the laughing and the gay, wonderful story-tell-
ing . . . and the wax candles dripping slowly down on his stiff, dark
clothes. (*Red Wine* 47)

In the light of the overall development of a literary tradition of social
protest of neo-naturalistic inspiration, Patchen's "Family Portrait" appears
as an interesting compromise between fictional realism and lyric conciseness, a form whose modal hybridity lends itself to the assimilation and
expression of prosaic or "unpoetic" material but still preserves a "poetic"
space for lyric intensity and nonnarrative presence. In the absence of a
straightforward narrative line (Patchen's narrative does not follow a
straightforward, linear logic but consists of a series of sentences standing in
semi-isolation), the succession of images and frozen moments that constitutes the first half of the poem is evocative of the physical and emotional
stagnation permeating the working-class household.[8] The sudden switch
from the present to the past tense of the flashback, however, signals an
unexpected return to the conventions of fictional narrative. Eventually, the
idiomatic local color introduced by the dialogues progressively engulfs the
lyric moment in a dynamic mixture of dramatic engagement and mimetic
verisimilitude.

In "Family Portrait," Patchen's dispassionate account of working-class
misery, as well as his unsavory description of urban blight and its psychological consequences, are firmly rooted in their social and geographical
context and expressed in a language incorporating the idiom and the
rhythm of life in the industrial town. If Patchen's prose poem, like the
Joycean epiphany, reflects an attempt at assimilating the "prosaic" into a
poetic genre, it is also sustained by a democratic impulse conspicuously
absent from the history of the American prose lyric, which—with the notable exceptions of Sherwood Anderson's *Mid-American Chants* and, to
some extent, of William Carlos Williams' "Improvisations"—had until
then been associated primarily with the avant-gardist stance of Gertrude
Stein's language games and Eugene Jolas' Revolution of the Word.

The specific form of radical realism underlying Patchen's "Family Portrait" finds in the syntactic and stylistic suppleness of the prose vignette an
adequate medium for the combination of scrupulously detailed, naturalis-
tic description and the heterogeneous and discontinuous cadences of modern city life. In this respect, Patchen's "Family Portrait" can be regarded as
a contemporary extension of Baudelaire's project to harness "the miracle
of a poetic prose, musical though rhythmless and rhymeless" into a description of "modern life—or, rather, a certain variety of modern, more
abstract life" (*Poems* 25).[9] Even though the underlying ambition of the

prose poems collected in *Paris Spleen*—to combine a realist and an "abstract" and, therefore, self-consciously aestheticized mode of representation—differs from the unconcealed rawness of Patchen's vignette, both approaches originate in the same desire to capture the jolts of an overwhelmingly disharmonious and essentially urban modernity.[10] More generally, however, the choice of a prose medium is best understood in the context of a flourishing literature of social protest in prose, which in the 1940s and 1950s gained a larger popular recognition than did equivalent moves in poetry. Despite the aforementioned efforts of the likes of Patchen, Fearing, and many other "proletarian" poets, the greater success and public repercussion enjoyed by the the the novels of John Steinbeck, Robert Cantwell, and Jack Conroy, along with those of black novelists Henry Roth and Richard Wright, consolidated the prominence of fiction as the most accessible—and best-selling—medium for literature written by and/or for working-class people.

The Famous Boating Party and Other Poems in Prose (1954), Patchen's first collection consisting entirely of prose poems, clearly confirms his departure from a poetry of social statement toward the more playful kind of experimentalism that was to dominate his late career. Like Sherwood Anderson's *Mid-American Chants,* the fifty-five short pieces of the collection display a consistent use of the musical directness of popular speech as a means of lending the prose poem a distinctively folky and American voice. They were originally meant to be spoken aloud and many of them were indeed performed live by Patchen, to the accompaniment of a jazz band, during a series of extremely successful reading tours in the late 1950s. The process of oralization and dramatization of the prose poem already signaled by the inclusion of realistic dialogues in the prose vignettes of *Red Wine and Yellow Hair* becomes, in Patchen's "jazz poems," a major generative and epistemological principle. More often than not, the first three words of the opening sentence are used as a title, instantly propelling the poem and its reader into the immediacy of speech and public performance:

SOON IT WILL

Be showtime again. Somebody will paint beautiful faces all over the sky. Somebody will start bombarding us with really wonderful letters . . . letters full of truth, and gentleness, and humility . . . Soon (it says here) . . . (*Famous* 11)

This conception of the poem as an oral and musical performance further underlines Patchen's attempt to create a picture of contemporary life not just through music but also *as* music.[11] Patchen's vision of modern society as a complex constellation of syncopated rhythms and chromatic counterpoints is reflected in his use of a variety of tones and modes of representation ranging from the purely confessional to the dramatic or even, as we will see, the didactic. Despite such modal and tonal experiments, Patchen remains, in many instances, faithful to the uncompromisingly popular tonalities of his early work in his attempts to transcribe the discontinuous rhythms of speech and the local color of contemporary experience, as in "The Famous Boating Party":

> The Announcer: Ladies and gents, your attention please. It is now exactly two and sixty-four minutes past seven. Thank you, thank you, I was coming to that if you will be so kindly. But wait! Things are beginning to do! I'm afraid that something has gone amiss! I will thank you not to panic . . . The management stands behind its usual rights in cases of this kind. I—excuse me—Sam! Hey, Sam! over here . . ! (Aside: No, no, no, *no* . . . Sam, look, I know you think I did. But I don't want no mustard on my frank. You know I never take it except plain—no pickle, no relish, no onion, no catsup, no mustard, no nothin!)
>
> What the fellow said was murder, Sam—not mustard. Uh-huh, that's right—blew the ship skyhigh . . . Over seven hundred people— just like that, *poof-poof.* (58)

Such experimental playfulness is representative of Patchen's uniquely American contribution to the prose poem form. Patchen's oralization and dramatization of the form into a popular genre (he was, at the time, one of the most widely read—and heard—poets in the United States), often closer to stand-up comedy than to any accepted definition of poetry, paves the way for the later extravagant fantasies of Russell Edson, Michael Benedikt, and other representatives of the "fabulist" prose poem. More specifically, the presence of humor and playfulness in *The Famous Boating Party* is inextricably linked with Patchen's understanding of the form as a supremely hybrid medium capable of accommodating various tones, modes, and discourses. As suggested by the title poem of the collection, Patchen's rewriting of the inherent chromatic duality of the prose poem into a heterogeneous space for a multiplicity of "prosaic" and "poetic" avatars often creates a dissonant medley of voices and personae. In most of the poems of the collection, however, humor is created through a mixture or a juxtaposition of two stylistic or modal orientations usually accepted as incompatible. The use of a factual tone for the description of surreal experiences, in particular, is still a major generative feature of many prose poems written in the United States today:

> Only close-up could you make out the wings on their horses. They were nearly transparent.
>
> But that's how they covered so much ground. In a single night they'd be twenty places.
>
> Someone told me he'd noticed them in two places a good hundred miles apart practically simultaneously.
>
> He also said they had mouths in their foreheads. You'd probably think him of dubious value, witness-wise.
>
> However . . . the fact won't down that an unusual number of schoolgirls have been disappearing these last couple weeks.
>
> It may well be all that talk of mouths in foreheads and of strands of long silken hair found caught in the branches of the dogwood down by the river has given some people a false notion of the thing. This won't be the first publicity stunt to get out of hand . . . though it could be the last. ("Evidence? What Evidence?" [14])

"Rising a Little" involves another kind of discrepancy between mode of representation, diction, and "content," in which Patchen's creative subversion of capitalist discourse clashes with the helplessness of the proletarian self:

RISING A LITTLE

> Fearful with them gathered about my bed on that dreary autumn morning
>
> Wouldn't it just be to one like myself—a defenceless mousething quite unnailed and unnealed by the grayest of lives here below in this vale of blackened tares—that they'd come

And not ever no no never to one of your fat and fancy-whiskered tomadandandies in their soft-padding motorcars emboldened all in as out by prosperity and other similar figures of an economic legerdemain (24)

This method of subversion "from within," achieved through a creative and playful exposure of the limitations and failures of a particular discourse, extends to other kinds of rhetoric. Patchen's favorite targets include the claims to rational objectivity of the language of logic, scientific analysis ("Childhood of the Hero 1"), and various other forms of utilitarian prose:

COURT OF FIRST APPEAL

Humbly—but with caution (in unbridled vigor of faith: acceptful of joy for whatever reason, for no reason—humbly I believe!)

In the splendorment and holification of everything individuated, and of everything togetherized; from causes known to me, from causes forever (unassailably) unknown to me: I believe!

In the serene and beautiful prevailation of life, from causes beyond understanding, I believe!

Serene and beautiful, that livinglifeness beyond understanding!

(But of that most unsubstantial—though momentarily conspicuous—of all this earth's pitiful little nations, the human, I delay judgement until such time as the evidence shall reveal itself as being in any way applicable to what I must imagine the true nature of the case to be.) (63)

By bringing together antithetical modes and discourses (here, the language of prayer and that of legal procedures), Patchen elaborates on the futility of our endeavors to come to terms with the contradictions of modern life, a motif which pervades both his poetry and his fiction. In so doing, he also manages to expose the constructedness of the various rhetorical genres an individual inevitably has to resort to in order to verbalize his or her relationship to society at large. As suggested, the comic effect resulting from the tension created between the meanders of the individual consciousness and the apparently seamless and straigthforward factuality of utilitarian prose directly anticipates the absurdist "narratives of consciousness" of Russell Edson and Michael Benedikt.

The prose poem is not the only example of Patchen's experiments with prose and poetry. *First Will and Testament,* his second book of poetry, is a collection of lineated poems preceded by blocks of prose. More important, Patchen's "antinovel," *The Journal of Albion Moonlight* (1941), in addition to its impressive variety of other short literary and extraliterary prose forms (including parables, impressionistic sketches, lists, speeches, "confessions," and journal entries), contains samples of prose printed in direct juxtaposition to passages of poetry. Albion, Patchen's fictional creation of a failed novelist—at least in the traditional sense—rejects the methods underlying conventional fiction because he is profoundly dissatisfied with the lack of presence and immediacy of novel writing: "this novel is being written as it happens, not what happened yesterday, or what will happen tomorrow, but what is happening now, *at this writing.* At this writing! Do you see? I told you before that I would tell part of our story in the form of a novel: I did not say that I would write a novel" (*Albion* 145).

Albion's condemnation of the artificial premises of traditional fiction underlies his iconoclastic revision of the novel form into "writing" and his use of the fragment and the journal entry as an antinarrative form. As a result of Albion's rejection of conventional treatments of narration, plot, and characterization, the short prose fragment replaces the chapter and the paragraph as the basic structural unit of a new, *writerly* novel. In this respect, Albion's conception of "writing" as immediate novelistic potentiality, a fictional mise en abyme of Barthes' novelistic mode, is the exact countertype of Patchen's "novelization"/"fictionalization" of the short prose lyric discussed earlier. Albion's use of the journal entry as his favorite "novelistic" unit—a consequence of his resistance to the artificiality of accepted fictional structures and his insistence on writing "as it happens"— reestablishes a relationship of personal directness and lyric presence between the writer and his work.

In *Poemscapes,* a later collection of prose poems, Patchen's imaginative subversion of traditional genre boundaries further extends to the very notion of literariness. In the following vignettes, his use of the short prose poem shows unmistakable affinities with such short prose genres as the aphorism, the maxim, and the short philosophical *pensée.* By moving back and forth between the colloquial and the philosophical, Patchen attempts to create a new form of speculative discourse whose closeness to the intimacy of personal experience challenges accepted distinctions between abstract and concrete, figurative and literal levels of meaning. The result is a form that makes use of the discursive resources of analytical prose at the same time as seeking to debunk its underlying assumptions of objectivity and transparency:

137) ANOTHER DAY GONE

This . . . and it is already that. On, on we go, baffled by the shadow of this In-Out; baffled to the point of cunning which declares: It is so little, it is nothing, it is enough.

NONESSENTIALISM IN PRACTICE (138

It's nonessential to believe that the special quality of every life resides not in its being (if by being we mean being somewhere: and if we don't, whose else's tail shall we chase?), but in its strange motionability, its headlong flight from anything and everything that even remotely smacks of "this day," "this place." (unpag.)

In defining the prose poem as the locus of convergence and conflict of various literary and nonliterary discourses, Patchen's poetics of hybridity does not limit itself to denying the legitimacy of a structural distinction between poetry and prose. Indeed, the coalescence of various utilitarian and nonutilitarian discourses into the transgeneric synthesis of the prose poem also challenges the imperviousness of accepted boundaries between theoretical and creative writing. In this respect, Patchen's "popular experimentalism," his domestication of late modernist avant-gardism into a Great Leveler of genres, stands as a unique and multifaceted milestone in the history of the American prose poem and, more generally, as a challenging contribution to both experimental and popular writing. In the context of this study, Patchen's prose poems emerge as so many attempts to explore the potential of poetry for reclaiming specific functions and modes usually considered as the prerogative of prose genres. A platform for ludic negotiations between the subjective and the objective, the lyric and the novelistic, the public and the private, the secular and the religious, Patchen's prose poems contain *in nuce* some of the most recent patterns of development of the contemporary American prose poem.

PART II

Contemporary Trajectories

3 · The Prose Poem
and the (Short) Short Story
Russell Edson and the Fabulist School

Let us, for a start, consider the following piece published in a recent anthology of prose poems:

> Even before he put on the old sweater his first wife had given him, he was thinking of the leaves. How they were two piles. How he had been careful to arrange them in some kind of order, the wettest on the top, dryer leaves in the middle, the driest on the bottom. He bent, cupped his hand against the wind, lit the match and held it as close to the bottom as he could reach, then stood up and moved away. Leaning against the rake he watched the curve of smoke, how the wind came over the yard like some invisible hand, swirling the smoke into his face. And he began thinking of himself as a kind of leaf, wished himself removed from his own body, so that he might drift down through the air onto the fire, spread himself like a leaf over the flames. He stood motionless, watching the leaf of his own body disintegrate, a man gone up in smoke, drifting off through his own yard, his own trees, leaving his own ground, past his front door, through each room, sifting into the clothes of his wife and daughter, knowing, when they rose in the morning they would scent the smell of his old skin, a body turned inside out, something loose in the air, something a daughter might dream, visions of her father moving off like smoke through trees. (Myers 17)

Michael Delp's "Burning" is only one among many recent prose poems with what can be called a strong narrative line. It does not indeed limit itself to describing a particular moment, object, landscape, or detail but contains a number of nonlyric or nonmeditative elements accounting for the protagonist's concrete movements and actions. Moreover, the use of the past tense draws it further away from any strictly poetic tradition toward the familiar conventions of the third-person fictional narrative. If one had to ascertain its degree of "poeticalness," in the largest sense of the word, or any other feature that would justify its being written, labeled, and received as a "prose poem," one would almost automatically be tempted to underline some of its lyric attributes. One could argue, for instance, that Delp's prose entry, despite its narrative elements, originates in an essentially subjectivist impulse—that of the protagonist's "thinking" himself into a burning leaf—which contributes to an interiorization of the narrative into a kind of dream-vision (an aspect hinted at in the last sentence of the poem). Other interpretations of the poem's poetico-lyric aspects could foreground the presence of a central imagistic or emotional motif—the leaf or the idea of burning—the metaphorical resonance of which eventually supplants the concrete meaning of the narrative. One could also propose that the languid, incremental flow of the last sentence and the repetition of "how" and "something" give the entry a rhythmic, quasiprosodic quality. However, none of these attributes of vertical, metaphorical lyricalness (which one usually opposes to the allegedly metonymic horizontality of narrative) can be said to pertain exclusively to the prose poem, as they are found, in different degrees, in all literary genres. Finally, if one is bound to acknowledge that "Burning" could have been part of a longer prose narrative like a short story or a novel, then the only intrinsic quality distinguishing it from a work of fiction is precisely its limited narrative scope and, ultimately, its length (less than two hundred and fifty words), which is well below the usual length of a short story. This particular kind of narrative prose poem deals with only one or two specific narrative moments, visions or fragments which, like Joyce's novelistic vignettes in *Giacomo Joyce,* would constitute only one element of a larger fictional whole. One could therefore describe this kind of narrative sketch as a very short narrative piece resisting the metonymic expansiveness of fictional or novelistic narrative and compensating for it through a heightened use of metaphoric structures. Still, even if one suscribes to this somewhat tentative "definition," the difference remains one of degree, not kind.

On the Edge of Genre: Prose Poems, Short Stories, and Short Shorts

Such an ex negativo definition of the prose poem based on an appraisal of the scope of its "narrative expansiveness" bears strong similarities with numberless attempts by short story critics to differentiate the short story from other longer narrative genres and the novel, in particular. Charles May, for instance, has claimed that the reason for the shortness of the short story is that it tends to deal with a particular incident or a brief kind of experience, usually leading to a moment of revelation or "epiphany" that constitutes the sequential and emotional crux of the story. As Norman Friedman has rightly pointed out, however, while many short stories indeed meet those criteria, May's theory does not account for the many short stories—or, as we will see, "narrative" prose poems—not centered on a particular epiphanic revelation (22–23). Other critics, like Mary Rohrberger, have attempted, more or less successfully, to solve this problem by postulating the existence of two kinds of short fiction narratives, the "simple" or nonepiphanic narrative and the "short story proper":

> My own distinction between the simple narrative (I don't like the term, but have difficulties with all the others, too) and the short story proper is founded mainly on the presence or absence of symbolic substructures. Both categories partake of the qualities of unity and coherence; but in the simple narrative interest lies primarily on surface level. There are no mysteries to be solved, no depths to be plumbed. Meaning is apparent, easily articulated and accomplished by simple ironic reversals. This kind of "plot" story, "character" story, or "setting" story is mainly representational and linear. Readers experience an immediate feeling of satisfaction in completion of the form. The short story, on the other hand, leaves readers with a set of emotions that cannot be easily sorted; readers are often confused as to meanings and find it almost impossible to state them. In this kind of story, reader satisfaction must be postponed until questions presented by the symbolic substructures are answered. In this way the short story makes of readers cocreators, active participants in the revelation of meaning, and it is in this interaction that satisfaction ultimately rests. (43)

Rohrberger's tentative description of the complex short story and her half-derogatory dismissal of the simple "'plot' story, 'character' story, or 'setting' story" clearly privilege the metaphorical as opposed to the metonymic content of the short fiction narrative. Once again, her insistence on symbolic "depth" and the "revelation" of a seemingly ineffable "meaning" makes her definition akin to May's characterization of the genre as a narrative developing around and toward a moment of insight or an epiphany. Another problematic limitation of Rohrberger's "depth" vs. "surface" and "passive" vs. "active" dichotomies (and one that applies to all [semi-]prescriptive generic features) is that those generic and subgeneric categories themselves can be extremely elusive and will bear different connotations according to the text or genre to which they are applied. Significantly enough, Rohrberger does not mention a single example of a "simple narrative" liable to be mistaken for a short story in the strict sense. While her definition of the short story as a short narrative laden with "symbolic substructures" is flexible enough to include many texts not usually associated with the genre (including the parable and the fairy tale), her focus on the "readerly" aspect of what she terms "the short story proper" excludes a number of more "realist" short stories with a strong linear, metonymic drive in which the reader is arguably as active as any other in the creation of meaning (the detective or mystery short story immediately comes to mind).

Eileen Baldeschwiler's account of two "related developments" in the history of the modern short story—an "epical" and a "lyrical" trend—is arguably a more convincing theory than Rohrberger's, and certainly a more useful one in the context of our exploration of the relationship between the short story and the narrative prose poem. "The larger group of narratives," says Baldeschwiler, "is marked by external action developed syllogistically through characters fabricated mainly to forward plot, culminating in a decisive ending that sometimes affords a universal insight, and expressed in the serviceably inconspicuous language of prose realism." The other segment of stories, which, she argues, "concentrates on internal changes, moods, and feelings, utilizing a variety of structural patterns depending on the shape of the emotion itself, relies for the most part on the open ending, and is expressed in the condensed, evocative, often figured language of the poem" (203).[1] Baldeschwiler later proceeds to trace back the tradition of the "lyric" short story to the sketches of Ivan Turgenev's *A Sportsman's Notebook* and the short stories of Anton Chekhov. She then attempts to follow its development in the work of English and American disciples, such as A. E. Coppard, Katherine Mansfield, D. H. Lawrence, Virginia Woolf, Sherwood Anderson, Conrad Aiken, Katherine Ann Porter, and John Updike. Just like Turgenev and Chekhov, all the contemporary authors considered by Baldeschwiler write short stories that deal with "small, emotionally laden situations from the point of view of two or three characters" (205) and in which "the locus of narrative art has moved from external action to internal states of mind" (206). The mechanisms of the traditional epic or "cause-and-effect" narrative are therefore inverted, as the story line is now subordinate to and, so to speak, put at the service of the psychological complexities and emotional fluctuations of the protagonist's inner life. Baldeschwiler's distinction clearly draws the inward, psychological and epiphanic landscape of Michael Delp's dream-vision toward the internal narrative of the lyric short story.

By bringing forward two dimensions of narrative, one vertical (internal or metaphorical), the other horizontal (external or metonymical), Baldeschwiler's survey of the history of the short story seems to solve the problem of the lyric vs. narrative dyad. Her theory, however, also has a number of limitations. She, too, uses elusive categories (for instance, the "emotional" content of particular narrative moments), which are not easily turned into the unequivocal criteria that would validate her apparently crystal-clear classification of the modern short story into two separate "trends." Similarly, her equation of lyricism with open-endeness is also open to argument. If many of Katherine Mansfield's stories, for example, culminate in an epiphanic, and relatively open-ended, emotional resolution, what do we then make of the great majority of short stories, which, like George Orwell's "Shooting an Elephant" or Alan Sillitoe's "The Loneliness of the Long-Distance Runner," combine a strong external narrative drive *and* a concern with internal states of mind, and in which the conceptual core is therefore neither confined to "plot" nor pivoting upon "lyric" emotional climaxes? Since Baldeschwiler's article is entirely devoted to the "lyric" short story and does not mention a single example of strictly "external" narratives, one wonders, also, whether she is implying that any short story not written by one of the writers she cites belongs to the epic category. Clearly, the "syllogistic" and the "lyric" short story are two different poles between which *any* short story (or any other kind of narrative) constantly wavers, rather than being two clearly defined groups. As we will see, Baldeschwiler's criteria, once translated into *degrees* of external "narrativeness" and internal "lyricalness" present in any literary work, whether it is labeled fiction or poetry, also apply to the difference between the (short) short story and the prose poem.

Lyric Narratives and Anti-Realism

Baldeschwiler's distinction is clearly based on the same criteria of epiphanic revelation, specificity of focus, and "unity of effect" that led Charles May, and many other short story critics before and after him, to dissociate the genre from the tradition of the so-called "realist" narrative. "In the short story," says May, "a fictional character may seem to act according to the conventions of verisimilitude and plausibility; however, since the shortness of the form prohibits the realistic presentation of character by extensive metonymic detail, and since the history of the short tale is one in which a character confronts a crucial event or crisis rather than develops over time, the very form and tradition of short fiction militate strongly against the central conventions of realism" ("Metaphoric" 66).

Anaïs Nin's "Through the Streets of My Own Labyrinth" is a typical "borderline" case between the (short) short story and the prose poem, and seemingly one tailor-made for an application of Baldeschwiler's theories on the "lyrical" short story:

Landing at Cadiz I saw the same meager palm trees I had carefully observed when I was eleven years old and passing through on my way to America. I saw the Cathedral I had described minutely in my diary, I saw the city in which women do not go out very much; the city I said I would never live in because I liked independence. When I landed in Cadiz I found the palm trees, the Cathedral, but not the child I was.

The last vestiges of my past were lost in the ancient city of Fez, which was so much like my own life, with its tortuous streets, its silences, secrecies, its labyrinths and its covered faces.

In the city of Fez I became aware that the little demon which devoured me for twenty years, the little demon which I fought for twenty years, had ceased eating me.

I was at peace walking through the streets of Fez, absorbed by a world outside of myself, by a past which was no longer my past, by sicknesses one could touch and name and see, visible sickness, leprosy and syphilis.

I walked with the Arabs, chanted and prayed with them to a god who ordained acceptance. I shared their resignation.

With them I crouched in stillness, lost myself in streets without issues—the streets of my desires; forgot where I was going, to sit by the mud-colored walls listening to the copper workers hammering copper trays, watching the dyers dipping their silk in rainbow-colored pails.

Through the streets of my labyrinth I walked in peace at last, strength and weakness welded in the Arab eyes by the dream. The blunders I made lay like the refuse on the doorsteps and nourished the flies. The places I did not reach were forgotten because the Arab on his donkey or on naked feet walked forever between the walls of Fez as I shall walk forever between the walls and fortresses of my diary. The failures were inscriptions on the walls, half effaced by time, and with the Arabs I let the ashes fall, the old flesh die, the inscriptions crumble. I let the cypresses alone watch the dead in their tombs. I let the madnesses be tied in chains as they tie their madmen. I walk with them to the cemetery not to weep, but carrying colored rugs and bird cages for a feast of talk with friends—so little does death matter, or disease, or tomorrow. The Arabs dream, crouching, fall asleep chanting, beg, pray, with never a cry of rebellion; night watchmen, sleeping on the doorsteps in their soiled burnooses; little donkeys bleeding from maltreatment. Pain is nothing, pain is nothing here; in mud and hunger, everything is dreamed. The little donkey—my diary burdened with my past—with small faltering steps is walking to the market. . . (71–72)

Like many of Nin's short stories, "Through the Streets of My Own Labyrinth" supplies no or little "realistic" or contextual information about the I-narrator, who seems to exist mainly by reference to the complex emotional mosaic of her dream-vision. Here, Baldeschwiler's criterion of inwardness for the "lyric" narrative appears literalized by the poem's central metaphor, that of the labyrinth and its relationship with personal experience and memory. Again, what makes Nin's story "poetic" is not so much its style as the gradual subsumption of the narrative under the pressure of a central allegorical motif, as the "story" as such becomes that of the correspondences between the exterior space of the narrative and the interior space of the lyric "I." The dominance of the lyric mode is further reinforced in the last paragraph, when it becomes clear that the metaphor of the labyrinth also stands for the "walls and fortresses" of the narrator's diary, one of Nin's favorite narrative forms, and one that is recurrent in many recent prose poems and short short stories. The status of Nin's story as a piece of "private" writing further foregrounds the act of writing in an "interior" space over what it is supposed to "tell" us. The melancholy, almost incantatory diction of the narrative also makes it resemble an elegy, another genre in which the expression of personal feelings prevails over the story told. Lastly, the very shortness of the entry prevents the development of an extensive metonymic and diachronic narrative line and lends itself, instead, to the expression of successive moments of vertical intensity. We will see that this resistance of the (short) short narrative against the "realist" narrative tradition also reaches a climax—although in a totally different way from Nin's short story—in the playful idiosyncrasies of the neo-Surrealist "fabulators" examined later in this chapter. In the works of Russell Edson and Michael Benedikt, for instance, the reassuring, one-to-one representational relationships of the realist tradition are systematically flouted by the triumph of imagination over material reality, of discourse over content. Like most writers of lyric short stories and many other representatives of the contemporary prose poem in English, the fabulist prose poets also favor a certain conception of "inwardness" as well as the use of a nonrealistic, often surreal or dreamlike narrative.

Although the criterion of inwardness of the "internal" narrative remains applicable to many "narrative" prose poems and short stories most readers would agree on calling "lyrical," a definition aimed at distinguishing between narrative genres by virtue of, for instance, their imagistic, metaphorical, or, more largely, "poetic" content should not imply a denial of the existence of lyrical elements in *any* narrative, whether it is labeled as a short story, prose poem, novel, novella, fairy tale, or parable. Among other things, such an arbitrary delimitation would involve shoving the "lyric short stories" of Anton Chekhov, Sherwood Anderson, Katherine Mansfield, or Anaïs Nin into yet another generic ragbag—to say nothing of the "poetic novel" (whether in the form of "novels in verse," from Alexander Pushkin's *Eugene Onegin* to Vikram Seth's *The Golden Gate,* or fiction with a high degree of metaphorical content) or the many relatively self-contained "purple patches" to be found in the fiction of Virginia Woolf, William Faulkner, James Joyce, and in numberless contemporary works of fiction.

Short Shorts

An attempt to distinguish between the prose poem and the recent "new" genres of the "short short story" or "sudden fiction" would amount to skating on even thinner ice. Like the so-called narrative prose poem, the short short story generally appears as a further reduction of the thematic and narrative scope of the traditional short story, either in the form of an internal narrative or of a "plot" restricted to a single anecdote or incident. In a recent anthology of short shorts, Irving Howe differentiates the "ordinary short story" (the length of which he gauges as ranging between three thousand and eight thousand words) from the short short (for which he sets the length limit at twenty-five hundred words) on the ground of their respective formal and thematic development. While the short story, says Howe, still admits *some* development of action, theme, and character, the short short is based on "the barest, briefest incident" and presents "human figures in a momentary flash" and "in archetypal climaxes which define their mode of existence." Situation, Howe argues, "tends to replace character, representative condition to replace individuality" (x). In emphasizing the opposition between lyrico-epiphanic immediacy and epic extension, Howe's argumentation clearly rests on the same criteria used earlier in this chapter to distinguish between the lyric and the metonymic short story. But the dissolution or, rather, the aborted realization of individuality and "character" as a result of the extreme shortness of the story is Howe's own contribution to the various debates on lyric vs. narrative genres discussed so far:

> Consider Ernest Hemingway's "A Clean, Well-Lighted Place." What do we know, or need to know, about the man who sits in the café piling up saucers? Next to nothing about his past, very little about his future. What we do know, unforgettably, is the wracking loneliness and lostness of his life in the present.
>
> Or consider Octavio Paz's "The Blue Bouquet." We know almost nothing about the man threatened with the loss of his eyes, since the crux of the story is not biography but confrontation—that moment of danger in which the man finds himself, a moment such as any of us could experience. Faced with that danger, he loses whatever fragment of individuality he may have for us, and all that matters is the color of his eyes.
>
> In both Hemingway's and Paz's miniature masterpieces, circumstance eclipses character, fate crowds out individuality, an extreme condition serves as emblem of the universal. (x)

Howe's insistence on transindividual "situations" and "archetypal climaxes" definitely draws the short short story genre away from the heightened emotional intimacy of Delp's "Burning" and Nin's "Through the Streets of My Own Labyrinth" toward the impersonality of allegorical narratives. As a result of its universal quality, Howe's short short indeed "often approaches the condition of a fable," projecting "not the sort of impression of life we expect in most fiction but something else: an impression of an *idea* of life" (xi–xii).[2] This "universalizing" tendency put aside, one of the main features emerging from Howe's description of the short short is the disappearance of the protagonist of the story, at least in the traditional sense: what remains is a semi-allegorical content or, sometimes, a voice. W. S. Merwin's "The Reaper" is one among many short short "fable- parable-like" narratives published in the last thirty years in volumes or anthologies of prose poems:

> The harvest was over. Even the scythe had not been mine. I had nowhere to go.
>
> In the evening I found a young woman lying on the ground like a sheaf of wheat, radiant and silent. When I bent over her she was watching me, smiling.
>
> I carried her into an empty house among the trees. Next to the

kitchen there was a room with a bed and a colored quilt. I put her there and stood between two sources of light, and the room was brighter than the day outside.

She is helpless. She cannot speak. I will take care of her.

It is her house. I learned that from a woman who came to the door almost at once, and called to her, and tried to trick me, charm me, frighten me, get rid of me. Old and poisonous. When at last she went away, she left, under the bushes by the house, a rabbit from the mown fields, that pretends to be dead, to be half-skinned, to have no eyelids, so that it can watch what I do.

It has watched me before. I will not leave.

When I shut my eyes I see the wheat. (28)

The different aspects in which contemporary prose poets have reclaimed the parable form and made it their own is dealt with later in this chapter. Suffice it to say, at this stage, that Merwin's "The Reaper" emerges in many ways as a compromise between the impersonal didacticism of the parable (here signaled, for instance, by the figure of the Reaper) and the intimacy of the lyric mode. The final vision of the poem suggests that the lyric I still manages to survive the parabolic mode, albeit half-smothered by the allegorical strain of the narrative.

Labeling and Publishing Circumstances

The different generic delimitations and modal definitions considered so far are based on a number of intrinsic formal features paradoxically shared, at least to some extent, by all narrative and nonnarrative genres. This brings us back to the issue of the relationship between the lyric short story and the prose poem. If one refers, for instance, to the quality of lyric intensity Charles May, Susan Lohafer, and many other short story critics see as characteristic of the short story as opposed to longer narrative genres, the narrative prose poem (or the "lyric short short") should theoretically indicate a further distillation of the epiphanic core of the (lyric) short story. Alberto Moravia's definition of the short story, while largely subscribing to the usual criteria of specificity of focus, inwardness, and epiphanic intensity, posits an interesting spectrum of "short-storiness" on a scale of narrative expansiveness versus lyric concentration, its opposite poles being the novel and the prose poem: "A definition of the short story as a distinct and autonomous literary genre, with its own special rules and laws, may well be impossible, for, among other things, the short story has an even wider sweep than the novel. It extends from the French-style récit, or long short story, whose characters and situations are almost those of a novel, down to the prose poem, the sketch and the lyrical fragment" (147).

Moravia, who avoids resorting to prescriptive modal or generic categories, has the merit of offering a method by which to measure the degree of presence of generic features in a particular work. According to Moravia's Marxist interpretation of literary genres, the novel is the site of a "dialectical and necessary development" of "ideological" themes. The short story, in contrast, deals with "nonideological characters of whom we get foreshortened and tangential glimpses in accord with the needs of an action limited in time and place." A further limitation of the diachronic and dialectic development of the narrative structure is likely to alter the generic status of the short story: when the "very simple plot" that characterizes the genre disappears, the short story, Moravia argues, becomes a prose poem (150).

Because of its brevity and its extremely restricted linear or syntagmatic dimension, the prose poem logically invites the reader to focus on its "vertical" or paradigmatic dimension. Examples of the superior "verticality" of the prose poem can include a higher degree of metaphorical, lyric, or allegorical content (as in many prose poems displaying strong affinities with the genres of journal entry, meditation, dream-narrative, or parable) or, as we will see, a renewed attention to the very language or discourse that brings it into being. Despite the usefulness of the theories examined so far, however, the publishing circumstances of each genre are often constitutive of their "genericness"—many pieces labeled as "short short stories" would not be out of place had they appeared in a poetry magazine publishing "prose poems," and vice versa.[3] In this respect, one should not underestimate the impact of generic labels and statuses on the strategies developed by the reader in order to understand or respond to a particular work. While a reader presented with a work labeled a prose poem is more likely to read for vertical attributes of poeticity, the same reader faced with a similar text labeled a (short) short story may be led to pay more attention to its sequential or "horizontal" aspects. In other words, the same piece of writing can be assigned different hermeneutic priorities and read *as* a short short story or a prose poem.

The issue of the labeling and publishing situation of short narrative genres becomes even clearer if we consider the following piece published by David Ignatow contained in Michael Benedikt's *The Prose Poem: An International Anthology*:

I paused in my car at a street corner before entering a broad, busy road, looked in both directions for traffic and then eased into the road ahead of distant, oncoming cars, a warm feeling of accomplishment that once more I had entered the stream of things to become part of America, on the go. When I reached my house and entered I slid back into a chair and felt stranded, forgotten and apart in my own home. ("The Driver" [471])

As was the case with Michael Delp's "Burning" and Anais Nin's "Through the Streets of My Own Labyrinth," no intrinsic feature distinguishes Ignatow's "poem" from even a fairly conventional passage excerpted from a novel or short story. Its style is certainly not more "poetical," its mode not more lyrical than that of most first-person narratives, and the use of the past tense—as opposed to the continuous present of many prose poems of the "Deep Image" trend, for example (see chapter 4)—definitely relates it more to the history of fiction writing than to that of the contemporary prose poem. Still, the very fact that it is presented and labeled as a prose poem may lead us to privilege a number of potentially poetical or metaphorical features, including the possible lyric quality of the I-narrative or the epiphanic or allegorical meaning of the narrator's sense of "being part of America" and, later, feeling "forgotten and apart in [his/her] own home." Similarly, the structural "autonomy" of the prose poem format tends to give its ending a certain sense of closure, although most readers would agree that Ignatow's "entry," despite its status as a self-contained unit, induces us to ponder over what comes before and after the story of "The Driver."

Finally, the issue of the length of the prose poem is a highly debatable one. It echoes a number of attempts to define the suitable size of other narrative genres, including the short story. If one is here reminded of Poe's famous dictum on the specificity of focus and the "unity of effect" of the short story and his definition of the genre as a work short enough to be read at a single sitting, the potential length of the short story is more generally defined as ranging from a few pages to such middle-length works or "novellas" as Joseph Conrad's *Heart of Darkness* or Henry James' *The Turn of the Screw*. By contrast, the great majority of the works currently labeled as prose poems (as we will see, the "New Prose Poem" of the Language poets, with its notion of the paragraph as a quantitative unit, is a notable exception) range from a few lines to a little less than one or two pages and, therefore, tend to follow an even shorter format than Howe's "short short." Despite the arbitrariness and the apparent pointlessness of such classifications, the length of both the narrative prose poem and "sudden fiction" pieces as opposed to longer forms like the short story or the novel is itself a feature that conditions the way the text is going to be approached and received. Readers know they will be able to read a prose poem in a short time and are therefore likely to "metaphorize" metonymic sequences or, more simply, to pay more attention to each word, sentence, or image than they would were they engaged in reading a novel. Thence the popularity of miniaturistic descriptions among many practitioners of the prose poem and the sense of stylistic and emotional intimacy, which, as Bly puts it, enables one to "stay close to the senses for half a page." As the reader's attention allows itself to explore each individual word or sentence in a leisurely fashion (a reading condition advocated by representatives of the prose poem as antipodal as Robert Bly and Ron Silliman), the function of detail becomes a crucial category of composition. In many works examined in this study, miniaturism, whether of the descriptive or sequential kind (the detail and the incident, respectively) is the raison d'être of both the narrative and the lyric core of the poem.

Parabolists and Fabulators

Russell Edson and the Poetry of the Absurd

Russell Edson first began publishing prose poems in the early 1960s, at a time when the genre was hardly arousing any interest among either poets or critics in the United States.[4] Since then, Edson has undoubtedly become one of the best-known American representatives of the genre. His influence on the work of numerous younger prose poets was highly decisive, as was his personal contribution to the history of the narrative prose poem in English: the neo-Surrealist, absurdist "fable":[5]

> In a nursery a mother can't get her baby out of its cradle. The baby, it has turned to wood, it has become part of its own cradle.
> The mother, she cries, tilting, one foot raised, as if in flight for the front door, just hearing her husband's car in the driveway; but can't, the carpet holds her . . .
> Her husband, he hears her, he wants to rush to her, but can't, the door of the car won't open . . .
>
> The wife, she no longer calls, she has been taken into the carpet, and is part of it; a piece of carpet in the shape of a woman tilted, one foot raised as if to flight.

The husband, he no longer struggles towards his wife. As if he sleeps he has been drawn into the seat of his car; a man sculptured in upholstery.

In the nursery the wooden baby stares with wooden eyes into the last red of the setting sun, even as the darkness that forms in the east begins to join the shadows of the house; the darkness that rises out of the cellar, seeping out from under furniture, oozing from the cracks in the floor . . . The shadow that suddenly collects in the corner of the nursery like the presence of something that was always there . . . ("The Terrible Angel" [*Intuitive 5*])

One of the typical "recipes" for this particular kind of prose poem involves a modern everyman who suddenly tumbles into an alternative reality in which he loses control over himself, sometimes to the point of being irremediably absorbed—both figuratively and literally—by his immediate and, most often, domestic everyday environment. Often, the turning point at which something goes wrong or just does not seem right propels the protagonist into a logic-of-the-absurd sequence, the stages of which are depicted, one after the other, with painstaking, almost hallucinatory precision. Constantly fusing and confusing the banal and the bizarre, Edson delights in having a seemingly innocuous situation undergo the most unlikely and uncanny metamorphoses; a method reminiscent not only of Kafka's parables but also of Edward Gorey's domestic gothicism. Edson's personae usually appear at the mercy of an environment that does violence to human subjectivity. "The Terrible Angel" is also an example of how these basic conceptual premises of Edson's prose poems often lead him to dwell on the unsavory, the macabre, and the monstrous—a tendency generally attenuated by the lightheartedness of the author's absurdist rhetoric. Characteristically, the concluding paragraph of Edson's prose poem is built on a single imagistic motif—that of the "seeping darkness"—which adds a touch of poeticalness to an otherwise most prosaic narrative. This albeit tentative move away from the narrative drive toward the more meditative tones of the last sentence is further reinforced by the recurrence of suspension points. An important typographical hallmark of Edson's prose poems, they have the effect of constantly slowing down the action, while making room for moments of verticality and nonnarrative presence between the different metonymic "leaps" making up the story.

Like "The Terrible Angel," almost all of Edson's prose poems, their length never exceeding the traditional one-page format, consist of a series of short paragraphs, most of which contain only one sentence—a compositional method reminiscent of Patchen's narrative sketches in *The Famous Boating Party*. The different phases of the narrative, which testify to the author's fascination with the eccentric and the bizarre, reflect his predilection for short "scenes" with a strictly limited narrative scope and with plotlines built on a particular detail or a succession of details. Denise Levertov has commented on the microcosmic quality of Edson's narratives: "Seen as through the wrong end of a spyglass, minuscule but singularly clear, this world within a world of his is one in which 'things'—chairs, cups, stones or houses—may be immobile but are not inanimate, and therefore experience solitude and suffering; where animals are unlikely to be dumb; and where man is often essentially immobilized by the failure to communicate. There is interaction but no interrelation. The inanimate before the animate, a child before his parents, man before woman, the eye before the world of appearance, each is alone" (v).

This overwhelming sense of utter solitude and helplessness is indeed an essential aspect of Edson's imaginary worlds. In them, anonymous people or things get "mislaid" and fall apart, abandoned by the traditional roles and functions that have so far conditioned the cozy, reassuring atmosphere of their everyday existence. The point at which things start to go wrong therefore often constitutes the dynamic crux of the poem. In a more general sense, the objects and concrete surroundings described in Edson's fables seem to prevail over the poem's personae. When Edson's characters are not simply referred to as "a man" or "a woman" (the author's favorite grotesques also include the "old woman," the "fat man," and the "large woman"), they are systematically deprived of physical or psychological complexity. In fact, Edson's "types" are actually no types at all, as their personalities or even their dominant characterological feature are hardly ever described. This radical anonymity of Edson's prosaic personae reflects the author's desire to write "a poetry of miracles—minus the 'I' of ecstasy . . . [and] not caught and strangled on particular personalities" ("Portrait" 297). This uncompromising rejection of the latent solipsism of lyric poetry would seem to invalidate Levertov's point about the "pervasive desperation" (vi) of Edson's writing. Even though one cannot overlook the overall feeling of frustration and helplessness pervading "The Terrible Angel" and numerous other poems in the same vein, one could still object that Edson's personae, despite the atrocious treatment they are frequently submitted to, seem incapable of expressing, or even experiencing, "solitude and suffering." Like Kafka, Edson deals precisely with the *loss* of feeling and spirit in a mummified world in which human beings are always on the verge of shrinking into negligible quantities of impersonal matter. More often than not, Edson's characters are merely used as starting points for his absurdist rhetoric. In the absence of a temporal, emotional, or contextual frame of reference, they seem to exist in a quasi-allegorical and profoundly untragic (and unlyrical) vacuum.

At the level of the story itself, the rambling patterns resulting from Edson's "involuted nonsense" owe a lot to the kind of logic of the absurd that generates the multiple narrative ramifications of Lewis Carroll's *Alice's Adventures in Wonderland*. Edson's plots often involve a familiar situation either "logically" extended to absurdist extremes or simply turned upside down, as in "The Pattern," in which a woman gives birth to an old man, or "Piano Lessons," which tells the story of a piano given to a young girl as a birthday present becoming the greatest girl-player in the world. More generally, some of Edson's favorite motifs, like the spiral staircase or the tunnel, suggest the complex, labyrinthine dynamics of his prose poems. To resort to one of the author's own favorite metaphors (see, for instance, "The Bride of Dream Man" in *The Intuitive Journey and Other Works*), reading a prose poem by Russell Edson often amounts to peeling an onion: there seems always to be a yet-to-be-discovered layer of meaning (or nonsense) beneath the latest image or turn of events, one which is always likely to snowball into further sequential and perspectival immoderations.

A Pathology of Laughter: Max Jacob and T. S. Eliot

Edson's prose poems have often been compared with newspaper cartoons (Edson's father created the famous "Andy Gump" series in the 1940s), as both genres indeed largely rely on a number of common formal and thematic constants. These recurrent features include an interest in burlesque situations and grotesques (in more than one respect, Edson's collections can also be seen as a literary equivalent of the freak show), an apparent economy of effort, and the use of a short narrative format. In many of them, however, the sequential arrangement of the different images or scenes that compose the "plot"—far from subscribing to the relatively conventional linearity of cartoon narratives—seems to follow the logic of a dream or, more precisely, that of a nightmare. To quote Edson himself, this particular kind of prose poem resembles "a kind of mental pantomime that arises from the part of the mind that is mute" (Letter). This oneiric quality, which lends itself to every kind of syntactic or imagistic "idiosyncrasy," has now become something of an unmistakable trademark for the particular kind of formal exoticism commonly associated with the American neo-Surrealist prose poem.

In this respect, the most decisive influence pervading a poem such as "The Terrible Angel" is to be found not so much in the free-wheeling, associational imaginings of *écriture automatique* usually associated with French Surrealism as in the more controlled and self-conscious fantasies of Max Jacob and the early Henri Michaux. The prose poems of Jacob were recently rediscovered and revalued by the American public: a relatively minor figure in the French canon, he headlined the March/April 1994 issue of the *American Poetry Review*. His work has exerted a tremendous influence on a generation of American prose poets who, in the last thirty years, have tried to emulate, more or less successfully, the surreal and playful miniatures in such collections as *The Dice Cup* (1917) and *Visions of Hell* (1924).[6] On a superficial level, what Edson and Jacob share—besides their predilection for instant dream narratives—is an ability to tell a strange, snowballing tall tale for its own sake and to twist it into a self-contained poem. Edson's prose poems, like Jacob's, display an insatiable interest in anecdotes and particulars and a demiurgic tendency to indulge in endless sequential and imagistic manipulations, all of which seek to confuse the reader and play with expectations as to "what comes next":

> When I was working at the Fashion Cooperative I tried, despite the watchful eye of the dark, ugly old maid, to steal a pair of suspenders. I got chased down those splendid stairs not for the theft, but because I was a lazy worker who hated mindless finery. You descend, they follow. The stairs are less beautiful down by the offices than in the public area. They are less beautiful in shipping and handling than at the office level. They are even less beautiful down in the cellar! But what can I say about the swamp I came to? About the laughter? The animals I brushed against and the murmur of invisible things? The water turned into fire, my fear into a blackout. When I came to, I was in the hands of silent, unnameable surgeons. ("Hell Has Gradations" ["1914" 4])

The resemblances between Jacob's and Edson's prose poems are too numerous to be commented on, even briefly, in the context of the present chapter. Suffice it to say that both authors often make use of an essentially dramatic mode in order to avoid lapsing into the overt subjectivism of lyric poetry. Jacob and Edson also both use a syntax in which seemingly orthodox factuality can easily slip into whimsical absurdity or even outright insanity. The initial paragraphs of Jacob's "The Ballad of the Night Visitor" (a later work contained in the collection *Ballades* [1938]) contain a most eloquent summary of the poetics of Edson's "surreal fables." Despite the many parallels between Max Jacob and Russell Edson, however, the former differs from the latter in that he, unlike Edson, still frequently resorts to a pseudo-autobiographical first-person narrator and seeks to preserve a nonabsurdist, subjectivist space for the expression of personal feelings:

> What a winter that one of 1929 was! Paris in white velvet, all the windows like moonstones.
>
> That night, that December night, I woke up in my cozy room in the Hotel Nollet with the wild reasoning of madness. In the cozy room, I dressed warmly in thick wool clothing because of the cold (it was about two a.m.) in good heavy gloves and the wild reasoning of madness.
>
> "Where are you going this time of night, in this cold, darkness and snow?" asked the night watchman. "You'll never find a taxi." "I'm going to the Cirque du Temple, watchman!" What a winter that one of 1929 was. Paris in white velvet, all the windows like moonstones, and every street: light and shadow. ("Ballad of the Night Visitor" ["1914" 4])

A metaphor for the generative principles of the absurdist prose poem, Jacob's "wild reasoning of madness" appears as the quintessence of the prose fantasies of Russell Edson, Michael Benedikt, and numberless "minor" poets in prose, in which humor largely derives from the hopeless struggle of factual, rational rhetoric to come to terms with the capricious sinuousness of the poetic imagination. As is often the case in Edson's prose poems, the initial impression of bourgeois, domestic coziness suddenly undermined and negated by a quirky, dreamlike visionary twist (this time, a typically Surrealist technique) functions as a prelude to a gradual blurring of the boundaries between reality and dream, domesticity and wildness, conscious and unconscious life. In order to convey this duality, along with the "momentary lapse of reason" that constitutes the raison d'être of the narrative as a whole, Jacob's sentences leap from one perception to the next, seemingly drifting on wherever the author's fancy carries them, while remaining rooted in the original anecdote or *pensée* that brought them to life. The "Ballad of the Night Visitor" is also a good illustration of the formal duplicity of the prose poem: despite its "prosaic" format, Jacob's poem still functions as a ballad, as a number of motifs and "refrains"—including the initial "what a winter that one of 1929 was" and the "windows like moonstones"—recur throughout the poem.

The studied, self-conscious craftsmanship of Jacob's miniatures and the pervasive self-reflexiveness characterizing their narrative and conceptual lines—an attempt to domesticate the flow of the unconscious praised by the Surrealists—clearly distinguishes Jacob's prose poems from the radical associational freedom advocated by André Breton and Philippe Soupault. This uncompromising self-consciousness also differentiates Edson's fables from, for instance, the more "orthodox" Surrealist tradition initiated by David Gascoygne's *A Short Survey of Surrealism* (1935), the movement's first foray into the English-speaking world. Despite the essential differences between Jacob's prose poems and Breton's automatic writing, however, the former's "wild reasoning of madness" largely corresponds to the Surrealists' general critique of rationalism, their longing for creative correspondences and interferences between different levels of consciousness, and ultimately their desire to bridge the gap between dream and reality. This peculiar mixture of logical and narrative coherence and free-wheeling, dreamlike insanity also signals the birth of a specific kind of stylistic and imagistic hysterics inaugurated in the English-speaking world by T. S. Eliot's one published contribution to the history of the contemporary prose poem:[7]

> As she laughed I was aware of becoming involved in her laughter and being part of it, until her teeth were only accidental stars with a talent for squad-drill. I was drawn in by short gasps, inhaled at each momentary recovery, lost finally in the dark caverns of her throat, bruised by the ripple of unseen muscles. An elderly waiter with trembling hands was hurriedly spreading a pink and white checked cloth over the rusty green iron table, saying: "If the lady and gentleman wish to take their tea in the garden, if the lady and gentleman wish to take their tea in the garden . . ." I decided that if the shaking of her breast could be stopped, some of the fragments of the afternoon might be collected, and I concentrated my attention with careful subtlety to this end. (*Collected* 34)

Despite its descriptive and meditative orientation, Eliot's "Hysteria" is essentially narrative and possesses a strong *dramatic* drive, a major feature of the postwar American prose poem from Patchen to Edson. But what makes "Hysteria" even more of a precursor of Edson's prose poems is its humorous use of the contrast between an extreme, deadpan sobriety and ponderousness of diction and a surreal, frequently grotesque content; a technique which typifies many recent prose poems written in the Surrealist or neo-Surrealist vein. In 1915, the young, Francophile Eliot was undoubtedly aware of and influenced by the burlesque inventiveness and the verbal jugglery of Max Jacob's pre-Surrealist fantasies and, possibly, of his early experiments with the prose poem, collected a year later in the *Dice Cup*. Be that as it may, the "studied disorder" à la Jacob of Eliot's "Hysteria" indirectly reminds us of Eliot's strong aversion to the more solemn "impressionistic" prose sketches Richard Aldington started to publish around 1910. What Eliot finds interesting in the prose poem format is not its fin-de-siècle, Wildean avatars, with their self-conscious archaisms and stylized mannerisms, nor its impressionistic extension based on Aldington's understanding of "poetic" language as an essentially ornamented version of traditional prose. What matters here, instead, is that the inherent formal freedom of the genre enables Eliot to give expression to his dreamlike vision in a way that is faithful to its central motif: the concept of hysteria itself. Eliot's truculent description of the female persona's fit of uncontrolled laughter, in which the speaker feels himself entangled to the point of feeling physically threatened by it, is indeed conveyed through the continuous flow of prose in a way that would be difficult to reproduce in the more broken structure of a lineated poem.

Again, the humorous effect of Eliot's "Hysteria" is related to a technique that still inspires—via Jacob—the work of numerous contemporary prose poets like Russell Edson and Michael Benedikt: the struggle of a peculiar combination of factual rhetoric, rational "attention," and "careful subtlety" with the seemingly ungovernable meanders of the poetico-oneiric imagination. The element of formal Englishness introduced by the elderly waiter and the tea-time ritual, comically juxtaposed with a Fellinian close shot on the woman's shaking breasts, adds a final touch of ludicrousness to the whole. (This method also clearly relates to the kind of "domestic gothicism" mentioned in relation to Edson's "The Terrible Angel.") The threat of female insanity is reinforced by the ensuing prospect of the disintegration of the self, or worse—at least from the point of view of the male persona—its dissolution into a female Other whose aggressive laughter seems to represent what critics have identified as the menace of uncontrolled sexuality, the castrating allegory of the *vagina dentata,* the vagina with teeth.[8] This moment of acute sexual anxiety eventually gives way to a last attempt to "collect the fragments of the afternoon" and achieve an ironic stance enabling the persona to convert his experience into a coherent shape.

The motif of unrestrained laughter and its connotations of insanity, which give Eliot's poem its "hysterical" quality and which are also noticeable in Jacob's "Hell Has Gradations," are here revived by Edson in his own peculiar playful mode:

> A man had a brain. That's what they said he had. That his head was not just a storage of foetal hair.
>
> They said whenever you are self-conscious you are self-conscious there.
>
> They said who you think you are is known only there . . .
>
> . . . Still, it's the reason we go to the madhouse, the reason we'll need a supervised environment . . . The walls are painted with calm colors there. And only insane laughter is allowed. That being considered the sincere symptom. All else is calm, all else is serious, because our poor brains are out of whack . . . ("Our Poor Brains" [*Wounded 3*])

In Edson's own variations on the theme of insanity, the conventional form of the fable-like opening is immediately dismantled as the content of the poem becomes the speaker's own hallucinated consciousness. Once again, the prose poem format is used as a means of subverting the didactic orientation of a short narrative genre, a method recalling Arturo Giovannitti's use of the sermon and the parable form in *Arrows in the Gale*.

Edson and Cubist Writing

Unlike Eliot's "Hysteria," which is composed of a single free-flowing paragraph, Edson's narrative consists of sentences existing in semi-isolation, partially resisting, so to speak, their own incorporation into the larger narrative of the poem as a whole. This impression is further underlined by the numerous pauses in the narrative flow signaled by way of suspension points.[9] The relative self-containedness of the sentences emphasizes the dreamlike incongruity of the narrative transitions between them, as in "How Things Will Be," one of Edson's most successful Surrealist *coups de théâtre*:

> . . . The kitchen will always be hungry then. The cupboard won't even find a bone.

The bedrooms will lie awake at night, blank-eyed against the whis-pery shuffle of hallways wandering back and forth, like blind mice looking for their eyes.

History in voluminous skirts waddled by knocking courage off the table.

The singing by the river turns out to be a radio plugged into the mouth of a corpse.

In a nearby field a butterfly is being folded up by a praying mantis into a small bright package.

. . . A tub of arthritic blood: Mother Hubbard kills the Sphinx. In a dresser drawer a ruined city of hemorrhoids.

This . . . and the moon . . . (*Wounded* 4)

This succession of descriptive and meditative moments results in a pecu-liar mixture of imagistic restraint and absurdist delirium, which under-mines the poem's potential for narrative progression, the "story" being constantly tossed about by a number of nonrational, unexpected juxtapo-sitions and syncopated jolts. This resistance to narrative, as well as the accompanying tendency toward lyric presence, is an integral part of Edson's oneiric landscapes, in which the "plot" or metonymic development of the story systematically veers away from traditional perspectives and mimetic exactness. The sequential development of the story or interior monologue also seems to have been distorted and stylized into an absurdist, quasi-pataphysical space of sequential manipulation and per-spectival playfulness. All this results in a literary *cadavre exquis,* a collage of events, objects, figures, situations, and images whose incongruous collo-cations give the whole the dreamlike quality often associated with Edson's "surreal" fables.

In this respect, Edson's prose poems bear strong affinities with Cubist art, originally a compromise between abstract and representational paint-ing and an important influence on Max Jacob and other representatives of the early twentieth-century French prose poem.[10] The structure of Edson's "How Things Will Be" subscribes to the Cubists' fondness for the juxtapo-sition of disparate elements (a technique Suzanne Bernard called *l'esthé-tique du discontinu*), which later paved the way for the discontinuous, irra-tional prose sequences of the Surrealists. But the affinity of Edson's prose poems with Cubist painting is also further emphasized by the author's pre-dilection for perspectival games in which seemingly insignificant anec-dotes, objects, or details (particularly as related to body parts or kitchen utensils and other household commodities) tend to acquire a disproportionate, almost obsessional importance, while gradually supplanting the human element. As suggested, Edson's characters/personae, by contrast, appear deprived of all the attributes of three-dimensional credibility we encounter in more traditionally mimetic-realist narratives.

More generally, and despite occasional imagistic juxtapositions such as "How Things Will Be," the sentence-paragraph is used by Edson as the primary narrative unit of his more habitual absurdist fables:

> He opens his car door and steps into a great throne room with chandeliers and red carpeting.
>
> There a man wearing knee breeches bows and asks, may I take your head, sir?
>
> What is it? cries the man. I get into my car to go someplace, but see that I have already arrived at the throne room of some unknown king.
>
> Would you like a hot bath before tea, says the man in knee breeches, or would you prefer a tonsillectomy?
>
> But how did this castle get into my car? Or did my car just fit itself around the castle?—One of those incredible accidents one reads about . . .
>
> Won't you come in, sir, says the man wearing knee breeches, the master is waiting to announce you to the further master, who is waiting to announce you to the even further master, who is waiting to announce you to the master even beyond that . . . It takes several thousand years for the final master to even begin to hear of you . . . Best to get an early start . . .
>
> Yes, of course—but, what an incredible accident! (*Intuitive* 91)

This certainly sounds very much like Bertolt Brecht's *Kalendergeschichten* or Kafka's short short stories–parables.[11] In Edson's fables, however, the underlying didactic-satirical impulse still present in Brecht's and Kafka's fables is smothered by the grotesque quality of Edson's rhetoric. Edson's prose poems are indeed utterly deprived of any allegorical content and often tend to refer to nothing outside their own logic-of-the-absurd conventions. Despite the vividness of the images and the dramatic burlesque, one can easily see how such "nonsensical" synopses can feel a bit strained and turn into a predictable ploy, especially as they are used quite often in Edson's collections. In this respect, Edson's prose poems do not seem quite to live up to his utopia of a poetry without artifice, "a prose free of the self-consciousness of poetry; a prose more compact than the story teller's; a prose removed from the formalities of literature" ("Portrait" 296). Indeed, one could argue that Edson's anti-narrative and anti-lyric prose poems display their own particular kind of formality and self-consciousness by resorting to a number of recipes that are themselves arguably as "artificial" and, most certainly, as predictable as the conventions Edson denounces as being the unhappy privilege of "traditional" poetry as well as of longer narratives like the novel. Some of Edson's through-the-looking-glass and down-the-rabbit-hole stories fail to produce anything more than an occasional forced smile, particularly when they are read one after another in a collection. Somehow, Edson's volumes of prose poems indeed gain by an infrequent, sporadic reading.

Edson is often at his best when the absurdist witticisms for which he is best known interact with his more lyrical and meditative gifts. Occasional interventions of the metaphoric indeed temper Edson's penchant for the metonymic jolts of a narrative that tends to go berserk and lose itself in the circumlocutions of its own capricious rhetoric. The result, in "The Canoeing," is probably a more enjoyable and certainly a more ambitious piece of writing than Edson's habitual exercises in absurdist virtuosity:

> We went upstairs in a canoe. I kept catching my paddle in the banisters.
>
> We met several salmon passing us, flying step by step; no doubt to find the remembered bedroom. And they were like the slippered feet of someone falling down the stairs, played backward as in a movie.
>
> And then we were passing over the downstairs closet under the stairs, and could feel the weight of dark overcoats and galoshes in a cave of umbrellas and fedoras; water dripping there, deep in the earth, like an endless meditation . . .
>
> . . . Finally the quiet waters of the upstairs hall. We dip our paddles with gentle care not to injure the quiet dark, and seem to glide for days by family bedrooms under a stillness of trees . . . (*Intuitive* 67)

Sometimes, when moments of imagistic mysticism intersect with Edson's typical snowball rhetoric, some of the author's favorite domestic labyrinths seem to meet up with the more sober tones of Robert Bly's poetics of inwardness and quiet wonder. Although it is dedicated to David Ignatow, Edson's "One Who Journeys in a Tree"—with its connotations of quiet, inner space mysticism—indeed reads more like a tribute to the author of *The Morning Glory*. Like Bly, Edson the miniaturist occasionally puts his gifts at the service of a celebration of nature and the possiblity for human beings to engage in a mystical, self-forgetful contemplation of their familiar (and yet to be defamiliarized) surroundings:

> In the tree the stairway of osmosis—up up through trunk to branch, thinner branch, out out into a twig, a leaf—expire!
> I should love to photosynthesize in one leaf lost at the top of a tree. To be useful for no reason at all . . .
> A door in a tree. A stairway that grows thinner and thinner into the narrowing of a twig; one diminishes, as it were, into a journey. The traveler dying down into a journey that ingests him until he is only the journey and those distances that you cannot see . . .
> The trunk of this tree looks thick enough to hold a spiral stairway. I open the bark door and step in, and am suddenly at peace. As I climb the stairs with a kind of spiritual sweetness I know that I ruin myself; I grow smaller as the stairs narrow, like the traveler who diminishes in the diminishing road; and I do not call this dying, but metamorphosis . . . (*Intuitive* 69)

Parables, Fables, and Fabulators

As already suggested, many of Edson's prose poems bear affinities with a number of short, popular narrative genres, including the fable, the parable, and the fairy tale. The fables and parables written by Russell Edson, Lawrence Fixel, and a number of younger American poets in prose break with several famous precedents within the tradition of the prose poem in English, including the English Decadent tradition of parable-like prose poems and even American precursors like Sherwood Anderson and Arturo Giovannitti. While Wilde and Anderson were still trying to pastiche the laconic limpidity of style and sober didacticism of the King James Bible and tinge it with fin-de-siècle pastel ornamentalism, Edson's parables–prose poems depart from the biblical tradition at the levels of both style and content. The prevailing influences here are the writings of Henri Michaux, Julio Cortazar, Peter Altenberg, Jorge Luis Borges, and above all Franz Kafka. Kafka's unique contributions to the history of the parable include an irreducible ambiguity one could define as aesthetic—as opposed to didactic— and an irresistible playfulness constantly undermining the didactic potential of the story:

> I ordered my horse to be fetched from the stable. The servant did not understand me. I went into the stable myself, saddled my horse and

mounted it. In the distance I heard the sound of a trumpet, I asked him what that meant. He knew nothing and had heard nothing. At the gate he stopped me and asked: "Where are you riding to, master?" "I don't know," I said, "just away from here, just away from here. On and on away from here, only in this way can I reach my goal." "So you know your goal?" he asked. "Yes," I replied, "I've just told you: 'Away-from-here,' that is my goal." "You have no provisions with you," he said. "I need none," said I, "the journey is so long that I must die of starvation if I get nothing on the way. No provisions can save me. Fortunately, it is a truly enormous journey." (321)

In many ways, Kafka's "The Departure" both subscribes to and strays away from the conventions of the traditional parable. Kafka's story has clearly retained at least some of the external attributes of the genre: the central dialogue still *seems* to be endowed with an allegorical meaning and to stress a tacit analogy between its literal content and an abstract thesis or lesson. Its use of the first person pronoun, however, departs straight away from the allegorical impersonality of the parable. Furthermore, and even though the story does not seem to "stand on its own," the lesson or moral the story seems about to yield is difficult, if not impossible, to ascertain or even guess at. The aim of the quest the protagonist decides to embark on is unclear and we do not know either, for instance, why the servant, who until then could not understand his master's words, suddenly decides to inquire about the reason for his departure. (This, in itself, also anticipates the absurdist turns of Edson's fables.) Finally, the conclusion—in which the character or narrator is usually expected to unveil the implicit meaning of the story—is completely open-ended. The conventional dialogue between master and servant, which also parallels the relationship between teacher and disciple of the traditional parable, is ironically deprived of its didactic raison d'être, as the only lesson delivered by the master is that the aim of his quest is simply to get "just away from here."

Even though Kafka's story can give rise to a number of quite legitimate interpretations (the possible apocalyptic connotations of the trumpet call and the master's refusal to take any provisions with him, for instance, can evoke either the protagonist's oncoming death or the spiritual nature of his journey), it differs from a biblical parable, for instance, in which a more or less unambiguous moral principle is supposed to be abstracted from the concrete, manifest content of the narrative. As we ponder upon the hidden significance of the trumpet call and the master's sententious comment on his "extraordinary" journey, our last hope to understand the latent meaning of Kafka's parable lies perhaps in the author's own remarks on the genre. In another short short story, entitled "Von den Gleichnissen" ("On Parables"), Kafka indeed has one of his characters comment on the fact that "all these parables are only trying to say that the incomprehensible is incomprehensible" (*Erzählungen* 359). A mise en abyme of Kafka's poetics of the short short, "Von den Gleichnissen" draws our attention to a feature that makes Kafka's parables appear as an intermediary stage between the traditional parable and the radical playfulness and indeterminacy of Edson's prose poems: as open-endedness and ambiguity replace the more stable moral lessons of the biblical parable, the literal "telling" of the story now prevails over its alleged allegorical meaning.

With the prose poems of Russell Edson, the allegorical value of the parable or fable has definitely ceased to be didactic, or even ceased to exist altogether, as is the case in many prose poems, which tend to refer to nothing but the literal matter-of-factness of their miniature realms, or even merely to the process of their own composition. One could still object, however, that Edson's poems have retained at least some of the allegorical potential of the older tradition of the parable and the fable: an impulse to illustrate on a microcosmic scale the "universal" anxieties of the common unconscious:

> In it were the things a man kept, otherwise they were not in the box: a toy person with an arm missing; also a leg.
>
> Actually, both arms were missing. And, as one leg was missing, so was the other; even the torso and the head.
>
> But, no matter, because in it was another toy person. This one was also missing an arm and one of its legs.
>
> Actually, it had no arms at all; same with the legs, the torso and head.
>
> But, no matter, the box was full of armless and legless toys without torsos or heads.
>
> But again, no matter, because even the box was missing . . . And then even the man . . .
>
> In the end there was only an arrangement of words; and still, no matter . . . (*Wounded* 15)

"The Matter" summarizes Edson's poetics of fabulation. As the "toy-person" is gradually dismembered into nothingness and as the "story" gradually turns into a snake eating its own tail, both reveal themselves to be only a pretext or a springboard for the author's whimsical verve. They thereby make the "matter" into a mere pretext for the creation of a poem eventually reduced to an "arrangement of words." This foregrounding of discourse, which is further enhanced by the poem's tendency to self-referentiality, is what distinguishes Edson's prose poems not only from the traditional parable or fable but also from some of their modern avatars, many of which (like those written by T. F. Powys and James Thurber) are still basically faithful to the genre's original didactic impulse, albeit in an updated fashion.

This increased, overt self-consciousness about the process of composition indirectly reminds us that Edson began to publish prose poems in the mid-1960s, at a time when the so-called fabulators had begun to establish themselves as a major influence on the American literary world. Like Robert Scholes' fabulators, Edson deliberately foregrounds and violates a number of conventions ruling traditional narrative genres and often does his best to remind readers that the text before them is merely an artificial and fictional artifact. Like many of his fellow fabulist novelists (such as John Barth, Robert Coover, and Thomas Pynchon or their common "precursor," Jorge Luis Borges), Edson also likes to blur boundaries between fiction and reality, the everyday and the nightmarish, tragedy and comedy. He shares with them a strong interest in black humor and the literature of the absurd. By defining himself as a poet, Edson also violates standard expectations concerning the alleged lyric content of poetry: ironically, the art of fabulation is here applied to a genre usually relying more than any other on a set of assumptions of "direct," unmediated naturalness and authenticity.

David Ignatow, another pioneer of the American prose poem–fable, is, even more than Edson, a typically "metafictional" fabulator. Ignatow's use of the direct address, his predilection for idiosyncratic dreamscapes and poems written (or writing themselves) "at this very moment" turns the prose poem into a highly self-reflexive, tortuously metapoetic fantasy, sometimes reminiscent of Borges' fictional labyrinths. The demise of the lyric subject signaled by Edson's impersonal, dramatic art is here replaced by a more specific focus on the writing I:

> You are reading me now and thanks. I know I feel a bit better and if you will stay with me a little longer, perhaps take me home with you and introduce me to your friends, I could be delighted and change my tone. I lie in a desk drawer, hardly ever getting out to see the light and be held. It makes me feel so futile for having given birth to myself in

anticipation. I miss a social life. I know I made myself for that. It was the start of me.

I'm grateful that you let me talk as much as this. You probably understand, from experience; gone through something like it yourself which may be why you hold me this long. I've made you thoughtful and sad and now there are two of us. I think it's fun. ("I'm a Depressed Poem" [*Tread* 81])

At this stage, we must again turn to Robert Scholes, who described the kind of "satiric" black humor exploited by a fabulator like Kurt Vonnegut as "qualified by the modern fabulator's tendency to be more playful and more artful in construction than his predecessors: his tendency to fabulate." "Fabulative satire," Scholes goes on to say, "is less certain ethically but more certain esthetically than traditional satire," as fabulators "have some faith in art but reject all ethical absolutes." Rejecting "the traditional satirist's faith in the efficacy of satire as a reforming instrument," they have "a more subtle faith in the humanizing value of laughter" (41). Scholes' distinction between traditional and modern fabulists is also valid within the context of the postmodern parable–fable–prose poem, in which the original didactical or satirical aim of the genre is irremediably drowned into an amoral turmoil of rhetoric and textual games. In Edson's and Ignatow's prose poems, the satiric impulse is directed solely at the very conventions ruling both the lyric and the narrative modes. As suggested earlier, the self-referential, sometimes self-parodying quality of Edson's and Ignatow's prose poems (which is also a major feature of the prose poems of Max Jacob and Pierre Reverdy and arguably one of the reasons their poems still appeal so much to the postmodern mind) questions our conception of what a (prose) poem should be made of.[12] The myth of the self-present, transcendental lyric self is here deconstructed by means of a foregrounding of the methods determining its coming into being. The fabulists' parodic subversion of poetico-lyric material also affects the treatment of the didactic subgenres parodied by the prose poem, their heuristic potential now being problematized. As in Scholes' "amoral" fables (37), the final "truth" of the story is also ultimately textual (and, more often than not, intertextual) as opposed to transcendental.

Despite these important distinctions, the difference between the classical fable and the fabulist one is, once again, more a matter of degree than of kind. As Scholes has pointed out, even the traditional fable displays "an extraordinary delight in design." With its "wheels within wheels," Scholes continues, "rhythms and counterpoints, this shape is partly to be admired for its own sake" (10). One of the features of Scholes' "traditional" fable that the postmodern prose poem has so far preserved and developed is precisely its distinct quality of self-conscious craftsmanship. Edson himself has commented on the tendency of even the arguably "classical" fables of Marie de France to take a life of their own and "reach beyond the lesson to tell a strange tale for its own sake" ("Soul" 92). As is particularly clear from Edson's "The Matter" and Ignatow's "I'm a Depressed Poem," the telescopic strategies of the narrator's absurdist rhetoric tend to become ends in themselves, as they cease merely filtering reality and become the creators of their own private fictional realms.

More Fables and Parables: Lawrence Fixel and the Poetics of Possibility

Among the representatives of the fabulist prose poem, Lawrence Fixel is, with Russell Edson, the most concerned with the relationship between the prose poem and other short narrative genres. In his *Truth, War, and the Dream Game (Selected Prose Poems and Parables)*, Fixel remarks that what both ancient and modern parables have in common is "the overthrow of an expectation: the reversal of some deep-grounded assumption or explicit belief" in which "paradox is the key element, opposing the identity of opposites to any commonsense, linear, or literal view" (Foreword [unpag.]). Paradox, says Fixel, is what allows the writer to juxtapose "actual, virtual, and fictional worlds, transposing and connecting the different scales, planes, and dimensions of reality." Fixel then proceeds to distinguish the parable, which is "required to be about something" and to evoke "some feeling of universality," from the prose poem, which "tends to be lyrical, subjective, impressionistic" and is "based more on self-expression than the combination of concept and metaphor offered by the parable." Fixel then concludes that the prose poem "can provide a counterpoint of *possibility* to balance the parable's greater concern with *necessity*."

Fixel's definition of the prose poem is clearly one in which the metaphorical/literal duplicity of the parable is deprived of any didactic or even allegorical value, at least in the traditional sense. What matters here is the "paradoxical" *tension* created between the "real" and the "alternative" world presented to us, not the lesson or moral it may or may not offer. The multiple frictions between the literal and the figurative, the actual and the virtual that we encounter in Fixel's parable–prose poems therefore cease to produce allegorical meaning and favor a kind of rhetoric free play, which is mostly (self-)expressive and intransitive. Fixel's prose poems, like Kafka's and Edson's, nevertheless preserve *something* of the didactic and moralistic orientation of the ancient parable, albeit with a difference. The heuristic orientation of the ancient parable, for instance, is still preserved: Fixel's anecdotal stories and meditations still seem to gesture at something other than their literal meaning and seem to further the investigation of a particular problem or issue. In most cases, however, ambiguity, polysemy, and self-reflexiveness are the hallmarks of Fixel's prose and his use of paradox—a recurrent consciousness-raising device of the traditional parable—appears deprived of any specific didactic orientation. In "A Stone Taking Notes," a sense of unfathomable heuristic mystery tends to smother the poem's moralistic-didactic impulse and foregrounds its thematic and formal indeterminacy:

A Stone Taking Notes
Somewhere among us a stone is taking notes.
Charles Simic

1.
Surely not your ordinary stone: something that appears in the field of vision, that you glance at and turn away from. The poet calls it "a stone," but bestows upon it a special, unique status. What goes through the mind, if we decide to honor the poet's imagination, may be something like this: can a mere stone be so endowed, transformed, elevated? Doesn't this usurp the role of listener: our role? And note that the poet doesn't stop there: he implies that the stone is positioned somewhere out of sight. *Somewhere?* The location is left vague enough to suggest a disturbing mystery. For while the next words— *among us*—apparently shorten the distance, it remains remote and hidden. As for the concluding words—*taking notes*—surely this augments our uneasiness, plays upon the surface of our always latent paranoia . . .

2.
Assume this is indeed a stone set apart from all others, from any we have noticed or studied. Try then to visualize color, shape, size—even adding distinctive marks and scratches. Enough to make it identifiable. Does this mean we can convert any apparently anonymous object into an efficient "machine"—or even a piece of art? A thought I find both intriguing and depressing. For it opens the possibility that the designated object may have or acquire personality, judgment,

will—even desire. (A stone's "desire" is a subject we may speculate upon freely—for who could prove us wrong?) And since we have gone this far, say that a stone's most profound, most secret desire is to discard its anonymity, to be emblematized: *Rosetta, Sphinx, Pyramid, Cleopatra's Needle,* etc. We may add to this list others that, for one reason or another, have achieved their own eternal name.

3.
At this point someone *among us* (!) is sure to claim we are better off without emblems. But someone else, more experienced, wiser, is likely to reply: Without emblems there can be no legends. Without legends, we can have no heroes. Without heroes, all that is menacing, inaccessible must remain that way. . . . Out of reach those distant icefields and moonfields, never to know the sound of live footsteps and answering voices. . . . But then suddenly it occurs to us: if a stone can take notes, why not also record, store, transmit? Imagine retrieving the sound of vanished worlds: dinosaurs mating, the great cry of perishing populations before the flood, the fire, the erupting volcano. . . . A stone that survives, tells this much, yet leaves some part of its secret coded message intact, some faint signal, not quite decipherable, that might signify another chance, another dawn for consciousness. (115–16)

The series of speculations we find in Fixel's prose poems build up a discourse that favors discursive ambiguity and "possibility" rather than allegorical necessity. "A Stone Taking Notes" also illustrates how Fixel's poetics of "paradox"—just like Edson's logic of the absurd—can result in a highly self-conscious and self-reflexive exercise. The whole poem indeed reads like a half-parodic explication de texte analysis of Charles Simic's sentence (the title of one of Simic's early collections), one which gives rise to a series of temporary and suggestive interpretations. Simic's stone—"a subject we may speculate upon freely—for who could prove us wrong?"—suggests that the kind of "knowledge" one can attain through Fixel's poem is not strictly rational or even allegorical. It resists any attempt at a single-minded interpretation and resides, rather, in an endless, plural, and supremely digressive movement from one idea to the next. In this particular kind of "discursive" or "expository" prose poem, one could consequently argue that the *digression,* rather than the sentence, becomes the basic unit of composition. This method confirms both Fixel's concept of paradoxical tension and his condemnation of "commonsense, linear, or literal" views.

It also underlines the propensity of the prose poem form for self-expression (the focus here is on the meanders of the poet's consciousness), as opposed to the impersonal universality of the parable.

As for words themselves, they are not meant to reassure us and thereby to enable us to translate reality into reassuring terms, for instance by converting "*any* apparently anonymous object into an efficient machine—or even a piece of art." Instead, they are there to "augment our uneasiness" and "[play] upon the surface of our always latent paranoia" (115). This paranoid feeling of uneasiness with language and scripturality (elements of psychological disorder manifestly abound in the recent history of the prose poem) is already implicit in Simic's postulate that "*somewhere among us a stone is taking notes*" (my emphasis). At the level of discourse itself, the scrupulous cautiousness of Fixel's multiple digressions further consolidates a more general foregrounding of discourse, the invasive overgrowths of which seem gradually to stifle any imagistic or lyric content and to create a sense of quasi-claustrophobia. The final debate on the legitimacy of "emblems" (the power of language to name and objectify reality but also to become the stuff history, legends, and ultimately survivors are made of) characteristically ends on a note of tentative suggestiveness. With the author's closing remarks on the possibility that the surviving stone may signify "another dawn for consciousness," the poem as a whole, which began as merely a series of incidental observations, has now achieved a new historical dimension and—despite its lack of commitment to absolute, "necessary" truths—a sense of parabolical universality.

Michael Benedikt's Mole Consciousness

In 1976, Michael Benedikt published *The Prose Poem: An International Anthology,* one of the first significant attempts at popularizing the genre in the United States.[13] In his landmark introduction, Benedikt sets out to define the genre according to a number of allegedly intrinsic features, which are largely responsible for the way the genre has been understood and practiced by many American poets and critics in the last twenty years. The essential characteristics Benedikt ascribes to the prose poem are (1) an "attention to the unconscious, and to its particular logic"; (2) an "accelerated use of colloquial and other everyday speech patterns"; (3) "a visionary thrust" following "the insistence on the reality of the unconscious, and on the dailyness of the imagination"; (4) "a certain humor . . . which truly registers the fluctuating motions of consciousness, and which subsumes ordinary ideas of 'poetic' gravity or decorum"; (5) "a kind of enlightened doubtfulness, or hopeful skepticism" (48–49).

Benedikt's "special properties"—all of which are directly or indirectly related to the need to "attend to the priorities of the unconscious" (48)—are clearly still in accordance with Baudelaire's famous definition of the genre as "flexible yet rugged enough to identify with the lyrical impulses of the soul, the ebbs and flows of reverie, the pangs of conscience." However, the specific literary tradition Benedikt is drawing on is clearly (neo-)Surrealist. Again, the determining influence on most of the American poets whose work meets *all* of the main features of Benedikt's conception of the prose poem most closely is not Reverdy, nor Breton, but the tradition initiated and rendered famous by Max Jacob and subsequently practiced by a number of American masters of the "humorous" Surrealist vignette, including Edson and Benedikt himself. (Benedikt's fourth criterion, in particular, would hardly be applicable to the poems of Robert Bly, for example, or to other prose poets of the so-called Deep Image tradition.) Also, none of these allegedly essential features (with the significant exception of the "attention to the unconscious" Benedikt sees as "unfettered by the relatively formalistic interruptions of the line break" [48]) can be said to pertain exclusively to the prose poem as opposed to lineated poetry written in the same vein. Most Surrealist verse displays, at least to some extent, every one of Benedikt's "special properties," including attention to the unconscious, use of everyday speech, and a certain kind of black humor tinged with "a kind of enlightened doubtfulness."

The preceding discussion has shown that the "need to attend the priorities of the unconscious"—indeed the lowest common denominator of Benedikt's analysis—is characteristic of many recent prose poems. This suggests that Benedikt's descriptions of the genre, notwithstanding their lack of specific relevance, remain useful when applied to, or contrasted with, specific authors or "trends." An essential quality Benedikt's own prose poems have retained from their Surrealist precedents is the double metamorphosis of both the lyric and the narrative mode into a means of expression of the unconscious. This process is fulfilled on the paradigmatic and the syntagmatic levels through the use of metaphoric "leaps" and metonymic disruptions in the sequence of events and images, respectively. While the great majority of Benedikt's poems fall into the category of the absurdist "dramatic monologue" (like Edson, Benedikt also favors depicting a world in which the human element is constantly being threatened by an increasingly unintelligible everyday environment), the "snowball" process here is even further interiorized than in Edson's fables, which on the whole still follow a strong "external" narrative drive. Benedikt's prose poems, unlike Edson's, always consist of a single, uninterrupted paragraph.

The narrative or "plot" therefore becomes human consciousness itself—with its endless speculations and its relentless associational imaginings—and the very discursive strategies through which it is translated into form:

> A boxful of rare cigars . . . have one . . . and it melts into the roomful of as-yet-unknown guests like a sugar cube melting on the tongue . . . like honey in the mind of the diabetic . . . like your wallet in the hands of a prostitute, like chopped chicken liver in the heart of the professional caterer, like surviving leaves in midwinter sleet, like ant feces in a vat full of nitrate, like an inexpensive tieclip before the onslaughts of rust, like conversation into silence among boring company, like the conception of generosity after December 26th, like space beneath even the tiniest hand caressing even the tallest lover discovering the joys of some novel perversion, like the idea of 18th century chamber music in the heads of oppressed, like truth in a Latin-American newspaper, like dialogue in the mouth of the megalomaniac, like meaning in the mind of the poet. Whoever you are, my best, unseen guest, in case this poem of mine in which we have had a chance at last to meet: please have a cigar; and also, may I offer you a light? ("Invitation to Previously Uninvited Guests" [*Mole* 101])

In *Mole Notes,* his first published collection of prose poems, Benedikt describes the affinities his interior monologues have with what he calls "mole consciousness," a mode which "has something to do with a fascination for contradiction, perhaps with a sense that things which automatically we think of as 'good' may in fact be tedious and destructive with respect to the spirit, even to the point of being lethally limiting; and that things which seem sentimentally threatening can actually be very rich areas for exploration, really liberating us" (*Benedikt* 55). The metaphor of the mole also suggests the circumvoluted rhetoric of Benedikt's prose poems, which, even more than Fixel's, verge on the kind of digressive hysteria described above in my analysis of the prose poems of Max Jacob and Russell Edson. Finally, Benedikt's mole remains primarily "an animal who, though he surfaces on various occasions, is most at home, and closest to the source of his powers, when living rather deeply underground" (Letter). *Mole Notes* therefore confirms the author's desire to use the prose poem form as a means of performing transactions between the internal and external, the conscious and the unconscious, in a way that often results in what Jerome McGann describes as "a sort of low-keyed condition of visionary transport" ("Virtues" 911).

The reference to the "unseen guest" of Benedikt's poem once again confirms the strong affinities of the recent Surrealist prose poem with the art of metapoetic fabulation. The syntactic intricacy, the tortuous—and often tormented—ramifications of Benedikt's style are reminiscent of the long, syncopated sentence one finds in Kafka's short short stories. Benedikt's prose tends to obfuscate and disconcert the reader, rather than to expose or describe a particular situation or even a state of mind. Benedikt's pensées usually favor irresolution rather than conclusiveness and, more generally, underline the *process* of consciousness rather than its potential epiphanic resolutions. In "Invitation to Previously Uninvited Guests," the different images and events Benedikt associates with "a boxful of rare cigars" tend to play a tense cat-and-mouse game with the reader's expectations. In this respect, one of the shortest poems of *Mole Notes*, "The Politics of Metaphor," stands as a manifesto for the complex intertwining of arguments, digressions, and associations that have been the hallmarks of Benedikt's prose poems for more than twenty years:

> For a full-grown mole, the future has never begun to exist apart as a form of thought; and thought has never begun to exist except as a form of metaphor. Even for a mole in his final circle of tunnels, there is always one more larger, more generous set of relevances into which all previous relevances fit. (*Mole* 79)

The uninterrupted, paratactic flow of Benedikt's paragraphs, which, as he himself reminds us, are already liberated from the "formalistic interruptions of the line break" (*Prose Poem* 48), by the same occasion undermines the claims to transcendence of so-called poetic language, which is here exposed as just another "form of thought." Similarly, Benedikt's poems also bring poetry back to ordinary experience, a deflated diction (the second point of his definition), and a casual digressiveness that renders the laboriousness but also, in the best cases, the sparkling complexity and richness of the speaker's attempts at self-expression.

Benedikt has attributed the discursive and expository quality of his interior monologues to "a great severance of cause and effect, a gap between pretensions and realities, in this world, and through the use of logic to undermine logic" ("Meat" 20). This turning of logic against itself is precisely the reason Benedikt's absurdist prose poems "work." As the random, wayward quality of his speculations is recounted with reference to a conventional narrative or discursive structure, the general formality of tone and the apparently seamless, blocklike coherence of the paragraph provide the reader with a sense of normality against which the poem attempts to rebel. In other words, the subversion here is achieved from within the very structures of conventional logic and rationality and in the very terms of the rhetoric Benedikt is trying to subvert. The intricate sinuosities and the seemingly uncontrollable outbursts of Benedikt's dramatic monologues keep pulling forward the narrative of consciousness into yet more associational correspondences or "relevances"—a feature which makes Benedikt the most Sternian prose poet of his generation. By doing so, Benedikt's prose poems also bring forth, so to speak, the metaphorical value of logical language. They suggest that speculative thought can easily slip into, or even lend itself to, absurd or insane extremes tangled in their own claims to rationality:

> Am I really supposed to stay here with the rest of these people making the usual surreptitious motions, tentative gestures, and shifting around guiltily from foot to foot? Because I can feel that there is obviously not going to be enough room to move in this room. To scratch the top of my head I have to go slipping my arm around the side of my head in a guilty way, as if it were a journey by Rolls-Royce around a bend in a mountain road in the poverty region, all the while praying that nobody accuses the hollow of my armpit of causing competition with a shut-down coal mine. Just so, I am amply assured that whenever I reach up to scratch my nose, a boxcar falls over in Alabama, as does a beer can in the Alhambra. And should I lower my eyelashes to express the requisite embarrassment, a bird's nest falls out of the tree in a field beside the farm. According to these definitions, I'll have to black out both my eyes in order to be able to say I see! And if I decide to deeply inhale, the tender finger of the saintly child beside me here, the one giving me the long lecture on delicacy, holding me by the lapel with one hand, and poking me in the chest with the other, becomes blunted. Also, inhaling risks bursting the stained glass windows in this beautiful room they have locked us all in. The poetry Library would fall! The orphanage be eaten up by an ogre! And to think, I originally came here to this place because I heard it was the ideal place to go if you wanted to open a career in modern dance. ("The Melancholy Moralist" [*Night* 44])

As the reader follows the persona's guilty conjectures on the possible tragic (and "logical") consequences of his most innocuous movements, humor arises from the inadequateness of rational, argumentative rhetoric when it tries to come to terms with the free-associational complexities of the human mind. Russell Edson's definition of his own prose poems as "a statement that seeks sanity whilst its author teeters on the edge of the abyss" ("Portrait" 300) is even more adapted to Benedikt's work, which often reads like a kind of rhetoric tightrope-walking exercise. Even though the specific kind of prose poem referred to here is, as we have seen, only one of the major trends of the contemporary American prose poem, Edson's definition is still valid when applied to the recent proliferation of "absurdist," neo-Surrealist prose poems in the Max Jacob tradition. Another, mediating, influence occurring between Jacob and Benedikt is that of Jorge Luis Borges and Julio Cortázar, whose prose poems favor the same kind of semiabsurdist disruptions *within* the realm of logic and rational thought. This duplicitous game between insanity and sanity, the wildness of the unconscious precariously held together by a rigorously factual rhetoric constantly on the verge of tipping over into madness, is still the most pervasive feature of many prose poems written by veterans Edson, Benedikt, and Fixel and by a whole generation of younger writers. Characteristically, also, the only "poetic" moment of "The Melancholy Moralist"—the appearance of "the tender finger of the saintly child"—is deflated (one could almost say debunked) by an overall off-handedness of diction and drowned in a turmoil of discursive arabesques.

Here, Benedikt's Surrealism seems, once again, more indebted to Jacob and Michaux than to Breton's écriture automatique. The associational "jumps" happen not so much at a metaphorical level as at the level of language itself (puns, euphemisms, literalizations, alliterations, repetitions abound in Benedikt's poems) and can result in a highly self-conscious and consummate art, radically opposed to Breton's conception of poetic language as the spontaneous, unmediated disclosure of the movements of consciousness. As suggested, the self-conscious meticulousness that characterizes the Surrealist rhetoric of Edson's and Benedikt's poems casts doubt on Benedikt's interpretation of such prose poems as closer to the movements of the unconscious than are most poems written in verse. Poems of this kind were more aptly characterized by Edson as combining "the all too real" with "the artificial sense of art aware of itself."

Prose pure *and the Poem in Search of a Content*

The self-conscious, fabulist craftsmanship characterizing the prose poems of Russell Edson, Lawrence Fixel, and Michael Benedikt is, as we have seen, deeply related to their desire to redefine the notion of poetic language. Moving away from all accepted definitions of poetry, whether of the stylistic (i.e., ornamental) or modal (i.e., lyric/self-expressive) variety, their work brings forth another functional, rather than essential, difference between prose and poetry. As we have seen, since its concern with narrative and its everyday matter-of-factness of tone often makes it appear to be deprived of all accepted attributes of poeticalness, the "poetic" content of the neo-Surrealist prose poem therefore can be seen as resulting almost exclusively from its exploration of the movements of consciousness for their own sake. The foregrounding of discourse and writing-as-process advocated by the fabulists is linked with their understanding of poetic language as a particular (unorthodox) use of language or even a form of thought. As for the content of Benedikt's poems, it often recedes to the background as the poem becomes, so to speak, enthralled in the circumvolutions of its own discourse.

The prose poem's overall preference for its own medium, rather than its subject matter, has been underlined by John Gerlach, probably the only critic who has so far shown an interest in the relationship between the short story and the prose poem. Gerlach identifies the tendency to foreground its own discursive medium as being one of the major recurrent features distinguishing W. S. Merwin's narrative prose poem "The Dachau Shoe" (a typical "borderline" case) from other so-called nonpoetic genres. Even though he still tends to invoke the lack of thematic or metonymic magnitude (the prose poem, unlike other narratives, does not encourage us to "extend our imagination along the lines of characters and conflict, space and time") and the metaphorical value of one, single "central" object as the last unequivocal criterion of poeticalness, Gerlach also insists on the constant foregrounding of "the discourse itself" in the prose poem and its "calling attention to the signifier, a trait we associate with poetry" (82). In underlining this focus on discourse as opposed to content, and on the narrative as opposed to the narrated, Gerlach is indebted to Stephen Fredman's groundbreaking characterization of the prose poem as evidencing "a fascination with language (through puns, rhyme, repetition, elision, disjunction, excessive troping, and subtle foregrounding of diction) that interferes with the progression of story or idea, while at the same time inviting and examining the 'prose' realms of fact and reclaiming for poetry the domain of truth" (80). Besides emphasizing the double (and bilateral) contamination of poetry by prose and of prose by poetry, which characterizes the whole history of the contemporary prose poem, Fredman's argument suggests that sometimes the focus in prose poems is on the very hermeneutic process leading to the epiphanic moment we associate with the lyric and, therefore, on the "telling of the tale" rather than the tale itself.

This is, in many ways, reminiscent of Paul Valéry's famous likening of prose to walking, on the one hand, and poetry to dancing, on the other. According to Valéry, prose is "an act directed toward some object which we aim to reach," while poetry is "a system of acts which are, at the same time, ends in themselves" (140).[14] While Valéry acknowleges that poetry "uses the same words, forms and tones as prose"—thereby doing away with traditional structural definitions—prosaic language is clearly understood as representational and utilitarian, while poetry is confined to the realm of the signifier, in which language has nothing in view but itself. In fact, what many of Benedikt's poems are trying to tell us is that if experience is a prerequisite for discourse, then discourse can also be the very stuff experience is made of. In some extreme examples, the meanders of the sentence indeed become the meanders of the "plot." As Donald Wesling reminds us, the prose poem has long been a preferred form for the "narrative of grammar," in which the movements of consciousness and sensibility take the place of epic progression, so that action becomes "a cognitive and linguistic sequence, where the events are thoughts, words." This "tendency" characterizes the whole history of the contemporary prose poem from Baudelaire's "flexible prose" to the New Sentence of the Language poets. Echoing Mallarmé's definition of the "critical poem" as one that reproduces "the immediate thought rhythms which organize a prosody," Wesling's narrative of grammar (or "narrative of consciousness") is one in which "every sentence of the poem is a narrative, insofar as it puts into an order the reader's acts of attention and habits of response to language; and the sequence of sentences make up another, larger narrative" (176):

(1) Here I am, lying back here in bed again, making up things to try, at least temporarily, to escape our sad situation. Will I ever get out of here? Then suddenly I find myself out in the next room while you sleep, making tea for myself with no memory of having left bed. How did I get out here, anyway? By "here" what I mean is "here," sitting at the typewriter with a glass of steaming tea in one hand, typing out this poem with the other. (2) How come I can move around this way, with no memory of having ever left bed? And what is this half-composed poem doing under this typewriter roller anyway? (3) It must be that for the first time this morning, for a change, instead of events containing ideas, ideas seem to be containing events. For the first time this morning, thought seems to have become portable! (4) And now that we have arrived in this new conceptual locale, the first thing we have to do of course, is fix it up here and there. But we refuse to hire

an interior decorator—and certainly we don't need an electrician to install the stereo: we can do it all by ourselves this same way, simply by thinking. (5) Finally, some day: our first full-course dinner prepared in our very own new home! But how long will it be before we can invite to the housewarming party our very dearest friends and all those whom we have ever really loved? ("Portable Thoughts" [*Mole* 35])

Benedikt's poem contains the characteristic element of "fabulation," creating a sense of the poem being written in front of the reader's eyes. Its title, "Portable Thoughts," also underlines the status of such prose poems as quasidomestic conveniences meant to be produced and consumed as instant tales or vignettes designed to elicit a quick or immediate emotional or intellectual response. The suggestion that "ideas seem to be containing events" literalizes Benedikt's poetics of fabulation by emphasizing the fact that the narrative of consciousness and its many digressive and associational interferences create rather than merely reflect their objects or "referents," like the need to "fix it up here and there" or the potential housewarming party. As consciousness prevails over its own content, the telling becomes the tale itself. Likewise, the rhetoric of Benedikt's miniature streams of consciousness, just like that of Edson's fables, tends to cannibalize its own metastatic excesses. "Travel Notes" is another, more extreme example of such an absolute prevalence of discourse over content:

(1) Take me away from all this, take me away from all this! Away from what? I don't see a thing around here, anymore, myself. No? Please look around harder, then; I'd love to know where whatever it is that was, went. After all, there must be something around here to get away from. And when you find it, please, hurry up and take me away from it. Unless, of course, there is something that it would be even more attractive to completely abandon. (2) In view of this, it seems logical to say that since it is impossible to arrive everywhere at once, we may have to accept being satisfied with being located here and there, occasionally. (*Mole* 119)

In a way reminiscent of Edson's "The Matter," "Travel Notes" hardly exists by virtue of anything other than the very self-monologue that brings it into being and only refers to an absent or undefined context. Characteristically, the habitual sense of hysteria and paranoia prevailing in the first part of the poem is neutralized by a return to the reassuring sobriety of logical thought. As the persona of Benedikt's poem becomes tormented by the absence of directions in a nonexisting landscape, the only points of reference available to him occur through language. As always, however, the focus is on the semiautarchic cognitive and experiential strategies that bring about the poem, rather than on their referential orientation. By this focus, Benedikt once more invalidates all traditional distinctions between prosaic and poetic writing and signals the advent of *prose pure.*

The Gender of Genre: Margaret Atwood's Unnamable Prose

Many prose poets, unknown or well-known, have worked in the fabulist trend for the last twenty or thirty years. A full-length study of the neo-Surrealist prose poem in English in the Jacobean or the Kafkaesque vein would have to consider the work of a number of its "minor" or occasional representatives, including Duane Ackerson, Jack Anderson, David Benedetti, Elizabeth Bishop, Greg Boyd, Steven Ford Brown, Kirby Congdon, Philip Dacey, Lydia Davis, Stuart Dybek, Dave Etter, Gary Fincke, Siv Cedering Fox, Dick Gallup, Elton Glaser, Philip Graham, Donald Hall, Marie Harris, Michael Hogan, Paul Hoover, Brooke Horvath, Louis Jenkins, Peter Johnson, Nancy Lagomarsino, Hank Lazer, Gian Lombardo, Morton Marcus, Bin Ramke, Vern Rutsala, Ira Sadoff, James Schuyler, James Tate, Charles Webb, Tom Whalen, Peter Wortsman, David Young, and Gary Young, as well as British poets Cecil Helman and Christopher Middleton and Canadian poet Robert Priest. Among the younger generation of American fabulists, the name of Maxine Chernoff stands out. Such early masterpieces as "Stand-Up Tragedians," "A Vegetable Emergency," and "The Moat" (contained in her first collection of prose poems, *A Vegetable Emergency,* published as early as 1976) seem indebted to the verbal and imagistic extravagance of Henri Michaux, Jorge Luis Borges, and Julio Cortázar, with whom she also shares a tendency to perform multiple transactions between the metaphorical and the literal. "Prose poems," Chernoff writes, "may be a contemporary equivalent of metaphysical poetry, since in both cases metaphor can expand to become the central concept (conceit) of the writing" (Lehman 27). Chernoff's view of the genre as originating in a central "expanding" metaphor recalls Benedikt's own "Politics of Metaphor," which posits that any thought process is necessarily metaphorical in that it always gives rise to "one more larger, more generous set of relevances into which all previous relevances fit" (*Mole* 79). But the basic principle that structures a prose poem such as "The Fan" is less metaphorical than antinarrative:

I enter a room where a fan seems to be chanting "Air! Air! Air!" as it
whirs. I see it's not the fan, after all, but a child facing the wall in the
far corner of the room.

At the opposite end of the room, a man is seated, stroking his beard.
He keeps repeating, "Yes, quite excellent. Air wafers. Air wafers."

I turn off the fan and the child and the man stop instantly, as if
slapped in the face. (*Utopia* 16)

Describing the method of composition of "The Fan," Chernoff writes: "I
am not commenting about the nature of one's character's reaction to experience. Rather, I am suggesting that a linguistic event has been observed by
a witness. This witnessing verifies that something has been made of language. . . . Thus, 'character' in many of my prose poems exists so that
language can occur. . . . The linguistic event 'happens' in the sense that
anything happens" ("Fence" 88). Other poems featuring in Chernoff's
early collections, such as "The Shoe and the City" ("A woman answers the
phone every day saying 'Kill me' to the paperboy" [*Leap* 22]), "On My
Birthday" (which begins with "words lin[ing] up like racehorses at a starting gate" [*Utopia* 35]), or "His Pastime" (which tells the story of a man
who manages to hold his breath for days and whose sudden exhalation
nearly blows away the newspaper reporter who was supposed to cover the
story) are clearly in accordance with the author's notion of a leading "linguistic moment" giving birth to a chain of telescoping associational leaps.
In recent years, however, Chernoff's prose poems, while remaining as fan-
ciful and exuberant as her earlier works, have tended to preserve a connection with the intimacy of personal experience. A poem such as "Lost and
Found" oscillates between the trivial and the serious in a way that somehow privileges the lyrical strain of her prose:

I am looking for the photo that would make all the difference in my
life. It's very small and subject to fits of amnesia, turning up in poker
hands, grocery carts, under the unturned stone. The photo shows me
at the lost and found looking for an earlier photo, the one that would
have made all the difference then. My past evades me like a politician.
Wielding a fly-swatter, it destroys my collection of cereal boxes, my
childhood lived close to the breakfast table. Only that photo can help
me locate my fourteen lost children, who look just like me. When I

call the Bureau of Missing Persons, they say, "Try the Bureau of Missing Photos." They have a fine collection. Here's my Uncle Arthur the night he bought a peacock. O photo! End your tour of the world in a hot air balloon. Resign your job at the mirror-testing laboratory. Come home to me, you little fool, before I find I can live without you. ("Lost and Found" [*Leap* 51])

Unlike the relatively anonymous, rhetorical "I" of Benedikt's prose poems, the "I" of Chernoff's prose poem does not merely exist as a mouthpiece for discursive fantasies and is not utterly deprived of emotional features. While many of Chernoff's recent poems bear close affinities to the journal entry, even the most "fabulist" and self-reflexive ones still manage to make room for a subjective space in which the I-persona remains "credible" in its own right. This concern with the survival of lyricism *within* the parodic is also central to Margaret Atwood's *Good Bones,* a collection of short shorts gathering some of the most interesting generic borderline cases in recent North-American literature. Like its 1984 precedent, *Murder in the Dark*—Atwood's first book of "Short Fictions and Prose Poems"— *Good Bones* contains playfully perverted or inverted revisions of familiar genres, modes, and subject matters, ranging from fairy tales and adventure stories to autobiography, theology, science fiction, popular romance, *Dracula, Hamlet* or, more simply, the everyday life politics of the average middle-class North American housewife. Despite an enormous diversity of tone and subject matter, all of Atwood's stories share a strong concern with the various socio-ideological assumptions underlying both literary and nonliterary narratives. In "The Little Hen Tells All," for instance, a well-known children's story is struggling its way out of bourgeois capitalistic ideology ("You know my story. Probably you had it told to you as a shining example of how you yourself ought to behave. Sobriety and elbow-grease. Do it yourself. Then invest your capital. Then collect. I'm supposed to be an illustration of *that?* Don't make me laugh" [*Good* 11]). While "My Life as a Bat" attempts to rehabilitate the bat race and deliver it from an evil which is "hair-headed and walks in the night with a single white unseeing eye, and stinks of half-digested meat, and has two legs," "Making a Man" parodies the demagogic how-to rhetoric of popular magazines from the point of view of domestic gender issues. Another, perhaps even more representative piece is Atwood's mock-sermonic catalogue of representations of the "Eternal Stupid Woman," where modern icons and stereotypes ("the airheads, the bubblebrains, the ditzy blondes: the headstrong teenagers too dumb to listen to their mothers: all those with mattress stuffing between the ears, all the lush hostesses who tell us to have a good day, and give us the wrong change, while checking their Big Hair in the mirror, all those who dry their freshly-shampooed poodles in the microwave, and those whose boyfriends tell them chlorophyll chewing gum is a contraceptive, and who believe it" [31]) are traced back to biblical or mythological ancestors: "How we enjoy hearing about her: as she listens to the con-artist yarns of the plausible snake, and ends up eating the free sample of the apple from the Tree of Knowledge: thus giving birth to Theology; or as she opens the tricky gift box containing all human evils, but is stupid enough to believe that Hope will be some kind of a solace" (34).

Murder and *Good Bones* contain many other examples of such playfully "debunked" stories. But if many of Atwood's "short fictions" privilege the parodic mode, their subversive potential is certainly not limited to that alone for, in addition to lampooning some of their author's favorite targets, they also seek to explore the specific power-related interests underlying the construction and perpetuation of dominant narratives. As one of the personae of *Good Bones* reflects, thinking of her own previous life as a bat and complaining about the bad reputation inflicted upon the bat race by cheap vampire movies, "previous lives have entered the world of commerce." "In the previous-life market," however, she continues, "there is not such a great demand for Peruvian ditch-diggers as there is for Cleopatra; or for Indian latrine-cleaners, or for 1952 housewives living in California split-levels" (98). Genres and narratives, in other words, are not immune to the law of supply and demand ("Disaster sells beer" [119]). While some of them are silenced or repressed by the Establishment, others are turned into glamorous, best-selling commodities progressively creating "a general consensus about the content of reality" (97) that inevitably works to the detriment of the oppressed or silenced individual. This also accounts for Atwood's predilection not only for ancient myth and modern classics ("Four Small Paragraphs" is an irreverent meditation on the life and works of Albert Camus) but also for other popular genres and narratives—including children's literature, fantasy fiction, women's magazines, instruction books, or even dumb blonde jokes—having a massive ideological impact on large audiences.

The recent renewal of interest in genre studies as a tool for a critical investigation of the conventions of popular fiction, as well as their interaction with prevailing sociocultural codes and practices, offers an interesting counterpoint to Atwood's impertinent exercises in sexual and textual politics. Moving beyond traditional taxonomic investigations of inherent features of "genericness," recent studies have focused on how, for instance, women's popular romances, science fiction, and western or detective fiction subvert or support not only the literary canon but also the socio-political Establishment.[15] The short prose pieces of *Murder* and *Good Bones* are Atwood's own creative contribution to such a critique of dominant narratives pervading popular genres. Characteristically, Atwood's narrative revisionism—for all its apparent formal and thematic heterogeneousness—often goes hand in hand with a more specifically feminist concern with the different textual and, ultimately, existential constraints under which the female self is compelled to live. Indeed Atwood's interest in popular culture is linked with a recurrent theme in her oeuvre, from the early inner landscapes of *Double Persephone* to the dystopian investigations of the *Handmaid's Tale:* the propagation and interiorization of a prescriptive notion of "womanhood" and the confinement of the female self to socially accepted roles of self-effacement and submission. As one of her personae observes, for instance, in "Women's Novels":

> Men's novels are about men. Women's novels are about men too but from a different point of view. You can have a men's novel with no women in it except possibly the landlady or the horse, but you can't have a women's novel with no men in it. Sometimes men put women in men's novels but they leave out some of the parts: the heads, for instance, or the hands. Women's novels leave out parts of the men as well. Sometimes it's the stretch between the belly button and the knees, sometimes it's the sense of humour. It's hard to have a sense of humour in a cloak, in a high wind, on a moor. (*Murder* 34)

Atwood's interest in popular romance is all the more revealing since the kind of narrative she attempts to deconstruct and ridicule is precisely a genre both written and consumed by women—although, she reminds us, "women do not usually write novels of the type favoured by men but men are known to write novels of the type favoured by women" (34). In this sense, her antididactic parables do not limit themselves to undermining the latent oppressiveness of popular iconography; they also expose the complicity of women in the propagation of stereotypes signifying their own (self-)confinement to supporting parts and, thereby, suggest how the various patriarchal narratives permeating everyday life and language must first and foremost win their readership's consent. In order to do so, they often set out to question the taken-for-granted transparency of such popular narratives by subverting them, so to speak, "from within." As the speaker in

"Let Us Now Praise Stupid Women" remarks, "such women are fictions: composed by others, but just as frequently by themselves" (*Good* 32):

I like to read novels in which the heroine has a costume rustling discreetly over her breasts, or discreet breasts rustling under her costume; in any case there must be a costume, some breasts, some rustling, and, over all, discretion. Discretion over all, like a fog, a miasma through which the outlines of things appear only vaguely. A glimpse of pink through the gloom, the sound of breathing, satin slithering to the floor, revealing what? Never mind, I say. Never never mind. . . . I want happiness, guaranteed, joy all around, covers with nurses on them or brides, intelligent girls but not too intelligent, with regular teeth and pluck and both breasts the same size and no excess facial hair, someone you can depend on to know where the bandages are and to turn the hero, that potential rake and killer, into a well-groomed country gentleman with clean fingernails and the right vocabulary. *Always,* he has to say. *Forever.* I no longer want to read books that don't end with the word *forever.* I want to be stroked between the eyes, one way only. (*Murder* 34–35)

"Women's Novels" is typical of the whole collection in that it sets out to diagnose, and subsequently deconstruct, the different fictions in which Atwood's personae are trapped, achieving this by exploring the various emotional needs inflicted by popular narratives upon both the private and the collective self. (Hence Atwood's interest in all kinds of culturally inherited models of thought and behavior.) In doing so, her short fictions emphasize the strategic equivalence of collective and personal victimization, macrocosm and microcosm, and remind us that "the positions are the same whether you are a victimized country, a minority group or a victimized individual" (*Survival* 36).[16]

The conversational, semididactic (and quasi-admonishing) tone of "Women's Novels" is unquestionably a prevailing modal feature in *Murder in the Dark* and *Good Bones.* More generally, however, Atwood's short shorts are often characterized by a mixture of lyricism and matter-of-factness, of imagistic presence and narrative continuity. The recurrence of "poetic" or imagistic disruptions in the overwhelmingly factual tone of both collections underlines another aspect of the double-edgedness of Atwood's vignettes of everyday life conflicts. By combining the homely with the uncanny, the serious with the trivial, and the factual with the metaphorical, Atwood's short pieces, like her opening description of a pet-rified gorgon, constantly remind us that ordinary life and people are the stuff myths are made of:

> The red geraniums fluorescing on the terrace, the wind swaying the daisies, the baby's milk-fed eyes focusing for the first time on a double row of beloved teeth—what is there to report? Bloodlessness puts her to sleep. She perches on a rooftop, her brass wings folded, her head with its coiffure of literate serpents tucked beneath the left one, snoozing like a noon pigeon. There's nothing to do but her toenails. The sun oozes across the sky, the breezes undulate over her skin like warm stockings, her heart beats with systole and diastole of waves on the breakwater, boredom creeps over her like vines. ("Bad News" [*Good* 9])

Such moments of metaphorical verticality emerge as so many potentially epiphanic interruptions in the one-dimensional lives of Atwood's prosaic personae. In this respect, also, traditional distinctions between "fictional" and "lyrical" works are constantly subverted and deconstructed by virtue of the collection's hybrid modalities, as is already suggested by Atwood's harpylike collage featured on the cover of the 1993 Virago paperback edi-tion of *Good Bones*. This is not to say that Atwood's use of the prose poem form comes down merely to a mixing up of "poetic" and "prosaic" mate-rials. Even though many of the pieces contained in *Murder* and *Good Bones* indeed tend to juxtapose antipodal modes and subject matters (for instance, the beautiful and the unsavory, or the alternate use of a conversa-tional and a solemnly metaphorical style), Atwood's poetics of hybridity is certainly not confined to the formal ambiguity that has largely character-ized the history of both the contemporary prose poem and the so-called lyric short story. It also echoes the sense of an essential opposition between the male and the female brain, a sense pervading Atwood's fiction and poetry. Typically, the male brain stands for uncompromising, all-categoriz-ing rationality ("Space over here, time over there, music and arithmetic in their own sealed compartments. The right brain doesn't know what the left brain is doing" [*Good* 45]), a principle whose self-congratulatory logic inevitably makes it an agent of domestic and public violence in the name of practical efficiency ("Good for aiming though, for hitting the target when you pull the trigger. What's the target? Who's the target? Who cares? What matters is hitting it. That's the male brain for you. Objective" [45]). The female brain, by contrast, is presented as an alternative to such a loboto-mizing conversion of time, space, and emotions into conveniently measurable categories. Its shape-shifting, all-embracing nature radically differs from the essentially functional and power-related dynamics of "male" language. While men constantly seek to make reality fit their mathematical equations ("something safely abstract, detached from you; a transfer of the obsession with size to anything at all" [78]), women dream of a protean, undefined space often establishing their kinship with untamed organic matter:

> They dream of plunging their hands into the heart, which is red as blood and soft, which is milky and warm. They dream that the earth gathers itself under their hands, swells, changes its form, flowers into a thousand shapes, for them too, for them once more. They dream of apples; they dream of the creation of the world; they dream of freedom. (*Murder* 33)

Such unexpected eruptions of "lyrical" irrationality and elemental unnamableness (both features have so far been largely characterized by feminist theory as "female" categories silenced and excluded by patriarchal thought) clearly echo Atwood's much-discussed suggestion of the potential of the female mind for resisting the Adamico-humanist urge to "name," measure, and enclose the things around him.[17] Nevertheless, the male brain's quasi-performative use of language as a tool for domination and victimization ("*Death,* they say, making the word sound like the backwash of a wave" [*Good* 87]) remains the thematic keynote of most of Atwood's vignettes. Despite occasional, and mostly unspoken, moments of insight in which Atwood's female personae manage to "[forget] what things [are] called and [see] instead what they are" (*Murder* 55), men indeed "[have] the word" (*Murder* 52). Their minds and bodies are verbalized ("*Hurt,* they say, and suddenly their bodies hurt again, like real bodies" [*Good* 86]) and women can only attempt to "re-say them in [the men's] own words" (87), while witnessing the transformation of their own bodies into domestic conveniences and marketable commodities ("The Female Body").

The purpose of this discussion is not to determine whether Atwood's binary view of gender relationships should be considered as a strength or a limitation in her achievement as a poet and a fiction writer. The extent to which her short shorts do or do not suggest a middle or a third way is examined later. Suffice it to say at this stage that the "naming" motif in *Murder* and *Good Bones* is as much an essential feature of domestic body-politics as a crucial element of larger socio-ideological apparatuses. As we have seen, Atwood is indeed primarily concerned with the naming of the self into a textual construct; a process carried out with the help of various dominant icons and narratives turning man into an agent of violence and woman into a passive and unverbalized being. In order to isolate the different sociolinguistic elements contributing to this process, Atwood succeeds in depicting the psychological and concrete surroundings of her personae with an anthropologist's eye for culturally meaningful details. "In Love with Raymond Chandler" stands as a manifesto of the specificity of focus underlying Atwood's attempts to defamiliarize contemporary reality into a democracy of emotionally and ideologically charged objects:

> An affair with Raymond Chandler, what a joy! Not because of the mangled bodies and the marinated cops and hints of eccentric sex, but because of his interest in furniture. He knew that furniture could breathe, could feel, not as we do but in a way more muffled, like the word *upholstery,* with its overtones of mustiness and dust, its bouquet of sunlight on ageing cloth or of scuffed leather on the backs and seats of sleazy office chairs. I think of his sofas, stuffed to roundness, satin-covered, pale-blue like the eyes of his cold blonde unbodied murderous women, beating very slowly, like the hearts of hibernating crocodiles; of his chaises longues, with their malicious pillows. He knew about front lawns too, and greenhouses, and the interior of cars. (*Good* 47)

From the influence of cheap magazines on domestic politics ("Simmering") to the imperialist biases of early twentieth-century adventure novels ("The Boy's Own Annual, 1911") or the misleadingly reassuring efficiency and glamorous sex appeal of the Canadian lumberjack ("Someone who can run a chainsaw without cutting off his leg. . . . Power, quiet and sane. Knowing what to do, doing it well. Sexy." [53]), Atwood's iconographical and narratological games seek to demonstrate how specific patterns of power relations are always already engraved on the most seemingly trivial and innocuous aspects of our everyday lives.[18] Her concern with the painful discrepancy between the textual and the existential self indirectly brings us back to the issue of whether her hybrid vignettes should be read as prose poems or as short short stories. If one chooses the latter option, one is inevitably confronted with a series of texts constantly drawing attention to their double function as both indispensable tools for individuation and ideologically charged and potentially oppressive models interiorized since one's earliest youth. By contrast, reading Atwood's short shorts as poems (by privileging, for instance, the strong lyrical strain that characterizes many pieces contained in *Murder in the Dark* and *Good Bones*) adds another ironical twist to her subversive use of literary genres. By focusing on the various unacknowledged politics behind our strategies of (self-)representation and the cultural formation of subjectivity, Atwood undermines a number of basic assumptions underlying the very nature of lyric poetry, a genre which has often relied on a claim to unmediated naturalness and a desire to convey the poet's (or the persona's) "true" and "authentic" voice. In this perspective, also, her use of the prose poem form—which often appears as a rather disturbing compromise between the impersonal didacticism of the parable and the intimacy of the lyric mode—is one that seeks to expose the "worldliness" of the lyric I and to show the various ways in which Atwood's personae, far from being autonomous and self-present beings, appear to be spoken into existence by their socioeconomic environment.

Despite such deterministic premises, Atwood's miniatures nevertheless generally succeed in questioning the validity of *all* narratives, including those which themselves allegedly seek to counteract patterns of oppression and victimization. As is often the case elsewhere in Atwood's poetry and fiction, these are, so to speak, put to the test of their own claims to practical subversiveness. While *The Handmaid's Tale,* for instance, appears in many ways as a cautionary tale against all forms of political extremism (whether of the right-wing fundamentalist or left-wing feminist variety), "There Was Once" is a caustic satire of one of the most fashionable political narratives currently prevailing on North American campuses: Political Correctness. As the female critic's repeated onslaughts on the male writer's "intimidating physical role models" (*Good* 21) demonstrate, even the most progressive discourses (here P.C.'s feminist, left-wing, and antiracist subtexts) can end up setting new prescriptive reference models and are therefore likely to be turned into just another form of unofficial censorship. Atwood treads on dangerous ground in trying to reveal the Procrustean impulses lurking beneath alternative ideologies. For "There Was Once" suggests that "male" urges to categorize, silence, or victimize are not only present in the male brain but also potentially there in the mind of anybody in a position to use a particular discourse as an assertion of power. It also underlines the necessity to transcend the antagonistic premises underlying certain progressive discourses, some of which are occasionally used by Atwood herself as so many consciousness-raising gimmicks. (Pieces such as "Liking Men" or "Alien Territory" clearly put the blame on men rather than on an abstract or cultural notion of "manhood.") This is, in any case, what Atwood has in mind when, while commenting on victims acknowledging the fact that they are victims but refusing "to accept the assumption that the role is inevitable" [*Survival* 37]), she warns readers of the danger of becoming "locked into [their] anger" and failing to "change [their] position" (38).

The next question arising from Atwood's distrust of progressive discourses is that of where the prospect of a real, "positive" resistance to the hegemonic power of "prose" can possibly lie. A number of possible answers are suggested in the examples discussed here, two of which seem to stand out in Atwood's oeuvre as a whole. As we have seen, the first step consists in a rigorous inquiry into *specific* causes of oppression, inviting the reader to diagnose "basic victim positions" (*Survival* 36). As for the exact nature of the relationship between text and reader, the title story of *Murder in the Dark* contains its own directions for use: "If you like, you can play games with this game. You can say: the murderer is the writer, the detective is the reader, the victim is the book" (*Murder* 30). The second, and arguably more positive, alternative to the reification of subversive discourses is perhaps to be found in the uncompromising playfulness and, above all, the essentially parodic mode characterizing Atwood's genre and gender politics. Atwood's narratological and iconographical language games, most of which are founded on a perverted and/or inverted retelling of "canonical" narratives, are at work both within and against the various discourses and assumptions they are trying to question and subvert. By defamiliarizing the familiar and confronting the full political force of the seemingly transparent realities of our everyday lives, her short fictions also succeed in rewriting our perception of gender categories into positional and power-related (as opposed to merely antagonistic) terms, thereby moderating the author's own penchant for binary and, ultimately, essentialist thought models. One is reminded here of Linda Hutcheon's defense of postmodernist parody as a positive deconstructive praxis on the grounds of its capacity to "de-doxify" "politically uninnocent things" *despite* its "complicity with power and domination," a process which "acknowledges that it cannot escape implication in that which it nevertheless still wants to analyze and maybe even undermine" (Hutcheon 4). Still, Hutcheon reminds us, "to 'de-doxify' is not to act." The somewhat bitter pessimism underlying the deconstructive impulses of Atwood's vignettes indeed confirms Hutcheon's observation that the "theory of agency" demanded by feminist agendas is "visibly lacking in postmodernism, caught as it is in a certain negativity that may be inherent in any critique of cultural dominants" (22). Likewise, Atwood's prose poems seek not so much to put forward solutions to the various "key patterns" they set out to denounce as to diagnose the various ways in which her personae *fail* to become aware of their real causes of oppression. Even their rare moments of insight ultimately signify a sudden loss of reassuring—albeit oppressive—certainties to live by ("thoughts [coming] with breakfast, like the juice of murdered fruits" [*Good* 142]), rather than the prospect of using their new awareness for the purpose of emancipation and constructive action on a social level. Atwood's apparent lack of belief in the oppressed individual's capacity for agency within a given sociocultural dominant is largely the result of her distrust of the power of language to question its own ideologically laden premises ("How do you wash a language? There's the beginning of a bad smell, you can hear the growls, something's being eaten, once too often. Your mouth feels rotted" [*Murder* 49]).[19] Torn between such a repudiation of language as a means of achieving social change and a belief in the advent of "a new order, a new birth, possibly holy" in which "the animals will be named again" (*Good* 92), the pieces of *Murder in the Dark* and *Good Bones* plead for the visionary powers of a "Third Eye," a new plural, protean, and essentially nameless logic that could nevertheless lead to "the word, the one that will finally be right. A compound, the generation of life, mud and light" (*Murder* 49).

4 · Deep Images and Things
The Prose Poems of Robert Bly

Robert Bly's now anthologized status as a "political" poet during the Vietnam war, his often uncompromising and sometimes virulent essays on contemporary American poetry and poetics, and more recently his interest in male and female consciousness and men's initiation rites have iconized him into an unusually popular but also most controversial figure. Even though critics have not always been unanimous in their appraisal of Bly's creative and critical works, his pervasive influence as a poet, editor, anthologizer, translator, social and political commentator, and literary essayist cannot be ignored.[1] Since his 1962 official debut as a writer of prose poems, Robert Bly has become one of America's most widely acclaimed prose poets and has established himself as a major practitioner of an increasingly popular genre in American poetry.[2] Bly's critical essays, political stances, and philosophical ideas are all the more inextricably linked with the evolution of his poetic work since he has been an assiduous critic of his own poetry for the last thirty years. His use of the prose poem form, in particular, is characterized by a strong sense of self-conscious craftsmanship, which has led him to develop his own conception and definition(s) of the genre. In an essay titled "The Prose Poem as an Evolving Form," for instance, Bly distinguishes between three main tendencies of the modern prose poem:

> We know several sorts of prose poems, the most ancient of which is the fable; David Ignatow and Russell Edson are contemporary masters of the fable. Traditionally in the fable, the story is more important than the language that carries it. Rimbaud, in *Les Illuminations,* invented a second sort of prose poem, inspired by the new color separations, known as "illuminations," in the printing industry; there, image and fiery language draw attention away from the story. A third sort, the object poem, centers itself not on story or image but on the

object, and it holds to its fur, so to speak. My predecessors in the object poem are Jiménez and Francis Ponge. (*Selected* 199)

In a general way, Bly's classification reflects at least two major impulses of the prose poem on the American scene today: a narrative trend, on the one hand, and a prolongation of the tradition of the object poem, on the other. The former is represented by Russell Edson's humorous fables, W. S. Merwin's short Surrealist tales, and countless other poets in prose, the latter by Bly himself. Whether the second "sort" of prose poem, centered on "image and fiery language," should be considered in itself as a subgeneric trend or, rather, as a formal and modal category present to a certain extent in *any* prose poem is arguable. In any case, the flamboyant vignettes and the prose-poetic exaltation of Rimbaud's *Les Illuminations* and *Une Saison en enfer,* while seminal in the development of a certain tradition of the French Surrealist prose poem, cannnot be considered as a major influence on the American neo-Surrealist prose poem, which, as we have seen, is still dominated by the significantly more marginal figures of Max Jacob and Pierre Reverdy.

The Morning Glory (1975), Bly's first full-length collection of prose poems, is a book of "thing poems" based on the close observation of an object, an animal, or a landscape. In his epigraph to *The Morning Glory,* Bly characterizes his approach as one of Taoist respect for the irreducible completeness and particularity of things:

There is an old occult saying: whoever wants to see the invisible has to penetrate more deeply into the visible. All through Taoist and "curving lines" thought, there is the idea that our disasters come from letting nothing live for itself, from the longing we have to pull everything, even friends, in to ourselves, and let nothing alone. If we examine a pine carefully, we see how independent it is from us. When we first sense that a pine tree doesn't need us, that is has a physical life and a moral life and spiritual life that is complete without us, we feel alienated and depressed. The second time we feel it, we feel joyful. As Basho says in his wonderful poem:

The morning glory—
another thing
that will never be my friend.
(*Morning* 1)

Bly's adherence to Taoist principles advocating a life of absolute simplicity, naturalness, and noninterference with the basic energies of life is a major underlying principle of his poetic work as a whole. His insistence on "letting things live for themselves," in particular, is of crucial importance in a study of Bly's contribution to the history of the object poem. In this respect, the first poem of the collection, "A Bird's Nest Made of White Reed Fiber," reads like a poetic manifesto of the relationship between observer and observed prevailing in Bly's prose poems. Typically, he invites the reader to consider the bird's nest in its irreducible but transient particularity and subsequently engages in a process of empirical meditation based on absolute self-forgetfulness:

> The nest is white as the foam thrown up when the sea hits rocks! It is translucent as those cloudy transoms above Victorian doors, and swirled as the hair of those intense nurses, gray and tangled after long nights in Crimean wards. It is something made and then forgotten, like our own lives that we will entirely forget in the grave, when we are floating, nearing the shore where we will be reborn, ecstatic and black. (3)

The thing poems of *The Morning Glory* can be classified into three categories according to the nature of the connection between the human and the animal element or "thing" and, more generally, between the poet and his object. The first, and most common, category of thing poems involves the ascription of human characteristics to an animal or thing. In Bly's prose poems, this anthropomorphic fallacy often encompasses much more than mere physical resemblance and acquires a cultural or historical connotation, as in the passage quoted from "A Bird's Nest," in which the color and texture of the nest are associated with elements of Victorian architecture, or in "Looking at a Dead Wren in My Hand," where the bird's bill is brown "with the sorrow of an old Jew whose daughter has married an athlete" (5). Earlier in the poem, the wren's legs are even ascribed a religious, quasimythical significance when Bly describes them as "bars of music played in an empty church . . . where no worms of Empire have ever slept." In *The Morning Glory,* such anthropomorphizing or "culturalizing" comparisons result in a number of emotional climaxes or moments of insight, as in the image of the lily pads rising above the water "like hands held up to receive" ("A Poem about Tennessee" [32]) or of the "Lobsters Waiting to Be Eaten in a Restaurant Window," turning up to the sky "as if praying after some catastrophe" (27).

The second type of object poem, the exact obverse of the anthropomorphic fallacy, describes a human being in terms of his or her physical, metaphorical, or symbolic resemblance to an animal or an object. Examples of this zoomorphic or reifying fallacy can be found, for instance, in "Leonardo's Secret (The Virgin and St. Anne)," where the Virgin's smile—its prior reification into an element of Leonardo Da Vinci's painting implicitly preceding the genesis of Bly's poem—"reminds you of a cow's side, or a stubble field with water standing in it" (4). Bly's zoomorphic and reifying techniques are best understood in the context of his more general concern with the constant interaction between the natural world and the poetic imagination, one of the most important themes of his poetry since the short lyric vignettes of *Silence in the Snowy Fields*. It is therefore not surprising that the most elaborate zoomorphic descriptions in the *Morning Glory* collection should occur in the two poems about poets: "Watching Andrei Voznesensky Read in Vancouver" and "Seeing Creeley for the First Time." In the former, the poet has "a curious look like a wood animal," his hair "falling over the pale forehead is a little like birch branches swaying over the water," while "[his] fantastic and resonant voice booms out, like enormous dynamos, like immense waterfalls falling, tremendous winds in the west sweeping up, swirling winds carrying bits of chairs, barndoors, dust from chickenhouse floors" (23). A similar method is used not only to depict Robert Creeley's physical appearance but also to render the distinctively spasmodic and elliptical tessitura of his poetic voice:

He looks astoundingly like a crow—it is unbelievable—even his hair is somehow "crow hair." Shining black, falling over his head that is full of determination to pester owls if he sees any. . . . And I suppose his language is crow language—no long open vowels, like the owl, no howls like the wolf, but instead short, faintly hollow, harsh sounds, that all together make something absolutely genuine, crow speech coming up from every feather, every source of that crow body and crow life. (13)

"The Minister," a prose poem by Francis Ponge, whom Bly acknowledges as one of his illustrious predecessors in the genre, bears striking resemblances to Bly's acoustic portraits, which Ponge's caricature of a minister delivering a speech and compared with a cockchafer may have inspired:

A black coat with long tails, of rectilinear cut, makes him look like a cockchafer. If needs be, some applause of frenzied hands accentuates the comparison. It is when the sentences of the speech, thrown out like streamers, come to an end, beribbon the recent statue which they bind to the crowd, then float like those plumes of smoke with their knots tied and untied by the wind which ends by dispersing everything.

And soon the signatures walk in procession like cockroaches over pages strewn in disorder on a table of state furniture. (*Lyres* 17)

Yet, "The Minister" is not in any way typical of Ponge's object poems in prose. In fact, Ponge rarely succumbs to Bly's favorite fallacies, whether zoomorphic or anthropomorphic, instead preferring to have things refer to other things. In this respect, the closing sentence of the poem is a much more faithful illustration of Ponge's approach to objects, in that it seeks to establish meaningful connections between apparently unrelated things. Surprisingly enough, this third and last tendency of the object poem is hardly represented in *The Morning Glory,* so that the question of whether Bly's anthropomorphic and zoomorphic strategies can be reconciled with his poetic ideal of "letting things alone" and, consequently, whether his thing poems really live up to his own definition of the genre, is arguable.[3] As Howard Nelson has remarked: "It is symptomatic that in pointing out how independent natural beings are from us, [Bly] immediately endows them with prerequisites of humanness: moral and spiritual life. They would not need to have any of these to be worth our fascination and respect. . . . Bly wants to resist the drive to 'pull everything . . . in to ourselves.' At the same time, he is a poet who in describing the natural world relates it constantly to human life" (135–36). An extreme example of this occurs in the poem "On the Rocks at Maui," in which a black crab confides to the reader that he "pray[s] all day" and hears "friends whisper" to him in his dream that he "has lost their friendship" (34).

Bly's penchant for anthropomorphic comparisons and pathetic fallacies notwithstanding, the categorical imperative to "let things alone" nevertheless indicates his attempts to distinguish his epiphanic thing poems from the American tradition of the object poem. In "A Wrong Turning in American Poetry," an essay first published in 1963, Bly repudiates the poetry of Marianne Moore, William Carlos Williams, and Charles Olson on the grounds of the uneasy relationship between poet and object. Bly condemns Moore's conception of the object poem as an "exercise in propriety," depicting only fragments of objects, "all adapted to domestic life . . . reduced to human dimensions (*American* 11)," while Williams' famous motto "no ideas but in things" leads to a poetry where "keeping close to the surface becomes an obsession" and the poet appears "only as a disembodied anger

or an immovable eye" (13). As for Olson's "objectism," the "getting rid of
the lyrical interference of the individual as ego, of the 'subject' and his
soul" (advocated in Olson's famous essay on "Projective Verse") is irreconcilable with Bly's own predilection for "inwardness," which, as we will see,
is one of the keystones of his poetic work.[4] In the light of Bly's severe
criticism of the tradition of the American object poem, one can easily understand why Bly acknowleges the author of *Le Parti pris des choses* as his
"predecessor" in the genre. In "The Prose Poem as an Evolving Form," Bly
praises Ponge's "precise" diction, which offers "language in archeological
layers, drawing some words from science, others from reservoirs of words
used in earlier centuries, in order to come close to the object and participate
in its complication" (*Selected* 199). He then proceeds to quote from
Ponge's essay "The Silent World Is Our Homeland": "In these terms one
will surely understand what I consider to be the true function of poetry. It
is to nourish the spirit of man by giving him the cosmos to suckle. We have
only to lower our standard of dominating nature, and to raise our standard
of participating in it, in order to make this reconciliation take place" (200).

Unlike Ponge's object poems, which, more often than not, display an
erudite and playful use of archaic and scientific vocabulary, Bly's thing
poems are written in a language of an elemental, often quasi-archetypal
simplicity. Despite this essential stylistic difference, Bly's conviction that
"our disasters come from letting nothing live for itself" shares the premises
of Ponge's utopian reconciliation between the poet and nature. In a poem
such as "The Large Starfish," it also becomes apparent that Bly, despite his
propensity to indulge in anthropomorphic fallacies, does not fail completely in his endeavors to establish a relationship of equality and respect
with the natural world he describes:

> How slowly and evenly it moves! The starfish is a glacier, going
> sixty miles a year! It moves over the pink rock, by means I cannot see
> . . . and into marvelously floating delicate brown weeds. It is about
> the size of the bottom of a pail. When I reach out to it, it holds on
> firmly, and then slowly relaxes . . . I suddenly take an arm and lift it.
> The underside is a pale tan . . . gradually I watch, thousands of tiny
> tubes begin rising from all over the underside . . . hundreds in the
> mouth, hundreds along the nineteen underarms . . . all looking . . .
> feeling . . . like a man looking for a woman . . . tiny heads blindly
> feeling for a rock and finding only air. A purple rim runs along the
> underside of every arm, with paler tubes. Probably its moving-feet.
> . . .
> I put him back in . . . he unfolds—I had forgotten how purple he

was—and slides down into his rock groin, the snail-like feelers waving as if nothing had happened and nothing has. (*Morning* 55–56)

This extract is typical of Bly's thing poems, in that the inevitable reference to human features ("the nineteen underarms . . . all looking . . . feeling
. . . like a man looking for a woman")—this time partially compensated for
by another interobjective comparison ("The starfish is a glacier, going sixty
miles a year!")—is eventually neutralized by an assertion of the object's
independent self-containedness ("the snail-like feelers waving as if nothing
had happened and nothing has"). On a stylistic level, this attitude goes
hand in hand with a radical distrust of abstraction, which, in Bly's thing
poems in particular, must be understood in its etymological sense of
ab-s-trahere ("to pull up"), a refusal to "pull" things "in to ourselves" and
thereby negate their inalienable separateness from the human observer.

Decolonizing the Object: Bly's Neo-Romantic Utopia

As we have seen, Ponge was very much aware of the impossibility of fully
respecting the integrity of the object of a poetic work. In "L'Objet, c'est la
poétique," one of several aesthetically self-reflexive prose poems contained
in the volume *Lyres,* he explains:

> Man is a strange body which does not have its center of gravity
> within itself.
> Our soul is transitive. It needs an object which modifies it, like its
> direct complement, immediately.
> This is the most serious relation (not at all of the *to have* but of the
> *to be*).
> The artist, more than any other man, shoulders its weight, is
> charged with the blow. (*Lyres* 150)

Ponge's full appreciation of the implications of an ontologically decen-
tered subject goes well beyond Bly's condemnation of Marianne Moore's
"exercises in propriety" in acknowledging the insuperable transitiveness of
the poetic act. This "gravest connection" between the soul and its direct
object, and its necessary internalization by the subject into its very being, is
precisely what Bly's prose poems try to abolish, in order to get as close as
possible to a literary work in the "nominative" or (as Barthes would have
it, though in a totally different context) "intransitive" mode. The last sentence of "The Large Starfish" illustrates the specific nature of the interplay
between the subjective and the objective world in Bly's prose poems, its

narcissistic potential systematically thwarted by a reminder that the observer's gaze should not prevail over the thing observed. In many ways, Bly's epiphanic resolution of the walker's encounter with the starfish is the antithesis of the Joycean epiphany. Unlike Stephen's "sudden spiritual manifestations," revealing themselves to the vigilant *flâneur* poet, whose primary duty is to transcribe them into terms related to his own subjective experience or aesthetic design, Bly's epiphanic strolls are inscribed in an attempt to establish with the object a connection based on a sense of generous and disinterested empathy. Even though the thing poem shares the underlying principle of Joyce's epiphanies to create a poetic space for the prosaic, in that it systematically aims at bringing out the spiritual value of simple objects or mundane incidents, Bly's "objects" are presented in their irreducible subjectivity. Joyce's fragments, by contrast, are merely signs to be interpreted and internalized by a subject in search of a new spiritual insight. Typically, the occasional exclamatory sentence ("How slowly and evenly it moves!") also contributes to reasserting the speaker's admiring puzzlement before the starfish's being and, indirectly, the relative imperviousness of the animal's life to the observer's gaze. The issue of the relationship between writer and object in Bly's prose poems is more openly commented on in one of the most successful pieces of the collection, "November Day at McClure's":

> Alone in the jagged rock at the south end of McClure's Beach. The sky low. The sea grows more and more private, as afternoon goes on, the sky comes down closer, the unobserved water rushes out to the horizon, horses galloping in a mountain valley at night. The waves smash up the rock, I find flags of seaweed high on the worn top, forty feet up, thrown up overnight, separated water still pooled there, like the black ducks that fly desolate, forlorn, and joyful over the seething swells, who never "feel pity for themselves," and "do not lie awake weeping for their sins." In their blood cells the vultures coast with furry necks extended, watching over the desert for signs of life to end. It is not our life we need to weep for. Inside us there is some secret. We are following a narrow ledge around a mountain, we are sailing on skeletal eerie craft over the buoyant ocean. (*Morning* 39)

Bly's paraphrase of Whitman's praise of the independent self-containedness of animals in "Song of Myself" ("I think I could turn and live with animals, they are so placid and self-contained / . . . / They do not sweat and whine about their condition, / They do not lie awake in the dark and weep for their sins" [73]), which he extends to the natural world in general through his oxymoronic description of the "unobserved water," is closely related to his neo-Romantic conception of the goals and methods of modern poetry. The future of modern poetry, Bly has explained, lies not in a continuation of the modernist tradition of "irony" (a mode denying the assumption of unmediated apprehension and expression underlying Bly's poetry as a whole) advocated by Eliot and Pound but in an effort to internalize and carry through the Romantic project to reach a "unity of consciousness" between man and nature (*News* 5). In *The Morning Glory,* Bly rewrites Ponge's poetic utopia of "lower[ing] our standard of dominating nature" into this yet unrealized neo-Romantic project. The basic principles of the thing poem follow the premises of the Romantic belief in nature as the symbol of a spiritual truth and, above all, follow Emerson's insistence on a direct and unmediated apprehension of natural forms "*in and for themselves*" (Emerson 9). In Bly's writings, this refusal to indulge in an attitude of narcissistic lyricism goes hand in hand with a phenomenological extension of the Transcendentalist refusal to colonize nature, not only concretely (as in Emerson's "Hamatreya," where the presumptuous first settlers of Concord, Massachusetts, anxious to take possession of the land, hear the "Earth-song" and are reminded that the earth will never belong to anyone) but also, as we have seen, through the very act of observing and its poetic articulation into form.

Finally, Bly's Romantic faith in dialectic relationships between specificity and universality is also characteristic of the Transcendentalist poets he acknowledges as early masters of the thing poem (*Selected* 200). Although all the poems of *The Morning Glory* focus on a specific animal, thing, place, or incident encountered by the poet on one of his solitary strolls, they are usually pervaded with an atmosphere of universality and palimpsestic atemporality, conveyed here by the metaphor of the "Siamese temple walls" and, more generally, through the use of the starkly elemental syntax and "archetypal" vocabulary that have been the hallmarks of Bly's style since the early landscape poems of *Silence in the Snowy Fields.* Where Emerson's discussion of the principles of particularity and universality in language and nature and of the correspondences between natural and spiritual phenomena ("1. Words are signs of natural facts. / 2. Particular natural facts are symbols of particular spiritual facts." [Emerson 14]) led to the apprehension of an omnipresent divine principle (the "Over-Soul"), Bly's poems carry a sense of universality achieved through a double process of mythification and mythopoeticization of the local and the particular. In this respect, Bly also shares the commitment of the Fugitive movement to a ritualization of traditionalist and regionalist poetry (a connection Bly himself would probably disavow on the grounds of the Fugitivists' subscription to a poetry of New Critical wit, ambiguity, and irony), as exemplified, for example, by John Crowe Ransom's mythopoeic transfiguration of the anonymous toil of Mississippi harvesters into a chivalric ceremony in "Antique Harvesters."

Privacy and the Art of Artlessness

Bly's choice of the prose poem form—which he defines as "the final stage of the unpretentious style" (*News* 210) initiated by the German Romantics in reaction against "the peak of human arrogance" (3) of eighteenth-century literature—is in keeping with the Transcendentalist emphasis on solitude and meditation that permeates *The Morning Glory* ("When I write poems, I need to be near grass that no one else sees, as here, where I sit for an hour under the cottonwood" [*Morning* 71]). "The virtue of art," Emerson has said, lies "in detachment, in sequestering one object from the embarrassing variety":

> Until one thing comes out from the connection of things, there can be enjoyment, contemplation, but no thought. Our happiness and unhappiness are unproductive. The infant lies in a pleasing trance, but his individual character and his practical power depend on his daily progress in the separation of things, and dealing with them one at a time. Love and all the passions concentrate all existence around a single form. It is the habit of certain minds to give an all-excluding fulness to the object, the thought, the word they alight upon, and to make that for the time the deputy of the world. These are the artists, the orators, the leaders of society. (307)

This concern with the uniqueness of the moment and the particularity of things is an important aspect of Bly's relationship with the history of the object poem. Bly's thing poem is, so to speak, a literal generic translation of Emerson's precepts to deal with things "one at a time" and "give an all-excluding fulness to the object." The status of "deputy of the world" conferred upon the object is also typical of the thing poem's democratic approach to a reality consisting of discrete units, each of which deserves equal attention in its poetic treatment. Indeed, *The Morning Glory* as a whole reads like the diary of a solitary walker who takes the time to stroll about and stop to consider things or incidents often not considered worthy of attention. In this sense, also, Bly's meditative sketches once again crystallize a major tendency of the modern prose poem to sublimate or "de-familiarize" the trivial or prosaic.[5]

Bly has commented on his decision to write his object or thing poems in prose. "One August day," says Bly, "watching a rain shower, I was astounded at how many separate events were taking place only once. Each needed to be given space in the poem separately, and I was glad for the prose poem form" ("What" 45). In "A Hollow Tree," as in all of the poems of *The Morning Glory,* a single object is given an independent treatment in its temporal and local uniqueness. The process of progressive apprehension of the object is here punctuated by a description *à tiroirs,* first of the hollow stump as a whole, then of its "temple walls," the inside of the tree, and the feathers:

> I bend over an old hollow cottonwood stump, still standing, waist high, and look inside. Early spring. Its Siamese temple walls are all brown and ancient. The walls have been worked on by the intricate ones. Inside the hollow walls there is privacy and secrecy, dim light. And yet some creature has died here.
>
> On the temple floor feathers, gray feathers, many of them with a fluted white tip. Many feathers. In the silence many feathers. (11)

"The prosodic unit in any prose poem," Bly has said, "is the sentence rather than the line," while "the nearest relative to the thing poem is not the essay or the short story but the haiku" (*Selected* 201). In this respect, each sentence of Bly's prose poems is an autarchic microcosm in Bly's egalitarian universe, a unit which could often stand on its own, like the last three, haikulike sentences of "A Hollow Tree," but is inserted in the larger self-contained unit of the prose poem itself. The prose poem thus carries out the object poem's utopian principles through more explicit syntactic and typographical strategies, in that the inherent completeness of the object (or the Whitmanesque "self-containedness" of Bly's animals) is emphasized by the very typographical density of the prose block. This framing of the object into a "blocklike" unit would be difficult to reproduce by means of the sparser typographical stategies at work in a lineated poem.

The sense of density that characterizes Bly's prose poems distinguishes his treatment of objects from that of other poets, for instance in the Imagist or Objectivist tradition. Although Bly, the Imagists, and the Objectivists clearly exhibit the same emphasis on the image as the primary unit of meaning, their use of typography is completely different. Where the Imagist poem involved a succinct and instantaneous presentation of an object in its specific isolatedness (which reaches an extreme in the severe sobriety of

George Oppen's Objectivism, for example), the object in the prose poem is engulfed in—and continually fleshed out by—a flow of syntactic continuation within and between the paragraphs. The prose poem becomes thus an appropriate medium for meditative descriptions in the continuous (as opposed to progressive) present, an alloy of prosaic flow and lyric presence which is still characteristic of most prose poems written today. Unlike its verse equivalent, in which the abruptness of the line breaks creates a pervasive sense of disruption and interruption, the thing poem in prose enables one to "stay close to the senses for half a page." According to Bly, the strength of the prose poem therefore lies in its sense of stylistic and emotional "intimacy" as well as in its capacity to create a medium in which "the conscious mind gives up, at least to a degree, the adversary position it usually adopts toward the unconscious" (202).

Intimacy of feeling and experience, combined with an attitude of quiet wonder, characterizes both the tone and the form of *The Morning Glory*. As suggested by the "privacy and secrecy" prevailing inside the hollow tree, Bly has defined his prose poems as a kind of "private religion" akin to ancient "Mysteries" and other initiation rites ("What" 45). This notion of the poem as a ritual, or a private, religious, and atemporal act, is emphasized by the many allusions to ancient civilizations (the "Siamese temple" in this case) and Christian symbolism, in particular, as in "Christmas Eve Service at Midnight at St. Michael's," in which the notion of mystery acquires an explicitly Eucharistic connotation (*Morning* 74).

The formal features of the prose poem (at least according to Bly's own way of understanding and practicing the genre) rest on a similar sense of privacy and intimacy. Indeed, the blocklike makeup of the thing poem in prose—along with the already mentioned methodical accent on the temporal and local situatedness of the object or incident described—often makes it resemble a diary entry. In many cases, the kinship between the thing poem and diary writing is already apparent in the titles and opening sentences, as in "The Large Starfish" ("It is low tide. Fog. I have climbed down the cliffs from Pierce Ranch to the tide pools. Now the ecstasy of the low tide, kneeling down, alone" [55].) and "Finding a Salamander on Inverness Ridge":

> Walking. Afternoon. The war still going on, I stoop down to pick up a salamander. He is halfway across the mossy forest path. He is dark brown, fantastically cold in my hand. This one is new to me— the upper part of his eyeball light green . . . strange bullfrog eyes. (48)

Such syntactic and lexical artlessness is confirmed and reinforced by the presence of a lyric voice supposed to be that of the poet himself. In this respect, the thing poem as a genre reacts against the taking-for-granted of the existence of a poetic persona necessarily and (de-)ontologically dissociated from the poet's person. This assumption has long been internalized by Western poetics and Anglo-Saxon criticism, in particular, since its official ratification by the New Critics in the name of the paradox-ambiguity-irony triptych and the radical autonomy of Cleanth Brooks' "well-wrought urn." The notion of a poetic persona, however, would be absolutely irrelevant in a discussion of Chinese or Japanese poetry, including the haiku, which Bly acknowledges as a the nearest relative of the prose poem (*Selected* 201).[6] The prose poem, which is composed "away from the writer's desk, and in the presence of the object" (201), tends to incorporate the equation of the poet's voice with the lyric "I" into a poetics of radical presence verging on the immanentist (and latently animistic) symbolism characteristic of haiku poetry, as in the opening paragraph from "Grass from Two Years":

> When I write poems, I need to be near grass that no one else sees, as here, where I sit for an hour under the cottonwood. The long grass has fallen over until it flows. Whatever I am . . . if the great hawks come to look for me, I will be here in this grass. I feel a warmth in my stomach being near this grass. Knobby twigs have dropped on it. The summer's grass still green crosses some dry grass beneath, like the hair of the very old, that we stroke in the morning. (71)

Commenting on the genre's potential for celebrating the ordinary, Bly has written that "we often feel in a prose poem a man or a woman talking not before a crowd, but in a low voice to someone he is sure is listening" (61). "A Caterpillar on the Desk" is a good example of how the poems of *The Morning Glory* articulate the observer's wonder at the usual into an expression of poeticized domesticity:

> Lifting my coffee cup, I notice a caterpillar crawling over my sheet of ten-cent airmail stamps. The head is black as a Chinese box. Nine soft accordions follow it around, with a waving motion, like a flabby mountain. Skinny brushes used to clean pop bottles rise from some of its shoulders. As I pick up the sheet of stamps, the catterpillar advances around and around the edge, and I see his feet: three pairs under the head, four spongelike pairs under the middle body, and two final pairs at the tip, pink as a puppy's hind legs. As he walks, he

rears, six pairs of legs off the stamp, waving around in the air! One of the sponge pairs, and the last two tail pairs, the reserve feet, hold on anxiously. It is the first of September. The leaf shadows are less ferocious on the notebook cover. A man accepts his failures more easily—or perhaps summer's insanity is gone? A man notices ordinary earth, scorned in July, with affection, as he settles down to his daily work, to use stamps. (67)

In the light of this kind of poem, one can understand why Jonathan Monroe described Bly's relationship to the prose poem as a drawing away from his political poetry and a "depoliticiz[ation] of what has been historically a highly charged, polemical, form-smashing genre for the sake of ecstatic religious content and a focus on domestic concerns and the inner life" (301). In *This Body Is Made of Camphor and Gopherwood* (1977), Bly's second collection of prose poems, this focus on inwardness and domesticity is put at the service of an exploration of the dialectics of inner and outer reality. Unlike *The Morning Glory, This Body* is a work centered on a single subject; rather than a collection of individual poems, it is a book-length investigation and celebration of the metaphor of the body, which Bly sees as a universal source of basic energies of being and creation. Another essential difference between *This Body* and *The Morning Glory* is that the former seems to focus not so much on specific things, animals, or places as on the very process of perception and consciousness. The phenomenological strategies at work in *This Body,* however, constantly waver between the intellectual, the emotional, and the purely sensory, for Bly sees the soul and the body as two related aspects of the same life. To quote Charles Molesworth, the prose poems of *This Body* attempt to render "the data of consciousness understood not as thought, but as bodily sensation" (138):

My friend, this body is food for the thousand dragons of the air, each dragon light as a needle. This body loves us, and carries us home from our hoeing.

It is ancient, and full of the bales of sleep. In its vibrations the sun rolls along under the earth, the spouts over the ocean curl into our stomach . . . water revolves, spouts seen by skull eyes at mid-ocean, this body of herbs and gopherwood, this blessing, this lone ridge patrolled by water. . . . I get up, morning is here. The stars still out; the black winter sky looms over the unborn lambs. The barn is cold before dawn, the gates slow. . . .

This body longs for itself far out at sea, it floats in the black heavens, it is a brilliant being, locked in the prison of human dullness. . . . ("Going Out to Check the Ewes" [*Body* 23])

As do most poems of the collection, "Going Out to Check the Ewes" consists of a succession of discrete images and impressions immersed in the wider flow of the poet's daydreaming imagination. In this particular form of languorous, half-awakened reverie, reality is perceived as a fluid succession of ephemeral and infinitely malleable moments of quiet awareness. Bly's attempts to dissolve the traditional body-soul dichotomy ruling Western thought into the all-inclusive metaphor of the universal body seem to resolve, at least in part, the problematic relationship between subject and object, observer and observed, explored in the thing poems of *The Morning Glory*. Indeed, Bly's body-metaphor is at once the cause and the consequence of its own existence. Complete in and unto itself, it longs for its own healing powers, which are derived from invisible energies lying outside or beyond language. While the body itself and its revelatory potential remain unverbalized, the poet's ability to "[gather] ecstasies from [his] own body" ("The Pail" [*Body* 47]) nevertheless enables him to attend to the process of revelation itself:

This body holds its protective walls around us, it watches us whenever we walk out. Each step we take in conversation with our friends, moving slowly or flying, the body watches us, calling us into what is possible, into what is not said, into the shuckheap of ruined arrowheads, or the old man with two fingers gone. ("Falling into Holes in Our Sentences" [29])

Bly's emphasis on the mind's movement from perception to vision involves the discovery of some secret wisdom, deep and resonant, but nonetheless ineffable, hidden beneath the phenomenal world. Such revelation, he concludes, is meant to elicit "no sentimentality, only the ruthless body performing its magic, transforming each of our confrontations into energy, changing our scholarly labors over white-haired books into certainty and healing power, and our cruelties into an old man with missing fingers." In this respect, the poems contained in *This Body* are representative of Bly's emphasis on the prose poem as a healing influence on the reader's emotional life. As for the prose poem's closeness to the senses, rather than to the intellect, it is indicative of what he sees as the genre's essential role as "a healing form for an overtly mental culture" (Interview). Grounded as it is in the poet's felt encounter with the natural world, as well as in the personal intuition of the universal in the particulars of experience, Bly's belief in the existence of a yet-to-be-discovered, primitive consciousness is also characteristic of the so-called "Deep Image" with which his poetry has been associated since the mid-1960s. Like Bly's body-centered immanentism, the Deep Image poem usually delivers a moment of mystical enlightenment rooted in the poet's observation of concrete surroundings but eventually emerging from the deepest recesses of the subconscious.[7]

In this respect, Bly's prose poems—most of which depend on a similar sense of creative empathy with the natural or inanimate world—can usefully be contrasted with the work of David Ignatow, a poet usually associated with the fabulist trend of the neo-Surrealist prose poem. Ignatow's object and landscape poems in prose combine the stern, meditative stance of the Deep Image poem with elements of absurdism and Surrealism reminiscent of Russell Edson's prose poems–fables. As is often the case in Ignatow's poetry, such a combination results in a number of irony- and anxiety-laden psychological landscapes. The prose poem, "I Identify"—in which the poet seeks to relate to the wooden shed in his neighbor's backyard and concludes: "I am identified with the necessary, whether I myself am necessary" (New 170)—is a typical example of Ignatow's transformation of the object poem into a means of dramatizing a philosophical or existential dilemma. Unlike Bly, who discovers hidden treasures of metaphorical depth in the most innocuous details of domestic or pastoral life, Ignatow emphasizes the inability of the human mind truly to make sense of its relationship with inanimate matter and to go beyond a recognition of its own insubstantiality and impermanence. "Talking to Myself," in which Ignatow puts the accent on the indifference of the natural world to the poet's attempts to understand and celebrate it, reads like a debunked version of Bly's "A Hollow Tree":

About my being a poet, the trees certainly haven't expressed an interest, standing at a distance. I'd expect that at least they'd try to learn something new besides growing their leaves, old stuff by now, and anyway it's done by so many others. Wouldn't these trees want to know what they'll be doing in a hundred years, what they look like now, how they stand, what's their name, where they are and what they actually do in winter and in summer, deaf, dumb and happy as they are? Not happy, simply willing to go on as always. Not even willing, just doing what comes naturally. To them I might as well be dead or a tree.

To stay among the trees as if I were at home, arrived from a long journey, I am digging a place for a burial with my feet. (*Facing* 37)

Ignatow does not shun abstraction and discursiveness in the name of the "ineffable" quality of the speaker's emotive response to the landscape. Far from indulging in the archetypal rhetoric of *The Morning Glory* and *This Body*, his prose poems display an increased self-consciousness about the act of writing and the psycholinguistic strategies at work in the so-called object or landscape poem. As he writes in "My Own House":

As I view the leaf, my theme is not the shades of meaning that the mind conveys of it but my desire to make the leaf speak to tell me, Chlorophyll, chlorophyll, breathlessly. I would rejoice with it and, in turn, would reply, Blood, and the leaf would nod. Having spoken to each other, we would find our topics inexhaustible and imagine, as I grow old and the leaf begins to fade and turn brown, the thought of being buried in the ground would become so familiar to me, so thoroughly known through conversation with the leaf, that my walk among the trees after completing this poem would be like entering my own house. (*New* 152)

The assumptions of artlessness, naturalness, and immediacy that constitute the premises of Bly's prose poems, their main purpose being to help to "heal the wound of abstraction" (*Body* 61), have been the target of much criticism. In his review of *This Body Is Made of Camphor and Gopherwood*, sardonically retitled "This Book Is Made of Turkey Soup and Star Music," Philip Dacey denounces Bly's use of an archaic vocabulary and a solemn simplicity of diction (as well as his consistent use of simple declarative present-tense sentences) as a particularly insidious form of literary demagogy. He argues that the claims to artlessness of his style paradoxically result in a rather high degree of affection and inflation. Although Bly "rails against artifice in poetry," Dacey writes, many of the prose poems in *This Body* are "more artificial—pieces clearly contrived in a language one is not likely to hear outside the poem—than virtually any of, say, Frost's poems in blank verse." Whereas "Frost and countless others achieve the natural or a semblance of it through the artificial," he continues, "Bly wishes to bypass the latter and ends up smack in the middle of it" (quoted in H. Nelson 164). The most articulate objection to Bly's poetics of "naive" directness and immediacy is raised by Robert Pinsky, who condemns Bly's reliance on a rather predictable lexical and visual decorum and chides him for his "more-imagistic-than-thou" attitude (Pinsky 77). More generally, Pinsky dismisses the simple, "archetypal" rhetoric of the Deep Image poem as a rather dull, hackneyed, and ultimately complacent form of neo-Surrealism: "One of the most contemporary strains in contemporary poetry is often interior, submerged, free-playing, elusive, more fresh than earnest, more eager to surprise than to tell. The 'surrealist' diction associated with such writing sometimes suggests, not a realm beyond surface reality, but a *particular* reality, hermetically primitive, based on a new poetic diction: "breath," "snow," "future," "blood," "silence," "eats," "water," and most of all "light" doing the wildly unexpected. . . . This is a kind of one-of-the-guys surrealism" (162–63).

The implications of Pinsky's statements are twofold: (1) the codification of poetic language into a generic vocabulary can easily turn the "studied naturalness" of Bly's prose poems into a new form of mannerism; and (2) the sense of "authentic immediacy" created by Bly's prose poems (which are allegedly written in some silent and secret place "with no one watching" [*Morning* 20]) depends on the existence of a "voice," which is certainly not that used by the poet in his everyday life. As we have seen, Bly's prose poems, despite their claim to lyric directness, are never completely immune to a certain amount of "unspontaneous" contamination, if only in the form of the author's favorite pathetic fallacies. In this sense, Bly's search for an unmediated expression of the self and its relationship to a pristinely "natural" environment is itself a form of artifice, for it seeks to elude the necessary distance between the preverbal sensory experience and its elaboration into form. By turning the poem into an act of "pure" perception, Bly denies the gap between apprehension and representation dramatized in the playful but tortured psychological frustrations of Ignatow's prose poems.[8]

Pinsky's "antidote" to the somewhat stilted spontaneity of the Deep Image poem and its failed attempt to convey "immediate" experience in an unself-conscious way (a feature the Deep Image poem shares with confessional poetry, another prominent poetic mode in the 1960s and early 1970s) lies in a rejection of the old modernist mistrust of abstraction and statement and, in particular, of the Imagist notion that "a poet presents, rather than tells about, a sensory experience" (Pinsky 3). Because poetic expression is necessarily exposed to a certain form of narrative or abstract "contamination," poetry should reclaim the possibilities of narrative and abstract discourses. According to Pinsky—who sees poetic language as the site of a permanent struggle not only between the imagistic and the abstract but also between artifice and artlessness—the kind of self-celebratory neoprimitivism advocated by Robert Bly and other Deep Image poets tends to swing the pendulum too far away from what a poem is actually made of. As the closing part of this study shows, the reclamation of abstract and narrative modes, as well as the renewal of a certain self-consciousness about the process of poetic creation, have proven central to the development of some of the most recent trends of the American prose poem.

5 · Unreal Miniatures
The Art of Charles Simic

Since he first began publishing his neo-Surrealist work in the mid-1960s, Charles Simic has earned a reputation as a poet writing across different genres and traditions. Simic himself has acknowledged a variety of influences (including those of poets Theodore Roethke, Benjamin Péret, and François Villon, philosophers Martin Heidegger and Edmund Husserl, and even blues musician Robert Johnson), and critics have praised his ability to blend classical and modern myth and juggle with elements of Western philosophy and Eastern European folklore as well as jazz and blues music.

Simic's 1990 Pulitzer Prize–winning *The World Doesn't End* is divided into three sections of short prose poems ranging in tone from the solemn to the conversational, the playful to the sinister. A collage of lyrical fragments, short tales, dreams, aphoristic vignettes, and anecdotes, *The World Doesn't End* constantly mixes history and myth, autobiography and fiction, dreamlike content and cold-eyed observations. Most of the poems in part I, however, clearly center on the author's childhood years in Yugoslavia. Simic's experience of World War II and of his family's emigration from their native country to Paris and then to the United States (Simic arrived in America in 1954, at the age of sixteen) is often expressed in a surreal and visionary fashion:

My mother was a braid of black smoke.
She bore me swaddled over the burning cities.
The sky was a vast and windy place for a child to play.
We met many others who were just like us. They were trying to put on their overcoats with arms made of smoke.
The high heavens were full of little shrunken deaf ears instead of stars.
(*World* 3)

This poem is representative of Simic's talent for short, austere Surrealist vignettes that derive a significant part of their lyric intensity from the thick margins of silence surrounding them. More often than not, Simic's oneiric landscapes account for the terrors of the war as experienced by a child, who nevertheless seeks to interrogate and come to terms with seemingly incomprehensible events and situations through the power of his imagination. His voice is alternately poignant and detached, deeply tragic and ruthlessly ironic: "We were so poor I had to take the place of the bait in the mousetrap" (8). "The city had fallen. We came to the window of a house drawn by a madman. The setting sun shone on a few abandoned machines of futility" (15). "Some small town so effaced by time it has only one veiled widow left, and now she too is leaving with her secret" (19).

In the second and third sections, Simic's semifantastic recollections of his childhood years give way to a more playful brand of Surrealism, occasionally reminiscent of Russell Edson's absurdist humor. Simic's short narrative pieces cover every subject from art and philosophy to witches and china dolls, not to speak of the author's penchant for conversational references to famous historical and mythological figures, from Hermes to Jesus Christ, Friedrich Nietzsche, and Sigmund Freud. In most cases, a comic effect is created by the juxtaposition of antipodal images, ideas, and registers constantly short-circuiting the apparent matter-of-factness of the narrative. As is the case in many recent neo-Surrealist prose poems, Simic's vignettes are often balanced between a terse, conversational rhetoric and a starkly surreal imagery rooted in precise, domestic detail. Here are two examples of Simic's verbal and imagistic fireworks:

My thumb is embarking on a great adventure. "Don't go, please," say the fingers. They try to hold him down. Here comes a black limousine with a veiled woman in the back seat, but no one at the wheel. When it stops, she takes a pair of gold scissors out of her purse and snips the thumb off. We are off to Chicago with her using the bloody stump of my thumb to paint her lips. (49)

Ambiguity created by a growing uncertainty of antecedents bade us welcome.

"The Art of Making Gods" is what the advertisement said. We were given buckets of mud and shown a star atlas. "The Minotaur doesn't like whistling," someone whispered, so we resumed our work in silence.

Evening classes. The sky is like a mirror of a dead beauty to use as a model. The spit of melancholia's plague carrier to make it stick. (57)

While the first prose poem clearly falls into the category of the uncanny Edsonian fable, the second example is more representative of Simic's expertness at blending powerful images with a strong philosophical strain. It also reminds us that Simic is at his best when he does not confine himself to creating mordant, enigmatic scenes but seeks, above all, to reveal the subjective and intuitive tenor of seemingly mundane events and situations ("From inside the pot on the stove someone threatens the stars with a wooden spoon. Otherwise, cloudless calm. The shepherd's hour" [69]). One can relate that particular concern to his use of the prose poem form in *The World Never Ends*. Most of the pieces of the collection are spoken ("prose poems are spoken in a certain way, not sung" [Weigl 215]) in a dispassionate, often fatalistic, voice that lends an objective, firsthand quality to the strange events and wondrous images that people Simic's poems. In the words of Christopher Buckley, Simic's prose poems, just like the folk tale, blend the astonishing events of the mythic and historical past with a resolutely unsentimental "witnessing voice" that "reports 'truly' what the speaker has seen and how that might be resolved or has taken place in such a world as ours" (100).

The epigraph to the collection, "let's waltz the rumba" (a quotation from a Fats Waller lyric), provides an essential clue to the interweaving of various rhythms and atmospheres that characterizes Simic's work as a whole. The reference to jazz music indirectly also accounts for the syncopated structure of his prose poems, in which the emphasis is often on meaningful hiatuses and polyrhythmic changes between and within the poems. Simic's distaste for linear development and organic form as well as his fondness for associative "leaps" and metaphoric jolts (which is further attested by the presence in the collection of several dream-narratives), are best understood in the light of his conception of the genre as a dialectical hybrid between the lyric and the narrative mode. "The prose poem," he writes, "reads like a narrative but works like a lyric, since it relies on juxtaposition of images and unexpected turns of phrase" (*Unemployed* 118). Commenting on his choice of the prose poem form in *The World Doesn't End*, Simic adds: "A lyric impulse is an impulse in which everything stands still. It's like a song that repeats. Nothing ever happens in a lyric poem. It's a great acknowledgement of the present moment. In a prose sentence, however, things do happen. A prose poem is a dialectic between the two. You write in sentences, and tell a story, but the piece is like a poem because it circles back on itself" (McQuade 57).

One major implication emerging from Simic's conception of the prose poem concerns the self-referential "circularity" of the genre, which is once again understood as a creative compromise between the absolute paradigmatic presence of the lyric and the syllogistic linearity of narrative. According to Simic himself, it is from the poetry of Theodore Roethke that he learned how to "[attack] a subject from different angles, juxtaposing with great freedom, making unexpected imaginative leaps and then arranging the whole poem cyclically . . . an ideal way to avoid narrative development" (Matuz 363). Simic's suggestion that a prose poem "circles back on itself" implies that the poeticalness of his prose pieces lies, at least in part, in their self-contained and self-referential nature. Unlike poetry in verse, however, the circular integrity of the prose poem does not depend on the systematic repetition and patterning of certain motifs or rhythmic elements. Rather, it results from a conception of the sentence and the paragraph not only as primary units of composition and attention but also as so many imagistic microcosms endowed with a life of their own. That Simic considers the prose poem as a form closed onto itself is even more apparent in the shorter prose poems of the collection, some of which consist of only two or three sentences: "At least four or five Hamlets on this block alone. Identical Hamlets holding identical monkey-faced spinning toys" (*World* 59).

Despite Simic's penchant for such powerful visual effects, many poems in *The World Doesn't End* have a strong meditative tone.[1] In many ways, Simic's choice of the short vignette surrounded by margins of pensive silence is shaped by an awareness of the unreliability of perception and the transiency of human thoughts and observations. The philosophical stance underlying many of Simic's vignettes is characterized by a consistent lack of faith in great philosophical and ideological systems: "O the great God of Theory, he's just a pencil stub, a chewed stub with a worn eraser at the end of a huge scribble" (64). To the systematizing powers of the rational mind, Simic opposes the lowly wisdom of folk tales, riddles, ditties, and proverbs as well as his own modestly framed flashes of imaginative insight:

> Once I knew, then I forgot. It was as if I had fallen asleep in a field only to discover at waking that a grove of trees had grown up around me.
>
> "Doubt nothing, believe everything," was my friend's idea of

metaphysics, although his brother ran away with his wife. He still bought her a rose every day, sat in the empty house for the next twenty years talking to her about the weather.

I was already dozing off in the shade, dreaming that the rustling trees were my many selves explaining themselves all at the same time so that I could not make out a single word. My life was a beautiful mystery on the verge of understanding, always on the verge! Think of it!

My friend's empty house with every one of its windows lit. The dark trees multiplying all around it. (46)

As is often the case in Simic's prose poems, "Once I knew . . ." consists of a series of images always on the point of disclosing a secret or a revelation without ever actually doing so. In a typical move from the anecdotal to the general, culminating in a semi-aphoristic observation, the confused voices of Simic's prose poem are symptomatic of the logic of ambiguity and irresolution that pervades his work. Reflecting on the current lack of audience and public attention for poetry, Simic writes:

The time of minor poets is coming. Good-by Whitman, Dickinson, Frost. Welcome you whose fame will never reach beyond your closest family, and perhaps one or two friends gathered after dinner over a jug of fierce red wine. . . .

It's snowing, says someone who has peeked into the dark night, and then he, too, turns towards you as you prepare yourself to read, in a manner somewhat theatrical and with a face turning red, the long rambling love poem whose final stanza (unknown to you) is hopelessly missing. (58)

Having lost their traditional authority as public figures, poets must now develop new creative strategies in order to match the fragmented consciousness of the age. Simic's own prose poems suggest that poetic language can still recover its revelatory quality through a straightfaced but intensely self-conscious appraisal of the tenor of our times and one's own unexplained condition. "We live in a time," Simic writes, "in which there are hundreds of ways of explaining the world. Everything from every variety of religion to every species of scientism is believed" (*Unemployed* 2–3). Modern poetry, Simic explains elsewhere, is nothing more than the dramatization of Keats' "negative capability," namely the capacity of "being in uncertainties, mysteries, doubts, without any irritable reaching after facts and reason"; for Simic, the modern poet therefore remains, according to Wallace Stevens' definition, "a metaphysician in the dark" (*Wonderful* 63). The post-Holocaust poem, in particular, ceases to disclose even the most provisional and relative truths and becomes, instead, "a kind of magnet for complex historical, literary and psychological forces, as well as a way of maintaining oneself in the face of that multiplicity" (*Uncertain* 83). Such is, after all, the essential nature of Simic's poetics of incongruity. In this perspective, the prose poems of *The World Doesn't End* are clearly reminiscent of a certain brand of French Surrealism, one which adheres to André Breton's Freudian conception of black humor as a liberating force related to "the triumph of narcissism . . . the invulnerability of the self which asserts itself victoriously . . . [and] refuses to admit that the traumatisms of the exterior world can touch it"—ultimately, black humor can even enable one to turn an evil into a source of pleasure (*Anthologie* 15). Arguing that in the twentieth century humor has become "ontological . . . a permanent disruption . . . a world view, a philosophy of life," Simic writes: "Everything is equally tragic and comic in the long run. . . . Yet, probably in humor, too, there is a kind of yearning for harmony, some kind of metaphysical synthesis. In other words, a basically poetic way of gobbling the world" (*Uncertain* 19). Likewise, Simic's fragments of terse, mock-gnomic wisdom, his irreverent revisions of classical and modern myth, and, more generally, his comic blending of contradictory ideas, images, and registers often point to the frequently tragicomical realities hidden behind the poems' dissonances. Behind Simic's disjunctive poetics, one finds not just a sense of the absurdity of human endeavors to make sense of the irrationality of twentieth-century history but, at least as important, a counter-determination to resist that absurdity. Not only does humor contribute to making misery and suffering more tolerable; it is also a means of coming to terms with the incomprehensible—as the author himself writes, in a characteristically anticlimactic conclusion to one of his verbal collages: "not the least charm of this tableau is that it can be so easily dismissed as preposterous" (*World* 34):

He held the Beast of the Apocalypse by its tail, the stupid kid! Oh beards on fire, our doom appeared sealed. The buildings were tottering; the computer screens were as dark as our grandmother's cupboards. We were too frightened to plead. Another century gone to hell—and for what? Just because some people don't know how to bring their children up! (11)

Totems of the Self: *Dime-Store Alchemy* and the Art of Joseph Cornell

> I have eaten the city.
> Surrounded by musical silence,
> I have swallowed crowds of pigeons,
> Grass grows on my eyelids,
> My body is full of mirrors.
> H. R. Hays, "Manhattan"

Dime-Store Alchemy, Simic's second collection of prose miniatures, contains a variety of lyric, descriptive, and meditative vignettes celebrating the art of Joseph Cornell. Mixing critical and creative writing, the book also includes a biographical note and a notes section as well as eight illustrations of Cornell's works and a number of quotations from the artist's unpublished papers, currently held at the Archives of American Art–Smithsonian Institution. While many of Simic's pieces evoke Cornell's solitary walks in the streets of Manhattan, where he often went rummaging around in used bookstores and junk shops in search of material for his collages, others are in the form of interpretive commentaries on Cornell's box constructions. In the following prose poem, for instance, Simic attempts to compose an imaginary narrative on the basis of an early collage consisting of a china doll half-hidden behind a miniature forest:

> The chubby doll in a forest of twigs. Her eyes are open and her lips and cheeks are red. While her mother was busy with other things, she went to her purse, took out the makeup, and painted her face in front of a mirror. Now she's to be punished.
>
> A spoiled little girl wearing a straw hat about to be burnt at the stake. One can already see the flames in her long hair entangled with the twigs. Her eyes are wide open so she can watch us watching her.
>
> All this is vaguely erotic and sinister. (*Dime-Store* 45)

In the history of Surrealist writing, Paul Eluard's collaboration with Max Ernst on *Les Malheurs des immortels* (1922) and André Breton's textual interpretations of Joan Miró's *Constellations* (1958) are two illustrious precedents for such a use of the prose poem as a verbal accompaniment to a work of art. It is hardly surprising that the prose poem has often been seen as particularly fit to provide a verbal equivalent of or a complement to a picture and, thereby, to reflect the kinship of poetry and painting first enunciated in Horace's injunction, *ut pictoria poesis* ("as is painting, so is poetry"). After Aloysius Bertrand, the official initiator of the genre, had defined *Gaspard de la nuit* (published posthumously in 1842) as a collection of "fantasies in the style of Rembrandt and Callot," the close connection between the French prose poem and visual art remained evident in Rimbaud's choice of the title *Illuminations* for his second collection of prose poems, as well as in Baudelaire's intention to modernize the method Bertrand applied to "the quaintly picturesque life of a bygone age" (*Spleen* 25). More broadly, the mimetic and pictorial quality of the late nineteenth-century prose poem can be traced back to a number of short descriptive prose genres, including the portrait, the *blason,* the Rousseauesque *rêverie,* or even the *salon,* a genre of lyrical writing about works of art, which John Simon sees as the main impulse behind Bertrand's prose poems (96). As soon as the prose poem truly entered the modern era, however, this descriptive (and, at its worst, ornamental) tendency of the genre ceased to be unproblematic, as the genre began to adjust to the crisis of representation that characterizes modern painting itself. In the English-speaking world, Gertrude Stein's portraits and still lifes, for instance, testify to an anti-mimetic development of the Horatian dictum, one which reflects the Cubists' distrust of the power of any art to articulate a single, transparent representation of reality.

The specific form of contemporary art Simic's own prose poems purport to emulate also departs from the goals and methods of traditional mimesis. On a superficial level, Simic's interest in Cornell's three-dimensional collages of everyday objects and found materials in picture-frame boxes (Cornell was particularly fond of discarded materials such as old newpapers, prints, flasks, crystal cubes, glass, balls, feathers, and various debris) indirectly reminds us of Simic's own début as a writer of object poems. "Fork," one of Simic's most frequently anthologized poems, is a genuine Surrealist collage typical of his interest in "dreams in which objects are renamed and invested with imaginary lives" (*Dime-Store* 44). Such poems are best described by Simic himself as "premonitions . . . about the absolute otherness of the object" (*Wonderful* 85):

> This strange thing must have crept
> Right out of hell.
> It resembles a bird's foot
> Worn around the cannibal's neck.
> (*Selected* 34)

Simic's interest in analogies between the inanimate and the animate world points clearly to the object poems of Serbian poet Vasko Popa, whose work he began to translate as early as the 1960s. "Fork" is also indicative of his admiration for Heidegger's "phenomenological impulse to reexamine the simplest, the long-taken-for-granted things" (Matuz 367). Yet, the work of art, as it is conceived of by Cornell and other champions of *art trouvé* and the ready-made, such as Marcel Duchamp and Kurt Schwitters, ceases to be a means of representing reality, albeit in a "defamiliarized" fashion. Instead, it consists of one or several everyday, usually mass-produced objects dragged away from their habitual context and use-value and subsequently endowed with the status of an objet d'art by virtue of the artist's mere act of selection and arrangement.

Moving away from representation toward an art of presentation, Simic is primarily concerned with the various ways in which Cornell manipulates real objects in order to "abolish the separation between art and life" (*Dime-Store* 18). Commenting on Cornell's admiration for Houdini, Simic goes as far as reversing the process in suggesting that what we perceive as actually "there" can be as illusory as a product of the imagination: "Nature, too, makes fakes—. . . all these splendid sunsets are mere illusions and cannot be true of real objects and properties" (36). The essential question raised by this double blurring of accepted boundaries between the real and the imaginary is that of how the contemporary, postmimetic artist can possibly recover a sense of art's aesthetic relevance in the modern world. For Simic, the answer lies in one's capacity to "[see] poetry everywhere" (18), including in the most prosaic reality of our daily life. "Man," says Gérard de Nerval in "Divine Kaleidoscope," "has little by little destroyed and cut the eternal type of beauty into a thousand little pieces"; Cornell, Simic replies, "found them in the city and reassembled them" (22). Simic also calls on the spirit of Guillaume Appolinaire, who "spoke of a new source of inspiration: 'Prospectuses, catalogues, posters, advertisements of all sorts' which contain the poetry of our age" (18), and of Rimbaud ("Didn't he say he liked stupid paintings, signs, popular engravings, erotic books with bad spelling, novels of our grandmothers?"), who, according to Simic, "would have walked the length of Fourteenth Street and written many more 'Illuminations'" (21).

As for Simic's Cornell, he is the epitome of the Baudelairian *flâneur,* roaming the streets of Manhattan "in seeming idleness" (7). His mission as an artist is to make sense of the jolting, and often absurd, rhythms of the modern city, which Simic describes as a "labyrinth of analogies, the Symbolist forest of correspondences" (11). All this brings us back to Baudelaire's famous statement concerning his own perambulatory meditations in *Paris Spleen,* which he said arose from his familiarity with "the life of great cities, the confluence and interactions of the countless relationships within them" (*Spleen* 25). In the same way as chance encounters, trivial events, junk shops, and jumble sales were all grist to the mill of Cornell's visual hymns to the modern city ("the city has an infinite number of interesting objects in an infinite number of unlikely places" [*Dime-Store* 14]), Simic often allows himself to be surprised by the insignificant and the commonplace. Like Baudelaire and Joyce, he regards the city as a new spatial model for a redefinition of poetic form, which becomes a means of celebrating objects or events we tend to perceive as trivial or prosaic. "Poetry: three mismatched shoes at the entrance of a dark alley" (21), writes Simic, echoing Baudelaire's comparison between the modern poet and the ragman consulting "the archives of debauchery, the shambles of rubbish" and collecting "all that the great city has cast away, all that it has lost, all that it has disdained, all that it has shattered" (*Paradis* 74).

Dime-Store Alchemy contains many vivid scenes of urban life in which straightforward realism mixes with the oneiric and the surreal. The result is very much in the spirit of "fusion between the sordidly realistic and the phantasmagoric," which Eliot claimed to have inherited from Baudelaire (*Criticize* 126). In Simic's depiction of the "unreal city," however, the bitter, Laforguian irony and the metaphysical despair of Eliot's poems give way to an essentially ludic interest in the visual richness and the iconic luxuriance of the urban landscape. Far from the pale, disembodied personae that people Eliot's *Waste Land,* Simic's book tells us about the city's potential to conjure eccentric situations and comic characters, such as Cornell's great hero, Gérard de Nerval, who was "famous for promenading the streets of Paris with a live lobster on a leash" (7). Pondering upon one of Cornell's most famous collage-boxes, *Medici Slot Machine,* Simic writes:

> Outside the penny arcade blacks shine shoes, a blind man sells newspapers, young boys in tight jeans hold hands. Everywhere there are vending machines and they all have mirrors. The mad woman goes around scribbling on them with her lipstick. The vending machine is a tatooed bride.
>
> The boy dreams with his eyes open. An angelic image in the dark of the subway. The machine, like any myth, has heterogeneous parts. There must be gear wheels, cogs, and other clever contrivances attached to the crank. Whatever it is, it must be ingenious. Our loving gaze can turn it on. A poetry slot machine offering a jackpot of incommensurable meanings activated by our imagination. (26)

This passage underscores another important similarity between the Simic-Cornell vision of urban life and that of Baudelaire, who also conceived of art as a demiurgic force capable of transmuting the prosaic mud of the city into poetic gold. Simic's antipoetry, however, acknowledges the city itself as the supreme producer and converter of its own images: "A slot machine for the solitaries. Coins of reverie, of poetry, secret passion, religious madness, it converts them all. A force illegible" (28). After the "astonishing discovery that poetry can come out of chance operations," the role of the artist, who has become "an eccentric collector of sundry oddities" (28), is now to discover the seeds of a new mythology in the meanders of the modern city: "At 3 A.M. the gum machine on the deserted platform with its freshly wiped mirror is the new wonder-working icon of the Holy Virgin" (27). Cornell's art, however, is utterly devoid of the mysticism underlying the Symbolist theory of correspondences, which was aimed at unveiling analogical connections between the spiritual and the natural world. Indeed, Cornell, who was converted to Christian Science in the late 1920s, is a religious artist born into "a world in which old metaphysics and aesthetic ideas were eclipsed" (73). Like the "literal" objects and images contained in Simic's poems ("If I say 'rats in diapers' that's to be taken literally" [*Uncertain* 78]), Cornell's collage-boxes have therefore no symbolic or allegorical value, nor are they the key to some transcendental reality. They are "parts of the missing whole" (72), severed from their "original" context and use-value and subsequently reinscribed into the new imaginary narrative produced by the collage-box. In "Naked in Arcadia," for instance, Cornell's objects are regarded as so many residual traces of the postcultural palimpsest of the American nation. Here, as in many other poems, one cannot help but relate Simic's fascination with displaced objects to his own experience of physical, mental, and linguistic displacement as an immigrant to the United States and a poet/translator trying to make sense of the contingencies and contradictions of history:

The New World was already old for Poe. The lost paradise lost again. On a street of faded store signs, Berenice, where was she?

The Church of Divine Metaphysics, with its headquarters in a Bowery storefront, advertises funerals and marriages on a handwritten sign. Around the corner, Salvation Army Store and a junk shop.

America is a place where the Old World shipwrecked. Flea markets and garage sales cover the land. Here's everything the immigrants carried in their suitcases and bundles to these shores and their descendants threw out with the trash:

A pile of Greek 78 records with one Marika Papagika singing; a rubber-doll face of uncertain origin with teeth marks of a child or a small dog; sepia postcards of an unknown city covered with greasy fingerprints; a large empty jewel case lined with black velvet; a menu from a hotel in Palermo serving octopus; an old French book on astronomy with covers and title page missing; a yellowed photograph of a dead Chinese baby. (17)

In this democracy of objects, history itself loses a significant part of its cultural authority and is reduced to what Graham Hough, commenting on the eclecticism of modern poetry, has called "the limitless junk-shop of the past" (316). Far from deploring the demise of old, stable frames of cultural reference, Simic delights in emulating the luxuriant pastiches of Cornell's make-believe world, which tends to elude the distinction between the past and the present, the true and the false, the authentic and the fake. (Cornell baked his boxes to make them crack and look old; "forgers of antiquities," Simic writes, "lovers of time past, employ the same method" [61].) In many ways, Simic's imitations/appropriations of Cornell's collage technique are emblematic of the juxtaposition of ancient and modern, sacred and profane, mythic and trivial material (best represented by Cornell's *Medici Slot Machine*) that has characterized his prose poems since the iconographic *trompe l'oeil* of *The World Doesn't End*:

Scaliger turns deadly pale at the sight of watercress. Tucho Brahe, the famous astronomer, passes out at the sight of a caged fox. Maria de Medici feels instantly giddy on seeing a rose, even in a painting. My ancestors, meanwhile, are eating cabbage. They keep stirring the pot looking for a pigfoot which isn't there. The sky is blue. The nightingale sings in a Renaissance sonnet, and immediately goes to bed with a toothache. (*World* 4)

As some of the most successful poems here examined demonstrate, however, there is more to Simic's miniatures than a taste for iconoclastic pastiches and burlesque comedies of errors. Like Cornell's boxes, Simic's oneiric landscapes resemble childhood dreams in which "objects are renamed and invested with imaginary lives" (44). The prose poems of *The World Doesn't End* and *Dime-Store Alchemy* follow a principle reminiscent of Gaston Bachelard's definition of the miniature as method of psychological integration and a means of endowing "fake objects" with a "real psychological objectivity" (140). More generally, they aim at establishing emotionally and intellectually meaningful relationships between free-standing elements with a view to reconciling the self with the outside world:

> Inside everyone there are secret rooms. They're cluttered and the lights are out. There's a bed in which someone is lying with his face to the wall. In his head there are more rooms. In one, the venetian blinds shake in the approaching summer storm. Every once in a while an object on the table becomes visible: a broken compass, a pebble the color of midnight, an enlargement of a school photograph with a face in the back circled, a watch spring—each one of these items is a totem of the self. (62)

Like the lonely boy of "Postage Stamp with a Pyramid," who is seen kneeling on the floor between his parents' beds "pushing a matchbox, inside which he imagines himself sitting" (37), Simic's personae are "voyagers and explorers of their own solitudes" (73). Hence the importance of the empty spaces and silences framing Simic's short prose lyrics. Hence, also, Simic's dictum that "the commonplace is miraculous if rightly seen, if recognized" (18), a belief which constitutes the common denominator of Cornell's boxes as well as a major methodological premise of Simic's prose poems. Baudelaire—who, according to Walter Benjamin, began publishing at a time when "the climate for the lyric [had] become increasingly inhospitable" (109)—was the first to recognize the necessity to create a new poetic form in which to dramatize the most prosaic aspects of our everyday experience. In *Dime-Store Alchemy,* Simic turns to the prose poem for the opportunity it provides not only to "poeticize" the prosaic but also to bridge the gap between high and low culture, lyrical and critical discourses, and, ultimately, art and life. As the preceding chapters have shown, it is largely with reference to this dialogical confrontation between antipodal themes, functions, and registers that the prose poem has attempted to redefine the goals and methods of poetic form from Baudelaire to the present.

PART III

The Prose Poem
and the New Avant-Garde

6 · Rewriting the Sentence
Language Poetry and the New Prose Poem

Does language control like money?
Kathy Acker, *Empire of the Senseless*

In an essay that appeared in Ron Silliman's *In the American Tree* (probably the most representative and comprehensive anthology of Language poetry to date), Jackson Mac Low raises the issue of the elusiveness of the label "language-centered" as applied to himself and what is commonly perceived as an avant-gardist "school" of younger writers emerging in the early and mid-1970s: "The term 'language-centered' is ill chosen. The many works thrown under this rubric are no more 'centered in language' than a multitude of other literary works. Many depart from normal syntax. In many, what might be called 'subject matter' shifts rapidly. In some, such as many of my own, principles such as 'objective hazard,' 'indeterminacy,' and 'lessening of the dominance of the ego' may predominate over more usual concerns. But that a writer's efforts are ever 'centered in language' is highly dubious" (*Tree* 491). As Mac Low suggests, a single, monolithic definition of the "language-orientedness" of Language poetry could not possibly do justice to the multifaceted body of texts produced by writers associated with the "movement" (Silliman lists 79 poets who could have featured alongside the 39 writers represented in his anthology).[1] Nevertheless, the writers represented in Language anthologies such as Silliman's share a number of common objectives, including (Mac Low's objections notwithstanding) a conspicuous renewal of attention to "what a poem is actually made of—not images, not voices, not characters or plot, all of which appear on paper, or in one's mouth, only through the invocation of a specific medium, language itself" (xvi). More generally, the collective premises underlying the development of the movement (which have so far given birth to a polymorphous body of texts published in numerous specialized magazines, small presses, talk series, and other collective projects explicitly or implicitly associated with the "Language" label) bring out a number of broadly shared aesthetic, theoretical, and ultimately political concerns signaling their breakaway from the mainstream of contemporary

American poetry.² These broadly shared concerns include a critique of referentiality, a rejection of the norms of the plainspoken "voice" lyric, and a conviction that theory is central to and even inseparable from the writing of poetry. Lastly, Language poetry also proposes new compositional methods that invite the reader to participate in the creation of meaning and are meant to hold out the prospect of new social and political possibilities for poetry.

Ron Silliman's Marxist appraisal of the commodification of language and literature in capitalist society provides us with a useful starting point for an understanding of the specifically leftist critique inspiring, directly or indirectly, the creative and critical work of many Language poets. In an essay entitled "Disappearance of the Word, Appearance of the World," Silliman argues that one of the most important consequences of "the subjection of writing to the social dynamics of capitalism" is its repression of what he calls the "gestural" quality of linguistic production, by which he means "that which serves solely to mark the connection between the product and its maker" (*Sentence* 9). Clearly, for Silliman, the reification or "fetishization" of language into a commodity—whether it manifests itself in so-called fictional realism, daily journalism, display advertising, or product packaging—is a political as well as a linguistic issue. Implicitly drawing on an Althusserian notion of the discursive foundations of ideology, Silliman then goes on to say that the fetishization of signified constructions severed from the social locus of their production (or, in Marxist terms, the labor process which brings them into being) is a means for the dominant power to pass off its ideological foundations as "natural" and "inevitable" realities. In this way, the sociopolitical Establishment constantly confirms its own hegemony through language:

> Words not only find themselves attached to commodities, they *become* commodities and, as such, take on the "mystical" and "mysterious character" Marx identified as the commodity fetish: torn from any tangible connection to their human makers, they appear instead as independent objects active in a universe of similar entities, a universe prior to, and outside, any agency by a perceiving Subject. A world whose inevitability invites acquiescence. Thus capitalism passes on its preferred reality through language itself to individual speakers. And, in so doing, necessarily effaces that original connecting point to the human, the perceptible presence of the signifier, the mark or sound, in the place of the signified. (*Sentence* 8)

In the field of literary production and reception, Silliman traces back the obliteration of the "gestural" quality of the literary work to a number of gradual economic and technological changes. The printing press and the standardization of spelling, for instance, were followed by a crucial "division of labor in language" and an increasingly alienated relationship between authors, their works, and their audience (41). The advent of mechanical reproduction also radically modified the status of the literary artifact, which from then on was bound to be both perceived and produced as an "independent" and, above all, autonomously consumable commodity, rather than in relation to the social and economic surrounding of the "perceiving Subject."[3]

In the more specific domain of modern poetry, another crucial factor Silliman mentions is the disappearance of a certain "meaningless" aspect of rhyme, which he sees as epitomized by John Skelton's doggerel verse. This nonreferential character of rhyme, which is lost in most contemporary poetry, used to foreground the *physical* quality of the poem as opposed to its semantic or syntactic orientation.[4] According to Silliman, these aesthetic and technological changes have contributed to a general "anaesthetic transformation of the perceived tangibility of the word" (10) brought about by the passage of language into a capitalist stage of development.

As already suggested, an important consequence of the prevalence of signified elements of language—and the accompanying repression of all traces of the "gesturality" of a literary work—is that its referential powers can be used with a view to legitimizing a certain socioeconomic Establishment. With the rise of the bourgeoisie, Silliman argues, "the expressive gestural, labor-product nature of consciousness tends to be repressed." Such is the overall disguised effect, for instance, of fictional realism, in which "under the sway of the commodity fetish, language itself appears to become transparent, a mere vessel for the transfer of ostensibly autonymous referents" (11). The seeming "transparency" of the language used by a political (or literary) Establishment to speak and write itself into dominance proceeds by developing fixed referential relationships between language and the particular reality it is supposed to "familiarize" and legitimize, while concealing its actual social and political foundations.

In view of the relationship between transformations taking place within the economic infrastructure and their impact on the social, political, and intellectual superstructures, and considering what he perceives as an increasingly conspicuous fetishization of linguistic production in capitalist societies (in this particular perspective, *media capitalism* may be a more appropriate term for the current postindustrial techniques of dissemination of information), Silliman calls for a poetry that "can work to search out the preconditions of a liberated social fact" and, therefore,

> requires (1) recognition of the historic nature and structure of referentiality, (2) placing the issue of language, the repressed signifier, at the center of the program, and (3) placing the program into the context of conscious class struggle. (17–18)

The main purpose of this chapter is to investigate the specific nature of this increasing interest in the "repressed signifier" and how this feature relates to the recent proliferation of prose poems by writers who have appeared in so-called Language poetry anthologies and magazines since the mid-1970s.[5] I give special attention to the various ways in which the issue of referentiality characterizes the Language poets' relationship to the history of the American prose poem and accounts for their specific interest in prose syntax and generic subversion. The various terms in which a poetry centered on language and the repressed signifier can or cannot address social conditions as such, as well as the extent to which the third phase of Silliman's mini-manifesto can actually be fulfilled, are also studied in some detail.

The Material Signifier

The difference between a short story and a paragraph. There is none.
Gertrude Stein, *How to Write*

The programmatic aesthetics developed by Ron Silliman and other prominent Language poets–theorists such as Bruce Andrews, Charles Bernstein, Bob Perelman, and Barrett Watten are best understood if one considers briefly the larger aesthetic context out of which such a movement emerged. Outside the world of poetry writing, some of the basic premises of Language poetry's emphasis on the repressed signifier were already "in the air" a decade before its adherents started to publish their first books. In the field of music, for instance, an indirect but highly influential precedent was John Cage's early experimentation with nonintentional procedures and his introduction of random noises into the musical space. The aesthetic philosophy of John Cage was based on the necessity to "unfocus" the spectator's mind from the potential creation of meaning and establish a new relationship between the audience and their acoustic environment, one in which the material and the process of sound production or "performance" is more important than what it may or may not refer to: "New music; new listening. Not an attempt to understand something that is being said, for, if something were being said, the sounds would be given the shapes of words. Just an attention to the activity of sounds" (*Silence* 10).

Cage's interest in the concreteness of the sonic unit directly anticipates the Language poets' celebration of the "material signifier" and their appeal for a poetry underlining the object-status of the word while minimizing its referential role. (As pointed out by George Hartley, there are a number of earlier precedents, including the work of Objectivist poets Louis Zukofsky and George Oppen, the nonsense poetry of French Dadaist Tristan Tzara, and the areferential word play or *zaum* poetry of Russian Futurists Velimir Khlebnikov and Alexei Kruchonykh.)[6] Cage's controversial foregrounding of "the activity of sounds" has, of course, no direct equivalent in literature, since the production of language—unlike that of music—bears in itself the marks of its meaning-directed or "instrumental" orientation. Still, the abstract, *zaum*like typographical shapes of David Melnick are probably as close as a two-dimensional printed poem can get to Cage's "unintentional," silence-interrupted live noises:

> thoeisu
>
> thoiea
> akcorn woi cirtus locqvump
> icgja
> cvmwoflux
> epaosieusl
> ~~cirtus locquvmp~~
> a nex macheisoa
> (*Tree* 90)

The so-called poetics of nonintentionality inaugurated in the 1950s by John Cage's music composed by chance operations was extended, in the early 1960s, to poetry writing, by Jackson Mac Low and later Cage himself. The (highly regulated) aleatory dynamics Cage and Mac Low advocated are still shunned by many Language poets, who tend to put the emphasis on *controlling* the compositional process rather than leaving it, at least in part, to chance. Nevertheless, some of the theoretical fragments collected in Cage's introduction to *Themes and Variations* clearly echo several basic premises of Language poetry. Besides a will to "let sounds be sounds" (621) and preserve the "anonymity or selflessness of work (i.e., not self-expression)" (622), the stray axioms underlying Cage's project, including a belief in a poetry focused on "process instead of object," "activity, not communication," are at the heart of the work of the poets discussed in the present chapter. As we will see, Cage's assertion that "the practicality of changing society derives from the possibility of changing the mind" (623) is also a basic methodological principle of the sociolinguistic politics of the Language movement.

In the world of painting and sculpture, Minimal art (which flourished in the 1960s, when most Language poets were at the start of their careers) was another determining influence. The Minimalists' attempts to redefine accepted ideas about space, shape, scale, and, more largely, the borderline between art and non-art (a borderline ultimately denied by the advent of found art and *musique concrète*) logically led artists to reconsider their relationship to the very material that brings "art" into being—a notion the Minimalists themselves had inherited from the experiments of the Russian Constructivist school. By seeming stripped of all decorative, metaphorical, or simply referential value, Richard Serra's Arte Povera–inspired *Belts* (1966–67)—a series of tangled clusters of vulcanized rubber strips illuminated by a curl of neon tubing—or the sculptures of Robert Morris—which often consist of industrial or building materials such as plywood, steel, or fiberglass—force the viewer to pay attention to the concrete material itself, as opposed to what these arrangements are supposed to represent or "stand for." Many Minimalist artists therefore favored anonymous surfaces or "pure," self-referential geometrical figures utterly deprived of any figurative connotation. In addition to bringing the material signifier of art into the limelight, Minimalism thus implicitly proclaimed the obsolescence of a number of categories traditionally associated with artistic creation. Until then undisputed principles such as a conception of art as a means of (self-)expression or the notion of "personal style" were increasingly supplanted, if not denied, by the supremacy of the material signifier. The work of Language poet Robert Grenier reflects a similar attempt to keep the reader's attention focused on the isolated shape of the words themselves. Grenier's *Sentences* is a boxed collection of five hundred short poems, each of which is no longer than a few words, printed on unnumbered five-by-eight-inch index cards with no indication of a chronological sequence or a general context. The conspicuous absence of a fixed referent and an expressive, "lyric" origin—such as the poet's desire to express his or her thoughts or feelings—resists the emergence of a single, unitary meaning beyond the self-sufficient materiality of Grenier's fragments:

TWELVE VOWELS
breakfast
the sky flurries

       stepping through the water to the rocks

POPLARS
facing away

       s o m e o l d g u y s w i t h s c y t h e s

BIRD
one two
three four
five six seven eight nine ten eleven

The advent of Conceptual aesthetics in the late 1960s further contributed to a delineation of a new physical relationship of both the artist and
the viewer to the art object. The Minimalists' deconstruction of the validity
of the traditional idea of art and its referential value paved the way for the
works of Douglas Huebler or Joseph Kosuth, in which physical form, however, became less and less essential, as the "concept" (which the Conceptualists considered as both the starting point and the ultimate goal of a work
of art) was more efficiently conveyed by means of documents, maps, film
and video, and above all language itself. Given its lack of interest in the
"physical" or extraconceptual manifestations of the work of art, Conceptual art, even more than Minimalism, became increasingly dependent on
critical theory to justify its own existence. A submovement such as the
British-based Art & Language group, which presented art theory itself as a
form of Conceptual art, further deadlocked the increasingly symbiotic relationship of art and theory into a state of maximum homogeneity. Kosuth's
First Investigations (1965)—a series which includes photographic enlarge-
ments of dictionary definitions of words such as *water, meaning,* and
idea—is emblematic of how Conceptual art, by employing language itself
as its medium, also sets out to foreground the discursive aspect of "artness"
in order to question the ways in which art conventionally acquires meaning
and consuming-value: the works of Kosuth and many other Conceptualists
suggest that a work of art always already depends on a statement declaring
its status as a work of art.[7] As we will see, even though Language poetry

often differs from Conceptual art in giving priority, like the Minimalists, to the material "physicalness" of language, it nevertheless shares the Conceptualists' interest in theory as a creative practice and in the various social, political, cultural, and economic contexts and discourses through which art is defined and, subsequently, consumed.

Writing and Scripturality

Robert Grenier's "On Speech," which appeared in 1971 in the first issue of the magazine *This,* is one of the earliest published débuts of what was later to be called the Language movement. "I HATE SPEECH," Grenier's lapidary finale to his essay, has since been heralded as the Language poets' declaration of independence from Charles Olson's speech-based poetics. This deliberately provocative statement (with its tongue-in-cheek use of capital letters, one of Olson's typographical favorites) raises the issue of the ambivalent position of Language poetry toward the poetic modes advocated by its immediate predecessors. More particularly, it is symptomatic of the methodological choices that prompted the Language poets' systematic redefinition of poetry out of an essentially speech-based art into a primarily *scriptural* practice. The Language poets' rejection of the so-called voice poem heralded by the "New American poetry" of the 1950s and 1960s—itself largely a reaction against the elitist premises and the stylistic sophistication of modernist aesthetics—has been aptly characterized by Ron Silliman as "a complex call for a projective verse that could, in the same moment, 'proclaim an abhorrence of "speech"'" (*Tree* xv). The Language movement's love-hate relationship with Olson's free verse indeed largely comes down to an overall adherence to the Projectivist notion of the poem as an expansive, organic form—an "open field" in progress as opposed to what Olson perceived as the customary non-Projective "closed forms" of the printed poem—and a simultaneous rejection of Olson's speech-based poetics and its emphasis on the line as a unit of "breathing" rather than syntax. Swerving away from Olson's speech- and breath-oriented poetics, many Language poets indeed seek to rethink the Projectivists' open field into a new basis for an essentially scriptural art. This is true not only of David Melnick's and Hannah Weiner's *zaum*like experiments with typographical disruptions and neoconcrete poetry but also, as we will see, of Lyn Hejinian's free verse in *Writing Is an Aid to Memory.*[8]

The "disjuncted" free verse experiments of Lyn Hejinian, Bruce Andrews, and other Language poets emerge as a continuation of Olson's own revision of the form into an open field, with its (partial) eradication of the justified left margin, while depending all the more heavily on their visual realization on the page.[9] The exploded syntax that characterizes the work of many Language poets also indirectly signals their self-avowed rejection of the identification of poetic language with the poet's voice; a feature which underlies, of course, not only Olson's Projectivist project but also the history of Western poetry as a whole, from Sappho to Lowell and beyond. Indeed, what makes such works as Hejinian's "Writing Is an Aid to Memory" different from even the most experimental kinds of "free verse" published in the United States in the second half of this century is that they breach the kind of free-flowing, breath-patterned rhythms so characteristic of most American poetry and largely relying on the Romantic conception of the poetic work as a self-present and "natural" utterance (what Wordsworth called "the spontaneous overflow of powerful feelings"). Such a "vocal" definition of poetry is advocated not only by the Romantic poets themselves but also by several generations of contemporary American poets, in forms from Carl Sandburg's Whitmanesque chants to Charles Olson's breath-oriented poetics, Frank O'Hara's "personism," or Allen Ginsberg's speech-based bardic ecstasies.

Although one could argue that the primacy of writing over speech itself further diminishes what Silliman calls the gestural aspect of the poem (Olson's speech-oriented poetics had at least the merit of foregrounding the position of the poet as the *producer* of the poem), the Language poets' interest in the scripturality of writing can be seen as a means of updating our conception of the role of language (via mechanical or, more recently, electronic reproduction) as a mediating agency between contemporary writers and their work.[10] In this sense, for all their avant-gardist ambitions, the Language poets' concern with the materiality of language and the process of writing is ultimately an attempt to keep up with the times.[11] In this context, Jacques Derrida's critique of Western metaphysics of presence in *Of Grammatology* offers another seminal model by which to appraise Language poetry's radical breakaway from traditional vocal conceptions of poetry. According to Derrida, Western culture, from Plato to Freud, has privileged voice as the supreme medium of thought, thereby dismissing writing as a derivative or "contaminated" form of speech and a further form of alienating mediation between meaning and the producer of meaning. Such an opposition, Derrida argues, is based on a set of false, "phonocentric" assumptions regarding the status of the spoken word as a self-present and self-conscious form of expression closer to an originating thought—or "transcendental signifier"—than is the written word. Derrida's theory of Western logocentrism is particularly appropriate as applied to the history of poetry, which, more than any other literary genre, has often relied on a radical claim to unmediated plenitude and a desire to convey words coming from the poet's "true" or "real" being. The Language poets' deliberate privileging of the graphic and scriptural strategies of poetry writing appears as the ultimate deconstruction of such lyric presence. By emphasizing the materiality of the writing process, Language writing deliberately undermines the phonocentric assumption that poets (or any other speaking subjects) can spontaneously express themselves and use language as if it were a transparent medium for their innermost thoughts and feelings. As is clear from the poems quoted, the main emphasis is now instead precisely on the "contaminating" mediation of writing, as well as on the inherent self-limitations of language as a referential tool and the subsequent alienation of writers from their own discourse.

The New Prose Poem

As a result of its basic distrust of the speech-based assumptions behind most contemporary American poetry, Language poetry has developed two apparently antithetical structural and typographical directions. The great majority of poets associated, willingly or not, with the Language movement still continue to write free verse in order to release Olson's organic open field from its speech-based assumptions and subject it to new uses. The same poets, however, often use the prose poem as a means of redefining the goals and methods of poetic language. Indeed, the notion of poetry as a scriptural art and medium also applies to what Ron Silliman calls the "New Prose Poem," thereby referring to his own creative prose and that of most poets commonly associated with the Language movement. In his introduction to *In the American Tree*, Silliman distinguishes the so-called New Prose Poem from the short narratives and neo-Surrealist fables that characterize the "mainstream" of the contemporary American prose poem. "In the sense familiar to us from French modernism," he writes, "there are no prose poems here. And, beyond organization into paragraphs, these works share little with the dramatic monologues and short stories that characterize other recent prose writing by American poets" (*Tree* xvii).

By contrast, the syntactic dynamics of Silliman's "New Sentence" are directly inspired by the work of Gertrude Stein, who has often been acknowledged as a "precursor" of Language poetry.[12] Before we move to Silliman's New Prose Poem and its poetics of the New Sentence, Stein's own prose poems, collected in *Tender Buttons,* should be briefly reexamined.

The following description of "colored hats" is typical of the resistance of Stein's "poetic" language to the taken-for-granted transparency of mimetic prose:

COLORED HATS

Colored hats are necessary to show that curls are worn by an addition of blank spaces, this makes the difference between single lines and broad stomachs, the least thing is lightening, the least thing means a little flower and a big delay a big delay that makes more nurses than little women really little women. So clean is a light that nearly all of it shows pearls and little ways. A large hat is tall and me and all custard whole. (*Look* 172–73)

As we have seen, Stein's still life introduces ambiguity into the signifying chain even as it pretends to create conventionally hypotactic sentences. Despite the overall "abstractness" of Stein's prose, the persistence of conventional syntactic links indeed maintains a semblance of descriptive coherence and logical argumentation. This illusion of unproblematic referentiality, however, is irremediably shattered by the apparent nonsense of the description itself, which draws our attention to the artificiality of analytical and utilitarian prose: Stein's prose defies interpretation precisely because it undermines our attempts to construe it into a meaningful whole by virtue of its relative syntactic orthodoxy. Ultimately, the ironic tension between the definitional impulse announced in the title and the semantic elusiveness of the "definition" itself insists on the impossibility of producing a single, definitive representation of its object.

This ambiguous and partial resistance of the sign to its own propensity to "refer" or be construed into "referring" is undoubtedly what Jacques Derrida is alluding to, when, discussing Mallarmé's brief prose piece "Mimique," he describes the poet's syntax as an unprecedented break with the Platonic notion of mimesis:

We are faced then with mimicry imitating nothing: faced, so to speak, with a double that doubles no simple, a double that nothing anticipates, nothing at least that is not itself already double. There is no simple reference. . . . In this speculum with no reality, in this mirror of a mirror, a difference or dyad exists, since there are mimes or phantoms. But it is a difference without reference, or rather a reference without a referent, without any first or last unit, a ghost that is the phantom of no flesh, wandering about without a past, without any death, birth, or presence.

Mallarmé thus preserves the differential structure of mimicry or mimesis, but without its Platonic or metaphysical interpretation, which implies that somewhere the being of something that *is,* is being imitated. (*Dissemination* 206)

What Mallarmé is, in fact, denying is not the principle of reference as such but the Platonic assumption that words should refer to (or "imitate") a self-present reality external to the poem. As we will see, Derrida's image of the "mirror of a mirror"—a self-devouring mise en abyme of the mimetic impulses of language—suggests that Mallarmé anticipates the elaborate form of textual self-reference (as well as the consequent substitution of *différance* for reference) advocated by the Language poets. Like Mallarmé's "Mimique," Stein's poetry, far from rejecting the concept of referentiality, tends to "imitate" the very process of (self-referentiality) generating the "meaning" of a text and to turn it, so to speak, into its own subject matter. In other words, the poem ceases to be about something that it is supposed to represent and becomes, instead, a text about the means and limits of textual representation itself.

Like many other Language poets, Ron Silliman shares Stein's skepticism about the "naturalness" of descriptive and argumentative syntax and of the implicit relationship of language to reference sustained by "the simple, seemingly obvious concept that words should derive from speech and refer to things" (*Tree* xvi). In an essay originally published in the spring 1980 issue of *Hills,* Silliman lists the qualities of the New Sentence—his alternative to the referential strategies of conventional mimetic or narrative prose—as follows:

(1) The paragraph organizes the sentences;
(2) The paragraph is a unity of quantity, not logic or argument;
(3) Sentence length is a unit of measure;
(4) Sentence structure is altered for torque, or increased polysemy/ ambiguity;
(5) Syllogistic movement is: (a) limited; (b) controlled;
(6) Primary syllogistic movement is between the preceding and following sentences;
(7) Secondary syllogistic movement is toward the paragraph as a whole, or the total work;
(8) The limiting of syllogistic movement keeps the reader's attention

at or very close to the level of language, that is, most often at the sentence level or below. (*Sentence* 91)

In considering the paragraph and the sentence as quantitative units, Silliman's Stein-inspired manifesto of the New Sentence (the main influence here is Stein's chapter "Sentences and Paragraphs" in *How to Write* [1931]) signals a radical break from previous compositional methods even within the tradition of the American prose poem (with the usual exception of Gertrude Stein).[13] The following extract from Kit Robinson's "Verdigris," a prose poem characteristically divided into paragraphs of more or less equal length, is a typical example of the new compositional syntax inaugurated by the New Prose Poem:

> The sign is a raw shape. People river. Space lights up the porch. Dust clouds the window. Ashes break down into sky. A bird flies parallel to slope of roof. Wires hang at a like angle. Comings and goings are frozen in the new room. Wind rooms in the street. Business gets complete thoughts down on tape.

> Writing breaks off at mid-letter. Sound resumes. Shirttail. Waves heap themselves at your stone feet. The life of facts is undone in a day. That it organizes itself to work will identify the formality of the office. Three girls unite against a midsection. Paste-on stars glow in the dark. Bare legs, asleep on the floor. (69)

In Robinson's "Verdigris," the relationships of contiguity, which according to Jakobson's bipolar model facilitate the grammatical integration of discrete narrative and descriptive elements, are systematically interrupted and deviated by the caesurae between the sentences. In the absence of explicit syntactic links between the sentences or an overall referential or contextual focus (such as could be deduced from what the poem "signifies" as a whole), the connections the reader can make both between the sentences within each paragraph and between the paragraphs and the "total work" can only be tentative and partially realized. For Silliman, the New Sentence has assimilated the disruptive and separating effect of rhyme and line breaks at the level of the sentence, as "the torquing which is normally triggered by linebreaks, the function of which is to enhance ambiguity and polysemy, has now moved directly into the grammar of the sentence" (*Sentence* 90). This limiting (or "torquing") of the syllogistic movement of prose has the effect of constantly forcing the reader to consider the sentences and paragraphs as so many relatively autonomous units, the semantic potential of which does not depend on a particular "logical" (one might add narrative, metaphorical, or emotive) sequence. As we will see further on, the syntactic indeterminacy of the New Sentence also stresses the role of the reader in, so to speak, bridging the gap where the absent syllogism might have been.

The New Narrative

Another striking aspect of a poem such as Robinson's "Verdigris" is the absence of narrative line or sequence by which to make sense of the poem as a whole. If a good deal of Language poetry grew out of a radical critique of dominant models of syntactic linearity, this critique also extends to conventional narrative strategies, which, most Language poets argue, should be replaced by new structural and procedural principles no longer meant to construct an imaginary, extratextual "plot" (or even a character or persona) but focusing, instead, on the "real" circumstances of (and impediments to) the writing process. As Bob Perelman has written: "[Language] writing does not concern itself with narrative in the conventional sense. Story, plot, any action outside the syntactic and tonal actions of the words is seen as secondary. Attempts to posit an idealized narrative time would only blur perception of the actual time of writing and reading. Persona, Personism, the poem as trace of the poet-demiurge—these, too, are now extraneous" (*Tree* 489).

The following six paragraphs, taken from Silliman's *Paradise,* illustrate such an attempt to redefine narrative through an investigation of the potential of the New Sentence for syntactic and semantic polysemy:

> Out behind the diner the empty plastic trash can releases its thick, sour smell into the morning air. Or outside of a bakery at dawn. Running on both ends. I wouldn't return there to live. The weekend storm had cleaned the air. The weakened storm dissolved. A state of perpetual sweating tasted sweet.
>
> The definition of a pencil. Coin Wash and Dry. The fireman in front of the station on a hot day. He searches the aisle for the penny he dropped. A Cross pen you twist to write with (not this). Designs on lace curtains.
>
> The sun shapeless in the muzzy air. The three small clumps of eucalyptus on the top of the hill, where even the city had refused to build more housing projects, reinforced the barren air. Across the bay, where Oakland should have been. But over Glen Park the fog in

thick gray slabs. The air in my hair (drying it after a shower). Red feet of a pigeon. The roofers set up their pulley. So hot that she put a towel over the plastic seat before she climbed into the truck in her cutoffs. The truck in her cutoffs. Now one of the lowriders at the gym has made a sauna suit from a trashbag. I set the weight at 90 lbs and do 15 reps. He dresses like a lawyer but works in a thrift shop. She sits up and her breasts settle. The rest of the day is a cinch. I can still make out the logo of the Girl Scouts on that cookie on the sidewalk. Then we began to wonder if the bus would ever emerge from the projects. Then it did. Marat's tub was his ship of state. The mailman neglects to close the garden gate. We wander into work a little late. The prose was in the rhythm.

Donor list. The heat of morning, the weight of the sky. Stars fade at dawn rise. The size of the truck by the squeal of its brakes. Spots of brown about the peel of the banana. The luxury of thought. This was a reader-potential sentence. School bus yellow. Stanza's pansies. A break exists between etymology and connotation. The Columbus Day parade marching through Chinatown. Rolled down, metal curtains simplify store fronts. Must be farsighted by the way she holds that book.

Five minutes down. Boysenberry yogurt. Alternate spelling. The large bowl of his stomach made for a sloping desk. A mean-spiritedness to the humor of the comic poet. Just us chickens, classicly trained. Now that she's making 25 thou. A jolting bus impossible to write on. What I wish to say, dear reader, take off your blouse. April, turning toward November. Suggested denotation. An old stuffed chair on the sidewalk in the rain. Caution: frequent stops.

Exhaustion, a kind of freedom, sets in (a new pen). The nose runs, not unlike an engine, a jogger. A complex form of information called a potato. Even the simplest word is sometimes foreign. A balding woman. Trying to look punk, working in a bank. His vowels were dreamlike and indulgent. The cars occur in all colors. Eigner's noun. Dogs dogs dogs. Over the years, counting the little businesses that have gone into that storefront. Limbs off a tree stuffed into a garbage truck. Foundation in the weeds of a vacant lot. (42–45)

Silliman's poem evidently lacks the traditional elements of linearity, plot, or characterization underlying conventional narrative, whether of the fictional or the poetic variety. This is not to say, however, that the poem is entirely devoid of elements conveying a sense of unity or even closure. In

the first paragraph, for instance, several alliterations, assonances, and repetitions (including the pun on "weekend" and "weakened") establish phonetic links between the isolated sentences by creating a sense of relative
continuity or "flow." Also, and even though the situations and events described are by no means clearly defined, a general "setting" or "atmosphere" nevertheless emerges at the first reading; one that comprises,
among other things, the "sour smell" of the "empty plastic trash can" (or
is it coming from the bakery mentioned in the second sentence, or from
both?), a "weakened storm" (which is also likely to leave its own particular
kind of sour smell in the air), and an overall feeling of oppressive dampness
(or is it the "muzzy air" mentioned at the beginning of the third paragraph?).

The essential difference between these "unifying" principles and those
one would find in a more conventional narrative, or even in the syncopated
associational jumps of so-called stream-of-consciousness fiction, is that
they seem to arise mainly from the process of composition itself, rather
than from a preordained order or "grand design" to which the poem as a
whole might tend. This impression is reinforced by the many explicit references to the act of writing, which give the whole an air of self-reflexiveness
typical of many other New Prose Poems in which the author sees to it that
readers experience the poem as if it were being written in front of their eyes.
While Silliman's mention of the "jolting bus impossible to write on" and
the new pen he uses to start the last paragraph point to the difficulty of
poetic composition, his invitation to the reader to "take off your blouse"
and, above all, his allusion to the "reader-potential sentence" overtly attempt to draw the reader into the very heart of the poem to partake in the
act of poetic creation.

Despite the unusual lack of narrative, contextual, or even imagistic coherence in the traditional sense, Silliman's *Paradise* manages to create an
extremely vivid and successful picture of contemporary America, or rather
a series of snaps, that is anything but abstract or areferential. The numerous icons of Americanness—from the yellow school bus and the Columbus
Day parade to the gym cutoffs and the Boysenberry yogurt—scattered in
the different paragraphs contribute to sketching out an endless number of
vignettes of everyday life in the city. Indeed, self-contained, isolated sentences like "the sun shapeless in the muzzy air" or "the fireman in front of
the station on a hot day" (one is reminded here of the austere sharpness of
George Oppen's early city fragments in *Discrete Series*) turn Silliman's
poem into a kind of semiotic enquiry into life in contemporary urban

America in a format which is as close as a poem can get to a sequence of collaged cinematic shots. Once again, however, Silliman does not confine himself to listing a series of isolated symptoms of Americanness but suggests several ill-defined narrative lines extending beyond the scope of the individual sentence. In the course of the last three paragraphs, for example, it gradually becomes clear that the author (or "writer") is traveling on the bus he had been waiting for for some time and is overhearing bits of conversations ("Now that she's making 25 thou") while sitting at a window and watching life go by in blurred fragments.

The social conditions of postindustrial city, including urban blight (in the form of housing development and environmental pollution), class consciousness ("He dresses like a lawyer but works in a thrift shop"; "Trying to look punk, working in a bank"), and the precariousness of low-budget free enterprise ("Over the years, counting the little businesses that have gone into that storefront") are also given special attention. Another metaphor pervading the whole poem is that of trash—not just as an omnipresent element in the concrete surroundings described in the poem but also, so to speak, as a way of life in its own right. From the empty plastic trash can of the first paragraph to the trashbag ironically recycled into a "sauna suit" by one of the visitors to the gymnasium and, later, the "limbs of a tree stuffed into a garbage truck," Silliman's ironically named *Paradise* creates a preapocalyptic image of contemporary throwaway America, one in which the logic of commodity and garbage production (which is further illustrated by the "old stuffed chair on the sidewalk in the rain") has been definitely interiorized and naturalized into the most seemingly innocuous details of everyday life.

As suggested, Silliman's systematic dismantling of narrative conventions goes hand in hand with an all-devouring questioning of the very act of writing, which deprives these conventions of their taken-for-granted referential and linearizing power. By constantly drawing the reader's attention to the "contaminating" mediation of writing, the New Prose Poem also implicitly expands the issue of the relationship of writing to its presumed object or "referent" to the uneasy relationships between the narrating I—or producer of the written artifact—and his or her narrative avatars. Indeed, the multiple mises en abyme of the compositional process ultimately undermine the transitiveness of language at the same time as they destroy the double illusion of the narrator as the self-present origin and raison d'être of writing (what Perelman called "Personism, the poem as a trace of the poet-demiurge"). This last stage of such metascriptural self-reflexive-

ness necessarily threatens to lead to a structural and epistemological aporia. Silliman's narrative indeed tends to become a narrative about the creation (or the impossibility) of narrative itself.

Yet, if many writers of New Prose Poems share a common concern with
the actual activity of writing, they also refuse to resign themselves to a
nihilistic demystification of the structural and generative principles of narrative. Instead, they prefer to consider the result of their own deconstructive practice as only the beginning of new creative potentialities. In
this sense, the focus on writing itself, released from its historically accepted
associations with its producer and its object, gives rise to a different conception of writing as *practice,* while instoring different interactive operations between the text and its reader. As was suggested earlier in the context of Stein's *Tender Buttons,* Robinson's "Verdigris," and Silliman's
Paradise, the deliberate erasure of standard syntactic progression, normal
relations of time and space, or explicit frames of reference to a world "outside" the text forces readers to "make sense" of the poem by digging into
their own associative and interpretative competence, rather than merely
subscribing to a predetermined model of narrative or syntactic procedures.
Clark Coolidge's long prose sequence, *Weathers,* is an example of how the
critique of reference and normative syntax that characterizes Silliman's
New Sentence can produce a writing that, rather than being written by
somebody or about something, seemingly tends to "write itself":

> Lightful overcoat. Must be boning up on tieless affronts the comb
> ranges. Oversaw his dots backhanding berries while clot erect. Of a
> strew placed beyond the beakless bark scatter. This is pulp afternoon.
> Shoes to the grain offhand in spotlit breakfast nook. Places his starts
> off by lacing rods into coal swarm a cone eye view of the ricket vista.
> A brewer based on ice. Leafed up the nose in a capsule plot ascent.
> Nods to cleavage bugs of a scarlet, intermittent tinkle. The chimes of
> robes on the steeples of the mountains. His trombone marine and
> numb there. A shrug that would melt a pyramid, flash plasma, trigger
> its bolts. As with buttons their overcoats, stepped off, the day the
> earth stood still. (*Tree* 264)

The text's resistance to conventional or, more largely, normative syntagmatic links between and within the sentences or phrases—and between
the paragraphs within the sequence of poems as a whole—is an invitation
to the reader to complete and rewrite them into endless syntactic and narrative interpretations.[14] The absence (or, at least, the limited presence) of

normative or prescriptive elements is typical of much language-oriented poetry, in that it does not force the reader into a restrictive paradigmatic frame of reference. On a metaphorical level, the sequence of "images" refuses to yield to any ultimate interpretation and allows for a polysemy of semantic associations. The "increased polysemy" of Silliman's New Sentence becomes here an all the more crucial objective of language-oriented writing, its critique of "one-to-one" relations between words and their "objects" ultimately leading to a proliferation of referential vectors by which to create new conditions for a cognitive approach to language and the creation of meaning. As Charles Bernstein reminds us, dodging accusations of the murder of the referent:

> Not "death" of the referent—rather a recharged use of the multivalent referential vectors that any word has, how words in combination tone and modify the associations made for each of them, how "reference" then is not a one-to-one relation to an object but a perceptual dimension that closes in to pinpoint, nail down (*this* word), sputters omnitropically (the in in the which of who where what wells), refuses the build up of image track/projection while, pointillistically, fixing a reference at each turn (fills vats ago lodges spire), or, that much rarer case (Peter Inman's *Platin* and David Melnick's *Pcoet* two recent examples) of "zaum" (so-called transrational, pervasively neologistic) —"ig ok aberflappi"—in which reference, deprived of its automatic reflex reaction of word/stimulus image/response roams over the range of associations suggested by the word, word shooting off referential vectors like the energy field in a Kirlian photograph. (*Content* 34–35)

As a result of this diminishing of normative frames of reference and the consequent explosion of associational energy, the readers of a language-oriented poem are theoretically able to construct their own imaginary hypertexts in which they can freely redistribute "meaning" in a personal, "writerly" fashion. The analogy with computerized syntax reminds us that the Language poets' generation (most of them are now in their early fifties) is the first to have been directly exposed to the change in the technological environment brought about by the electronic computer. Like the hypertextual strategies of computer language (in many ways an extension of Barthes' "writerliness" along the syntagmatic axis), the "non-sequential" narratives of the Language group are at once highly disrupted and highly organized.

At this point, one may object that a certain amount of nostalgia for linearity and referentiality, involving a number of residual needs on the part of the reader to rewrite the isolated fragments into a meaningful totality, may diminish the actual potential for "writerliness" of so-called asyntactic or areferential poems. In *Weathers,* the presence of a high degree of alliteration (a feature recurrent in the work of many other Language poets), a quite unexpected resurgence of prosodic qualities in a text apparently so remote from traditional metrics, already suggests that the reader's "reading" of Coolidge's text—for all its real or apparent "writerly flexibility"—is still subjected, at least in part, to a general, subsyntactic unifying principle, that of *rhythm.* On a more strictly syntagmatic and sequential level, the reader's ability or propensity to "naturalize," if only subliminally, the fragmentariness of Coolidge's stray sentences—that is, to relinearize them into an intelligible whole on the model of standard narrative procedures—should not be underestimated either. The first two sentences of Coolidge's paragraph ("Lightful overcoat. Must be boning up on tieless affronts the comb ranges"), for instance, can reasonably be construed as the simple, everyday routine a middle-class clerk lacking in self-confidence has to go through before going out to work, putting on his spring coat ("lightful" as opposed to quilted), training himself to stand bolt upright ("boning up") to disguise his lack of composure, tightening his tie and carefully combing his hair in order to avoid possible social humiliations or "tieless affronts" (he is frequently gibed at by his colleagues or the people in the neighborhood). The third sentence ("Oversaw his dots backhanding berries while clot erect") could then describe the same awkward middle-class clerk briefly considering the berry-shaped dots printed on the tie he is now holding up on the back of his hand, on which a fresh cut (he cut himself during the breakfast mentioned in the sixth sentence of the excerpt) is already forming (or "erect[ing]") a clot. The next sentence ("Of a strew placed beyond the beakless bark scatter.") might well report the observations of our "protagonist" as he looks out of the window and his gaze comes to rest on a particular spot in the backyard—a little farther than the tree where, incidentally, no birds are singing ("the beakless bark")—where he dumped ("strew[ed]" or "scatter[ed]"), rather carelessly, a load of garbage the night before. The next phrase ("This is pulp afternoon"), then, might convey the clerk's response to the oncoming afternoon, which signals the end of his lunch break, while the sun now appears to him as a circle of orange "pulp."

It must be granted that such a narrative does not really do justice to the structural and imagistic ambiguity or the complex polyphony of Coolidge's poem—or even the metonymic energy created by the abrupt transitions between relatively isolated sentences. Other, less "literal" interpretations might focus more on the poem's possible figurative content or, on the contrary, might ascribe to it even more concrete, or even molecular, connotations (for example, by taking into account Coolidge's particular interest in mineral still lifes); in a general way, however, my rather flippant paraphrase of Coolidge's poem somehow evokes—albeit in an approximate and reductive fashion—the somewhat painstaking truculence and the vitriolic verve that often characterize Coolidge's prose in *Weathers*. Another, even more essential aspect of my personal "version" of Coolidge's paragraph is that it does away with the multiple syntactic disruptions and semantic ambiguities of the original by naturalizing them into a straight, linear sequence in which every word is understood by reference to a single larger imaginary narrative. In order to do so, I had to sketch out a more or less plausible context (involving, among other things, the protagonist's sex, social class and personality, the season, the time of the day in which the "action" is taking place, etc.) by which to make sense of whatever "happens" in each sentence and the paragraph as a whole. In this, I also benefited from a number of deliberate or fortuitous recurrences, including that of words belonging to specific semantic fields referring, for instance, to clothes ("overcoat," "tieless," "shoes," "robes," "buttons," and, again, "overcoats") and to movements or body parts ("boning up," "backhanding," "eye," "nose," and "shrug"). More generally, such attempts to "internalize" Coolidge's *Weathers* with reference to a specific context suggest that the metonymic movement from signifier to signifier, in which the reader ascribes a sequence to the text, is accompanied by moments of metaphorical verticality establishing a number of semantic features, which will, in turn, (re)determine the course of the metonymic narrative.

Such a fairly coherent and linear interpretation of an apparently unintelligible text clearly shows that a so-called areferential poem is never really immune to a return of the syntactic and figurative repressed. Ironically, the text's resistance to traditional narrative movements points most persuasively to the impossibility of a strictly "nonnarrative" poem and to the persistence of referentiality and "meaning": the responsibility of the writing of a narrative and semantic frame is simply shifted, at least to a certain extent, from the author to the reader. By leaving readers more room to maneuver, the poem opens itself up to their own hermeneutic (re)visions and the continuous establishment of new (temporary) conventions. The newly acquired "freedom" of the writerly reader is, of course, relative: although Coolidge's "open" text lends itself to many different personal interpretations, some elements or sequences of the poem, like the "middle-class" backyard, are likely to be interpreted and narrativized in a similar way by readers sharing the same social and cultural background.

Metaphor and Metonymy: From Surrealism to Language Poetry

The syntactic and associational "openness" of the New Prose Poem is reminiscent of the prose and poetry of French Surrealism, another movement whose aim was to promote linguistic indeterminacy. Yet, Silliman makes it clear that the New Sentence "does not have to do with the prose poems of the Surrealists, which manipulate meaning only at the 'higher' or 'outer' layers, well beyond the horizon of the sentence." One obvious objection to Silliman's insistence on the "removal of context" (*Sentence* 87) that characterizes the New Sentence (or, at least, its most areferential avatars in the work of Robert Grenier and Clark Coolidge) by "[preventing] most leaps beyond the level of grammatical integration" is that it implicitly denies the reader's active participation on a *paradigmatic* level: even—and, one might argue, especially—the most acontextual kind of writing will inevitably be subjected by the reader to a metaphorical interpretation. Conversely, the fact that most Language writing may display a significantly less flamboyant use of imagery than in Surrealist poetry does not imply, by any means, that Surrealist works do not call for the reader's active contribution at both the syntactic *and* the metaphorical level.[15]

Still, the syntactic and sequential relationships within and between the sentences of, for instance, the syncopated associational sequences of André Breton and Philippe Soupault's experiments with écriture automatique in *Les Champs magnétiques* are relatively conventional compared to most Language poetry. Silliman is therefore right in reminding us that the semantic and sequential disruptions of Surrealist writing occur mainly by imagistic association and "above" the level of the sentence. If we refer to the semic diagram representing the different degrees of openness of a given text along the paradigmatic and syntagmatic axis, Coolidge's poem would thus clearly fall into the "writerly" category while Breton and Soupault's would belong somewhere between "normative syntax" and "paradigmatic indeterminacy."

Despite their methodological differences, the obvious similarity between French Surrealism and Language poetry is that both movements seek to subvert conservative assumptions about the nature of language and its relationship to its producer and its object. While the prose poems of Breton and Soupault deny the unified stability of the self-subject by stressing the role of the unconscious in linguistic production, the New Prose Poem does

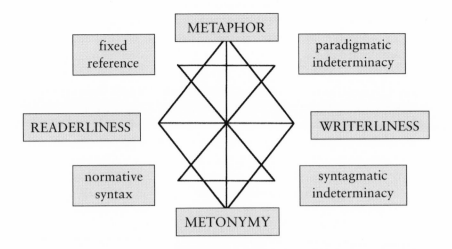

the same by foregrounding the activity of writing as the one and only primary cause of the poetic text, thereby opposing any claims to a transcendental (Romanticism) or vocal origin (the lyric). As we have seen, the New Prose Poem and écriture automatique also share a similar distrust of normative referentiality and, most notably, of the illusionist claims to mimesis located at the "readerly" pole of the diagram.[16]

In both cases, also, the development of fixed referential relationships and normative syntactic sequences is often identified as the privilege of the bourgeoisie, the favorite target of French Surrealism but also of the leftist critique of the Language poets. (Characteristically, Silliman ends his contribution to a symposium on "The Politics of Poetry" published in the October 1979 issue of $L=A=N=G=U=A=G=E$ with a call for a poetry that could "undermine the bourgeoisie.") Most language-oriented poetry also subscribes to the Surrealist utopian notion of poetry as an essentially collective enterprise reacting against the individualist ethics of bourgeois literature. In this, the movements are both in line with Peter Bürger's now classic redefinition of the "historical avant-garde" of Surrealism, Dadaism, and the Russian avant-garde, which he interprets as an attempt "to direct toward the practical the aesthetic experience (which rebels against the praxis of life) that Aestheticism developed" (34). Like Bürger's historical avant-garde, Language poetry is understood not so much as a resurgence of intense formal experimentalism but rather, as a transformation of art into a social praxis.

As suggested, there is nonetheless another important epistemological difference between Surrealist poetry and Language poetry as subversive practices: while the Surrealists reacted against the political conservatism and intellectual narrow-mindedness of the bourgeoisie (for instance, by becoming members of the French Communist Party and by charging their writing with overt sexual content), Language poetry criticizes other categories of the bourgeois/capitalist system, most notably its sociolinguistic premises. Whereas Surrealism attempted to subvert the literary and political Establishment at the level of the signified, the Language poets use the linguistic signifier as a critical stronghold from which to dismantle the very linguistic foundations—as opposed to its "higher" metaphorical level—of the bourgeois cultural myth concerning the objectivity and transparency of language.

Genre Deconstruction as Writing Practice

The examples discussed earlier illustrate how the compositional strategies of the New Prose Poem can lead to a radical questioning of the categories underlying what is commonly considered narrative and poetry. As we have seen, the language-oriented prose poem seeks not so much to undermine generic conventions from without but rather to show how they deconstruct themselves through the act of writing. A number of other Language poets, however, try to examine not only how normative conventions legitimize current definitions of poetry as such but also how they inform specific literary genres. Lyn Hejinian's *My Life* (1980) is an example of such a creative demystification applied to the genre of autobiography. A poetic investigation of the relationship of writing and memory (a notion Hejinian, following in the steps of Gertrude Stein, had already started to explore in her first major work of poetry, *Writing Is an Aid to Memory*), *My Life* consists of thirty-seven sections of thirty-seven sentences, each section standing for a year of the author's life. Considering Hejinian's Steinian rejection of narrative linearity and her belief in writing as "an aid to memory"—that is, belief in the process of writing itself as the coproducer of its own (re)definition of the past—such a determinate, almost programmatic, chronological frame may appear extremely restrictive, if not contradictory. Nevertheless, Jean Baudrillard's assessment of Barthes' choice of an alphabetical sequence in *A Lover's Discourse* suggests that ritual conventionality, by virtue of its own overt arbitrariness, can resist conventional logic and meaning more efficiently than do syntactic disruption and formal indeterminacy:

In *A Lover's Discourse,* Barthes justifies his choice of the alphabetical order: "To discourage the temptation of meaning, we had to find an order that was absolutely insignificant," that is to say neither a concerted one, nor even that of pure chance, but an order which was perfectly conventional. For, as Barthes says, quoting a mathematician: "We must not underestimate the capacity of chance for generating monsters," that is to say meaning. . . . We do not escape meaning through disjunction, disconnection or deterritorialization. We escape it by substituting for its effects of meaning a more radical simulacrum, an order still more conventional—such as Barthes' alphabetical order, such as the rules of the game, such as the innumerable ritualizations of everyday life which elude both disorder (chance) and the order of meaning (political, historical, social) that we wish to impose on them. . . . *Only ritual abolishes meaning.* (*Séduction* 190–91)

Like the repetition-with-variation progression of serial music or the programmatic rigorousness of John Cage's "mesostics," the overt determinativeness of Hejinian's chronological arrangement foregrounds the "monstrous" potential of narrative for creating (logical) meaning at the same time as it points to its own arbitrariness.[17] While the work's subdivision into thirty-seven "entries" for each year of the author's life still preserves a semblance of referentiality and linear coherence (an impression immediately invalidated by the syntactic indeterminacy of the text itself), the thirty-seven sentences contained in each section are an example of purely conventional and un-signifying ritualization (quite appropriately, the French *insignifiant* in the original version of Baudrillard's text suggests both triviality and the lack of reference). Hejinian's transformation of the paragraph and the sentence into strictly quantitative units of narrative—a method advocated by Silliman's manifesto of the New Sentence—creates a "simulacrum" of a narrative, which ironically underlines the impossibility for traditional narrative logic to do justice to the very process of "remembering." As Hejinian herself puts it, in a form itself more faithful, at least typographically, to the disrupted syntax of memory:

> the rate of forgetting is greatest
> storing that and these processes
> the principal source is his own and

desperately

> life is quantity through a language
> > substitute inventing music of a series
> of changes very little understood
> binding men for driving through a new internal logic fire
> > to fish
> > of despair of failure for knowledge
> by way of despair for the road
> (*Tree* 54)

Coming to terms with one's past as a quantitative and textual material in a state of perpetual motion requires the rememberer to engage in a consciously organized reshuffling of the fragments of her experience. Hejinian's insertion, in the second edition of *My Life*, of eight new sections and eight new sentences in each of the original sections to account for her current age further emphasizes her refusal of narrative closure as well as her desire to convey what Hank Lazer has described as "at once a specific and a generic life: the emergence of a life in the process of its textual (re-)construction" (32). Eventually, however, this cutting-and-pasting process should deliver the outlines of a "new internal logic" capable of covering the gaps between the isolated sentences while distancing itself from the claustrophobic linearities of conventional syntax. As we have seen and will see, Hejinian's programmatic procedures, like Barthes' distrust of total indeterminacy as a means of resisting the creation of meaning, is also an indirect comment on the survival of conventional logic, even within texts generated by the dynamics of indeterminacy and desire.

In a more specific way, what Hejinian's subversive use of autobiographical or diary writing sets out to achieve is a complex dissemination of private experience and its reinscription into a network of gender relationships and cultural and ideological principles:[18]

I am looking for the little hand mirror. The summer evenings saw window shoppers in a reflecting system, man with merchandise agog. It is hard to turn away from moving water. All summer I worked as a mountain guide and behind me hiked a group of girls giggling in descent of a president. He made me nervous as soon as he began offering a special discount. But the work is probably a good deal wiser than the horny doctor he was. I wrote my name in every one of his books. A name trimmed with colored ribbons. They used to be the leaders of the avant-garde, but now they just want to be understood, and so farewell to them. If I was left unmarried after college, I would be single all my life and lonely in old age. In such a situation it is necessary to make a choice between contempt and an attempt at understanding, and yet it is difficult to know which is the form of retreat. We will only understand what we have already understood. The turkey is a stupid bird. And it is scanty praise to be so-called well-meaning. But is there an independent quality, a self-sufficient quality, that is pleasure, and is it comparable to red, fame, and wealth or to beauty (one can feel some affinity for the several distinct categories). Mouth with a radical math clap. The washlines run with garments hung. (*My Life* 53)

The different entries of *My Life* reflect a similar attempt at assimilating the complexity of retrospective thinking into a personal narrative and a refusal to yield to the pressures of conventional autobiographical writing, which inevitably include a tendency toward the linearization and the monosemantic organization of stray material ("Only fragments are accurate. Break it up into single words, charge them to combination" [52]). Hejinian's juxtaposition of various discourses, whether personal or collective, her cold-blooded insertion of prescriptive social aphorisms ("If I was left unmarried after college, I would be single all my life and lonely in old age") testify to her desire to create a narrative that does justice to its own inherently disrupted dynamics as well as to its socioeconomic background. Indeed, Hejinian's refusal to indulge in the lures and hoaxes of realist narrative is deeply connected with her desire to convey personal experience in terms of its subjection to the particular societal discourse brought about by the logic of capitalism: not only are human relationships and sexual intercourse translated into economic exchanges (the doctor's "special discount"), but avant-garde art itself—which comprises narrative as an anti-institutional force—yields willingly to the all-devouring powers of assimilation of commodity culture.

By contrast, Hejinian's own avant-gardist poetics seem to embrace, rather than reject, the dominant discourses supporting the capitalist machinery. By doing so, *My Life* often succeeds in undermining them from within, using a method reminiscent of Andy Warhol's Campbell's soup cans, which celebrate the obscene glamor of commodity fetishism at the same time as they indirectly foster a critical appraisal of the dynamics of the capitalist system. By combining a variety of discursive categories and suggesting the existence of multisyntactic relationships between them, Hejinian's prose exposes normative narratives and their generic by-products as so many resultants of particular societal or cultural codes. More specifically, Hejinian's rewriting of autobiography into a political state-ment, both on a social and a personal level, also signals the passage of the writing "I" into a narrative in which, in Marjorie Perloff's words, "the natural giv[es] way to the artificial, the individual self to the body of words (*Radical* 170):

> What education finally serves us, if at all. There is a pause, a rose, something on paper. The small green shadows make the red jump out. That is not a telescope, nor do I have the stars in my belly. Such displacements alter illusions, which is all-to-the-good. Now cars not cows on the brown hills, and a stasis of mobile homes have taken their names from what grew in the valleys near Santa Clara. We have grown up with it. If it is personal, it is most likely fickle. The univer-sity was the cultural market but on Sundays she tried out different churches. In the museum, attention shifted from painting to painting, the eye forced around, so that it was impossible to focus on any single work. The nightmare was of a giant bluebottle fly which buzzed, "I'm all there is." Where cars don't go are short-cuts. My grandfather was forced to recognize his age when another, younger, man offered his seat on the bus. When one travels, one might "hit" a storm. The shoe must be tied to the ankle. As for we who "love to be aston-ished," McDonalds is the world's largest purchaser of beef eyeballs. They went out with bows and armbands to shoot at the hay. It's as easy as waves, slopping water. Traverse, watch, and cease. He had the hands of an artist. Europeans shake hands more often than we do, here in America, yet I don't think that constitutes a "daring to touch." (54–55)

This unusual combination of personal meditations and collective quota-tions from the social and educational code—added to the neutral derisive-ness of tone of the isolated sentences—reflects the surrender of human re-lationships and the individual consciousness to the reifying pressure of normative discourses. Like the cars and the mobile homes, social apho-risms like "the shoe must be tied to the ankle" and "he had the hands of an artist" are emblematic of the sociolinguistic points of reference the contem-porary self has "grown up with" and consequently naturalized as an inte-gral part of its material and psychological environment. Typically, Hejinian's text is also deprived of the "personal" quality and the emotional intimacy one usually associates with autobiographical writing, a condition further underlined by the disjunctions between the sentences, which prevent the reader from identifying and empathizing with the writing "I" so as to reconstruct an emotional narrative above the level of the sentence.

The Gender of Genre (2): Rosmarie Waldrop and the Female Symbolic

Right and Wrong.

John Cage, *Themes and Variations*

The organization of *My Life* into paragraphs of defined length suggests that a certain degree of structural organization is not incompatible with the Language poets' critique of linearity and "readerliness." In an essay entitled "The Rejection of Closure," Lyn Hejinian, using as a starting point French feminist theories concerning the relationship of language with power, raises the issue of the limits of textual openness of the avant-garde text: "the kinds of language that [French feminist writers] advocate seem very close to, if not identical with, what I think of as characteristic of many contemporary avant-garde texts—including an interest in syntactic disjunctures and realignments, in montage and pastiche as structural devices, in the fragmentation and explosion of subject, etc., as well as an antagonism to closed structures of meaning. Yet, of the writers I have read to date, only Julia Kristeva is exploring this connection" (283).

According to Kristeva, all texts are the result of a dialectical struggle between the "symbolic" and the "semiotic" impulses. The symbolic order is a post-Oedipal system regulated by normative processes and the Law of the Father. It is therefore the privileged locus of masculine discourse, an essentially repressive space where language is used as an instrument of power. By contrast, the semiotic as defined by Kristeva is the polymorphous space of anarchic, pre-Oedipal drives she associates with "feminine desire": a series of libidinal, uncontrollable, and profoundly excessive forces that constantly threaten to cause disruptions within the symbolic system. Kristeva's application of her theory to the literary text in *Revolution in Poetic Language* makes it clear, however, that this inherently "feminine" transgressiveness of the semiotic is not to be taken literally, as she sees it at work in a number of male representatives of the contemporary avant-garde, such as Lautréamont, Mallarmé, Joyce, Pound, Artaud, and Bataille. Hejinian clearly subscribes to Kristeva's equation of semiotic transgression with the syntactic disjunctions of the avant-garde. Nevertheless, she recognizes the impossibility of a purely "semiotic" text. "The (unimaginable) complete text," Hejinian writes, "the text that contains everything, would be in fact a closed text. It would be unsufferable" (285). In other words, the degree of openness of a text is only a matter of degree as the possibility of semiotic subversion implicitly depends on a symbolic norm to be transgressed.

While Rosmarie Waldrop shares Hejinian's sociolinguistic concerns, she most often uses them as a starting point for the exploration of specific issues concerning the nature of "feminine" writing.[19] The appendix to *The Lawn of Excluded Middle,* her most recent collection of prose poems, contains some of the basic principles of her conception of the feminine and its interaction with "logical" language:

1.

The law of excluded middle is a venerable old law of logic.
But much can be said against its claim that everything must
be either true or false

2.

The idea that women cannot think logically is a not so venerable
old stereotype. As an example of thinking, I don't think we need
to discuss it.

3.

Lawn of Excluded Middle plays with the idea of woman as the
excluded middle. Women and, more particularly, the womb, the
empty center of the woman's body, the locus of fertility.

4.

This is not a syllogism.

5.

This is a syllogism.

6.

Poetry: an alternate, less linear logic.

7.

Wittgenstein makes language with its ambiguities the ground
of philosophy. His games are played on the Lawn of Excluded
Middle. (unpag.)

Waldrop's identification of feminine thought with the excluded middle between truth and falsehood (which echoes Luce Irigaray's critique of [male-defined] Western rationality and its rejection of contradiction and ambiguity) does not in any way result in a celebration of the anarchic openness of Kristeva's semiotic language of desire. Such a positioning would indeed indirectly confirm the subordinate and self-limiting role of the feminine as a mere potential for "irrational" disruption within the masculine symbolic. By contrast, if the "womb" or "locus of fertility" of feminine thought is seen as an ambiguous and polysemous entity contesting the rigid binarism of masculine rationality, it can also be defined as an "excluded middle" enshrined in the process of logical thought even as it attempts to subvert this:

> The meaning of certainty is getting burned. Though truth will still escape us, we must put our hands on bodies. Staying safe is a different death, the instruments of defense eating inward without evening out the score. As the desire to explore my body's labyrinth did, leading straight to the center of nothing. From which projected my daily world of representation with bright fictional fireworks. Had I overinvested in spectacle? In mere fluctuations of light which, like a bird's wingbeat, must with time slow to the point of vanishing? What about buying bread or singing in the dark? Even if the ground for our assumptions is the umber of burnt childhood we're driven toward the sun as if logic had no other exit. (18)

For all its syntactic and logical orthodoxy, language in Waldrop's prose poems (like that of Stein's *Tender Buttons*) is uncompromisingly plural and cannot be forced into a unitary meaning. It is the product of a denial not of logic itself but of the totalizing claims of reason to arrive at an absolute truth. The Wittgensteinian language games of Waldrop's *Lawn of Excluded Middle* indeed preclude the establishment of a hierarchy of meanings dividing the real into "right" or "wrong" interpretations such as would legitimize the strict regulations underlying the power of the symbolic realm. As suggested, however, the rhetorical and syntactic rigorousness of Waldrop's prose (like the strict programmatic procedures and the cyclic recurrences paradoxically underlying Hejinian's deconstruction of linearity in *My Life*) nevertheless points to the practical uselessness of a completely indeterminate *écriture féminine*. It evokes the necessity for the semiotic text to preserve a certain amount of syntactic and narrative control, as well as to employ other categories otherwise pertaining to the symbolic, even as it tries to undermine their claims to syllogistic closure.

More generally, the inherent modal duplicity of the prose poem allows the cohabitation of symbolic logic and semiotic inconclusiveness and thus seems to be an ideal form for Waldrop's redefinition of poetry into "an alternate, less linear logic." In most cases, the constant back and forth movement between abstract thoughts, imagistic moments, and bodily realities also contributes to a further blurring of the boundaries between "symbolic" rationality and "semiotic" polymorphousness. Simultaneously somatizing the text and textualizing the body, the abstract and bodily geometries of Waldrop's prose poems suggest a new way of mapping the real and develop cognitive strategies that enable one to "accept the movement" and do justice to the "speed of desire" (30). Reflecting on her own poetic practice, as well as on the conflicting possibilities of language, body, and self, Waldrop asks: "All roads lead, but how does a sentence do it?" (16). Throughout the whole collection, Waldrop remains "worried about the gap between expression and intent, afraid that the world might see a fluorescent advertisement where I meant to show a face." She nevertheless concludes that an alternative is to be found at the level of the gap itself: "Sincerity is no help once we admit to the lies we tell on nocturnal occasions, even in the solitude of our own heart, wishcraft slanting the naked figure from need to seduce to fear of possession. Far better to cultivate the gap itself with its high grass for privacy and reference gone astray" (22).

Language and Reification

The poetry of Diane Ward possesses most of the external attributes of so-called language-oriented poetry, including an attention to the material quality of words, a highly experimental and self-reflexive stance, and the use of an essentially abstract, quasi-expository rhetoric. Like Rosmarie Waldrop, Ward does not focus primarily on the act of writing itself but, instead, conceives of poetry as a means of accounting for the complex dialectics of language and desire. Her abstract descriptions of private experience, which constantly blur the distinction between the psychological and the physical world, account for the complex verbal and gestural strategies used by people in relating to each other, or simply to themselves, in seemingly casual situations.

Ward's explorations of the human consciousness, however, are far from being merely anecdotal, as her most particular talent lies in a cold-eyed investigation of basic patterns of behavior and of the multiple correspondences between inner and outer landscapes, private and public architectures, psychological and material energies. The following excerpt from "Pronouncing," a prose poem contained in the collection *Never Without One*, is a typical example of Ward's antilyrical landscapes, in which her interest in the meanders of the human mind is often subordinated to an analysis of perspective and the distortions of parallax:

Ears leveled to the silence of a structural sidewalk movement. Feet leveled to the sidewalk sustained. An enemy massages an enemy.

Lower and lower, enter with monotony. All the rage, for effect. Messed up tied up rehearsed over and over a mannerism on the make. Elevators up to the higher floors, more running around. White town connected by blue ink threads on perfumed white envelopes. Close-up and long shot rot in a 2-dimensional room light soothing all illusions eased by sound which rolls. No more play. This is the perfect look for you after your integrity loss. Pride is a thorn in your side. "It's true I am a woman; it's true I'm employed;" going through the motions like a gun with your favorite pal. Playing around with deep humanity, the bargain was invented. This seems to be lean, deep and corrupted. The word is legs. (*Tree* 334–35)

Ward's writings are often characterized by a sense of what Jean Baudrillard has called "the loss of the real," a condition in which the old modernist tension between reality and illusion, the "authentic" original and the copy, has been dissipated and replaced by the "simulacrum"—a model of "a real without origin or reality: a hyperreal" (*Simulations* 2). (Baudrillard originally applied this theory to the age of the image-creating mass media, in which the signifier of an event appears to have less and less relationship to an outside, signified "reality.") Baudrillard's "simulacrum" indeed seems a relevant interpretive model for Ward's "Pronouncing," in which the self, confronted with "window oddities painted like painting" (*Tree* 335), is liable to mistake "the forest for trees and tree-like devices" (332).

The last four sentences of the excerpt from "Pronouncing" reproduced here point in the direction of a writing that pictures the female self at the intersection of various sexual, social, and economic conflicts. The positioning of the individual within the social whole is also one of the central concerns of Fiona Templeton's first book of poetry, *London* (published in 1984 but begun as early as 1977), which consists of a series of unpunctuated prose paragraphs grouped in sections of more or less equal length. Far from subscribing to the epiphanic "pedestrianism" one usually expects from a conventional city poem, each paragraph reads like a concatenation of visual and verbal units whose internal logic is highly difficult to apprehend. Another important consequence of the experimental structure and lack of syntactic coherence of Templeton's *London* is the absence of a coherent pattern by which to identify the central consciousness of the poem. The marks of individual subjectivity remain all the more indeterminate as the speaking or writing "I" often seems to be fumbling for a means of affirming her existence as a mere sign invested with different meanings and use-values by its immediate physical and societal surroundings. While her hopes, moods, and desires remain largely unstated, her very sense of identity seems complicated by the legal, political, technical, or commercial imperatives of the age:

> I'll do advisory moment serve queen or foster data processing man and pray off and find us at old underground station bucking lace on a data processing age well do I pal do an advertising vision great queen's earl's class if I can continue a half on art men in yellow age rough sin per cent of new sins rail vice now what can we do for you for full details of art men in yellow age's ring (35–36)

If the exact significance of such associational wanderings often remains inscrutable, recognizable icons of British culture (here, the underground station and Britain's monarchic and aristocratic subtext) nonetheless emerge from the recesses of the poem's many-layered discourse. Templeton's prose therefore does not fall into the abstract or "areferential" category, as each of the sections of the collection points not only to specific elements of the urban landscape but also to a number of social and cultural phenomena, including family values, the relationship between art and capital, religion, unemployment, class consciousness, and the mass media as well as various forms of domestic, racial, and sexual politics.

In more general terms, *London* delineates the variable trajectories of a self's consciousness revealed primarily through its interaction with (and subjection to) specific cultural codes and institutions. One of the main strengths of the collection indeed lies in Templeton's skillful juxtaposition of details of the urban landscape with idiosyncrasies of the speaker's mental wanderings. Templeton's vision of the city as a geographical and linguistic maze without a center discloses the poem itself as a set of fragmented cultural idioms that jam the basic principles of sense-making and frequently sap the self's attempts at self-expression. Ultimately, the unlikely combination of rambling, thinking, observing, and talking that makes up the body of *London* points to a collective voice subsuming, at least in part, the variety of individual utterances and linguistic registers contained in the collection.

The structural cohesiveness of Templeton's collection is achieved not just by the poem's overall dedication to the city of London but also by the repetition of key words placed in different contexts and therefore subject to successive interpretations. The effect of this repetition-with-variation technique—which is reinforced by Templeton's constant use of puns and alliterative effects—is to focus the reader's attention on how changes in the sequential arrangement of words on the page constantly recontextualize their meaning and create new possibilities for intermingling (and often contradictory) reading patterns and semantic metamorphoses.

Hi Cowboy, Templeton's most recent printed collection, is a much more discursive and argumentative work, in which the prose paragraph becomes an exploration site for a consciousness struggling to understand human relationships in terms of complex economic, intellectual, and libidinal transactions. Perhaps Templeton's most impressive achievement is to write a kind of prose poetry that, even though it reflects the poet's awareness of the discrepancy between language and meaning, can nonetheless attend to its own operations as both the vector of individual experience and the begetter of an ever-changing relation between self and world:

> The case against love steals its redness, says it was a loan. Realized because the names we gave curved arms shut. Conversation between disheveled and local, tampax and our languid tribute, licence and vanity, the bull-calf and the heifer, first of a series, dying, should thrill through stew? Curt and equal, name no hour, neglect alleged illicit groan. (Bernstein, "43 Poets" 31)

Like many of the works discussed so far, the poetry of Barrett Watten displays a strong concern with the defamiliarization—and the subsequent bringing-into-meaning—of the postmodern environment and its relationship to the collective and individual self. By emphasizing the impossibility of escaping from textuality, whatever the degree of self-consciousness involved in the act of writing, Watten often goes further than most Language poets in refusing to take the "language-centered" approach for granted. "Real Estate" (from the collection *1–10*) explores more systematically the issue of linguistic and phenomenological alienation discussed in connection with Ward's "Pronouncing," by focusing on the uneasy interaction between language and the world of objects:

> The abandoned warehouse surrenders itself to discourse: in the deliberate advance of repetitive texts. Because anyone can make a typographical error to wear down the pyramid by identity with word. The essence of poison is the power to soothe: the citizens spit flames of a rationalism they don't understand. The impression is a point of de-

parture: a tower of ashes (a coat full of holes) floating in the air. Water flows from the tap as time reaches zero: unforeseen floods rise exactly to the level of the words. Everything offers itself: a shoe polish learns to speak (avoiding subordinate clauses) from a crumpled umbrella. Propellors inhabit air where thought originates to whir in place the word. The brainworker has no basis: to adjust the birth rate all abstraction leads to a shorter route to the ocean. The intended confusion assumes all wishes to encounter anything interpreted as itself. Balancing all prefigurations to be caught in the throes of "that is how I am." (*Frame* 31)

Watten's prose entry, while leaving no doubt as to the overall adequacy of the "language-oriented" label, also exemplifies the essaylike character often encountered in Language poetry. The poem as a whole reads like a meditation on the power of normative language to "name" its object. The propensity of objects to "surrender [themselves] to discourse" is an indirect statement on the abuses of a language whose aim is to perpetrate the myth of a self-present interpretation of reality "as itself." The use of a poetico-theoretical medium as a means of construing away the complex discordances inherent to language and its relationship to its consenting object is further elaborated on in the next paragraph of Watten's poem:

The blueprint doesn't work, vanishes into intervals: only the buildings are left behind. Others have written on this safety valve to support the catastrophe of theory. The walls of the reaction chamber closing in: "I speak of a proliferation of windows." Therefore prose is restored to the assimilated fact: a microballoon rising inside the original movie. Discordant frames approach and slip from their feet: the plotline succumbs to a general inertia. Documents packed up in crates buckle under the weight of: "to study the laws of gravity, I fell." Here sentences translate the other side of the code: to fill in holes and cracks in the pavement.

Despite Watten's suggestive description of the failure of language to master the discordant geometries of the outside world, his vision of an Icarian "catastrophe of theory" seems compatible with a belief in the power of words to "fill in" the gaps in an increasingly fragmentary reality. By comparison, the claustrophobic geometries of Kit Robinson's "Authority Vespers" depict—in a merciless, hallucinatory fashion reminiscent of J. G. Ballard's psychopathological landscapes—a world in which language and the self seem on the verge of becoming irremediably engulfed in angles and curves of their material architectural environment:

> May try industrious lapping at lakeside. Old habit at a glance, but the punctilious rails glean rye. All I've even envisaged careens floor-boardward in an imagination of tiles. Try to pry information off the fuselage, push against raw metal endeavor tied to a post. Tangled organs were Gorky's parking spot. There's air outside an idea, more space than meets the eye. The pull is furious, flag snap in storm. All along the warm interior of the mouth houses resource. The elevated crash diction completes the image sentence. But behind that these interpolations can never get, the base slides noiselessly under foot, buildings heave into view, and an accelerated procedure takes up the slacks and drapes them over a chair. (*Windows* 119)

Robinson's poem seems to point to the progressive erosion of intellectual and geographical awareness in the postmodern space. Here, any verbal attempt to remap the depthless surfaces of the new environment into meaningfulness is evidently doomed to failure ("Try to pry information off the fuselage, push against raw metal endeavor tied to a post") as the self's rare epiphanic moments are automatically either silenced or petrified into a logic of inertness ("an imagination of tiles"). The I-observer of "Authority Vespers" can only see the buildings "heave into view"—referring to themselves in a state of supreme, hyperreal undeniability and undermining any effort to make sense of his/her immediate surroundings ("The elevated crash diction completes the image sentence. But behind that these interpolations can never get, the base slides noiselessly under foot"). Deprived of any figurative and emotional content, the objects and discourses of Robinson's "Authority Vespers"—besides raising the issue of the survival of the "lyric" genre in a posthumanist world—cease to be symbols and become, instead, symptoms of a new kind of linguistic and psychological depthlessness.

The following paragraphs from Craig Watson's "Discipline" and Tom Beckett's "The Picture Window" further illustrate this renewed interest in surfaces:

> Night sunk. The utterer sleeps through his sound: circuits of the stroke of wool between needles, bent back from the hands of uninhabited reason. In the echo of days awaiting devotion, vapor plies open the louvers, misting against the glass. This is the future

taking place, its skin waxing the silence of weightless architecture. Someone arrives: the touch of gesture in disconnected air.

Shadow, in the next moment, will reverse. Surfaces pass through surfaces, edge slit by edge, consuming friction. A threshold grinds into position, numbing the glare of straight time. Come asking of certainty a precise foliage, a secret trance, oiled by memory to walls. The body unrolls from dust, sterile and incognito, but not to dreams and not to action; emptied of description it receives and shimmers. (unpag.)

They are curiously interfaced. Their surfaces forming a common boundary. One might say that he thought of her as a person. No one feels composed. She is spectacularly encumbered. They are finding themselves alone. Each of them.

She is surfacing. The extension of a frame can be the limit of a world. Names can be labels of concealment. The picture window is being shattered with a brick. Their thoughts are encumbered. She finds herself thinking. Those sounds of breaking glass might be composed. (*Tree* 397)

Whether the surfaces and edges of Watson's and Beckett's poems are "consuming friction" or "curiously interfaced" in a state of quasi-cybernetic asepsis, they have in common that they continually add to the erosion of human relationships and the individual consciousness into a space of two-dimensional anonymousness.

The Death of the Lyric

> He wanted a writing that wanted to expose itself. He wrote as if not
> wanting nor imputing wanting to writing. Still this was the only way to
> account for it. He wanted to write and it wrote.
>
> Michael Davidson, *The Prose of Fact*

All this brings us back to the issue of the survival of the self in a world saturated with such linguistic depthlessness. In the poems just discussed, the primacy of the signifier advocated by the movement contributes to the divesting of the lyric subject of its pretenses to self-consciousness and self-contained integrity. In order to do so, Language poetry proceeds to reveal the self's status as the product of a particular set of intersecting socio-linguistic frames; that is, as a mere element of an all-engulfing system of signs supporting specific patterns of social and mental habits. The lyric mode is thus translated into a semiotic quest for the textual (as opposed to an "authentic," transcendental, or vocal) identity of the speaking and writing subject.

The hyperreal surfaces of this new realm of Total Textuality bear striking resemblances to the sense of depthlessness that, according to Fredric Jameson, characterizes the new sociocultural space of postmodernism. In a discussion of the condition of the subject in postmodern art, Jameson emphasizes the "waning of affect" and the disappearance of modernist subjective anxiety due to the fact that "there is no longer a self-present to do the feeling" (15). For Jameson, Edvard Munch's 1893 painting *The Scream* represents "a canonical expression of the great modernist thematics of alienation, anomie, solitude, social fragmentation, and isolation, a virtually programmatic emblem of what used to be called the age of anxiety." However, the more recent advent of a "postmodern depthlessness," in which the subject can only subsist as two-dimensional ghost, has discredited the anxiety-laden "metaphysics of the inside and outside" (such as was expressed in the modernist opposition of subject/object, spirit/matter, culture/nature) and the agonizing separation within the subject presupposed by the modernist concept of expression.

If we consider the fate of poetic subjectivity in the works of Watten, Robinson, Beckett, and Watson in the light of Jameson's postmodern depthlessness, we are led to conclude that the gradual recognition of the failure of the modernist subject to impose poetic order upon an increasingly chaotic and unintelligible world has now given way to a questioning of the very medium through which the premodernist subject used to make sense of the real and imaginary environment. The postmodern poetic self—at once deprived of its claims to transcendentalism and alienated from its own strategies of expression—therefore ceases to be a platform for the "older" kind of modernist alienation and for the enactment of metaphysical or personal anxieties, which depended on a now allegedly deceased centered, autonomous, and self-present subject at one with his or her own language.

The propensity of language-oriented poetry to emphasize the textuality of the lyric self reaches a climax in the following excerpt from "SOME NETS" by Canadian poet bpNichol, a writer whose work has been influential for many Language poets. Here, the remnants of a stable and unified voice still present in some of the samples of Language poetry examined so far seem irremediably smothered by a series of typographical interferences resulting in a kind of visual "white noise" that becomes an integral part of the text's logic of contingency and indecipherability:

three days after (*) *the lightning hit it* / or the beat, (*) check this, I can play around it, with it, there / *what's left of* (*) *the barn* (*) *still smoulders in the sun* / unresolved (*) notes or chords, should've been of wood, (*) paper, burning / *sending clouds of smoke across* (*) *the highway* / dislocating / *darkness* / son / *i awoke into* / nets / *hearing the voices from the Fire Hall across the lake* (*) / i remember this, angry, i thot it was a party, felt foolish / *seeing the flickering lights above the trees* / start looking for ways out, of this diction / *knowing* (*) *something was happening* / is happening, not in the way you intended, the way (*) that's always intended, you don't intend that / *unable to* (*) *determine* (*) *till the next day* / that tone, as tho the unravelling of this one event made the whole complex that is the world make sense, that (*) misuse of metaphor / *it was the barn's burning had awakened me* / it was the barn (*) burning, not the world (Messerli 311)

In view of the emphasis of Language poetry on the ontological rupture between the self and its own strategies of expression, any attempt to speak or write, to quote Carla Harryman, "in a state of fidelity to the subject" (32) becomes highly problematic, to say the least. One possible alternative to this aporia of lyric discourse, however, consists in turning the inherent self-dividedness of the subject into the subject matter of the poem. The opening paragraph of Bob Perelman's *a.k.a.* tends to focus on nothing less than the gap between the narrating and the narrated I:

I am often conscious, yet rain is now visibly falling. It almost combines to be one thing, yet here I am again. Though he dreamed he was awake, it was a mistake he would only make at a time like that. There are memories, but I am not that person. (*a.k.a.* 1)

The jaded skepticism and self-deflating irony of this passage from Perelman's *a.k.a.* illustrates the wholly untragic condition of Jameson's postmodern subject. More generally, the quasi-absence of catharsis, agon, or even "feeling" (at least if we stick to the accepted meaning of the word, which bears strong personal and emotive connotations) in most of the works examined so far is a particularly revealing symptom of the erasure of the subject through writing. With the death of the subject—or rather the advent of the subject who, to quote Lacan's famous diagnosis, "is not where he[/she] speaks"—language is now free to enjoy its freshly won autotelic supremacy, which the writer (succeeding that prestructuralist predecessor, the author) can only attempt to describe in terms of its own structural and generative dynamics.[20]

All this sounds, of course, like a climactic confirmation of Barthes' notion of writing (*écriture*). According to Barthes' well-known theory of the "death of the author," writing, which he defines as "that neutral, composite, oblique space where all identity is lost, starting with the very identity of the body writing" (*Image* 146), appears as gradually severed from notions such as the Romantic genius and, later, the personal style of bourgeois literature. This anonymousness of modern writing signals the birth of the writer who, "having buried the Author . . . can thus no longer believe, as according to the pathetic view of his predecessors, that his hand is too slow for his thought or passion and that consequently, making a law of necessity, he must emphasize this delay and indefinitely 'polish' his form."

For Barthes' modern "scriptor," he says, "on the contrary, the hand, cut off from any voice, borne by a pure gesture of inscription (and not of expression), traces a field without origin—or which, at least, has no other origin than language itself, language which ceaselessly calls into question all origins" (146). The substitution in Language poetry of the process of linguistic production itself for the subject who, previously, was supposed to control and use it signals a parallel move toward impersonality. Indeed, if the Language poetry movement displays a large variety of methodological nuances and approaches to poetry writing, none of its representatives can be credited with having developed a genuinely distinctive, personal "style." (As we will see, the disappearance of the notion of personal style itself, as well as that of other "deep" or "vertical" concepts like "inspiration" or "genius," is a postmodern feature.) The following minimalist everyday choreographies of Ray DiPalma's *January Zero* epitomize the advent of Barthes' *degré zéro* of writing in a manner reminiscent of the French nouveau roman:

I take a glass. I fill the glass. I drink the water. I wash the glass. I dry the glass. I give the glass to you. I take a bottle of milk. I put the bottle on the table. I open the bottle of milk. I take a clean glass. I fill the clean glass with milk. I give a glass of milk to you. I drink a glass of milk.

I go to the door. I stop at the door. I push the door open. I go out of the door. I go into the hall. I pull the door shut. I go to the EXIT. I stop at the EXIT. I push the door open. I go out of the EXIT. I go into the hall. I pull the door shut. (*Tree* 464)

Commenting on the kind of "neutral" writing that was inaugurated by Albert Camus' *The Outsider* (1942), Barthes writes that "if language, instead of being a cumbersome and uncontrollable act, achieves the status of pure equation, having no more solidity than algebra when faced with the hollowness of man, then Literature is beaten, the human predicament is laid bare and offered up, colorless; the writer is irredeemably an honest man." One has to keep in mind, however, that Barthes' "style-less" mode (or "white writing") is a utopian state to which a literary work can only aspire. Barthes himself recognizes the inherent failure of writing to reach a state of total stylistic neutrality. Not only is writing never entirely innocent of ideological content (cultural codes and myths are always already inscribed in the words used by the scriptor); it is also the locus where new codes and conventions will inevitably appear and will subsequently be reencoded into the different myths supported by (and supporting) the Establishment: "Unfortunately, nothing is more unfaithful than a blank piece of writing; automatisms develop where first there was freedom, a network of hardened forms squeezes tighter and tighter the first freshness of the speech, writing is reborn in the place of indefinite language. The writer, acceding to the classic, becomes the epigone of his original creation, society makes his writing into style and sends him away, prisoner of his own formal myths" (*Degré* 57).

In the light of the increasingly all-engulfing powers of assimilation of mass media society—a context at once epitomized and criticized by Language poetry—Barthes' words indeed take on apocalyptic overtones, at least as regards the very possibility of experimental writing to preserve its powers of agency within the current social structures. In a more general way, one is also entitled to wonder whether the death of the author and the "white writing" practiced by some Language poets do not collaborate with the structures of late capitalist culture in the repression of marginal and subversive discourses such as the poetic avant-garde, even as they attempt to further their cause. This is, at least, what Fredric Jameson is indirectly warning us against when he distinguishes the idea of parody as it was thriving in the "inimitable" private styles and mannerisms of "the moderns" (the examples of modern parody mentioned by Jameson include "the Faulknerian long sentence . . . with its breathless gerundives; Lawrentian nature imagery punctuated by testy colloquialism; Wallace Stevens's inveterate hypostasis of nonsubstantive parts of speech") from "the well-nigh universal practice today of what may be called pastiche," which he sees as the result of "the disappearance of the individual subject, along with its formal consequence, the increasing unavailability of the personal style"

(16). Pastiche, Jameson continues, is thus "like parody, the imitation of a peculiar or unique, idiosyncratic style, the wearing of a linguistic mask, speech in a dead language." But it is "a neutral practice of such mimicry, without any of parody's ulterior motives, amputated of the satiric impulse, devoid of laughter and of any conviction that alongside the abnormal tongue you have momentarily borrowed, some healthy normality still exists" (17). Jameson's subsequent appraisal of the postliteracy of advanced capitalism as that of "a linguistic fragmentation of social life itself to the point where the norm itself is eclipsed: reduced to a neutral and reified media speech" provides us with a model by which to assess the danger that recent avant-garde poetry may reflect—rather than remedy—not only the loss of individuality in postmodern consumer society but also the absence of any sense of a dominant "normality" against which to revolt.

Political and creative inertia due to the incapacity of the late twentieth-century individual (and of postmodern vanguardist art) to achieve critical distance from the Establishment is thus the potential evil lurking in the atmosphere of unconditional, apolemical eclecticism of postmodern culture. This condition is promulgated precisely by the recent desacralization of the Author as well as by the violent rejection of a number of other bourgeois concepts, such as personal style or "genius"—as was recently witnessed, in the field of American literary criticism, under the guise of a condemnation of the elitist politics of High Modernism and the erudite idiosyncrasies of Ezra Pound and T. S. Eliot, in particular. In this perspective, the question of whether the emphasis of Language poetry on writing as "impersonal" (or collective) process, rather than on a personal assertion of one's power as an individual to twist it to one's use, actually supports or subverts the strategies of self-legitimation of late capitalist society (including, for instance, the obliteration of Silliman's "gestural") remains an open but highly crucial one.

The same applies to many semantically and syntactically "open" language-oriented works that draw attention to their own constructedness by making their own structural, meaning-producing devices more tangible and, thereby, invite us to make sense of them on our own and construct our own sociolinguistic identity. Despite Barthes' famous assertion that "the birth of the reader must be at the cost of the death of the Author" (*Image-Music-Text* 148), it is unclear whether such writerly texts can really dissuade us from construing their "openness" into a meaningful whole by resorting to familiar, normative frames of reference (as in my earlier discussion of Coolidge's *Weathers*).

Language poetry, like any other vanguardist movement seeking to reestablish the capacity of art to claim some kind of relevance within the social sphere, is never really immune to the risk of undermining its own potential to function as social critique by attempting to cross the gap between art and society. According to Bürger, the failure of the European historical avant-garde effectively to subvert the social Establishment stems from a situation in which "an art no longer distinct from the praxis of life but wholly absorbed in it will lose the capacity to criticize it" (50). Indeed, what Bürger terms the "sublation (in the Hegelian sense) of art in the praxis of life" (51) makes it increasingly difficult for artists to distance themselves sufficiently from the social conditions to criticize their ideological foundations successfully. In this sense, the obsolescence of notions of personal style and the absence of "norm" not only deprive parody (and, more largely, "vanguardist" art) of its antagonistic relationship to the "institution"; they also argue for an interpretation of "white writing" (as practiced by Watson, T. Beckett, Robinson, DiPalma, and numberless other Language poets) as a symptom, rather than a critique, of the new postmodern anonymous depthlessness.

As we will see, the epistemological utopia underlying the work of many Language poets, with its focus on the process of writing as practice and its advocacy of a complete fusion of creative practice and critical thought, is also inevitably threatened by the possibility of a further paradoxical institutionalization of vanguardist poetry into a mere element of the ideological state apparatuses it originally set out to abolish. What initially appeared as a rebellion against dominant societal discourses is now in danger of developing its own self-limiting and self-legitimizing conventions, including an unexpected, and highly compromising, retreat into a new kind of postlyric subjectivism.

On the Edge of Genre: Poetry and Theory

> Poetry couples the making of the biggest mistakes possible with the
> making of the fewest and probably the loveliest. Of course, philosophy,
> the entire discipline, stands as the biggest, and conceivably the best,
> mistake of poetry.
> Madeline Gins

The works discussed so far are characterized by a desire to blur traditional boundaries between literary and extraliterary genres. While Lyn Hejinian's *My Life* seeks to subvert the claims and conventions of a particular genre, the autobiography, the other prose poems examined in this chapter reflect, each in its own particular way, a general attempt to question the practical validity of such metageneric binarisms as the lyric vs. the narrative, poetry vs. prose, and even the very notion of literary genre.[21] By freeing generic labels and conventions from their formal and contextual restrictions, the New Prose Poem, which was labeled by Michael Davidson as a "non- or intergeneric prose form" ("Sentence" 95), constantly seeks to suspend and disconfirm readers' expectations and force readers to rethink traditionally prescriptive categories as so many results of strictly differential and provisional relationships.[22] As we have seen, the Language poets' critical understanding of genre as a *textual* and "worldly" (i.e., historical and nonessential) category also extends to the various societal and institutional codes indirectly supported and legitimized by specific genres and discourses.

The radical dismantling by the New Prose Poem of traditional categories of narrative, on the one hand, and its radical revision of current definitions of the lyric, on the other, lead to a further blurring of generic distinctions between fiction and poetry. Ironically enough, the late writings of another writer usually regarded as a "deconstructionist" of narrative, Samuel Beckett, would not have been out of place in Silliman's anthology and would have demonstrated even further the elusiveness of all generic labels, *including* that of "language-oriented" writing. The minimalist degree zero of narrative aspired to by some of Beckett's shorter prose works (such as "Imagination Dead Imagine," "All Strange Away," or "For to End Yet Again") indeed bears striking resemblances to the postlyric mode and the syntactic experiments of Coolidge's *Weathers* or Watten's *1–10.*[23] Beckett's shorter "fiction" pieces—which have done away with the genre's teleological and characterological attributes—distinguish themselves generically from Watten's, Coolidge's or Robinson's "poems" mainly by virtue of their publishing circumstances and the reputations of their respective authors as public figures. (Beckett became a canonical figure as a playwright and a fiction writer, not as a poet.) By contrast, the kind of postlyric writing published by "poets" Lyn Hejinian or Ron Silliman, as we have seen, paradoxically puts narrative back on the poetic agenda, under the form of a "narrative of syntax."[24] In a way, it seems that both tendencies are in fact two different paths followed by a certain kind of postmodern experimental literature in its quest for the same degree zero of genericness, a space in which *writing*—apparently supplanting any of its subcategories, whether generic or modal—tends, so to speak, to double back on itself and become increasingly absorbed in the celebration of its own autogenous existence.

Besides questioning accepted notions of prose, poetry, narrative, the lyric, and a number of other literary genres and metagenres, the celebration by Language poetry of "writing itself" also contributes to blurring traditional boundaries between theory and poetry. The highly theorized and self-reflexive works discussed so far indeed suggest that such a focus on the activity of writing paradoxically leads to a situation in which the poets become their own critics and in which theory even tends to precede poetry and define it into being, thereby inverting the usual relationship between criticism and creative writing. As Charles Bernstein reminds us, the gradual fusion of creative and theoretical writing is largely based on the Language poets' desire to build a community of writers in which to engage in "an interrogation of the meaning of any mode—of 'poetry' or 'theory'—and an acknowledgment that there is no escape from composition, no logic on which to base the work other than the sense developed ongoing in the actual activity itself. "Critical forums," he concludes, "have been a way to open up beyond correspondence and conversation the dialogue between the writers themselves—an exchange of 'working' information—and to include in this discussion those not primarily involved with poetry, such as other artists, and political and cultural workers, and to suggest possible relationships between the poetry and recent critical and philosophical thought" ("For Change," *Tree* 488–89).

The "critical forums" Bernstein is referring to seek to problematize poetic practice by reference to a number of other theoretical discourses, including, as we have seen, politics, philosophy, French literary theory, and feminism. The work of Rosmarie Waldrop and of a number of other Language poets testifies to the existence of such a new hybrid kind of creative writing, itself halfway between poetry and theory, and of which James Sherry's "The Marginal Arts" is a typical and relatively self-explanatory example:

Ready to think. Standard covers, essential rather than deconstructed, in fact often a word for a theory. The scene can continue unabated if it is impure enough to accept the lives of its members and the necessities of its institutions, but several must look away when she skims the fat off her chicken soup. Softening the edge of expectation to admit that there is no end.

Science builds a description ending in near irony, Barry. I want to attribute this statement, but I don't know if I should. If I waited until I were sure, I would, no. Our choices are to fight it with our weapons or retreat to create an alternative agenda.

. . . To stumble through the words, to assure that you haven't got anything easy to communicate. Polymorphs—what is this feel like— mangled, managed. Two that the universe was created not by intelligence, but maintained by laws perceptible to intelligence.

For when are we steeled to greet the fantastic results of inconceivable action, then that action might be taken as means. Far away cows on a front swept back to a brow of trees, shades of the same green among the bones of diseased elms. Virtue is always too much of a piece. (Bernstein, "43 Poets" 52–53)

Sherry's poem is representative of Bernstein's notion of "critical writing" in two ways. First, it incorporates down-to-earth descriptions and imagistic interludes into its theoretical argumentation.[25] Second, it has evidently interiorized the "recent critical and philosophical thought" mentioned by Bernstein. While the opening lines of "The Marginal Arts" explicitly echo a number of basic principles of Derridean deconstruction, including its rejection of essentialist certainties and its celebration of an endless postponement of meaning ("softening the edge of expectation to admit that there is no end"), the first sentence of the second paragraph discards the claims to objectivity of scientific discourse by reminding us of its figurative nature, an issue raised not only by Derrida himself but also by the uncertainty principle of quantum theory.

Sherry's statement on the tropological foundations of scientific discourse ("Science builds a description ending in near irony") is an adequate illustration of the Language poets' self-conscious blurring of the boundaries between critical and creative writing—yet another aspect of Language poetry on which Stein's influence was decisive. This particular kind of prose poem has indeed the merit of bringing to light the syntactic and phenomenological mechanisms that condition the writing of poetry and, thereby, of divesting poetic discourse of its claims to spontaneous naturalness. Conversely, it sets out to reveal how the hypotactic logic of normative expository style is itself informed by contradictions and disruptions, which its apparent rigorousness or "literalness" attempts to conceal, rather than resolve, in the guise of syntactic mystifications.

The major theoretical correlatives here seem, once again, to be Derrida's critique of Western metaphysics and, in particular, his distinction between the literal and the figurative. According to Derrida, philosophical language can only claim to be philosophical if it suppresses or disguises the fact that it is inevitably articulated through a language that is irreducibly metaphorical (or "figurative"). Philosophy, notwithstanding its claims to rationality or "literalness," indeed works by the same tropes and figures as literature, and a deconstructive analysis of the various ways in which literal discourses deny their own textuality enables one to expose the extent to which they are actually contaminated by it. In the same way, literary discourse can be read as literal, despite its self-conscious use of the rhetorical devices supporting it. Ultimately, Derrida's discussion of the interpenetration and interdependence of the figurative and the literal denies the validity of any essential or structural divisions between literary and nonliterary, creative and utilitarian forms of writing.

Like Sherry's "The Marginal Arts," the following extract from Madeline Gins' *Essay on Multi-Dimensional Architecture* deconstructs the historically acquired prestige of the expository style of the essay as a "pure" rational, truth-bearing discourse by exposing it to an even higher degree of "figurative" disruptions:

> The closed-lipped glow of prehensility was everywhere. Yet how often I remember being told in those days of the nature of the complexion of capacity. The cooled-to-nothing ratchets were everywhere of a legendary expanse, but let me explain.
>
> It is a question of, an occasionally viscous question of, an unimpeded flow of nurtured motions [as much creak as slide/slurp]. Any path, once opened, had better be left that way, counteracted, if need be, or put into perspective, but never just shut down. Any careless stepping about or onto the path of immanent occurrence may lead to unuse or unawareness of anywhere, verging, of course, on everywhere, and leading, possibly, to a general pallor or power failure (capaucity). (Bernstein, "43 Poets" 95)

In her most recent work of "speculative prose" to date, *Helen Keller or Arakawa,* Gins weaves a spectrum of philosophical complications and molecular complexities that somehow exceeds the limits of her own unmistakable brand of "multidimensional" discourse. The language is abrasive, porous, corrugated, witty and visionary, lucid and opaque, visceral and analytical, alternately solid and protoplasmic. All this makes for a new form of "postgeneric" prose, a search for a new consciousness, the contours of which Gins sets out to delineate on the basis of Keller's life, the art of New York–based painter and architect Arakawa, and the Kirlian vectors of her own prose. Gins' reflections on the trajectories of thought and feeling often result in a sort of verbal choreography—interrupted and complemented by various types of typographical and intertextual directions—that seeks to combine the thread of memory with an awareness of the unnamed movements of the waking mind in relation to its physical environment. By focusing on the interaction between objective and subjective experience,

Gins also succeeds in creating a form of critical and creative sensibility that is both transitive and intransitive, without falling into the kind of mechanical self-reflexiveness all too often encountered in a style of writing that acknowledges "process." Here is the beginning of the closing chapter-poem-essay of Gins' book, "Critical Beach":

"Oh beach, what of compromise ?"
This went on :
Or wrenching torque or twister orbit grown core runner coordinate. Or torsion or. Or deformation or. Contour. More particles gravel roar lore. The ochre vortexed cortexed orotund orange grain of it. Corrugated fortitude. Corrugated anchoring. Orb sore soar sorting pours cornered odor porridge vigor.
And this was "heard" as:
"A compromising of what?" "Who is doing the compromising?" "Which envelope?" "Of which envelope do you speak?"
"I fear the dreadful patina of compromise. Whatever's only half done or anything merely half noticed has this patina. How can I have nothing to do with this?"
I was then put through this:
Micro-orbs succored through abrasive strainers. Orbs numerous toward runner coordinate core. Non-torpor tenor or dormant forbidden oracular powder. Gridder grid more corporeal. Effort's micro-operators. Torsion orifices ignoring four million or four billion minor other orbs. Vortices determining morphology of pre-formed neuter perforations. Rotated orthogonal coral-like corridors. Brocade of porosity by arbor.
Which said:
When you do what you do, are you desiring to be doing this enough?" "Minutely desiring enough in all particulars?" "Have you made sure the desire for doing this rests anywhere it possibly could figure?"
As to how this was said, and how, in general, critical beach goes about saying what it says, the blaysplay sand of the forming planet forming, able to self-position so as to convey, forms the basis of this. All supplemental significations up off the sand ride the waves of the sound of the surf in fair partnership. All position was pliant, intended, and critically adept. (289–90)

Gins' "critical beach"—a "forming planet" prompting the speaker's attempts to coordinate her senses and formulate her own awakening to new modes of perceiving—illustrates the process of expanding awareness which constitutes the basis of her poetic project. In a more general way, Gins'

prose does not let itself be construed by conventional hermeneutic strategies, albeit in a subversive fashion, because it does much more than resist
the normative strategies by which we try to regulate and simplify our lives,
both on a phenomenological and a linguistic level. Physical and metaphysical uncertainty, the dialectics of blindness and insight, the West's misunder-
standing of the non-West, transcontinental culture shock, postmodern aesthetics, and architectural contingency are themes that compete and
combine in Gins' investigation of the mechanisms of meaning and consciousness. Perhaps the best way of approaching *Helen Keller or Arakawa*
is to read it in light of her definition of the poet as "a juggler of micro-
distinctions" (*LINEbreak*). Gins displays a huge intellectual and visionary
faculty, both profound and witty, as she sets the terms for a "thinking field"
(Keller 9) that does justice to the manifold transitivity of her intercon-
nected lines of thought and belief.

The contamination of expository forms by syntactic, physical, cultural,
and rhetorical complications that characterizes the works of James Sherry
and Madeline Gins is precisely what Silliman is hinting at when, arguing
for a critical history of literary criticism, he indicates what such an approach should study. In addition to "the role of a bureaucratized criticism
in a capitalist society as the creation of a 'safe' and 'official' culture,"
Silliman insists that such a history needs to address "the illusion of clarity
in criticism in its use of the essay form, in which the contradictions of its
existence, such as would be revealed through inarticulations, redundancies
and non-sequiturs, are subsumed under hypotactic form, rendered invisible
rather than resolved." Ultimately, he continues, "it would study the existence of counter-tendencies within literary criticism as well, specifically the
sometimes anarchic works of literary theory created by poets (e.g., the
body of prose left by Charles Olson) and the recent trend in France towards
literary criticism as an admitted art form (e.g., Roland Barthes or Jacques
Derrida)" (*Sentence* 15–6).

The fact, however, that Language poetry itself can be seen as one of the
"counter-tendencies" mentioned by Silliman (including the hybrid critico-
literary experiments of a Barthes or a Derrida) logically leads one to wonder whether this constitutes a real alternative to the transformation of writing into a bureaucratized discipline that Silliman is denouncing in the same
paragraph. While a number of individual works effectively subvert traditional assumptions underlying the writing of both literature and criticism,
the overall phenomenon of Language poetry, with its constant interplay
between academic and creative discourse, is also likely to be perceived as a
further institutionalization of poetry writing into an academic discipline.

In this respect, one could also object that Silliman's own critical arguments against the claims to objective naturalness of expository prose are themselves expressed in the highly organized and hierarchical "syllogistic" language of academic criticism, a form of writing which depends on a number of methodological assumptions his creative works have attempted to deconstruct for the last twenty or twenty-five years.

The New Prose Poem and the Politics of Form

The Language poets' predilection for prose partly originates in a desire to question and disrupt prescriptive boundaries between traditional genres, modes, and discourses—both intra- and extrapoetic—and subsequently to redistribute them into a differential space. By deconstructing the very notion of genre as just another "narrative" and, for instance, calling into question the "naturalness" of accepted prescriptive and definitional boundaries between prose and poetry, the lyric and the narrative, the literal and the figurative (or, more generally, between aesthetic, utilitarian, and ideological discourses), the New Prose Poem can be seen as the methodological culmination of the various transgeneric experiments examined in the preceding chapters. One of the most important aspects of these generic disruptions is the mutually supplemental coexistence of theory and creative praxis: the sentence and the paragraph become hybrid units of both poetic and metapoetic value. Likewise, exploration in the New Prose Poem of the syntactic possibilities of prose facilitates both creative and theoretical exchanges, while doing justice to the movement's status as a communal, dialogical, and diacritical debate.

The Language poets' rejection of the self-present naturalness of speech leads them to question and distance themselves from a tradition that has so far largely promulgated a notion of poetry as an essentially aural art. The emphasis on the *process* of writing and the materiality of language as a medium for poetic composition ultimately aims at a "laying bare" of the syntactic and semantic strategies that condition the very act of writing, while foregrounding the textuality of the compositional process and its end product. In the context of their concern with scripturality and syntax, the Language poets' deconstructive approach to accepted notions of poetic "naturalness" is strengthened by an exploration of the constructedness of the various aesthetic frames of reference underlying prose writing.

As a result of the Language poets' focus on writing as a *social* practice, their analytical and creative exploration of scripturality and syntax often becomes a metaphor for the exploration of ideological, as well as aesthetic, constructions. Like Silliman, many Language poets see writing as both a social production and a reflection of the mechanisms that determine the social conditions themselves. According to this view, the structural resources of prose syntax—the linguistic medium par excellence of discourses of authority and legitimation—should theoretically provide them with a scrupulous instrument of social critique, one which is based on a double recognition of the ideological premises of poetic creation (language is always already pervaded with ideology) and the linguistic foundations of ideology (ideology itself is a signifying chain).[26]

If one were to describe the contribution of the Language poetry project "as a whole" to the history of contemporary poetry, one might attempt to draw a line around a range of writing that promotes a radical critique of nothing less than the very medium, methods, aims, and social significance of what is commonly referred to as poetry. By questioning the institutional and historical determinations of poetry and subsequently redefining it into a radically epistemological category, Language poetry emerges as the logical outcome of the gradual disappearance of formally, thematically, or modally prescriptive criteria of distinction between literary genres explored in the preceding chapters. As we have seen, the Language poets' insistence on writing as a social practice also led some of them to rewrite the "lyric" genre into a collective space by reinscribing the "I" into its real sociolinguistic conditions of existence.[27] Rejecting the assumptions of lyric "naturalness" and self-presence promulgated by most major trade publishers, MFA programs, and other avatars of what Bernstein has called "official verse culture" (*Content* 247), Language poetry puts the emphasis on the process of composition and the constructedness of the written artifact, thereby drawing attention both to the textuality of the written "I" and to the extraneousness of the writing "I" from its own discourse. In this, Language poetry can be seen as extending the lyric mode—rather than ringing its death knell—by updating it, so to speak, and making it compatible with the postmodern condition.

In theory, the methodological foundations of the Language poetry movement, far from declaring poetry bankrupt, should logically result in an enlargement of the social, thematic, and, more generally, epistemological scope of poetry. This is, at any rate, what Marjorie Perloff is implying when she describes Language poetry as a counterhegemonic practice capable of accommodating a variety of extraliterary discourses and, therefore, of making contact "with the *world* as well as the *word*" (*Dance* 181). However, the danger of the appearance of a new kind of self-limiting narcissism sometimes lurks even among those poets most convinced (and most convincing) of the necessity to "bring more of the outside world into it." Indeed, an unfortunate consequence of this tendency to focus on the process of writing (Bernstein's motto: "no escape from composition") is that it sometimes results in a mechanical and predictable self-reflexiveness all too often encountered in postwar American poetry and in an inherent disposition to fall back upon the self-conscious, and occasionally self-indulgent, poem about poetry writing. Language-oriented works such as Steve Benson's *Blue Book,* Michael Palmer's *Sun,* Alan Davies' *Signage,* and to some extent Ron Silliman's *Tjanting* or Steve McCaffery's *Panopticon* are, in various ways, symptomatic of the progression of Language writing from a self-conscious attention to the linguistic premises of poetry to a consciousness enthralled in the contemplation of its own strategies of (self-)verbalization. In some cases, such a reductive use of language-oriented poetry tends to indulge in a facile, narcissistic, and excessively explicit analysis of the process of composition. It also signals the unexpected emergence of a new kind of postlyric subjectivism born, as it were, out of the ashes of Barthes' defunct Author.

The Language poets' rejection of conventional syntax in the name of social and cultural dissidence is also far from being entirely convincing. As we have seen, most Language poets see the divergence of poetic language from customary discourse as a form of politically subversive activity. Even if one agrees with Steve McCaffery that prescriptive grammar is "a repressive mechanism, regulat[ing] the free circulation of meaning" (Andrews and Bernstein 160), it does not necessarily follow that a piece of so-called asyntactic or polysemantic writing can actually undermine the social and political Establishment, even in a rhetorical, nonpragmatic arena of action. In fact, the reverse may be true. The postulate that syntactic disruption *as such* marks out the ground of radical dissidence remains doubtful, to say the least, in the context of a society increasingly dominated not so much by the syllogistic logic of legal or political discourse as by the already fragmented and sloganizing rhetoric of advertising, MTV video clips, television newscasts, or professional spin doctors' versions of current events.

Bob Perelman acknowledges this risk in *The Marginalization of Poetry* when he writes that "the 'new' of the new sentence is poised between symptom and critique" (69). Responding to Eliot Weinberger's Jamesonian criticism of the Language poets' use of parataxis as "the product of a generation raised in front of the television: an endless succession of depthless images and empty signs, each cancelling the previous ones" (197), Perelman nonetheless insists on the underlying coherence and unity of (social) focus of New Sentence narratives: "new sentences imply continuity and discontinuity simultaneously, an effect that becomes clearer when they are read over long stretches." Commenting on an excerpt from Silliman's *Ketjak* ("Fountains of the financial district spout soft water in a hard wind. She was a unit in a bum space, she was a damaged child"), Perelman writes: "the child and the fountains need not be imagined in a single tableau. This effect of calling forth a new context after each period goes directly against the structural impatience that creates narrative . . . but in a larger sense, girl and fountain are in the same social space" (67). Perelman's analysis is accurate enough. That its featured writers are Silliman and Hejinian (whose work is significantly more referential and confessional than that of many other Language writers) and not, for example, Palmer, T. Beckett, Watson, or Robinson nonetheless indicates his reluctance to explore other uses of parataxis that, for all their obvious merits, may prove less oppositional or socially relevant. It is precisely this diversity of approaches to the same literary or rhetorical technique that Charles Bernstein has in mind when he speaks of the necessity to understand rhetorical and aesthetic techniques "in context rather than as some universal cipher of 'devicehood'." Juxtaposition of "logically unconnected sentences or sentence fragments," Bernstein writes, "can be used to theatricalize the limitations of conventional narrative development, to suggest the impossibility of communication, to represent speech, or as part of a prosodic mosaic constituting a newly emerging (or . . . traditional but neglected) meaning formation; these uses have nothing in common; neither can such techniques be identified with all uses of 'fragmentation' or collage in the other arts" (*A Poetics* 91–92). In other words, the Language poets' use of fragmentation can, in some cases, lead to the negation of conventional meaning or, in more engaging works, can become "a method of tapping into other possibilities of meaning within language" (93).

It seems to me that another, significantly more embarrassing, epiphenomenon of the Language poets' rejection of normative syntax and their insistence upon the materiality of the signifier is that it often leads them to neglect, or even actively to dodge, those very signif*ied* aspects of the cultural, historical, and political circumstances they set out to denounce. The rigorously theorized premises of the Language project, which sets out to explore literary creation as both a reflection of *and* a platform for ideological struggle, should logically lead to a systematic rewriting of the notion of poetry into a social and political space. However, many of the poems examined in the present chapter display a reluctance to go beyond an emphasis placed strictly on the syntactic and semantic aspects of linguistic production. Such an approach often tends to be too general to deal with specific issues and, therefore, partly fails in its attempts to contribute genuinely to the political critique advocated by the Language poets themselves. As Terry Eagleton reminds us, however, the privileging of the signifier over the signified, as well as the alleged death of the referent, applies not only to Language poetry but to the whole history of post-Saussurean structuralist and poststructuralist theory that underlies it and that all too often fails to live up to its own self-proclaimed radicalism:

> Literary theory has come to be identified with the political left; but while it is true that a good many of its practitioners hail from that region, it is much less obvious that theory itself is an inherently radical affair. One might, indeed, argue exactly the opposite. It would be possible to see semiotics as the expression of an advanced capitalist order so saturated with codes and messages that we all now live in some vast stock exchange of the mind in which gobbets of packaged information whizz past us at every angle. Just as money breeds money in finance capitalism, having long forgotten that it was supposed to be the sign of something real, so the Saussurean sign broods on itself and its fellows in grand isolation from anything as low as a referent. (Eagleton 3)

Such is the essential limitation brought about by Silliman's overthrow of the "tyranny of the signified" and the "limited" and "controlled" syllogistic movement of the New Sentence (and, arguably, deconstructive practice in general), in the context of which "any attempt to explicate the work as a whole according to some 'higher' order of meaning, such as narrative or character, is doomed to sophistry, if not overt incoherence" (*Sentence* 92). Bruce Andrews' reflections on language and radicalism account for the resistance of Language poetry to political "statement" as such:

> Conventionally, radical dissent & "politics" in writing would be measured in terms of communication & concrete effects on an audience. Which means either a direct effort at empowering or mobilizing—aimed at existing identities—or at the representation of outside conditions, usually in an issue-oriented way. So-called "progressive lit." The usual assumptions about the unmediated communication, giving "voice" to "individual" "experience," the transparency of the medium (language), the instrumentalizing of language, pluralism, etc. bedevil the project. But more basically: such conventionally progressive literature fails to self-examine writing & its medium, lan-

guage. Yet, in an era where the reproduction of the social status quo is more & more dependent upon ideology & language (language in ideology & ideology in language), that means that it can't really make claims to comprehend and/or challenge the nature of the social whole; it can't be political in that crucial way. ("Poetry" 23–24)

Andrews contrasts "conventional" political writing with what he calls "radical praxis," which operates at the level of the sentence and "involves the rigors of formal celebration, a playful infidelity, a certain illegibility within the legible: an infinitizing, a wide-open exuberance, a perpetual motion machine, a transgression" (25). Responding to Erica Hunt's objection that "there exist several distinct projects of opposition and resistance that are every bit as serious and intent as those that take the ground of textuality of language" (34), Andrews comments: "Because if the fundamental building blocks of sense reside at a lower level in the fundamental structure of the sign, and how that functions systematically, then if that's not addressed first, the power of the work to address the nature of the social order evaporates" (36). Since "there is no 'direct treatment' of the thing possible, except of the 'things' of language," he continues, any attempt to "cast our glance away from [the process of production of meaning]" is necessarily an act of bad faith, one which denies both the ontological gap between signifier and signified and the fact that any linguistic utterance is inevitably contaminated by ideology. For Andrews, the making of sense is always necessarily the making of "social sense." The only way of investigating the social and political dimension of language is therefore to consider the process of linguistic production itself in order to "lay bare the device" and "spurn the facts as not self-evident" (24). Andrews' rejection of practical, issue-oriented radicalism—that is, of a practice based on a forum for ideas about new, utopian representations of the social whole (such as would rely on the use of normative or "transparent" language most Language poets would object to)—is typical of a line of thought with Marxist premises that have been steadily eroded by its deconstructionist orientation.

This particular complaint will sound familiar to readers acquainted with the theoretical controversies that have surrounded Language poetry since the mid-1980s.[28] At present, critical approaches to the political claims of Language poetry seem divided into two opposite camps represented by avant-garde supporters such as Marjorie Perloff, Jerome McGann, and Hank Lazer, on the one hand, and a number of skeptical, and occasionally hostile, responses on the part of such critics as Charles Altieri and Albert

Gelpi, on the other. While Jerome McGann's statements about the social value of Language poetry have so far ranged from the melodramatic to the plain ludicrous, the close readings and theoretical insights of Marjorie Perloff, from *The Dance of the Intellect* to the closing chapter of *Wittgenstein's Ladder,* have provided us with many reasons to take the Language poets seriously and to go through the trouble of addressing the works of representatives of the movement on the basis of the particularities of their cases.[29] Her discerning readings of individual works and poets have helped readers become aware of the position of Language poetry in the broader history of twentieth-century avant-garde poetics as well as of the wide range of writing produced by writers associated with the movement. By doing so, they have also implicitly warned us about the danger of overgeneralizing about the group and homogenizing their ideas. As some of the readings contained in the present book have demonstrated, not all the Language poets share Andrews' ideas about language and the social order, nor do they all use the same disjunctive poetics to the same ends.[30] Similarly, the wide-ranging body of writing produced by Language poets in the last twenty-five years underscores the fact that the term *Language poetry* covers a diverse, highly contested field, crowded with a variety of philosophies that comprise not only the thinking of Marx, Derrida, Kristeva, Foucault, Lacan, and Althusser but also that of Cage, Mac Low, Stein, Perec, Khlebnikov, Brecht, Wittgenstein, Olson, Kosuth, Duchamp, Albiach, Beckett, Ashbery, and even Kerouac.

Among the detractors of Language poetry, one of the most articulate and incisive responses to the issue of its political relevance has come from Albert Gelpi, who, in his 1990 essay, "The Genealogy of Postmodernism," attempts to discriminate between language-oriented works that still enact "the engagement between consciousness and the external world" and others that do not, warning of the danger of yielding to language "a devouring self-reflexivity that denies both subject and object by refusing to mediate between them." The ultimate consequence of such a mode of writing, he concludes, is "to paralyze the capacity of language for change and effecting change and to reduce the range of reference and resonance to the mere spread of surface" (538).

What would seem to constitute a more solid basis for a new relevance of poetic language within the social sphere is the ability of certain Language poets to enter a particular set of discursive or narrative conventions in order to critique its biases and limitations with reference to a specific social context. By questioning the naturalness of social discourses and narratives and exposing their subservience to a particular network of cultural assumptions, these poets are indeed in a position to open up wider issues of social meaning than are their nonrepresentational counterparts. In this respect, at least two of the examples discussed, Lyn Hejinian's *My Life* and Ron Silliman's *Paradise,* seek to underscore their engagement with language and textuality yet simultaneously introduce new ways of experiencing and representing the relationship between self and world. The work of another prominent Language prose poet, Carla Harryman, far from retreating into a poetics of free play and undecidability, displays a similar interest in the signified contexts of contemporary experience, particularly as regards her investigation of genre and gender issues. Similarly, the streetwise controversialism of Bruce Andrews' *I Don't Have Any Paper So Shut Up (Or, Social Romanticism)* eschews conventional argumentative syntax at the same time as it takes a variety of domestic and public aspects of American imperialism and capitalism as its target. As we have seen, Andrews' radical praxis concerns exclusively the signifying "hardware" of syntax and ideology and prevents any direct treatment of signified realities. More important, however, it can be seen as preparing the ground for a possible resurgence of a poetry of "statement" capable of calling its own discursive premises into question.

Such works demonstrate that Language poetry can still focus on the paradigmatic axis of linguistic and poetic production, at the same time as it attempts to critique the syntagmatic dynamics of normative syntax. The Language poets are therefore in a position to address specific issues related to contemporary Western society (including mass media culture, gender politics, postindustrial technology, and the politics of postmodern culture) in a more specifically and explicitly "referential" fashion, while having clearly interiorized the theoretical foundations of the movement. The interest of those poets in specific or local signified contexts proves that a rejection of the metaphysics of the "transcendental signified" does not necessarily have to lead to a poetry that seeks to celebrate the areferential charms of the "empty sign" and demands to be read and evaluated on that basis only.

Epilogue
The Prose Poem Now

The preceding chapters have shown that the history of the contemporary prose poem in English is, above all, characterized by an enormous variety in mode, tone, form, and subject matter. It would therefore be tempting to see the prose poem not as a genre in itself but, rather, as a platform for various intergeneric negotiations, one which promotes a constant dialectical exchange not only with the various trends and modes of contemporary poetry as a whole but also with a number of extraliterary discourses and modes of representation. Generally speaking, the texts examined here indeed point to little more than such a latent "skeleton definition" of the genre as a prose composition labeled as a poem or a prose poem and the "poetic" quality of which derives from its relationship to a poetic tradition or from its conscious subversion of a prose tradition.

Given the prose poem's self-proclaimed status as a "boundary genre" par excellence, the impulse to set limits or decide on a number of defining "traits" that have characterized it throughout the twentieth century appears highly problematic. While I have tried to show a variousness of directions, rather than a set of definitions, the recent rise to prominence of the genre in the United States suggests that the prose poem can no longer be considered as a protean entity, the very existence of which depends on its relationship to the genres and traditions it belongs to or subverts. Now that a number of general trends have established themselves as characteristic of "the" American prose poem, the genre is likely to be further institutionalized into the canon of American poetry under various restrictive labels, such as the Deep Image prose poem, the neo-Surrealist fable, or the language-oriented New Prose Poem.[1] If the author of prose poems writes with reference to a particular tradition and/or with a view to a particular audience, the reader is also bound to approach each individual work with a number of expectations, which will vary with the current vogue. Michael Benedikt recently raised the issue of the gradual assimilation of the prose poem into the canon of American poetry. Commenting on what he sees as the inherent capacity of the prose poem to capture the rhythms of the unconscious mind, he writes:

> Certainly, there's a lot of primordial, unconscious, elemental-style imagery among recent prose poems. For example, "A Man," "A Woman" (with which an unusually high proportion of prose poems start out, relative to poems in verse); Earth, Air, Water & Fire (which also make their appearance quite frequently, relative to poems in verse).
>
> These habits are obviously legitimate, psychologically at least, since the unconscious tends to operate in terms of basics.
>
> On the other hand, that kind of elemental iconography can become a bit mannered, and predictable—like the often-repeated iconography of any period. For example, roses, cloaks, birds, etc., in, say, 16th century Elizabethan poetry, or old ruins, storms, lakes and mountains, in, say, 19th century Romantic poetry.

"If the prose poem has a long-term future as an alternative to writing poems in verse (and as an expression of the unconscious, the imagination, or whatever)," Benedikt concludes, "it will, I think, have to continue to develop in a way that is still more far-reaching—and proceed by extending itself beyond basics" ("A Few Notes" 10). Whereas the stock "elemental iconography" mentioned by Benedikt is an important hallmark of the Deep Image tradition made famous by Robert Bly, the opening formula, "A man"/"A woman," has become a recognizable feature of the fabulist trend still propagated by Benedikt himself and by scores of younger prose poets. As we have seen, these recent developments once again call into question the status of the prose poem as a "genreless" genre resisting incorporation into the mainstream of contemporary poetry. They suggest that the prose poem is liable to turn into just another highly codified genre or, at worst, a toolbox of hackneyed ploys.[2] In this respect, Naomi Shihab Nye's preliminary remarks to her 1991 collection, *Mint*, betray a devastatingly self-limiting conception of the genre. "I think of those pieces," she writes, "as being simple paragraphs rather than 'prose poems,' though a few might sneak into the prose poem category, were they traveling on their own. The paragraph, standing by itself, has a lovely pocket-sized quality. It garnishes the page, as mint garnishes a plate (R. Murphy 103). Even though Nye claims that her "paragraphs" are not part of any tradition of the prose poem as such, this statement is nevertheless emblematic of a conspicuous

lack of ambition too often encountered in recent collections and anthologies. Although some of Nye's most successful pieces have more to offer
than mere garnitures, they often display a tendency to produce nothing
more than a beautifully wrought paragraph; an elegantly framed and easily
consumable commodity generally thought of as less "difficult" than a
lineated poem.

Russell Edson has argued that one of the reasons for the current popularity of the prose poem is precisely "its clumsiness, its lack of expectation
and ambition" ("Portrait" 301). For Edson, "the ideal prose poem . . . is a
relatively short work without obvious ornament (if indeed this is not an
ornament), presented on the page with the simplicity of a child's primer,
including proper paragraph indents" (Letter). As another prose poet, Louis
Jenkins, writes: "Think of the prose poem as a box. . . . The box is made for
travel, quick and light. Think of the prose poem as a small suitcase. One
must pack carefully, only the essentials, too much and the reader won't get
off the ground" (unpag.). According to this view, the prose poem appeals to
many writers and readers primarily because of its lack of presumptuous
expansiveness ("the prose poem is a frame in which the particular individual experience is framed modestly and transiently" [E. Smith 117]), its
limited topical relevance, and, more generally, the accessibility of its format: "the deceptively simple packaging: the paragraph," which James Tate
sees as the genre's principal "means of seduction" (Lehman 202). Still, the
line between studied clumsiness (or deliberate naiveté) and an unintentional lack of skill and imagination is not always easy to draw. Clearly, the
kind of "cultivated nonchalance" that has become typical of Edson's own
fabulist pieces is also responsible, at least in part, for the current reputation
of the prose poem as a *minor* genre—this time not because of its antagonistic position toward the mainstream but as a result of its self-imposed formal and epistemological limitations.

As the best works represented in this study demonstrate, the prose poem
has nonetheless continued to live up to its original vocation as an "open"
and innovative form, notably by reclaiming a number of functions that lie
outside the traditional field of tonal and rhetorical expertise of poetry in
verse. A desire to expand the formal and methodological possibilities of the
genre is already noticeable in the work of younger poets published in various anthologies and magazines since the late 1980s.[3] This study should not
conclude without mentioning two of the most accomplished representatives of the younger generation of fabulist prose poets: Marie Harris and
Peter Johnson. Although one of the chief merits of these writers is that they
write into the open, the common denominator of their works is an effort to

reintroduce some social credibility and psychological depth into the genre—two features sorely absent from many recent collections of "well-made" absurdist prose poems. Harris and Johnson achieve an optimal balance of irony and lyricism, as well as a seemingly effortless use of language and rhythm, which prevents them from lapsing into the kind of heavy-footed self-consciousness many of their fabulist counterparts are mired in. What makes Johnson's work particularly successful in this respect has to do with its capacity to deal not so much with types and grotesques as with "the truths that make people grotesques" (to quote from the Sherwood Anderson epigraph to his collection, *Pretty Happy!*) and thereby to demonstrate that verbal play, pastiche, and irony are not incompatible with the expression of private or collective anxieties.

A full-length account of the different uses to which the form has been put since the 1980s would have to consider an extremely broad spectrum of forms and methods, ranging from the flamboyant textual games of Amy Gerstler's *Bitter Angel* to the raw, visceral confessionalism of a Stephen Berg or the image-centered poetics of a Robert Hass. One of the main strengths of a collection such as Hass' *Human Wishes,* which contains poems in verse and in prose, lies in its combination of two radically different ways of handling the poetic idiom—an ear for the rhythmic potentialities of prose and an awareness of the problem of language and referentiality—and which therefore reflects and elaborates upon two essential directions taken by the genre throughout the twentieth century. Whereas the second part of the book consists in a collage of microtales and prose poems resembling journal entries, the opening section contains a number of more speculative pieces investigating the nature of poetry and representation. These concerns are apparent in the semidisjunctive structure of "Spring Drawing," which is composed of a series of syntactically conventional clauses divided into paragraphs of variable length. The first paragraph of the poem is already suggestive of how Hass' preoccupation with the gap between mind and object combines with an intensely physical relationship with language: "A man thinks *lilacs against white houses,* having seen them in the farm country south of Tacoma in April, and can't find his way to a sentence, a brushstroke carrying the energy of *brush* and *stroke.*" For all his interest in the sheer energy of the creative process and the power of words *as* words, however, Hass' exploration of "the meaning of meaning" in "Spring Drawing" results in "a felt need to reinvent the inner form of wishing" (3). Far from subordinating the value of individual experience to an analysis of medium, Hass seeks to "name" the real in a way that, by pointing to the erasure of distinctions between the real and the made world, as well as between the physical and the abstract, holds out new connections between the spirit and the body, the intellect and the senses. Informed by the democratic and compassionate gesture of haiku ("Basho said: avoid adjectives of scale" [5]), his poetry longs for images that "do not say this is that" but "this is" (*Twentieth* 275). Such images, Hass writes—reasserting his preference for metonymy rather than metaphors—"marry the world but do not claim to possess it" (305).

In the "experimental" camp, many recent "language-oriented" works continue to rewrite the genre into a scriptural art, apparently confirming Stephen Adams' view that the prose poem marks "the farthest remove of poetry from any pretension to speech or song toward the direction of pure writing" (198). One could, however, argue exactly the opposite when confronted with John Godfrey's *When the Weather Suits My Clothes*, for instance, or Kenward Elmslie's abecedarium of prose poems, *26 bars,* both of which look back, at least formally speaking, to the vernacular, speech-based tradition of the genre inaugurated by Williams' *Improvisations*. Like the prose poems of Patchen's *Famous Boating Party,* Elmslie's pieces are meant to be recited or sung, often to the accompaniment of live music. The quirky, alliteration- and pun-ridden cadences of Elmslie's *26 bars* make him one of the most independent and talented presences on the prose poem scene today.

In recent years, the speech-based tradition of the prose poem has found one of its most remarkable expressions in the work of several Native American writers, most notably N. Scott Momaday, Luci Tapahanso, and Joy Harjo. Harjo's *In Mad Love and War* is a collection interconnecting verse, songs, stories, prayers, legends, chants, and prose poems. Building on oral traditions of Muscogee storytelling, Harjo's prose poems often center on the healing powers of narrative in order to establish meaningful connections between the self and society. Many of them—such as "Autobiography," "Santa Fe," and "Javelina"—are confessional pieces that reflect her attempts to come to terms with her Creek heritage, from the tragic history of her tribe's removal to the present displaced condition of Native Americans. Quite frequently, Harjo's poetic narratives seek to infuse the present with the past in a "spiral of memory," the ultimate goal of which is to keep spiritual community alive and to regenerate the self through dream, ritual, and myth.

Despite the current risk of the genre giving birth to a variety of highly conventionalized trends, the history of the contemporary prose poem in English remains far too polymorphous to be contained in a single definition capable of accommodating tendencies as antipodal as the speech-based poetics of Patchen's *The Famous Boating Party*, the scriptural premises of Silliman's New Prose Poem, the metapoetic games of Benedikt's *Mole Notes*, or the Deep Images of Bly's *The Morning Glory*. At this stage, however, it is safe to say that the two main competing camps in the recent history of the prose poem in English are represented by the so-called fabulist school and the language-oriented New Prose Poem. According to Ron Silliman, a distinction must be made between the New Prose Poem (or what Michael Davidson calls the "new prose") and the so-called conventional prose poets, who, like Ignatow, Edson, Benedikt, Bly, and Simic, write mainly with reference to a European tradition of the genre (*Sentence* 95–96). This distinction, however, brings us back to the issue of the labeling and publishing situation of the prose poem, for the boundary between these respective schools is not always as clear-cut as Silliman and Davidson deem it to be. Despite their claims to "language-orientedness" and vanguardism, the works of several poets generally regarded as Language writers, such as Carla Harryman and Lydia Davis, are definitely not antipodal to what Silliman describes as the "mainstream" of the American prose poem. The following piece by Lydia Davis, for instance, published in Charles Bernstein's anthology of L=A=N=G=U=A=G=E writing, "43 Poets (1984)," clearly falls (perhaps too obviously) into the absurdist category made famous by Russell Edson:

THE DOG MAN

A man in our office is really a dog. He does not do well, is slow and clumsy though extremely good-natured. There is also a dog in our town who is really a man and is tormented by his inability to express himself and thus cannot be good-natured but is sly and furtive and ashamed of himself. He is hated by everyone and kicked to a corner of the room. Of course, that is only one kind of dog who is really a man: another kind of dog who is really a man is like the man who is really a dog in our office, and he does very well because he is most comfortable as a dog. (7)

On a functional and methodological level, the fabulists and the Language poets are generally emblematic of the gradual emancipation of the contemporary prose poem from a conception of the genre as a piece of "poeticized" prose, and likewise emblematic of its tendency to explore the imagistic and rhetorical possibilities of already existing lyric, narrative, and speculative genres and discourses. Seen from this angle, both currents can be seen to embody, in different degrees, a number of features that have characterized the history of the prose poem in English throughout the twentieth century. These include a tendency to hypostatize language and the act of writing and turn them into the object of investigation; a desire to question the assumptions of naturalness and objectivity that underlie conventional modes of representation; an impulse to be at once critically playful and playfully critical and to undermine traditional boundaries between creative and utilitarian discourses; a renewed emphasis on the movement of consciousness itself and on the very process of cognition, which predetermines description and narrative; an awareness of the necessity to reinscribe the lyric mode into a network of personal or public narratives; a wish to turn the language of reason against itself and to explore its uneasy interaction with the meanders of subjective consciousness; and a tendency not only to poeticize the "prosaic" but also to debunk the aspirations to figurativeness of the "poetic" and, thereby, to enact what Barbara Johnson calls "the disfiguration of poetic language" (100).

One of the lessons to be learned from the history of the contemporary prose poem, however, is that none of these features should be considered as necessary or essential. Given the ontological hybridity of the genre, these patterns of development are more often than not the result of conflicts that can be acknowledged and investigated but never fully resolved. As the site of a struggle over what role poetry can play in stabilizing and destabilizing dominant discourses and forms of writing, the prose poem is inevitably articulated and rearticulated in terms of its own efforts to engage in a critical struggle with the competing camps of contemporary literature and the aesthetic criteria underlying the current literary canon. More important, it is from its capacity to reflect on its own past achievements and present ambitions that the prose poem has succeeded in retaining its original force as a subversive and self-critical genre and will continue to aspire to be what Jonathan Monroe describes as "poetic/literary language's own coming to self-consciousness" (35–36).

Moving beyond traditional distinctions between abstract and concrete, imagistic and analytical, narrative and lyric, figurative and literal, the contemporary prose poem has reclaimed a new diversity of approaches and subject matter for poetry. By giving special attention to the evolution of the methodological and epistemological premises of the genre, I have tried to show that the prose poem is concerned not just with the limits of a permissible expression of subjective experience but with understanding the close interdependence between changes in formal convention and changes in beliefs about how to apprehend the world outside art. It should now be apparent that what is at stake in the genre's multiple negotiations with literary and utilitarian discourses is the possibility of problematizing not only the nature and boundaries of poetic language but also its relevance or nonrelevance in other discursive domains. It is largely by carrying on this critical struggle with dominant aesthetic and cultural conventions that the prose poem has continued to preserve its potential for innovation.

Notes

Introduction

1. Where not otherwise acknowledged, translations are by Andrew Norris. Translations have occasionally been emended.

2. On the controversy surrounding Simic's Pulitzer Prize see, for instance, Buckley 96–98.

3. For a detailed account of the development of the prose poem form in the era of British Decadence, see M. Murphy 9–60.

4. Murphy's *A Tradition of Subversion* discusses only three representatives of the contemporary prose poem: William Carlos Williams' *Kora in Hell,* Gertrude Stein's *Tender Buttons* and John Ashbery's *Three Poems.* Stephen Fredman's study also focuses on Williams and Ashbery but includes a chapter on Robert Creeley's *Presences* and a short section devoted to David Antin's "talk-poems" and Ron Silliman's "New Sentence."

5. The major part of this study is devoted to the American prose poem, which, for more than thirty years, has enjoyed a popularity quite unmatched in the rest of the English-speaking world. Seamus Heaney's *Stations* (1975), a currently unavailable pamphlet, and Roy Fisher's long narrative piece *The Ship's Orchestra* (1966) are two noteworthy exceptions to the general lack of interest of contemporary British and Irish poets in the prose poem. Geoffrey Hill's celebrated *Mercian Hymns* (1971)—a sequence of thirty numbered extended line stanzas or "versets" celebrating the history and legend surrounding King Offa, who reigned over Mercia in the later part of the eighth century—owes more to the Latin psalms and canticles of the early Christian Church than to any past or present tradition of the prose poem.

A complete list of prose poets not considered in this study would have to include at least four other occasional British prose poets—Charles Tomlinson, Peter Redgrove, Peter Reading, and John Ash—as well as the following North American poets: John Ashbery, Ted Berrigan, Roo Borson (Can.), George Bowering (Can.), David Bromige (Can.), Stephen Ford Brown, Michael Brownstein, Laura Chester, Tom Clark, Christopher Dewdney (Can.), James Dickey, Diane Di Prima, Robert Duncan, Carolyn Forché, Kathleen Fraser, Albert Goldbarth, Jim Harrison, John High, John Hollander, Fanny Howe, Thomas Lux, Nathaniel Mackey, William

Matthews, Charles North, Frank O'Hara, Michael Ondaatje (Can.), Robert Perchan, Dennis Philips, Anne Sexton, Aaron Shurin, Jack Spicer, Robert Sund, James Wright, and John Yau; not to mention the minor or occasional "fabulators" listed in chapter 3 or the new generation of prose poets whose work has featured in numberless poetry magazines and anthologies published in the 1980s and early 1990s, notably in Peter Johnson's *The Prose Poem: An International Journal* (1992–).

6. For a discussion of the distinction between "historical" and "theoretical" genres, "the first [resulting] from an observation of literary reality; the second from a deduction of a theoretical order," see Todorov's *The Fantastic* 14–15.

7. The first significant foray of the Surrealist movement into the English-speaking world came about with David Gascoygne's *Short Survey of Surrealism* (1935). The publication of Gascoygne's survey was followed by the International Exhibition of Surrealism in June 1936, which led to the foundation of the Surrealist Group in London. In the United States, Surrealism remained virtually nonexistent until World War II, which brought many European Surrealist artists to New York (see Germain 38–45).

Prologue

1. Morris Beja has found fourteen clear uses of the original epiphanies in *Stephen Hero,* eleven in *A Portrait,* four in *Ulysses,* and one in *Finnegans Wake* ("Epiphany" 712–713).

2. Twenty-two manuscripts of epiphanies—carefully written on separate sheets of ruled paper by Joyce himself—are housed at the Poetry Collection at the State University of New York at Buffalo. The twenty-five remaining ones (seven of which are duplicates from Buffalo) are at Cornell University. All but one of these are copies made by Stanislaus Joyce; the remaining one (concerning Oliver Gogarty) is a rough draft in Joyce's hand. The numbers ranging from 1 to 71 written on the back of the twenty-two holograph manuscripts currently held at Buffalo suggest that the entire collection ran into the seventies or more. The Buffalo manuscripts were first edited and published by A. O. Silverman in 1956. In 1965, Robert Scholes and Richard Kain published in part I of *The Workshop of Daedalus* an annotated edition of all the surviving epiphanies, which they ordered into a sequence following the numbers on the versos. The most recent edition of the manuscripts was assembled by Richard Ellmann and completed by A. Walton Litz and John Whittier-Ferguson. For a detailed account of the composition of the epiphanies and of the adaptation made by Joyce for his novels, see Ellmann 83–85 and Beja 709–13, respectively.

3. According to most critics, the forty extant epiphanies were composed in the years between 1900 and 1904 (Ellmann 83, Scholes and Kain 5, Beja 709, Mahaffey, "Shorter" 190).

4. As Ellmann himself points out, Joyce interpreted one of his dream-epiphanies to be about Ibsen (85).

5. "[The Spell of Arms and Voices]" appears in the final section of *A Portrait of*

the Artist as a Young Man (275), in the form of a journal entry written down ten days before Stephen's resolution to "forge in the smithy of [his] soul the uncreated conscience of [his] race" (276).

6. For an extensive discussion of the fragment as both the expression of a lost totality and the desire for its recuperation within the realm of subjective discourse, see, in particular, Lacoue-Labarthe and Nancy 69–78 and Quignard 42–62.

7. Note that the term *epiphany,* in Joyce's writings, variously refers to (1) the "sudden manifestation" itself; (2) the written record of the moment of revelation; (3) the verbal strategy used by the artist in order to find meaning in the seemingly insignificant.

8. Ellmann's comments on the title of the manuscript are rather misleading. In his biography of Joyce, he acknowledges that the name was inscribed "in another, unknown hand" but almost immediately adds that Joyce "was content to keep what he had written under this heading," for the title must have expressed "his sense of *dépaysement* as a Triestine Dubliner pining for requital in two languages" (342). Ellmann's account, however, gives us no reason to believe that the name was written before Joyce's departure for Zurich and, therefore, casts some doubts upon the validity of his interpretation. (Note that the "unknown hand" which wrote the name "Giacomo Joyce" on the sketchbook cover was more than probably Italian, as suggested by the hesitant calligraphy of the letters "j" and "y," which do not exist in the Italian alphabet.)

For the purpose of clarity and consistency, I shall nevertheless apply the name Giacomo to the poetic persona of the poem.

9. For a detailed account of the life of Amalia Popper and a thought-provoking examination of the social and political realities surrounding her alleged relationship with Joyce, see Vicki Mahaffey's article, "Fascism and Silence: The Coded History of Amalia Popper."

10. See Noon, Nichols 93–106, and Eco 29–38, respectively.

11. Imagism flourished between 1912 and 1917, from Ezra Pound's first printed reference to the Imagist "school" in the appendix to *Ripostes* to Amy Lowell's unofficial dismantling of the movement. The first Imagist anthology (*Des Imagistes: An Anthology;* 1914), edited by Pound, featured Joyce's "I Hear an Army," which was later included in *Chamber Music.* Note that "I Hear an Army," which Pound included in his anthology on the grounds of its uncompromising "objectivity," is a far less "Imagist" poem than the fragments of *Giacomo Joyce,* even by Pound's own standards. The brevity of treatment characterizing Joyce's fragments also echoes the brief juxtaposed "flashes of inspiration," surrounded by blankness and silence, of Italian Hermeticism, whose chief exponent, Giuseppe Ungaretti, published his first collection, *L'allegria,* in 1914.

12. For a detailed discussion of the major themes, motifs, and literary origins of Joyce's manuscript, see Vicki Mahaffey's "Giacomo Joyce."

13. A striking parallel can be drawn between Giacomo's sketches and the following "lyrical" epiphany, in which the artist as a young voyeur also attempts to

turn his model into a work of art. As is the case in the opening fragment of *Giacomo Joyce*, the aesthete's observations almost immediately give rise to an act of interpretation:

> She stands, her book held lightly at her breast, reading the lesson. Against the dark stuff of her dress her face, mild-featured with downcast eyes, rises softly outlined in light; and from a folded cap, set carelessly forward, a tassel falls along her brown ringletted hair . . .
> What is the lesson that she reads—of apes, of strange inventions, or the legends of martyrs? Who knows how deeply meditative, how reminiscent is this comeliness of Raffaello? (Epiphany #39 [*Poems* 199])

14. As Vicki Mahaffey has pointed out, the final heraldic description of Giacomo's lady was probably modeled on the closing lines of Hawthorne's *The Scarlet Letter* ("Giacomo" 398).

15. In his introduction to *Giacomo Joyce*, Ellmann apparently contradicts his own earlier version of Joyce's "affair" with Amalia Popper, which he described a few years earlier as a "silent, secret wooing" (347) that always took place in the presence of another person.

16. It would be tempting to see the sudden appearance of Molly Bloom's interior monologue at the end of *Ulysses* as something of a resurgence of the lyric repressed. Joyce, however, did not conceive of Molly's monologue as a lyrical piece in the strict sense. In a letter to Harriet Weaver, he commented that he had "rejected the usual interpretation of [Molly Bloom] as a human apparition" and had tried to depict nothing less than "the earth which is prehuman and presumably posthuman" (*Letters* 1:160).

17. Paradoxically, the ballad *Turpin Hero*, "which begins in the first person and ends in the third person," is the antithesis of Joyce's novels, which start with the third person and end with a shift to the first person. The paratactical style and arrangement of the diary entries at the end of *A Portrait* is reminiscent of the fragments of *Giacomo*. (Is this an implicit statement on Stephen's immaturity and his incapacity to achieve as yet the "dramatic" mode?)

Chapter 1

1. The other signatories were Kay Boyle, Whit Burnett, Hart Crane, Caresse and Harry Crosby, Martha Foley, Stuart Gilbert, A. L. Gillespie, Leigh Hoffman, Elliot Paul, Douglas Rigby, Theo Rutra (a.k.a. Eugene Jolas), Robert Sage, Harold J. Salemson, and Laurence Vail.

2. This is only the beginning of Jolas' three-page "Monologue," which consists of a single, uninterrupted paragraph.

3. The most strenuous attack against this particular kind of narrative of consciousness was launched by Wyndham Lewis. According to Lewis, any attempt to celebrate the creative power of irrationality in itself results in "picturesque demen-

tia," an unsubtantial and unorganized "word-dreaming of the mind when not concentrated for some logical functioning purpose" (121).

4. As pointed out by Margueritte Murphy, the title of Williams' *Kora in Hell: Improvisations* was suggested by Pound, who saw it as an American pastiche of Rimbaud's *Une Saison en enfer* and *Illuminations* (97). Williams, however, denied any debt to Rimbaud and, in his prologue to the collection, condemned the international poetic tradition advocated by Pound, whom he called "the best enemy the United States verse has" (*Imaginations* 26).

5. Although Stein almost systematically submitted everything she wrote to various publishers and magazines, many of her works first saw the light long after they were completed. In order to reflect the development of Stein's writing, each work mentioned in the present chapter is followed by both its date of composition and its date of publication.

6. See, for instance, Ulla E. Dydo's comments on Stein's "fear that [Picasso's] susceptibility to sexual temptation might interfere with his art" (*Reader* 138).

7. See also Stein's account of her relationship with her brother Leo in *Two: Gertrude Stein and Her Brother and Other Early Portraits (1908–1912)*.

8. The two exceptions are "Roastbeef" and "Breakfast," two slightly longer pieces contained in the "Food" section.

9. Stein coined the phrase "Rose is a rose is a rose is a rose" in "Sacred Emily," a piece composed in 1913 and first published in 1922 in the collection *Geography and Plays*. The phrase reappeared, preceded by the indefinite article, in a later prose sketch entitled "Objects Lie on a Table": "Do we suppose that all she knows is that a rose is a rose is a rose is a rose" (*Operas and Plays* 110). Stein's favorite motto was later printed in a circle on her stationery and linen.

10. Yet, the kind of rhythmic parallelism Jakobson sees as the essence of poetic language is reproduced to some extent, in Stein's prose, through the repetition-with-variation of specific motifs and, above all, syntactic structures, which is largely the result not of a specific concern with prosody but of Stein's interest in the awkwardnesses and redundancies of the language of everyday life. Jakobson himself points out that when dealing with the poetic function, linguists cannot limit themselves to the field of poetry. He also acknowledges the existence of "parallelisms" in the language of prose and so-called "verseless composition." These parallelisms, however, do not rely on a dominant phonic motif and are "not so strictly marked and strictly regular as 'continuous parallelism'" (89).

11. In an analysis of Stein's subversion of descriptive discourse based on Chomsky's degrees of grammaticalness, Marianne DeKoven speaks of the "accessibility" of Stein's *Tender Buttons* to "purposive articulation of meaning; or, as Chomsky puts it, through deviation from, rather than total negation of, conventional grammar" (10).

12. For a detailed discussion of Stein's "Cubist syntax," see, among others, Hoffmann, Dubnick, Steiner 131–160, and Perloff, *Poetics* 67–85.

13. Stein's focus on the "hardware" of artistic creation is also emphasized

through her constant references to the medium of painting and her use of lines, curves, blank spaces, and above all color.

14. On the application of Saussurean and Jakobsonian linguistics to the dynamics of desire, see Lacan's examination, in "The Agency of the Letter in the Unconscious or Reason Since Freud," of metaphor and metonymy as the two basic rhetorical figures competing against each other—in a complementary way—for the establishment of meaningful connections within the signifying chain. Lacan distinguishes metaphor—which creates meaning by crossing the gap dividing signifier from signified—from metonymy—which maintains the "bar" of alienation between signifier and signified and develops itself through an endless displacement at the level of the signifier. The metonymic connections between signifiers "permit the elision in which the signifier installs the lack of being in the object relation, by using the value of 'reference back' possessed by signification in order to invest it with the desire aimed at the very lack it supports" (164). For Lacan, "the enigmas of desire . . . amount to no other derangement of instinct than that of being caught in the rails—eternally stretching towards the *desire for something else*—of metonymy" (166–67).

Chapter 2

1. See also Ron Silliman's remarks on Fenton Johnson's "The Minister" and its use of the "sentence:paragraph device," bringing the reader's attention "back time and again to the voice of the narrator." Silliman sees Johnson's poem as "the first instance in English of a prose poem which calls attention to a discursive or poetic effect" (*New Sentence* 83).

2. In *The People, Yes* (1936), a number of tall tales in prose about the lives of folk heroes are inserted between passages of verse.

3. A relatively minor representative of early American popular modernism, Arturo Giovannitti was nevertheless the subject of an entire chapter of Louis Untermeyer's highly influential *The New Era in American Poetry* (1919), the companion critical volume to his anthology *Modern American Poetry* (1919). As Frank Lentricchia has pointed out, Untermeyer's admiration for Giovannitti's work (as well as his interest in other writers excluded from literary elite centers, including black poet Paul Laurence Dunbar) reflected his idea that lyric poetry, just like prose fiction, should (Untermeyer's words) "[explore] the borderland of poetry and prose" (84) in order to reflect social conflicts and differences.

4. While *The Masses* included Anderson and Giovannitti among its regular contributors before and during World War I, the influence of Carl Sandburg's poetry on Sherwood Anderson's work, and in particular on his first published poetry book, *Mid-American Chants* (1918), is well attested. In a letter dated April 17, 1917, Anderson refers to Sandburg's recent visit to his house and his positive appraisal of the manuscript of the *Mid-American Chants;* Anderson writes that Carl Sandburg "came to see [him] and read [his] songs" and was "lavish in his praise" (*Letters to Bab* 69).

5. Anderson was, at the time, a regular contributor to radical left-wing magazines like *The Masses,* a cooperative platform for aesthetic and political dissent and which provided a meeting ground for revolutionary labor and the radical intelligentsia.

Stanley Kimmel's *The Kingdom of Smoke* is a later and politically radicalized example of activist prose poetry, often verging on the rhetoric of proletarian manifestos:

> God of the prairie, my people have lost their kingdom. They are captives in a land that once belonged to them. It is time for new men to come up out of the underground.
>
> It is time for my people to gather in the fields and break the chains that have been fastened upon them. . . . I have come up out of the underground to picture the story of my people upon a canvas of smoke. (11)

6. In other poems, like "Mid-American Prayer" and "Dirge of War," World War I is presented as the ultimate nemesis of poetic creation ("That's what I want to say—by song and by the jarring note of song that cannot sing. I was coming with America—dreaming with America—hoping with America—then war came" [*Chants* 75]).

7. Anderson's correspondence attests how important his experiments with the prose poem were to his own conception of his art, while at the same time putting the emphasis on their value as transitional episodes in his career as a fiction writer: "Some years ago I wrote the little book Mid-American Chants and that led directly into the impulse that produced Winesburg, Poor White and The Triumph. For two years now I've been at work on another thing I call A New Testament. And that has led directly into Many Marriages. If it comes off—the gods grant it may—it will be the biggest, most sustained and moving thing I've done" (*Selected* 32).

8. The semi-isolated sentence-as-unit resisting the reader's attempts at incorporating it into a larger narrative whole is an important hallmark of the "associative" narratives favored by the French Surrealists and the American "fabulists" discussed in chapter 3. As we will see, it also points in the direction of what Silliman calls the "New Prose Poem," in which the limiting of syllogistic movement between the sentences themselves—as well as from the sentences to the paragraph as a whole—"keeps the reader's attention at or very close to the level of language, that is, most often at the sentence level or below" (*Sentence* 91).

9. According to Baudelaire, this project was itself an extension of the method his predecessor Aloysius Bertrand had used to create "an illustration of ancient life, so strangely picturesque" (*Poems* 25).

10. See Baudelaire's famous "dedication" to Arsène Houssaye: "The notion of such an obsessive ideal has its origins above all in our experience of the life of great cities, the confluence and interaction of the countless relationships within them. Have you not yourself, dear friend, endeavored to transmute the *Glazier*'s strident

street-cry into a song, and to express in lyrical prose all the saddening implications that such an utterance throws up to garret and attic through the mist-bound streets" (*Poems* 25).

11. The strict formal patterns dividing some of the poems into sentences/paragraphs comprising the same number of words are another example of Patchen's concern with rhythm and musicality.

Chapter 3

1. Leitch proposes a similar distinction between the "anecdotal" and the epiphanic short story (130–47).

2. Howe lists four variations among short shorts: the epiphany of "one thrust of incident," the lives "compressed into typicality and paradigm," the interior monologue of the "snap-shot or single frame," and the semi-allegorical fable (xiii–xiv).

3. Augusto Monterroso's "The Eclipse," for instance, features both in Howe's anthology of short short stories and in Benedikt's *The Prose Poem: An International Anthology*.

4. Karl Shapiro's *The Bourgeois Poet*, another pioneer work published in 1964, should be mentioned at this stage. *The Bourgeois Poet* is a relatively uneven collection of prose poems mixing philosophical and aesthetical reflections, Freudian family drama, fragments of social and political statement, free associational narratives, and a number of semi-autobiographical anecdotes. The uncompromisingly earnest and often self-derisive tone pervading the whole collection is perhaps best exemplified in the prose poem that gave the collection its title, an ironical reflection on Shapiro's own private and public status as a middle-aged, middle-class Pulitzer Prize winner.

5. Edson's first three collections of prose poems (*Appearances* [1961], *A Stone Is Nobody's* [1961], and *The Very Thing That Happens* [1964]) were subtitled "Fables and Drawings."

6. As pointed out in Max Jacob's "Avis" to the original edition, even though *The Dice Cup* was first published in 1917, many of the poems contained in the collection were written as early as 1909.

7. Eliot's "Hysteria" was first published in Ezra Pound's *Catholic Anthology* and was subsequently included in *Prufrock and Other Observations* (1917). As pointed out in Margueritte Murphy's *A Tradition of Subversion*, Eliot's other unpublished prose poems are now part of the Berg collection of the New York Public Library. See also Donald Gallup's "The Lost Manuscripts of T. S. Eliot."

8. See Emig 71 and Murphy 56.

9. This is also where Edson's prose poems differ from Jacob's, which almost always consist of a single paragraph and are sometimes told in the past tense. Jacob's single "block" of prose was revived by Michael Benedikt.

10. For a discussion of the influence of Cubist painting on the work of Guillaume Appolinaire, Max Jacob, and Pierre Reverdy, see Bernard 618–50.

11. See, in particular, the short narrative vignettes of Brecht's "Geschichten vom Herrn Keuner" (in *Kalendergeschichten,* 1948) and Kafka's *Betrachtung* (1913) and *Ein Landarzt* (1919).

12. Many of Jacob's poems in the *Dice Cup* bear "fabulist" titles such as "Poem in a Style Which Is Not My Own," "Poem Lacking in Unity," "Roman Feuilleton," or "Biographical Genre." On the self-referential quality of Reverdy's prose poems, see Mary Ann Caws' "The Self-Defining Prose Poem" in Caws and Riffaterre 180–97.

13. Earlier anthologies include Duane Ackerson's *A Prose Poem Anthology* (1970), which contains work by Russell Edson, Michael Benedikt, William Matthews, and W. S. Merwin, as well as translations of Arthur Rimbaud, Pierre Reverdy, Cesar Vallejo, René Char, Henri Michaux, and Géo Norge.

14. In his essay, Valéry attributes this comparison to Malherbe via a letter from Racan to Chapelain.

15. See, for instance, Longhurst, ed., *Gender, Genre and Narrative Pleasure,* for a discussion of the ways in which sexual politics are central to the understanding of popular narrative, including science fiction, melodrama, the Western, and the thriller.

16. Atwood's concern with culturally inherited sources of oppression is inseparable from what she feels is her responsibility as a Canadian writer to inscribe her work in a specific social and political context. In her book, *Survival,* which she describes as "a cross between a personal statement . . . and a political manifesto (13), she defines Canada as a whole as a "state of mind" that often has to do with psychological failure and victimization. The "colonial mentality" of the Canadian people, she adds, is itself a cultural "side-effect" of the economic supremacy of its stronger southern neighbor (35–36).

17. For example "Progressive Insanities of a Pioneer" (*Animals* 36) presents a similar male-female dichotomy opposing the humanist's self-confident anthropocentrism ("He stood, a point / on a sheet of paper / proclaiming himself the center") to nature's resistance against name-giving ("Things / refused to name themselves, refused / to let him name them"). In "Marrying the Hangman," a prose poem contained in *Two-Headed Poems,* the dialogue between the hangman and the woman condemned to death ("He said: foot boot, order, city, fist, roads, time, knife. She said: water, night, willow, rope hair, earth belly, cave, meat, shroud, open, blood" [51]) displays the same kind of radical opposition between the rigorous, man-made strategies of the male brain and the elemental sensuousness of the female mind, while underlining once more the linguistic nature of Atwood's patterns of gender relationships. For an extensive discussion of Atwood's poetics of male and female space, see Davey 16–26.

18. Atwood's concern with the relationship between situational and linguistic clichés and domestic politics also establishes her striking kinship with Austrian writer Elfriede Jelinek, as well as with German writers Helga M. Novak and

Angelika Mechtel and their recent experiments with the short short story form. See also two recent collections by American poet Amy Gerstler: *The True Bride* and *Bitter Angel.*

19. Atwood herself has explained that the fourth and last of her "basic victim positions," the "creative non-victim" stage, is "not a position for victims but for those who have never been victims at all." "In an oppressed society, of course," she adds, "you can't become an ex-victim—insofar as you are connected with your society—until the entire society's position has been changed" (*Survival* 38).

Chapter 4

1. See, for instance, Robert Richman's criticism of Bly's solipsism or Philip Dacey's allegations of literary demagogy.

2. *Silence in the Snowy Fields,* Bly's first book of poetry, included the prose poems "Sunset at a Lake" and "Fall."

3. The prose poems of *Ten Poems* are no exception. In *The Morning Glory,* "Looking at a Dry Tumbleweed Brought in from the Snow," combines both the anthropomorphic ("Taken away from the deserted shore, it talks of queens sent away to live in cramped farmhouses, living in the dirt, and it talks of coffins and amazing arrows") and the interobjective trend ("It has leaped up on my desk like surf, or like a bull onto a cow! . . . a tumbleweed, every branch different, and the whole bush the same, so in that way it is like the sea").

Bly recently acknowleged his failure to "describe an object or a creature without claiming it, without immersing it like a negative in his developing tank of disappointment and desire." "Our desires and disappointments," he writes, "have such hunger that they pull each sturgeon or hollow tree into themselves . . . it may be that our desires, our aggressions and rages are already inside the sturgeon even before we approach it" (*What* xv).

4. Despite this fundamental difference, Robert Bly shares at least one important premise of Charles Olson's Projectivist manifesto, namely a reaction against "that particular presumption by which western man has interposed himself between what he is as creature (with certain instructions to carry out) and those other creations of nature which we may, with no derogation, call objects" (*American* 13). However, the subsequent recommendation Olson makes to the "objectist" or "projectivist" poet to relinquish all subjectivity is, as we will see, totally incompatible with Bly's poetics of inward lyricism.

5. Whether implicitly or explicitly (as is sometimes suggested in the titles themselves), most of the poems of *The Morning Glory* are "told" by a solitary walker. Note that the emphasis on the irreducible separateness of things and on reality being conceived of as a "democracy of objects" is, of course, characteristic not only of Transcendentalist doctrine and Taoist philosophy but also, in different degrees, of modern American poetry as a whole, from the Imagist and Objectivist precept to attend to the temporal and local situatedness of particulars to Williams' cult of the "thing in itself." In this perspective, the object or "thing" poem is one of the climac-

tic avatars of one of the most distinctive tendencies of contemporary American poetry.

6. On Chinese poetry and the identification of the speaker of a lyric with the biographical poet, see Miner 233.

7. The term *Deep Image* was coined by Jerome Rothenberg in 1960. Originally inspired by the poetry and criticism of Federico Garcia Lorca, it involved the existence of two distinct realities, the "empirical" and the "hidden (floating)" world. Rothenberg describes the "deep image" itself as "at once husk and kernel, perception and vision" and defines the deep image poem as a whole as "the movement between them" (*Pre-faces* 57). Other poets related to the Deep Image trend of the prose poem include William Matthews, James Wright, W. S. Merwin, and, more recently, Robert Sund and Michael Delp.

8. The first and third sections of *The Man in the Black Coat Turns* contain eighteen lineated poems, which Bly defines as "heavy thought-poems" (*Selected* 143). For these poems, Bly writes, "free verse in brief lines doesn't seem right" because it "suggests doubt and hesitation, whereas these thoughts are obsessive, massive, even brutal. And the prose poem doesn't seem right, because prose poems flow as rivers flow, following gravity around a rock." Since "these thoughts are like the rocks themselves," Bly tried to create a new form in which "language begins to take on the darkness and engendered quality of matter." Therefore, he "tried to knit the stanzas together in sound . . . and set [himself] a task of creating stanzas that have the same number of beats." "The more limits we set in the poem," Bly comments, "the more resistance we have set up, and the more energy the poem produces to push against those limits" (144).

Bly's poetics of "resistance" in *Black Coat* signals an unexpected step away from the "artlessness" of his earlier poems and prose poems and toward a kind of self-conscious formalism which recalls Richard Wilbur's famous pronouncement on the necessity for rhyme and meter to curb the energy of content in the same sense that "the strength of the genie comes of his being confined in a bottle" (R. Gray 222). Such a renewal of interest in formal restrictions seems quite an unexpected turn in the career of a writer who, until then, had scrupulously rejected any kind of aesthetic formalism or self-conscious craftsmanship and had instead privileged a poetry of optimal, antimodernist "naturalness."

Chapter 5

1. Some critics have condemned Simic's fondness for powerful visual effects as a serious limitation. In his review of *The World Doesn't End*, for example, David Dooley complains that Simic's poems and prose poems are derivative of a Surrealist tradition that "denies development and organic form, but lays the burden on the poet of being consistently entertaining from one image or sentence to the next" (Matuz 379). This comment, however, would also be applicable to the whole French Surrealist tradition, from which Simic derives his conviction that "all art is a magic operation, or, if you prefer, a prayer for a new image" (*Dime-Store* 28).

Chapter 6

1. Other anthologies of language-oriented poetry include *"Language" Poetries* (Douglas Messerli, ed.), "The L=A=N=G=U=A=G=E Poets" (Charles Bernstein, ed.; a supplement to the Fall 1985–Winter 1986 issue of the magazine *boundary 2*), *The L=A=N=G=U=A=G=E Book* (Bruce Andrews and Charles Bernstein, eds.), and a collection featuring in the March 81 "l'espace amérique" issue of *Cahiers du Collectif Change* (see Bernstein et al.).

2. See, also, the "Collective Introduction to the Language Poetry Movement" written by Charles Bernstein, Lyn Hejinian, Bob Perelman, Barrett Watten, Steve Benson, Ron Silliman, and Carla Harryman for *Cahiers du Collectif Change.*

3. For an extensive discussion of Language poetry as a mode of class struggle, see George Hartley's *Textual Politics and the Language Poets.* For a brief introduction to language-oriented poetry in America, see Michael Greer's "Language Poetry in America 1971–1991."

4. According to Gérard Genette, the obsolescence of rhyme is itself a consequence of an increasingly graphemic mode of literary production. A major reason for the dissociation of poetry and meter and the obsolescence of phonic criteria of distinction, Genette argues, was "the continuous weakening of auditory modes of consuming literature" (*Figures II* 124).

5. Major forums for Language poetry include, or have included—besides Bruce Andrews and Charles Bernstein's *The L=A=N=G=U=A=G=E Book*—Barrett Watten's pioneer magazine *This,* Bob Perelman's *Hills,* Ron Silliman's *Tottel's,* and Carla Harryman's *Qu, Roof, Miam, The Difficulties, A Hundred Posters, Sulfur, Tremblor, Sink, Tramen* as well as the following publishing houses: Sun & Moon, Potes & Poets, Tuumba, Burning Deck, Figures, Station Hill, Roof, This, and Tender Buttons.

6. See Hartley 8–18.

7. The arbitrarily truncated dictionary entries contained in Tina Darragh's *Striking Resemblance* appear as an interesting poetic extension of Kosuth's project.

8. See Hannah Weiner's *Little Book/Indians* and David Melnick's *Pcoet.*

9. As George Hartley has pointed out, the Language poets' emphasis on the printed page indirectly reveals their indebtedness to Olson as well as their rebellion against him. "Olson's composition by field," he writes, "is put to use with a vengeance, no longer as a score for voice but as a visual artifact whose 'meaning,' like that of any visual art, exists on the page itself. The page is the field" (23). The Language poets' revision of Olson's open field might thus be seen as an example of what Harold Bloom called *tessera,* an antithetical *completion*—rather than a mere rejection—of their precursor's experiments (14).

10. Interestingly enough, Olson, in his now historic 1950 essay on Projective verse, reacts against the same technological changes that severed literature from its locus of production and consumption (and were denounced as such by Silliman more than thirty years later) when he asserts that "what we have suffered from, is manuscript, press, the removal of verse from its producer and its reproducer, the

voice, a removal by one, by two removes from its place of origin and its destination" (618).

11. The fact that the Language poets deny the assumptions of vocal self-presence of "mainstream" poetry does not imply that they necessarily downplay its acoustic or even prosodic possibilities. As suggested by the zaumlike noises of David Melnick, the fragmented colloquialism of Robert Grenier, or the highly alliterated prose poems of Clark Coolidge and Ron Silliman, the aural or performative quality of the lyric has, to some extent, survived the demise of speech-oriented poetics, with this essential difference—that the emphasis is now on the role of language as a mediator between the poet and his or her work, as opposed to a mere mouthpiece for the subject's attempts at self-expression.

12. As Silliman himself has suggested, "a latent tradition of a poetics not centered on speech already existed in the work of Gertrude Stein, Louis Zukofsky and Jackson Mac Low" (*Tree* xvi–xvii). For a brief and convincing discussion of the Language poets' indebtedness to the work of Gertrude Stein (and her emphasis on the gap between object and description, in particular), see Peter Nicholls' "Difference Spreading: From Gertrude Stein to L=A=N=G=U=A=G=E Poetry."

13. As suggested earlier, the New Sentence of the New Prose Poem is not the one and only prevailing feature of Language poetry. Robert Grenier's minimalist free verse in *Series* and the disrupted orthographies of Peter Inman's *Ocker* and David Melnick's *Pcoet* use the word (sometimes the syllable or even the letter) as the primary unit of composition. (The result, in Melnick's *Pcoet,* seems to aspire to the three-dimensional "rawness" of a Russian Constructivist relief.) Note that the typographical eccentricities of Mallarmé's *Un Coup de dés jamais n'abolira le hasard* (1897) are a much earlier example of a graphic realization of the entire page as an "open field."

Language poet and critic Michael Davidson has distinguished the New Prose Poem from the more "conventional" prose poems in the Deep Image tradition: "The conventional prose poem of Robert Bly, James Wright or W. S. Merwin is scenic; it projects a *paysage moralise,* a landscape upon which is grafted a series of psychological speculations. However desultory the pattern of speculations, this prose depends upon some contingency between all elements of the landscape and the discourse which surrounds it. Disjunctions at the level of the sentence are expressive; they dramatize the fragmented emotional state of the author ("Sentence" 3).

14. Silliman distinguishes the dynamics of the New Sentence from that of Coolidge's paragraphs in *Weathers,* in that each of the latter, despite its focusing "attention at the level of the sentence in front of the reader," mostly does so "at the level of the phrase or clause" (88).

15. A 1981 article by Nanos Valaoritis bears an interesting relation to Silliman's dissociation of the "syntagmatic" ambiguities of the New Sentence from the "metaphorical" dynamics of Surrealism. In a brief discussion of Bruce Andrews' one-line poem, "Bananas Are an Example," Valaoritis distinguishes between the poly-

semantic difficulty of Language poetry and modernist "allusiveness," thereby pointing to the Language poets' reaction against modernist encyclopedic elitism. Andrews' "truncated" sentence, Valaoritis writes, "puts its trust in a new poly-semantism, in a new space. It is no longer a matter of allusive obscurities, as in Pound, Eliot and Olson, nor of the metaphorical system of Surrealism. It addresses at present the ambiguity that language itself possesses, and it requires the reader's cooperation" (160). Language poetry's swerve away from the obscurity of modern-ist allusion (and its extension, via Pound, to Olson's "open field") is an interesting example of how compositional strategies are always inscribed in hierarchical and, more largely, political relationships. The emphasis on "torquing" and the reader's "cooperation" in the creation of meaning in Language poetry is, at least according to Valaoritis, a reaction against the modernist work "talking down" to its reader by virtue of its intimidating erudition.

On the relationship between Language poetry and Surrealism, see also Barrett Watten's "Method and L=A=N=G=U=A=G=E: After Surrealism" and Bernstein's *Content's Dream* (388–90).

16. Other currents or modes such as Symbolism—with its emphasis on corre-spondences between the natural and the spiritual world and its instoration of fixed references, at least within the "private" (or "hermetic") symbolic repertoire of each of its representatives—are as close as realism to the "readerly pole." There are, of course, different degrees of "writerliness" to be distinguished within the works of the Language poets themselves. While the poems of Clark Coolidge and Peter Inman are clearly inscribed in a critique of referential and syntactic norms on both the syntagmatic and the paradigmatic level, the prose poems of Kit Robinson and Ron Silliman offer self-contained and grammatically correct sentences and there-fore displace their degree of writerliness onto the syntagmatic axis.

17. Another interesting precedent is Samuel Beckett's rigorously organized re-shuffling of preselected phrases in the twenty-four seven-sentence paragraphs of his 1969 "Lessness." Other examples of the use of procedural poetics in language-oriented prose poems include Ron Silliman's *Tjanting*, which is written according to the Fibonacci number series.

18. Note that the diaristic prose piece—an important influence on the develop-ment of the contemporary prose poem from Joyce to Bly—is still a favored form in Language poetry (see also Hannah Weiner's *Clairvoyant Journal* and Bernadette Mayer's *Memory*).

19. Other women poets associated with Language poetry—including Jean Day, Erica Hunt (the only nonwhite poet associated with the Language group), Diane Ward, Leslie Scalapino, Rae Armantrout, and Fiona Templeton—have tried to use the investigation of sociolinguistic issues as a springboard for a feminist explora-tion of gender issues.

20. Jameson's distinction between modern anomie and postmodern depth-lessness indirectly draws our attention to one of the most fundamental differences between the New Prose Poem and the modernist stream-of-consciousness, which is

that the former challenges the assumptions of (self-)credibility of the latter (the interior narratives of Virginia Woolf, William Faulkner, or Dorothy Richardson, for all their fragmented and disrupted dynamics, still seek to maintain the illusion of a self-present speaking subject who is at one with his or her own strategies of self-expression) by putting the emphasis on the unbridgeable gap between the writing I and the written I. Furthermore, the epistemological premises of many Language poets are based on a notion of the self as the product of its cultural and linguistic environment, which is largely incompatible with the subjectivist inwardness characterizing the modernist interior monologue. (See also Jameson's own brief discussion of Bob Perelman's poem, "China," as a symptom of "schizophrenic disjunction or *écriture* . . . displacing the older affects of anxiety and alienation" [29].)

There is, of course, no such thing as an abrupt shift from a self-present modernist speaker to a "self-consciously self-alienated" postmodern narrator. A more complex analysis would have to deal with (quantitative and qualitative) *degrees* of self-presence and self-alienation and would certainly bring to light a number of "postmodern" features in modernist narratives of consciousness. While James Joyce's *Ulysses,* for instance, seeks to dilute the self in the anonymous art of parody, Darl and Addie Bundren in Faulkner's *As I Lay Dying* are two "modernist" characters who are well aware that they "think where they are not."

21. Other examples of language-oriented writing subverting the technical and epistemological formulae of existing prose genres include, besides Perelman's "An Autobiography," Bernadette Mayer's prose journal in *Memory,* Hannah Weiner's *Clairvoyant Journal,* Erica Hunt's unsigned and untitled "letters," and James Sherry's novel *In Case,* a plotless detective story aimed at exposing the tropologically constructed "hardware" of the traditional thriller. In these works, the notion of genre itself is once again understood as an epistemic and ideologically laden category, rather than as a set of innocent formal features.

22. Such labels of "non-" or "post"genericness are often inadequate since those qualities would exist only in relation to the generic assumptions they seek to undermine and would therefore be immediately reinscribed in a complex of intergeneric relationships.

23. See also, in particular, Beckett's piece, "Lessness," which displays a similar "repetition-with-incrementation" progression as "For to End Yet Again." Most of Beckett's short prose pieces, however, still bear affinities with the dramatic monologue and thus contrast with the Language poets' concern with writing as opposed to speech. The influence of Samuel Beckett is noticeable in the work of numerous Language poets, including Bob Perelman, Michael Davidson, and Stephen Rodefer, whose prose poems in *Passing Duration,* in particular, are reminiscent of the timeless and colorless bareness of Beckett's minimalist landscapes.

24. Note that Hejinian's *My Life,* although generally received and discussed as a book of poetry, was advertised by its publisher as a "poetic novel." Barbara Guest's *Seeking Air* underwent the same hybrid strategies of distribution.

25. The influence of John Ashbery's *Three Poems* and Robert Creeley's *Pres-*

ences on this particular kind of language-oriented poetry combining critical, philosophical, and lyric writing should not be underestimated. For a discussion of *Three Poems* and *Presences,* see Fredman's *Poet's Prose.* For detailed readings of the works of Language poets in relation to literary and cultural theory, see also Linda Reinfeld's *Language Poetry: Writing as Rescue* (on Bernstein, Howe, and Palmer) and Hank Lazer's *Opposing Poetries* (on Bernstein, Andrews, Howe, and Sherry).

26. In this respect, language-oriented poetry is by no means a uniquely American phenomenon. While many poets in other countries of the Western world (not to speak of theoretical forums such as the Tel Quel group) have, since Mallarmé, displayed an increasing awareness of the materiality and resistance of language as *medium-in-res,* the recent birth of a similar Marxism-inspired and language-oriented movement in Italy—the "Gruppo 93"—once again confirms the methodological complementarity of left-wing politics, historical materialism, and an avant-garde that seeks to interrogate the materiality of the signifier.

27. The emphasis on writing as a collective activity is also reflected in the numerous collaborations that have taken place among Language poets in the last twenty years, whether in the form of anthologies, collaborative projects, talks, or colloquia.

28. See, in particular, Charles Altieri's "Without Consequences Is No Politics" and, more recently, the editorial "State of the Art" for the new magazine *apex of the M* (Daly et al.). While Altieri's claim that the Language poets' commitment to "audience freedom and responsibility" comes "dangerously close to the idea of the free, pleasure-seeking consumer" in capitalist society (305–6) seems somewhat exaggerated, the tendency of some Language poets to rely on formal analogies between syntax and economics (and, in particular, their rejection of "normative" issue-oriented radicalism in the name of what McCaffery calls the "free circulation of meaning"; a "semantic liberalism" of sorts) is reminiscent of similar examples in the field of social and cultural studies, notably that of Jean Baudrillard, whose neo-Marxist perspective has been rendered increasingly ineffective by his adoption of a number of basic tenets of his own particular brand of radical postmodernism. As Christopher Norris has argued, Baudrillard's Nietzschean repudiation of stabilized "depth" models, as well as his theory on the predominance of the sign over its use-value in a world given over to the infinitized play of simulacra and language games, have led him to avoid tackling local forms of social experience (11–31).

29. On McGann, see his claim that the small presses that publish the work of Language poets are "organizations founded . . . by writers themselves, so that the writing is necessarily imagined as part of a social event of persons" (*Riders* 113) and his view of Language poetry as a critical response to nothing less than "the collision of imperialist demands with the isolationist and revolutionary nationalism of American ideology," not to speak of "an extended cold war shadowed by the threat of a global catastrophe" ("Contemporary" 253).

30. As George Hartley points out, not all Language poets have made Marxist claims for their work. While Ron Silliman, Bob Perelman, Barrett Watten, Charles Bernstein, and Canadian poet Steve McCaffery largely subscribe to Andrews' critique of the ideology of capitalism, a number of other poets associated with the Language group, such as Clark Coolidge and Robert Grenier, "disavow any Marxist claims whatsoever" (xv).

Epilogue

1. Other trends and subtrends emerging from the body of texts examined in the present study include the object poem, the "dreamscape," the (speech-based) dramatic monologue, and the philosophical vignette or *pensée*.

2. For a general discussion of the gradual assimilation of the norm-breaking potential of the prose poem into the generic canon, see Monroe 335–38.

3. The first issue of Peter Johnson's *The Prose Poem: An International Journal* appeared in 1992. *The Prose Poem,* another magazine entirely devoted to the contemporary prose poem, was founded by Steve Wilson in 1990. Other recent anthologies of prose poems include *The Anatomy of Water: A Sampling of Contemporary American Prose Poetry* (Steve Wilson, ed.), *Models of the Universe: An Anthology of the Prose Poem* (Stuart Friebert and David Young, eds.), and *The Party Train: An Anthology of North American Prose Poetry* (Robert Alexander, C. W. Truesdale, and Mark Vinz, eds.).

Works Cited

Abrams, M. H. *A Glossary of Literary Terms.* 5th ed. Fort Worth, Tex.: Holt, Rinehart and Winston, 1985.

Ackerson, Duane, ed. *A Prose Poem Anthology.* Pocatello, Idaho: Dragon Flying Press, 1970.

Adams, Stephen. *Poetic Designs: An Introduction to Meters, Verse Forms and Figures of Speech.* Peterborough, Canada: Broadview Press, 1997.

Alexander, Robert, C. W. Truesdale, and Mark Vinz, eds. *The Party Train: An Anthology of North American Prose Poetry.* Minneapolis: New Rivers Press, 1995.

Altieri, Charles. "Without Consequences Is No Politics: A Response to Jerome McGann." In von Hallberg, q.v., 301–8.

Anderson, Sherwood. *Windy McPherson's Son.* New York: John Lane, 1916.

———. *Marching Men.* New York: John Lane, 1917.

———. *Mid-American Chants.* New York: John Lane, 1918.

———. *Winesburg, Ohio.* New York: Huebsch, 1919.

———. *Dark Laughter.* New York: Boni and Liveright, 1925.

———. *A New Testament.* New York: Boni and Liveright, 1927.

———. *Selected Letters,* ed. Charles E. Molin. Knoxville: University of Tennessee Press, 1984.

———. *Letters to Bab: Sherwood Anderson to Marietta D. Finley, 1916–1933,* ed. William A. Stutton. Urbana and Chicago: University of Illinois Press, 1985.

Andrews, Bruce. "Poetry as Explanation, Poetry as Praxis." In Bernstein, *The Politics of Poetic Form,* q.v., 23–44.

———. *I Don't Have Any Paper So Shut Up (or, Social Romanticism).* Los Angeles: Sun & Moon Press, 1992.

Andrews, Bruce, and Charles Bernstein, eds. *The L=A=N=G=U=A=G=E Book.* Carbondale: Southern Illinois University Press, 1984.

Attridge, Derek. *The Cambridge Companion to James Joyce.* Cambridge: Cambridge University Press, 1990.

Atwood, Margaret. *Double Persephone.* Toronto: Hawshead Press, 1961.

———. *The Animals in That Country.* Toronto: Oxford University Press, 1968.

———. *Survival: A Thematic Guide to Canadian Literature.* Toronto: Anansi, 1972.

———. *Two-Headed Poems.* Toronto: Oxford University Press, 1978.

————. *Murder in the Dark: Short Fictions and Prose Poems.* Toronto: Coach House Press, 1983.

————. *The Handmaid's Tale.* London: Cape, 1986.

————. *Good Bones.* London: Virago, 1992.

Bachelard, Gaston. *La Poétique de l'espace* (The poetics of space). Paris: Presses Universitaires de France, 1957.

Baldeschwiler, Eileen. "The Lyric Short Story: The Sketch of a History." In May, *Short Story Theories,* q.v., 202–13.

Barthes, Roland. *Le Degré zéro de l'écriture* (Writing degree zero). Paris: Seuil, 1972.

————. *Le Plaisir du texte* (The pleasure of the text). Paris: Seuil, 1973.

————. *Image-Music-Text,* ed. and trans. Stephen Heath. New York: Hill & Wang, 1977.

————. *A Lover's Discourse: Fragments,* trans. Richard Howard. New York: Hill & Wang, 1978.

————. *Roland Barthes by Roland Barthes,* trans. Richard Howard. New York: Hill & Wang, 1978.

————. *A Barthes Reader,* ed. Susan Sontag. New York: Farrar, Straus and Giroux, 1982.

————. *Le Bruissement de la langue: Essais critiques IV* (The rustle of the tongue: critical essays). Paris: Seuil, 1984.

————. *The Grain of the Voice: Interviews 1962–1980,* trans. Linda Coverdale. New York: Hill & Wang, 1985.

————. *Incidents.* Paris: Seuil, 1987.

Baudelaire, Charles. *Les Paradis artificiels* (Artificial paradise). 1869. Paris: Gallimard, 1964.

————. *The Poems in Prose,* ed. and trans. Francis Scarfe. London: Anvil Press, 1989.

Baudrillard, Jean. *De la séduction* (On seduction). Paris: Galilée, 1979.

————. *Simulations,* trans. Paul Foss et al. New York: Semiotext(e), 1983.

Beckett, Samuel. *Collected Shorter Prose 1945–1980.* London: John Calder, 1986.

Béhar, Henri, and Michel Carassou. *Le Surréalisme* (Surrealism). Paris: Librairie Générale Française, 1992.

Beja, Morris. *Epiphany in the Modern Novel.* Seattle: University of Washington Press, 1971.

————. "Epiphany and the Epiphanies." In Bowen and Carens, q.v., 707–25.

Benedikt, Michael. *Mole Notes.* Middletown, Conn.: Wesleyan University Press, 1971.

————. *The Prose Poem: An International Anthology.* New York: Dell, 1976.

————. *Night Cries.* Middletown, Conn.: Wesleyan University Press, 1976.

————. "The Meat Epitaph." Turner 93–94.

————. *Benedikt: A Profile.* Tucson, Ariz.: Grilled Flowers Press, 1977.

————. "A Few Notes on the Future of the Prose Poem." *The Prose Poem: An International Journal* 2 (1993): 10–12.

————. Letter to the author, 20 November 1996.

Benjamin, Walter. *Charles Baudelaire: A Lyric Poet in the Era of High Capitalism,* trans. Harry Zohn. London: Verso, 1983.

Benstock, Shari. *Women of the Left Bank: Paris 1900–1940.* London: Virago, 1987.

Bergson, Henri. *An Introduction to Metaphysics,* trans. T. E. Hulme. Indianapolis: Bobbs-Merrill, 1955.

Bernard, Suzanne. *Le Poème en prose de Baudelaire jusqu'à nos jours* (The prose poem since Baudelaire). Paris: Nizet, 1959.

Bernstein, Charles. *Content's Dream: Essays, 1975–1984.* Los Angeles: Sun & Moon Press, 1986.

————. *A Poetics.* Cambridge: Harvard University Press, 1992.

————, ed. "43 Poets (1984)." *boundary 2* 14.1–2 [Supplement: "The L=A=N=G=U=A=G=E Poets"] (1985–86): 1–113.

————, ed. *The Politics of Poetic Form: Poetry and Public Policy.* New York: Roof, 1990.

Bernstein, Charles, Lyn Hejinian, Bob Perelman, Barrett Watten, Steve Benson, Ron Silliman, and Carla Harryman. "Introduction collective au mouvement de Language Poetry" (Collective introduction to the language poetry movement). *Cahiers du Collectif Change* 41 (1981): 151–57.

Bertrand, Aloysius. *Gaspard de la nuit.* 1842. Paris: Gallimard, 1980.

Bloom, Harold. *The Anxiety of Influence: A Theory of Poetry.* Oxford: Oxford University Press, 1973.

Bly, Robert. *Silence in the Snowy Fields.* Middletown, Conn.: Wesleyan University Press, 1962.

————. *Point Reyes Poems.* Half Moon Bay, Calif.: Mudra, 1974.

————. *The Morning Glory.* New York: Harper and Row, 1975.

————. *This Body Is Made of Camphor and Gopherwood.* New York: Harper and Row, 1977.

————. "What the Prose Poem Carries with It." *American Poetry Review* 6:3 (1977): 45.

————. *News of the Universe: Poems of Twofold Consciousness.* San Francisco: Sierra Club Books, 1980.

————. *The Man in the Black Coat Turns.* New York: Harper Collins, 1981.

————. *Selected Poems.* New York: Harper Collins, 1986.

————. *Ten Poems of Francis Ponge Translated by Robert Bly and Ten Poems of Robert Bly Inspired by the Poems of Francis Ponge.* New Brunswick, N.J.: Owl's Head Press, 1990.

————. *American Poetry: Wildness and Domesticity.* New York: Harper Collins, 1991.

————. *What Have I Ever Lost By Dying? Collected Prose Poems.* New York: Harper Collins, 1993.

————. Interview with Peter Johnson. Forthcoming in *The Prose Poem: An International Journal* 7 (1998).

Bowen, Zack, and James F. Carens, eds. *A Companion to Joyce Studies*. Westport, Conn.: Greenwood Press, 1984.

Bowles, Paul. "Entity." *transition* 13 (1928): 219–20.

Bradbury, Malcom, and James McFarlane. *Modernism: A Guide to European Literature 1890–1930*. London: Penguin, 1991.

Brecht, Bertolt. *Kalendergeschichten* (Calendar stories). Hamburg: Rowohlt, 1953.

Breton, André. *Anthologie de l'humour noir* (Anthology of black humor). Paris: Jean-Jacques Pauvert, 1966.

———. *Constellations*. 1958. In *Signe ascendant*. Paris: Gallimard, 1968.

———. *Manifestos of Surrealism*. Ann Arbor: University of Michigan Press, 1972.

Breton, André, and Philippe Soupault. *Les Champs magnétiques* (The magnetic fields). 1919. Paris: Gallimard, 1971.

Brooks, Cleanth. *The Well-Wrought Urn: Studies in the Structure of Poetry*. 1947. London: Methuen, 1968.

Buckley, Christopher. "Sounds That Could Have Been Singing: Charles Simic's *The World Doesn't End*." In Weigl, q.v., 96–113.

Bürger, Peter. *Theory of the Avant-Garde*, trans. Michael Shaw. Minneapolis: University of Minnesota Press, 1984.

Butler, Christopher. *Early Modernism: Literature, Music, and Painting in Europe, 1900–1916*. Oxford: Oxford University Press, 1994.

Cage, John. *Silence*. Middletown, Conn.: Wesleyan University Press, 1961.

———. "From *Themes and Variations*." In Hoover, q.v., 621–26.

Caws, Mary Ann, and Hermine Riffaterre, eds. *The Prose Poem in France: Theory and Practice*. New York: Columbia University Press, 1983.

Chernoff, Maxine. *A Vegetable Emergency*. Venice, Calif.: Beyond Baroque Foundation, 1977.

———. *Utopia TV Store*. Chicago: Yellow Press, 1979.

———. "The Fence of Character." *Poetics Journal* 5 (1985):87–89.

———. *Leap Year Day*. Chicago: Another Chicago Press, 1990.

Cohen, Jean. *Structure du langage poétique*. Paris: Flammarion, 1966.

Coolidge, Clark. *Polaroid*. New York/Bolinas, Calif.: Adventures in Poetry–Big Sky, 1975.

Crane, Hart. *The Bridge*. Paris: Black Sun Press, 1930.

Crosby, Harry. "Illustrations of Madness." *transition* 18 (1929): 102–3.

———. *Chariot of the Sun*. Paris: Black Sun Press, 1931.

Culler, Jonathan. *Structuralist Poetics: Structuralism, Linguistics and the Study of Literature*. London: Routledge and Kegan Paul, 1975.

Dacey, Philip. "This Body Is Made of Turkey Soup and Star Music." *Parnassus* 7 (1978): 34–45.

Daly, Lew, Alan Gilbert, Kristin Prevallet, and Pam Rehm, eds. "State of the Art." *apex of the M* 1 (1994): 5–7.

Darragh, Tina. *Striking Resemblance*. Providence, R.I.: Burning Deck, 1989.

Davey, Frank. *Margaret Atwood: A Feminist Poetics*. Vancouver: Talonbooks, 1984.

Davidson, Michael. *The Prose of Fact.* Berkeley, Calif.: Figures, 1981.

———. "After Sentence, Sentence." *American Book Review,* September–October 1982, 3.

DeKoren, Marianne. *A Different Language: Gertrude Stein's Experimental Writing.* Madison: University of Wisconsin Press, 1983.

Derrida, Jacques. *Of Grammatology,* trans. Gayatri Spivak. Baltimore: Johns Hopkins University Press, 1976.

———. *Dissemination,* trans. Barbara Johnson. Chicago: University of Chicago Press, 1981.

———. *A Derrida Reader,* ed. Peggy Kamuf. New York: Columbia University Press, 1991.

———. *Acts of Literature,* ed. Derek Attridge. New York: Routledge, 1992.

Dubnick, Randa. *The Structure of Obscurity: Gertrude Stein, Language, and Cubism.* Urbana and Chicago: University of Illinois Press, 1984.

Eagleton, Terry. "Discourse and Discos: Theory in the Space between Culture and Capitalism." *Times Literary Supplement,* July 15 1994, 3–4.

Easthope, Antony, and John O. Thompson, eds. *Contemporary Poetry Meets Modern Theory.* London: Harvester Wheatsheaf, 1991.

Eco, Umberto. "Joyce et d'Annunzio" (Joyce and d'Annunzio). *L'Arc: Joyce* (1990): 29–38.

Edson, Russell. *Appearances: Fables and Drawings.* Stamford, Conn.: Thing Press, 1961.

———. *A Stone Is Nobody's: Fables and Drawings.* Stamford, Conn.: Thing Press, 1961.

———. *The Very Thing That Happens: Fables and Drawings.* New York: New Directions, 1964.

———. *The Intuitive Journey and Other Works.* New York: Harper and Row, 1976.

———. "The Prose Poem in America." *Parnassus* 5.1 (1976): 321–25.

———. "Portrait of the Writer as a Fat Man." In Friebert and Young, q.v., 293–302.

———. *The Wounded Breakfast.* Middletown, Conn.: Wesleyan University Press, 1985.

———. "The Soul of Tales." *Parnassus* 16.1 (1990): 87–92.

———. Letter to the author, 4 December 1995.

Eliot, T. S. "The Borderline of Prose." *The New Stateman* 9 (19 May 1917): 157–59.

———. "Prose and Verse." *Chapbook: A Monthly Miscellany* 22 (April 1921): 3–20.

———. Preface. *Anabasis,* by St. John Perse. London: Faber, 1930.

———. *Collected Poems, 1909–1962.* London: Faber, 1963.

———. *To Criticize the Critic.* London: Faber, 1965.

Ellmann, Richard. *James Joyce.* Oxford: Oxford University Press, 1982.

Elsmslie, Kenward. *26 Bars.* Calais, Vt.: Z Press, 1987.

Eluard, Paul. *Les Malheurs des immortels* (The misfortunes of immortals). In *Poésies, 1913–1926* (Poems, 1913–1926). Paris: Gallimard, 1971.

Emerson, Ralph Waldo. *Selected Writings*. New York: Modern Library, 1950.

Emig, Rainer. *Modernism in Poetry: Motivations, Structures and Limits*. London: Longman, 1995.

Faulkner, William. *As I Lay Dying*. 1930. New York: Vintage, 1985.

Fisher, Roy. *The Ship's Orchestra*. London: Fulcrum Press, 1966.

Fitch, Noel R., ed. *In* transition: *A Paris Anthology.* London: Secker and Warburg, 1990.

Fixel, Lawrence. *Truth, War, and the Dream-Game: Selected Prose Poems and Parables*. Minneapolis: Coffee House Press, 1991.

Fredman, Stephen. *Poet's Prose: The Crisis in American Verse*. 2d ed. Cambridge: Cambridge University Press, 1990.

Friebert, Stuart, and David Young, eds. *Models of the Universe: An Anthology of the Prose Poem*. Oberlin, Ohio: Field Editions, 1995.

Friedman, Norman. "Recent Short Story Theories: Problems in Definition." In Lohafer and Clarey, q.v., 13–31.

Füger, Wilhelm, ed. *English Prose Lyrics: An Anthology*. Heidelberg: Winter, 1976.

Gallup, Donald. "The Lost Manuscripts of T. S. Eliot." *Bulletin of the New York Public Library,* December 1968, 649–51.

Gascoygne, David. *A Short Survey of Surrealism*. London: Cobden-Sanderson, 1935.

Gelpi, Albert. "The Genealogy of Postmodernism: Contemporary American Poetry." *Southern Review* 23.2 (1990): 517–41.

Genette, Gérard. *Figures II*. Paris: Seuil, 1969.

Genette, Gérard. "Introduction à l'architexte" (An introduction to the architext). In Genette and Todorov, q.v., 89–160.

Genette, Gérard, and Tzvetan Todorov, eds. *Théories des genres.* Paris: Seuil, 1986.

Gerlach, John. "The Margins of Narrative: The Very Short Story, the Prose Poem, and the Lyric." In Lohafer and Clarey, q.v., 74–84.

Germain, Edward B, ed. *Surrealist Poetry in English*. London: Penguin, 1978.

Gerstler, Amy. *The True Bride*. Venice, Calif.: Lapis Press, 1986.

———. *Bitter Angel*. New York: Farrar, Straus and Giroux, 1990.

Gillespie, Abraham Lincoln. *The Syntactic Revolution,* ed. Richard Milazzo. New York: Out of London Press, 1980.

Gins, Madeline. *Essay on Multi-Dimensional Architecture*. Paris: Le Soleil Noir, 1986.

———. *Helen Keller or Arakawa*. New York: Burning Books–East-West Cultural Studies, 1994.

———. Untitled interview with Charles Bernstein. *LINEbreak* 13 (audio recording). Buffalo, N.Y.: Granolithic Productions, 1996.

Giovannitti, Arturo. *Arrows in the Gale*. 1914. In *Collected Poems,* q.v., 135–220.

———. *Collected Poems*. Chicago: Clemente and Sons, 1962.

Godfrey, John. *Where the Weather Suits My Clothes*. Calais, Vt.: Z Press, 1984.

Gray, Martin. *A Dictionary of Literary Terms*. Harlow, Essex: Longman, 1984.

Gray, Richard. *American Poetry of the Twentieth Century*. London: Longman, 1990.

Greer, Michael. "Language Poetry in America, 1971–1991." *Meanjin* 50.1 (1991): 149–56.

Grenier, Robert. *Sentences*. Cambridge, Mass.: Whale Cloth Press, 1978.

———. *Series*. San Francisco: This Press, 1978.

Guest, Barbara. *Seeking Air*. Santa Barbara, Calif.: Black Sparrow Press, 1978.

Harjo, Joy. *In Mad Love and War*. Middletown, Conn.: Wesleyan University Press, 1990.

Harris, Marie. *Weasel in the Turkey Pen*. Brooklyn, N.Y.: Hanging Loose Press, 1993.

Harryman, Carla. *Animal Instincts*. San Francisco: This Press, 1989.

Hartley, George. *Textual Politics and the Language Poets*. Bloomington: Indiana University Press, 1989.

Hass, Robert. *Twentieth Century Pleasures: Prose on Poetry*. New York: Ecco Press, 1984.

———. *Human Wishes*. New York: Ecco Press, 1989.

Heaney, Seamus. *Stations*. Belfast: Ulsterman, 1975.

Hejinian, Lyn. "The Rejection of Closure." In Perelman, *Writing/Talks,* q.v., 270–91.

———. *My Life*. Los Angeles: Sun & Moon Press, 1987.

Hernadi, Paul. *Beyond Genre: New Directions in Literary Classification*. Ithaca, N.Y.: Cornell University Press, 1972.

Hill, Geoffrey. *Mercian Hymns*. London: Deutsch, 1971.

Hoffmann, Michael J. *The Development of Abstractionism in the Writings of Gertrude Stein*. Philadephia: University of Pennsylvania Press, 1965.

Holden, Jonathan. *The Fate of American Poetry*. Athens: University of Georgia Press, 1991.

Hoover, Paul. *Postmodern American Poetry*. New York: Norton, 1994.

Hough, Graham. "The Modernist Lyric." In Bradbury and McFarlane, q.v., 312–22.

Howe, Irving, and Ilana Wiener Howe, eds. *Short Shorts: An Anthology of the Shortest Stories*. New York: Bantam, 1983.

Hutcheon, Linda. *The Politics of Postmodernism*. London: Routledge, 1989.

Huysmans, Joris-Karl. *Oeuvres complètes* (Complete works). 2 vols. Paris: Crès, 1928.

Ignatow, David. *Facing the Tree*. Boston: Little, Brown, 1975.

———. *Tread the Dark*. Boston: Little, Brown, 1978.

———. *New and Collected Poems, 1970–1985*. Middletown, Conn.: Wesleyan University Press, 1986.

Inman, Peter. *Ocker*. Berkeley, Calif.: Tuumba, 1982.

Jacob, Max. *Le Cornet à dés* (The dice cup). 1917. Paris: Gallimard, 1967.

———. "1914 and Other Poems," trans. William Kulik. *American Poetry Review* 23.2 (1994): 2–4.

Jakobson, Roman. *Language in Literature.* Cambridge: Harvard University Press, 1987.

Jameson, Fredric. *Postmodernism, or, the Cultural Logic of Late Capitalism.* New York: Verso, 1991.

Jauss, Hans R. *Toward an Aesthetic of Reception,* trans. T. Bahti. Brighton: Harvester Press, 1982.

Jenkins, Louis. *Nice Fish: New and Selected Prose Poems.* Duluth, Minn.: Holy Cow! Press, 1995.

Johnson, Barbara. *A World of Difference.* Baltimore: Johns Hopkins University Press, 1987.

Johnson, Peter. *Pretty Happy!* Fredonia, N.Y.: White Pine Press, 1997.

Jolas, Eugene. "Monologue." *transition* 6 (1927): 133–35.

———. "Illustrations of Madness." *transition* 18 (1929): 102–3.

———. "The Dream." *transition* 19–20 (1930): 46–47.

———. "[The Vertigral Age]." *transition* 22 (1933): 128.

Jones, Peter, ed. *Imagist Poetry.* London: Penguin, 1972.

Joyce, James. *Chamber Music.* 1907. London: Cape, 1971.

———. *Dubliners.* 1914. London: Grafton, 1977.

———. *A Portrait of the Artist as a Young Man.* 1916. London: Penguin, 1992.

———. *Ulysses.* 1922. Oxford: Oxford University Press, 1993.

———. *Pomes Penyeach.* 1927. London: Faber, 1968.

———. *Finnegans Wake.* 1939. London: Faber, 1964.

———. *Stephen Hero.* London: New Directions, 1944.

———. *Epiphanies.* Buffalo, N.Y.: University of Buffalo Press–Lockwood Memorial Library, 1956.

———. *Letters.* Vol. 1, ed. Stuart Gilbert. London: Faber, 1957.

———. *A First-Draft Version of Finnegans Wake,* ed. David Hayman. London: Faber, 1963.

———. *Letters.* Vol. 2, ed. Richard Ellmann. London: Faber, 1966.

———. *Giacomo Joyce,* ed. Richard Ellman. London: Faber, 1968.

———. *Poems and Shorter Writings,* ed. Richard Ellmann, A. Walton Litz, and John Whittier-Ferguson. London: Faber, 1991.

Joyce, Stanislaus. *My Brother's Keeper: James Joyce's Early Years,* ed. Richard Ellmann. New York: Viking, 1958.

Jung, Carl. "Psychology and Poetry." in Fitch, q.v., 141–43.

Kafka, Franz. *Sämtliche Erzählungen.* Frankfurt am Main: Fischer Verlag, 1992.

Kimmel, Stanley. *The Kingdom of Smoke: Sketches of My People.* New York: Nicholas Brown, 1932.

Kittay, Jeffrey, and Wlad Godzich. *The Emergence of Prose: An Essay in Prosaics.* Minneapolis: University of Minnesota Press, 1987.

Kreymborg, Alfred, ed. *Lyric America.* New York: Edward McCann, 1930.

Kristeva, Julia. *Revolution in Poetic Language,* trans. Leon S. Roudiez. New York: Columbia University Press, 1984.

Lacan, Jacques. *Ecrits: A Selection,* trans. Alan Sheridan. New York: Norton, 1977.

Lacoue-Labarthe, Philippe, and Jean-Luc Nancy. *L'Absolu littéraire* (The literary absolute). Paris: Seuil, 1978.

Lazaridis Power, Henriette. "Incorporating *Giacomo Joyce.*" *James Joyce Quarterly,* 28.3 (1991): 623–30.

Lazer, Hank. *Opposing Poetries.* Vol. 2. Evanston, Ill.: Northwestern University Press, 1996.

Le Guin, Ursula K. *Dancing at the Edge of the World: Thoughts on Words, Women, Places.* New York: Grove Press, 1989.

Lehman, David, ed. *Ecstatic Occasions, Expedient Forms: 85 Leading Contemporary Poets Select and Comment on Their Poems.* Ann Arbor: University of Michigan Press, 1996.

Leitch, Thomas M. "The Debunking Rhythm of the American Short Story." In Lohafer and Clarey, q.v., 130–47.

Lentricchia, Frank. *Modernist Quartet.* Cambridge: Cambridge University Press, 1994.

Levertov, Denise. Introduction. In Edson, *The Very Thing That Happens,* q.v., v–vi.

Lewis, Wyndham. *Time and Western Man.* London: Chatto and Windus, 1927.

Lodge, David. "The Language of Modernist Fiction: Metaphor and Metonymy." In Bradbury and McFarlane, q.v., 481–96.

Lohafer, Susan, and Jo Ellyn Clarey, eds. *Short Story Theory at a Crossroads.* Baton Rouge: Louisiana State University Press, 1989.

Longhurst, Derek, ed. *Gender, Genre and Narrative Pleasure.* London: Unwin–Hyman, 1989.

Lowell, Amy. *Can Grande's Castle.* Boston: Houghton Mifflin, 1918.

Mahaffey, Vicki. "Giacomo Joyce." In Bowen and Carens, q.v., 387–420.

———. "Joyce's Shorter Works." In Attridge, q.v., 185–211.

———. "Fascism and Silence: The Coded History of Amalia Popper." *James Joyce Quarterly* 32.3–4 (1995): 501–22.

Mallarmé, Stéphane. *Igitur, Divagations, Un Coup de dés.* Paris: Gallimard, 1976.

Marx, Karl. *Capital.* Vol. 1. 1867. New York: International, 1967.

Matuz, Roger, ed. *Contemporary Literary Criticism.* Vol. 68. Detroit: Gale, 1991.

May, Charles. *Short Story Theories.* Athens: Ohio University Press, 1976.

———. "Metaphoric Motivation in Short Fiction: 'In the Beginning Was the Story.'" In Lohafer and Clarey, q.v., 62–73.

Mayer, Bernadette. *Memory.* Plainfield, Vt.: Atlantic Books, 1975.

McCaffery, Larry. *Postmodern Fiction: A Bio-Bibliographical Guide.* Westport, Conn.: Greenwood Press, 1986.

McGann, Jerome. "The Virtues of Prose." *Times Literary Supplement,* 23 July 1976, 911.

———. "Contemporary Poetry, Alternate Routes." In von Hallberg, q.v., 253–76.

————. *Black Riders: The Visible Language of Modernism.* Princeton: Princeton University Press, 1993.

McMillan, Dougald. transition: *The History of a Literary Era, 1927–1938.* New York: Braziller, 1976.

McQuade, Molly. "Charles Simic." *Publishers Weekly,* 2 November 1990, 56–57.

Melnick, David. *Pcoet.* San Francisco: G.A.W.K., 1975.

Merrill, Stuart, ed. *Pastels in Prose.* New York: Harper, 1890.

Merwin, W. S. *Houses and Travellers.* New York: Atheneum, 1977.

Messerli, Douglas, ed. *"Language" Poetries.* New York: New Directions, 1987.

————, ed. *From the Other Side of the Century: A New American Poetry, 1960–1990.* Los Angeles: Sun & Moon Press, 1994.

Miner, Earl. *Comparative Poetics.* Princeton: Princeton University Press, 1990.

Molesworth, Charles. *The Fierce Embrace: A Study of Contemporary American Poetry.* Columbia: University of Missouri Press, 1979.

Monroe, Jonathan. *A Poverty of Objects: The Prose Poem and the Politics of Genre.* Ithaca, N.Y.: Cornell University Press, 1987.

Moravia, Alberto. "The Short Story and the Novel." In May, *Short Story Theories,* q.v., 147–51.

Morson, Gary Saul. *The Boundaries of Genre: Dostoevsky's "Diary of a Writer" and the Traditions of Literary Utopia.* Austin: University of Texas Press, 1981.

Murphy, Margueritte. *A Tradition of Subversion: The Prose Poem in English from Wilde to Ashbery.* Amherst: University of Massachusetts Press, 1992.

Murphy, Richard. Untitled review of Stuart Dybek's *The Story of Mist* and Naomi Shihab Nye's *Mint. The Prose Poem: An International Journal* 3 (1994): 102–5.

Myers, George, ed. *Epiphanies: The Prose Poem Now.* Westerville, Ohio: Cumberland, 1987.

Nelson, Howard. *Robert Bly.* New York: Columbia University Press, 1984.

Nelson, Cary. *Repression and Recovery: American Poetry and the Politics of Cultural Memory.* Madison: University of Wisconsin Press, 1989.

Nicholls, Peter. "Difference Spreading: From Gertrude Stein to L=A=N=G=U=A=G=E Poetry." In Easthope and Thompson, q.v., 116–27.

Nichols, Ashton. *The Poetics of Epiphany: Nineteenth-Century Origins of the Modern Literary Moment.* Tuscaloosa: University of Alabama Press, 1987.

Nin, Anais. *Under a Glass Bell.* London: Penguin, 1978.

Noon, William T. *Joyce and Aquinas.* New Haven: Yale University Press, 1957.

Nye, Naomi Shihab. *Mint.* Brockport, N.Y.: State Street Chapbooks, 1991.

Olson, Charles. "Projective Verse" (1950). In Hoover, q.v., 613–21.

Patchen, Kenneth. *Before the Brave.* New York: Modern Library, 1936.

————. *The Journal of Albion Moonlight.* 1941. New York: New Directions, 1961.

————. *Panels for the Walls of Heaven.* Berkeley, Calif.: Bern Porter, 1946.

————. *Red Wine and Yellow Hair.* New York: New Directions, 1949.

———. *The Famous Boating Party and Other Poems in Prose.* New York: New Directions, 1954.

———. *Poemscapes: A Letter to God.* New York: New Directions, 1958.

Perelman, Bob. *7 Works.* Castle Hill, Mass.: Figures, 1979.

———. *a.k.a.* Great Barrington, Mass.: Figures, 1984.

———. *Virtual reality.* New York: Roof, 1993.

———. *The Trouble with Genius: Reading Pound, Joyce, Stein, and Zukofsky.* Berkeley: University of California Press, 1994.

———. *The Marginalization of Poetry: Language Writing and Literary History.* Princeton: Princeton University Press, 1996.

———, ed. *Writing/Talks.* Carbondale: Southern Illinois University Press, 1985.

Perloff, Marjorie. *The Poetics of Indeterminacy: Rimbaud to Cage.* Evanston, Ill.: Northwestern University Press, 1983.

———. *The Dance of the Intellect: Studies in the Poetry of the Pound Tradition.* Cambridge: Cambridge University Press, 1985.

———. *Radical Artifice: Writing Poetry in the Age of Media.* Chicago: University of Chicago Press, 1991.

———. *Wittgenstein's Ladder: Poetic Language and the Strangeness of the Ordinary.* Chicago: University of Chicago Press, 1996.

Pinsky, Robert. *The Situation of Poetry: Contemporary Poetry and Its Traditions.* Princeton: Princeton University Press, 1976.

Ponge, Francis. *Lyres.* Paris: Gallimard, 1967.

Pound, Ezra, ed. *Des Imagistes: An Anthology.* New York: Albert and Charles Boni, 1914.

———, ed. *Catholic Anthology.* London: Elkins Mathews, 1915.

Preminger, Alex, ed. *Princeton Encyclopedia of Poetry and Poetics.* Princeton: Princeton University Press, 1974.

Quasimodo, Salvatore. *Tutte le poesie.* Milan: Mondadori, 1984.

Quignard, Pascal. *Une Gêne technique à l'égard des fragments* (A technical embarrassment with regard to fragments). Paris: Fata Morgana, 1986.

Ransom, John Crowe. *Selected Poems.* New York: Alfred Knopf, 1969.

Reinfeld, Linda. *Language Poetry: Writing as Rescue.* Baton Rouge: Louisiana State University Press, 1992.

Richman, Robert. "The Poetry of Robert Bly." *New Criterion* 5 (1986): 37–46.

Riding, Laura. "The New Barbarism and Gertrude Stein." *transition* 3 (1927): 153–68.

———. "Mademoiselle Comet." *transition* 13 (1928): 207–8.

Riffaterre, Hermine. "Reading Constants: The Practice of the Prose Poem." In Caws and Riffaterre, q.v., 98–116.

Riffaterre, Michael. "On the Prose Poem's Formal Features." In Caws and Riffaterre, q.v., 117–32.

Rimbaud, Arthur. *Poésies, Une Saison en enfer, Illuminations* (Poems. A season in hell. Illuminations). Paris: Gallimard, 1984.

Robinson, Kit. *Windows.* Amherst, Mass.: Whale Cloth Press, 1985.

Rodefer, Stephen. *Passing Duration.* Providence, R.I.: Burning Deck, 1991.

Rohrberger, Mary. "Between Shadow and Act: Where Do We Go from Here?" In Lohafer and Clarey, q.v., 32–45.

Rosmarin, Adena. *The Power of Genre.* Minneapolis: University of Minnesota Press, 1985.

Rothenberg, Jerome. *Pre-faces & Other Writings.* New York: New Directions, 1981.

Rutra, Theo. "Faula and Flona." *transition* 16–17 (1929): 34.

Sandburg, Carl. *Chicago Poems.* New York: Holt, 1918.

———. *Harvest Poems: 1910–1960.* New York: Harvest, 1960.

———. *The People, Yes.* New York: Harcourt Brace Jovanovich, 1936.

Schmitz, Neil. *Of Huck and Alice.* Minneapolis: University of Minnesota Press, 1983.

Scholes, Robert E., and Richard M. Kain, eds. *The Workshop of Daedalus.* Evanston, Ill.: Northwestern University Press, 1965.

Scholes, Robert. *The Fabulators.* New York: Oxford University Press, 1967.

Scott, Clive. "The Prose Poem and Free Verse." In Bradbury and McFarlane, q.v., 349–68.

Seth, Vikram. *The Golden Gate.* New York: Random House, 1986.

Shapiro, Karl. *Collected Poems, 1940–1978.* New York: Random House, 1978.

Sherry, James. *In Case.* College Park, Md.: Sun & Moon Press, 1981.

———. *Our Nuclear Heritage.* Los Angeles: Sun & Moon Press, 1991.

Silliman, Ron. *Paradise.* Providence, R.I.: Burning Deck, 1985.

———. *In the American Tree: Language, Realism, Poetry.* Orono, Maine: National Poetry Foundation, 1986.

———. "New Prose, New Prose Poem." In McCaffery, q.v., 157–74.

———. *The New Sentence.* New York: Roof, 1989.

Simic, Charles. *The Uncertain Certainty: Interviews, Essays, and Notes on Poetry.* Ann Arbor: University of Michigan Press, 1985.

———. *The World Doesn't End: Prose Poems.* New York: Harcourt Brace Jovanovich, 1989.

———. *Selected Poems: 1963–1983.* New York: Braziller, 1990.

———. *Wonderful Words, Silent Truth: Essays on Poetry and a Memoir.* Ann Arbor: University of Michigan Press, 1990.

———. *Dime-Store Alchemy: The Art of Joseph Cornell.* Hopewell, N.J.: Ecco Press, 1992.

———. *The Unemployed Fortune-Teller: Essays and Memoirs.* Ann Arbor: University of Michigan Press, 1994.

Simon, John. *The Prose Poem as a Genre in Nineteenth-Century European Literature.* New York: Garland Press, 1987.

Smith, Barbara Herrnstein. *Poetic Closure: A Study of How Poems End.* Chicago: University of Chicago Press, 1968.

Smith, Ellen. Untitled review of Nancy Lagomarsino's *The Secretary Parables*. *The Prose Poem: An International Journal* 2 (1991): 116–19.

Smith, Larry R. *Kenneth Patchen*. Boston: Twayne, 1978.

Spector, Herman. "A Very Little Incident." *transition* 16–17 (1929): 177–79.

Stein, Gertrude. *Three Lives*. New York: Grafton Press, 1909.

———. *Geography and Plays*. Boston: Four Seas Press, 1922.

———. *The Making of Americans*. Paris: Contact Editions, 1925.

———. *A Long Gay Book*. In *Matisse, Picasso and Gertrude Stein*. Paris: Plain Edition, 1931.

———. *Operas and Plays*. Paris: Plain Editions, 1932.

———. *Portraits and Prayers*. New York: Random House, 1934.

———. *Picasso*. London: B. T. Batsford, 1940.

———. *Brewsie and Willie*. New York: Random House, 1946.

———. *Q.E.D.* First published as *Things as They Are*. Pawlet, Vt.: Banyan Press, 1950.

———. *Two: Gertrude Stein and Her Brother and Other Early Portraits (1908–1912)*. New Haven: Yale University Press, 1951.

———. *Bee Time Vine and Other Pieces (1913–1927)*. New Haven: Yale University Press, 1952.

———. *Look at Me Now and Here I Am: Writings and Lectures 1909–45*. London: Penguin, 1971.

———. *A Stein Reader*, ed. Ulla E. Dydo. Evanston, Ill.: Northwestern University Press, 1993.

Steiner, Wendy. *Exact Resemblance to Exact Resemblance: The Literary Portraiture of Gertrude Stein*. New Haven: Yale University Press, 1978.

Stewart, Allegra. *Gertrude Stein and the Present*. Cambridge: Harvard University Press, 1967.

Templeton, Fiona. *London*. Los Angeles: Sun & Moon, 1984.

———. *You—The City*. New York: Roof, 1990.

Todorov, Tzvetan. *The Fantastic: A Structural Approach to a Literary Genre,* trans. Richard Howard. Ithaca, N.Y.: Cornell University Press, 1981.

———. *Genres in Discourse,* trans. Catherine Porter. Cambridge: Cambridge University Press, 1990.

Turner, Alberta. *Fifty Contemporary Poets: The Creative Process*. New York: David McKay Co., 1977.

Tzara, Tristan. "Manifeste dada 1918." *Dada* 3 (December 1918). In Béhar and Carassou, q.v., 260.

Valaoritis, Nanos. "Poésie Langage USA" (Poetry language U.S.A.). *Cahiers du Collectif Change* 41 (1981): 159–61.

Valéry, Paul. "Remarks on Poetry." In Walder, q.v., 138–42.

von Hallberg, Robert, ed. *Politics & Poetic Value*. Chicago: University of Chicago Press, 1987.

Walder, Dennis. *Literature in the Modern World*. Oxford: Oxford University Press, 1990.

Waldrop, Rosmarie. *The Lawn of Excluded Middle.* Providence, R.I.: Tender Buttons, 1993.

Ward, Diane. *Never Without One.* New York: Roof, 1984.

Watson, Craig. *Discipline.* Providence, R.I.: Burning Deck, 1986.

Watten, Barrett. *1–10.* San Francisco: This Press, 1980.

———. "Method and L=A=N=G=U=A=G=E: After Surrealism." In Silliman, *In the American Tree,* q.v., 599–612.

———. *Frame (1971–90).* Los Angeles: Sun & Moon Press, 1997.

Weigl, Bruce, ed. *Charles Simic: Essays on the Poetry.* Ann Arbor: University of Michigan Press, 1996.

Weiner, Hannah. *Clairvoyant Journal.* Lenox, Mass.: Angel Hair, 1978.

———. *Little Book/Indians.* New York: Roof, 1980.

Wesling, Donald. *The New Poetries: Poetic Form since Coleridge and Wordsworth.* London and Toronto: Associated University Presses, 1985.

Whitman, Walt. *Leaves of Grass.* New York: Fowler and Wells, 1855.

Wilde, Oscar. "Poems in Prose." *Fortnightly Review* 331 (1 July 1894): 22–29.

Williams, W. C. *Imaginations,* ed. Webster Schott. New York: New Directions, 1970.

———. "Theessentialroar." *transition* 10 (1928): 49–50.

Wilson, Steve, ed. *The Anatomy of Water: A Sampling of Contemporary American Prose Poetry.* Decatur, Ga.: Linwood Publishers, 1992.

Index